S0-AZD-087

The Strategic Constitution

The Strategic Constitution

ROBERT D. COOTER

PRINCETON UNIVERSITY PRESS

PRINCETON, NEW JERSEY

Copyright © 2000 by Princeton University Press
Published by Princeton University Press, 41 William Street, Princeton,
New Jersey 08540
In the United Kingdom: Princeton University Press, 3 Market Place, Woodstock,
Oxfordshire OX20 1SY
All Rights Reserved

Second printing, and first paperback printing, 2002
Paperback ISBN 0-691-09620-1

The Library of Congress has cataloged the cloth edition of this book as follows

Cooter, Robert.
The strategic constitution / Robert D. Cooter.
p.   cm.
Includes bibliographical references and index.
ISBN 0-691-05864-4 (cl. : alk. paper)
1. Law and economics. 2. Constitutional law—Philosophy. 3. Game theory. I. Title.
K487.E3 C667 2000
342'.01—dc21
99-058556

British Library Cataloging-in-Publication Data is available

This book has been composed in Times Roman

Printed on acid-free paper. ∞

www.pupress.princeton.edu

Printed in the United States of America

2   3   4   5   6   7   8   9   10

THIS BOOK IS DEDICATED TO
ILC AND LWC

BRIEF CONTENTS

DETAILED CONTENTS

LIST OF ILLUSTRATIONS

LIST OF TABLES

PREFACE AND ACKNOWLEDGMENTS

WHEN TOLSTOY decided to write a novel about the "Decembrist Revolt" of 1825 against Tsar Nicholas, he began setting the stage by describing Napoleon's invasion of Russia in 1812. One thousand pages later at the end of *War and Peace* a minor character appears whom Tolstoy intended to be the main character in the original, unwritten novel. Life is what happens while you are planning something else.

Comparing the great to the small, I planned a book on public law and economics, the first two chapters of which would concern constitutional law and economics, but I could not summarize succinctly a field that barely exists. So I ended up writing this book, which is a systematic account of constitutional law and economics as it exists today. I develop an original conception of democracy while synthesizing the application of economics and political science to constitutional law. I try to write in a way that is accessible to students and scholars from different disciplines. The book should be suitable for use in a class for advanced undergraduates, law students, or graduate students. Each chapter contains problems and exercises to test and deepen the reader's understanding.

I have taught parts of this book to students at Berkeley for several years. I have benefited from their comments, especially those by my teaching assistants Noah Baum and Neil Siegel. Winand Emons and Omri Yadlin, who taught from the book in successive years visiting Berkeley, gave me valuable comments and saved me from some errors.

I participated in intensive discussions on comparative topics in constitutional law at a conference in Saarbrucken in 1995. I presented early drafts of parts of this book in 1996 and 1998 when I lectured to European doctoral students and faculty in Switzerland at Studienzentrum Gerzensee, Stiftung Der Schweizerischen Nationalbank. I have also benefited from discussions at the annual meeting of the European Association of Law and Economics, the Latin American and Caribbean Law and Economics Association, and annual meetings of the Comparative Law and Economics Forum.

Discussions with Geoffrey Brennan and Phillip Pettit during my visit at the Australian National University in July 1998 forced me to elevate the generality of my analysis. Bruno Frey prompted me to rethink my views about direct democracy. My thanks to Debby Kearney of the Boalt Library reference staff for being a master detective and finding many references based on few clues from me. Thanks for various comments and help along the way to Chris Swain, Dhammika Dhamapala, Eric Rasmussen, Sandy Hoffman, and Georg von Wangenheim. Finally, I wish to thank Geoffrey Garrett and Bruce Chapman, whose thoughtful reviews of the manuscript's first complete draft gave me a fresh perspective on my project, and also Peter Dougherty of Princeton University Press.

The Strategic Constitution

Taking Consequences Seriously: Introduction

> Nothing is clear-cut around here except the forest.
> —*Don Costello, tribal court judge in Oregon*

JUST AS the bishop is the highest authority in a cathedral, so the constitution is the highest law of the state. Below it lie statutes and below statutes lie regulations, policies, orders, and decisions, as depicted in figure 1-1.

The constitution is the state's highest law in several respects. First, the constitution is more *general* than most other laws. Constitutions allocate basic powers to officials and recognize fundamental rights of citizens, whereas most legislation regulates behavior or implements policies. Second, the constitution *trumps* other laws in the sense that the constitution prevails whenever it contradicts another state law.[1] Third, the constitution is usually more *entrenched* than other laws in the sense of being harder to change.

The first two traits of constitutions relate to the third trait. As a law becomes more general and powerful, changes in it cause greater disruption. To avoid disruptions, general laws should change more slowly than specific laws.[2] Consequently, changing a constitution usually requires more burdensome procedures than enacting a statute or making a regulation. Figure 1-2 depicts the typical relationships between the generality of laws and the transaction costs of changing them.

A recent book surveying constitutional theory begins by saying, "The trouble with constitutional law is that nobody knows what counts as an argument."[3] As the highest law, the constitution is the logical beginning of the state's legal power. Law posts enough road signs for a knowledgeable traveler to find his way. Above the constitution, however, law runs out and the traveler enters "a place where the eyes of man have never set foot."[4] Being highest, constitutional law evokes the best efforts of scholars and political commentators. Being located where law runs out, constitutional arguments are subtle and evasive. History, philosophy, religion, politics, sociology, and economics hover above the constitution as depicted in figure 1-1. Scholars and officials disagree over how to use these sources for making and interpreting constitutions.

---

[1] Some scholars believe that international law trumps national constitutions. Perhaps international law is above national constitutions, like the pope is above the bishop.

[2] The absence of constitutional stability motivated this Russian joke: "In 1992 a customer entered a bookshop and asked for a copy of the Russian constitution. The shopkeeper replied, 'Sorry, but we don't carry periodicals.'"

[3] Gerhardt and Rowe 1993, p. 1.

[4] The Beatles' *Magical Mystery Tour*.

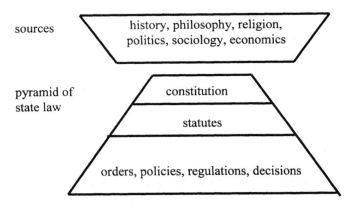

sources

pyramid of
state law

Fig. 1-1 Pyramid of State Law and Its Sources

In spite of these disagreements, some kinds of arguments should prove compelling to everyone. Political constitutions can cause suffering on a vast scale or lay the foundation for a nation's liberty and prosperity; thus, making, amending, and interpreting constitutions is a political game with high stakes. To help people win this game, theory should explain the constitutional causes of liberty and prosperity. By predicting the consequences of fundamental laws, constitutional theory can inform the public, guide politicians, and improve the decisions of courts. Predictions about the consequences for human welfare of alternative understandings of the constitution should count as arguments for everyone.

As currently practiced, constitutional theory mostly concerns the history and philosophy of constitutional texts. Some legal scholars, who find the sources of constitutional law in history, interpret a constitution by scrutinizing the original understanding of its makers. Other scholars insist on interpreting all laws

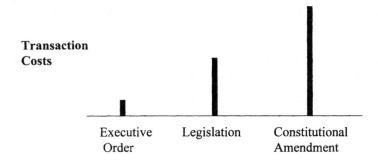

Fig. 1-2 Transaction Costs of Changing Laws

according to their plain meaning.[5] Still others examine the philosophical, moral, or religious inspiration for a constitution. These approaches clarify a constitution's normative commitments, such as the vision of individual autonomy inspiring constitutional rights.

Wittgenstein wrote, "Philosophical problems can be compared to locks on safes, which can be opened by dialing a certain word or number, so that no force can open the door until just this word has been hit upon, and once hit upon any child can open it."[6] Much of moral and political philosophy proceeds by searching for the right words for ideas. Like philosophy, constitutional theory devotes much of its energy to setting concepts straight. The right word can unlock conflation and set thought free.

The meaning of the words and the philosophy of its makers, however, cannot predict the response of people to a law. From the viewpoint of a person who takes consequences seriously, constitutional theorists look too hard for the right words and not hard enough for the real causes.[7] Constitutional theory needs more models and less meaning. After preaching his Sunday sermon in nineteenth-century Boston, a liberal minister overheard a conservative congregant remark, "Beans in a bladder. No food today for hungry souls." Similarly, consequentialists leave the banquet of constitutional scholarship while still hungry for predictions.

Philosophers and economists sometimes feel an affinity for each other based on their mutual commitment to rationality. More often, however, they feel antipathy over different conceptions of rationality. By confusing economics and utilitarianism, philosophers sometimes imagine that they can identify fatal flaws in economic reasoning without troubling to learn the subject.[8] Conversely, by confusing moral commitments with preferences, economists sometimes imagine that they can dismiss philosophical traditions far older than economics without troubling to learn the arguments for and against relativism.[9] Although I admire moral and political theory, I also think that constitutional theory is too preoccupied with philosophical arguments and methods.

Instead of examining history or clarifying normative commitments, this book takes another tack. An individual sometimes gains an advantage in social life by making a commitment. An individual commits by arranging his affairs so that he cannot benefit from violating the commitment. To illustrate, a person commits to keeping a promise by signing a legal contract so that breach costs him more than performance. Similarly, citizens can gain an advantage when the state commits to a constitution. A state commits to a constitution by arranging

---

[5] Law and economics scholars have debated whether a law should be interpreted according to its plain meaning (Macey 1986) or in light of its underlying political bargain (Easterbrook 1994).

[6] Wittgenstein 1993, p. 175. Quoted in the conclusion to Summers 1998.

[7] Rawls asserts (1971) that utilitarianism does not take differences between individuals seriously, and this claim apparently inspired Ronald Dworkin to title his book *Taking Rights Seriously*.

[8] Note that the ordinalist tradition in economics explicitly rejects the tradition of Bentham.

[9] A student once said to me, "I'm doing ok in everything except philosophy. My professor has his philosophy and I've got mine."

institutions so that each official or political faction expects to lose from violating the constitution. As depicted in figure 1-2, the constitution usually represents a society's strongest legal commitments. Once established, a constitution creates incentives for officials and citizens to do things or refrain from doing them. Although the tumult of politics and the particularities of history obscure these incentive effects, I try to uncover them by using economics and political science.

The modern state possesses many monopoly powers, including the power to make laws and collect taxes.[10] In a democracy, popular elections direct state powers, either directly through referenda or indirectly through elected officials. Democracy is thus a system of popular competition for directing the state's monopoly powers. The scope and breadth of political competition distinguishes democracy from other forms of government.

Competitive elections make government respond to citizens much like competitive markets make the economy respond to consumers. I believe that electoral competition provides the best guarantee that the state will give citizens the laws and public goods that they prefer. This belief, plus the definition of democracy as popular competition for directing the state's monopoly powers, implies that democracy is the best form of government for satisfying the political preferences of citizens.

Unlike democracy, a ruling family (monarchy), a powerful individual (dictatorship), a priestly caste (theocracy), a vanguard party (communism), a dominant social class (aristocracy), or a self-perpetuating bureaucracy insulates itself from popular competition. Following the language of economics, these noncompetitive forms of government can be described as different types of monopoly. Democracy is competitive government, and the alternatives to democracy are monopoly government. Monopolies typically provide their owners with exceptional profits at the expense of other people. As the most encompassing power within its domain, the state is potentially the most profitable monopoly for anyone who can control it and the most dangerous for everyone else. Regardless of its form, political monopoly is the enemy of democracy.

In general, the public benefits from organizing competition for control of a monopoly (Demsetz 1968). Constitutions can organize political competition in different ways, as illustrated by the contrast between direct and indirect democracy, federal and unitary states, unicameral and bicameral legislatures, and president and prime minister. According to opinion polls, citizens rate the performance of their political systems differently from one country to another. This book concerns alternative democracies, not alternatives to democracy. While I assume that democracy is the best form of government for satisfying the preferences of citizens, I show that some organizational forms dominate others in particular circumstances. By "dominate" I mean "provides more satisfaction to the citizens."

To compete in politics, a person should decide what to do by anticipating how others will respond. For this reason, political competition is strategic. Economics

[10] North makes the point concisely: "A state is an organization with a comparative advantage in violence, extending over a geographic area whose boundaries are determined by its power to tax constituents" (1981, p. 21, as quoted in Voigt 1997a).

provides the best models for predicting strategic behavior. This book analyzes democratic constitutions by using models of strategic behavior developed for markets and adapted to politics. I will use strategic theory and the available data to address such questions as these:

Example 1: A constitution can provide one or many elected governments. For example, Japan has a unitary state and Australia has federalism. How does the number of elected governments affect the supply of public goods? How many elected governments is optimal?

Example 2: The British prime minister can order members of her party in Parliament to enact legislation, whereas the U.S. president must bargain with the House and Senate over a bill. Does this difference explain why British courts and ministries are less daring than U.S. courts and agencies? How much judicial and administrative daring is best for the citizens?

Example 3: Imagine that a property owner applies for a building permit and, as a condition for receiving the permit, the planning authority demands the donation of ground for a public walkway. The property owner sues in court alleging an unconstitutional taking of private property. How will the court's decision influence future bargaining between developers and town planners? How much protection of private property is best for the supply of private and public goods?

In answering such questions, social science aspires to replace intuitive judgments with proofs. Unlike explicating the meaning, history, and philosophy of texts, scientific proofs require data.[11] Relatively few social scientists do empirical research on constitutional law, however, and the legal issues mutate quickly. When theories and events outrun data, arguments fall short of the standards of proof desired in social science.

When social scientists draw legal conclusions from limited data, many lawyers get uncomfortable. These same lawyers, however, are perfectly comfortable when traditional legal scholars draw conclusions from no data at all.[12] Lawmakers would do better to use imperfect empirical analysis than perfect nonempirical analysis. It is better to cut bread with a dull knife than a perfect spoon. By using available data to make predictions about constitutions, I cannot offer conclusive proofs, but I can improve the quality of argument.

Strategic behavior presupposes individual rationality. Unlike economists, psychologists often deny that individuals are rational, and sociologists often deny that groups aggregate the behavior of individuals. The rational, individualistic methodology used in this book remains controversial among some psychologists and sociologists. I also evaluate the state by its ability to satisfy the preferences

---

[11] Two data jokes:

"For a lawyer, one anecdote is empirical evidence, and two anecdotes are data."

"What is the empirical method in the economic analysis of law? Torture the data until it confesses."

[12] Joke: How does a lawyer do a longitudinal study? He asks himself the same question tomorrow.

of its citizens. Unlike economists or utilitarians, many political theorists deny that preference satisfaction measures the performance of a state. Regardless of whether the reader ultimately accepts or denies the positive methodology of individual rationality and the normative standard of preference satisfaction, I hope that the reader will appreciate my attempt to work these ideas pure as applied to constitutional democracy.

In the days of sailing ships, the crew on a long voyage included a carpenter, who sometimes repaired the hull while the ship was still at sea. Most boards could be removed one at a time and replaced, even though removing all of them at once would sink the ship. Like the ship's carpenter, economists can analyze laws one at a time and propose improvement. This approach puts every law within reach, even fundamental laws like the constitution. Eventually the economic approach can contemplate wholly new legal structures. This book analyzes constitutions one provision at a time and also contemplates wholly new legal structures.

In this introductory chapter, I will discuss the origins of strategic theory, describe some techniques of analysis, explain the policy values underlying these techniques, and finally describe the structure and contribution of this book.

Origins

Several intellectual traditions inspire the strategic approach to constitutions. First, political theorists who write in the contractarian tradition typically view the constitution as a bargain among political interests, much like a business contract is a bargain among economic interests. In terms of figure 1-1, contractarian choice occurs at the level located above the constitution ("preconstitutional choice"). Contractarians typically assume the absence of any particular constitution and then explain how to choose one. This style of argument flourished in the eighteenth century when revolutions in America and France transformed politics, and it eventually became moribund by the early twentieth century. James Buchanan and Gordon Tullock revived contractarianism in their classic book, *The Calculus of Consent: Logical Foundations of Constitutional Democracy* (1962),[13] which was followed by John Rawls's magisterial *A Theory of Justice* (1971) and Robert Nozick's incisive *Anarchy, State, and Utopia* (1974).

The second tradition inspiring this book is the economic analysis of law. Joseph Schumpeter distinguished between economic analysis based on formal theory and economic thought based on informal reasoning.[14] As applied to law, economic thought is old, whereas economic analysis is new. Ronald Coase's 1960 article on nuisance law, "The Problem of Social Cost," marks the conventional beginning of the economic analysis of law. Guido Calabresi's *The Costs of Accidents: A Legal and Economic Analysis* (1970) extended economic analysis to torts, and Richard Posner's *Economic Analysis of Law* (1972) sketched the

---

[13] J. Buchanan's subsequent writing on the logic of constitutions includes Buchanan 1975; Buchanan 1990; and J. Buchanan 1991.

[14] Schumpeter 1986, pp. 38–39.

complete subject. Publications using economic analysis subsequently exploded in such fields of law as contracts, property, torts, regulation, corporations, and crimes.[15] Although there are two specialty journals and a few published books,[16] the economic analysis of constitutional law remains thin.

This book draws on a third tradition called "public-choice" or "collective-choice" theory. "Public choice" refers to the fact that governments ideally allocate resources to public goods, whereas private markets ideally allocate resources to private goods. "Collective choice" refers to the fact that democracy requires a group of people to decide together by voting, whereas an individual can decide on his own whether to buy toothpaste or soybean futures. (For a good survey of public choice or collective choice as applied to constitutional law, see Voigt 1996.)

Collective-choice theory uses economic models of rational behavior to explain the workings of political institutions, including majority rule and representative government. Kenneth Arrow's brilliant and perplexing book *Social Choice and Individual Values* (1951) pioneered the modern application of economic analysis to voting. Amartya Sen explicated this book in *Collective Choice and Social Welfare* (1970). Duncan Black was another pioneer, whose insights were synthesized in *The Theory of Committees and Elections* (1958) and extended by Anthony Downs in *An Economic Theory of Democracy* (1957). William Riker's *The Theory of Political Coalitions* (1962) took a somewhat different approach to elections by emphasizing coalitions among parties. Mancur Olson's *The Logic of Collective Action: Public Goods and the Theory of Groups* (1965) analyzed the influence of money on politics as a free-rider problem. Dennis Mueller summarized these various traditions in *Public Choice* (1979; revised 1989) and related them to constitutions in *Perspectives on Public Choice* (1997), as did Daniel Farber and Philip Frickey in *Law and Public Choice: A Critical Introduction* (1991). A thoughtful, recent contribution is Jerry Mashaw's *Greed, Chaos, and Governance: Using Public Choice to Improve Public Law* (1997).

American political scientists adopted another label to describe their application of economic models to politics. John Ferejohn, Matthew McCubbins, Ken Shepsle, and Barry Weingast (to name but a few) refer to themselves as "positive political theorists." This label stresses the difference between the positive task of explaining how politics actually works and the normative task of philosophizing about how politics ought to work. Thus positive political theorists distinguish themselves from philosophers who traditionally dominated political theory in American universities. Positive political theorists have used game theory to explain specific political institutions that few economists understand. Shepsle and Mark Bonchek's *Analyzing Politics: Rationality, Behavior, and Institutions* (1997) provides a readable overview of positive political theory.

---

[15] For an overview of the economic analysis of law, see the two leading textbooks: Cooter and Ulen 1996 and Posner 1992. For a statistical study of its influence and success, see Landes 1993.

[16] The journals are *Constitutional Political Economy* and the *Supreme Court Economic Review.* Books include Siegan 1980; J. Buchanan 1991; and Mueller 1996.

In addition to these approaches, the fourth influence on this book is comparative law and economics. In Berkeley, Berlin, and Bombay, microeconomics is the same and law is different. Economic theory can analyze different legal systems in neutral language. As Hein Koetz said, "Economic rationales do not lose their persuasive power at national boundaries."[17] Most law and economics scholars in Europe inevitably use comparative methods in their research,[18] and a substantial body of comparative research now exists for several areas of law and economics,[19] including some writing on comparative constitutional law and economics (Schmidtchen and Cooter 1997).

Since statistical research on constitutional law is so limited, I often use observations as evidence. Observing different constitutions in different countries provides better evidence than does observing a single country. For this reason, I join Bruce Ackerman in appealing to scholars to remedy the underdevelopment of comparative constitutional law (Ackerman 1997). (As described in the preface, I collected comparative observations by lecturing on early drafts of this book at various international meetings.)

TECHNIQUES

According to a conventional definition, law consists of obligations backed by sanctions. Lawmakers often ask how people will respond to modifying an obligation or a sanction. To illustrate, lawmakers might ask, "If the constitution requires the state to compensate the owners of land taken for public projects, will private investment in real estate increase?" Before the 1960s, lawyers answered such questions in much the same way as they would have in 60 B.C.—by consulting intuition and any available facts. After the 1960s, price theory, which is mathematically precise and econometrically confirmed, gave more exact and reliable answers. Price theory was applied to law by reinterpreting legal sanctions as prices. The application of price theory to law constitutes much of the early economic analysis of law.

Many constitutional powers and rights, however, do not have explicit sanctions attached to their misuse or infringement. For example, a constitution may prescribe how to enact a law without specifying punishments for circumventing the procedure. Or a constitution may guarantee freedom of religion to the individual without specifying how to protect its exercise. The absence of a sanction poses an obstacle to analysis by using price theory.

---

[17] Koetz 1997.

[18] For examples, see the selected papers from the annual meeting of the European Association of Law and Economics, which are published each December in the *International Review of Law and Economics*.

[19] For corporations and finance, see Buxbaum 1991; for administrative law, see Rose-Ackerman 1994; for property, see Hansmann and Mattei 1994; for contracts, see Koetz 1997; in general, see Mattei 1996; for developing nations, see Bruno and Pleskovic 1997 and Buscaglia, Rotliff, and Cooter 1997.

Even without explicit sanctions, however, constitutions create incentives amenable to economic analysis. To see why, consider an analogy to the famous board game Monopoly. Its rules specify prices (e.g., the initial buying price of "Marvin Gardens") and moves (e.g., rolling the dice determines how far a player must advance), but not sanctions for breaking the rules (e.g., no punishment is specified for advancing "seven" when the dice say "six"). Even without explicit sanctions, the fundamental rules provide the framework for competing in the game of Monopoly. Similarly, a democratic constitution provides a framework of rules for competing in the game of politics. An effective constitution constrains and channels political competition.

In interactive games, the players form strategies by anticipating the moves of other players. To illustrate, a player in American football often runs around the right side as a decoy to fool the other team while the player carrying the ball runs around the left side. In contrast, a mountain climber never starts up the south slope as a decoy to fool the mountain while the main party ascends the north slope. Football is strategic and mountain climbing is nonstrategic. Perfectly competitive markets have too many transactions for any one person to affect the price, so price theory usually assumes that actors behave nonstrategically. In contrast, game theory analyzes strategic behavior, which typically involves small numbers of competitors.[20]

Just as perfectly competitive markets have too many transactions for any one person to affect the price, general elections have too many voters for any one voter to affect the election. In competitive markets and general elections, the large number of actors usually prevents individuals from acting strategically. In these circumstances, price theory provides an adequate analytical tool. This book adapts price theory to analyze some problems of constitutional law involving nonstrategic behavior, such as voting in general elections.

Law and politics, however, often involve small numbers of actors who behave strategically. To illustrate, litigants in court and candidates in elections form strategies by anticipating the moves of their opponents. This book adapts game theory to analyze problems of constitutional law involving strategic behavior. In moving from price theory to game theory, this book reflects a movement in the recent history of economic analysis.

Early in the development of the economic analysis of law, theorists learned to simplify games by treating strategy as one of the "transaction costs" of interacting with other people.[21] From this perspective, the need for strategy merely raises the price of engaging in an activity. Treating strategy as a price dramatically simplifies analysis, which is especially useful at a problem's begin-

---

[20] In general, see Baird, Gertner, and Picker 1994 and Rasmusen 1994. Note that organizing large numbers of people into hierarchies with a small number of leaders can result in strategic behavior, as when hostile generals lead large armies in war.

[21] The technique of treating strategic behavior as a cost was developed in the most famous proposition in the economic analysis of law called the Coase Theorem. This theorem has several versions, one of which asserts that *bargaining succeeds so long as transaction costs are low*. See Coase 1960 and Cooter 1982.

ning. (Readers familiar with the Coase Theorem, which is a license to postpone strategic analysis, will recall how it simplified the early economic analysis of property and tort law [Coase 1960].) In the end, however, strategic behavior does not resemble the price of toothpaste, soybean futures, or any other good sold in a competitive market (Cooter 1982). Buyers usually treat the prices of these goods as beyond their control, whereas politicians anticipate the response of their rivals. A full explanation of interaction among small numbers of competitors, such as litigants and politicians, must model their choice of strategies. Instead of applying price theory by treating strategy as a cost, a more satisfactory analysis requires game theory.

VALUES

Many of the predictions in this book are neutral with respect to political values. To illustrate, Duverger's Law predicts that two-party competition emerges when seats in the legislature are filled by plurality voting in winner-take-all elections. This prediction does not say whether two-party competition is better or worse than many-party competition. Politicians, administrators, judges, and voters often want to go beyond neutrality and predict the effects of law on policy values. By "policy values," I mean the values that figure prominently in debates about public policy. By "policy science," I mean a body of reliable predictions about policy values. Debates about public policy often rely on false or doubtful predictions. Policy science improves the quality of public debate by supplying reliable predictions about policy values.

Economists are experts on two kinds of policy values: efficiency and distribution. More than other social scientists, economists understand how laws influence the production and distribution of income and wealth across groups of people. For example, economists in nineteenth-century England contributed to a great policy debate by predicting the effects of repealing the "Corn Laws" (tariffs on imported wheat). The predictions focused on national wealth and the distribution of income across social classes.[22] Given that a policy science predicts the consequences of policy on public values, economics is the policy science that specializes in efficiency and distribution. (I distinguish several concepts of "efficiency" and "distribution" in chapter 2.)

These two values have different political foundations. Everyone concedes that pursuing good ends efficiently is better than pursuing them inefficiently. No one publicly advocates wasting money. In contrast, people of different political persuasion disagree sharply over distribution. Some people favor using the state to increase equality by redistributing income, and others object to compulsory income redistribution. Some economists take sides in this debate, either advocating equality or protesting redistribution. Other economists strive for neutrality by predicting the effects of different policies on distribution without advocating any particular goal ("parameterizing"). Still other economists confuse the

---

[22] Classical papers on tariffs and taxes are in Musgrave and Peacock 1967.

discussion by insisting that efficiency is the only value that belongs to economics as a science.[23] These pure positivists spread confusion because predictions about redistribution are central to economics, and redistribution is a controversial value.

In this book I comment on distribution when a constitutional provision clearly affects economic equality or poverty. Constitutions drafted before the first half of the twentieth century usually say nothing about redistribution explicitly. These constitutions often limit the means of redistribution by protecting property rights explicitly. In contrast, some democratic constitutions drafted after the creation of the welfare state include welfare rights, as discussed in chapter 11. To illustrate, the constitutions of South Africa and some post-communist countries provide for "positive rights" such as housing, pensions, and education. Instead of entitlements enforceable in court, constitutional rights to welfare currently resemble aspirations. These rights provide goals without providing implementation. Regardless of the constitution, modern democracies typically follow an old tradition in economics by imposing progressive taxes on everyone and transferring income to the poorest citizens.[24] Since welfare states mostly pursue redistributive goals through legislation, not through constitutions, redistributive goals occupy a modest part of this book.

Liberty, which provides the individual with the freedom to choose, is another important constitutional value that connects with economic theory. Each person knows his own wants better than others do. Consequently, individuals satisfy their preferences best when given freedom to choose. For these reasons, a constitution that aims to satisfy the preferences of individuals must give them liberty. (The connection between liberty and efficiency is discussed in chapters 11 and 12.) Liberty for citizens requires limiting the powers of government. The quest for power by many politicians knows no limits. When law and ambition collide, ambition sometimes destroys law. To illustrate, Spain suffered forty-three coups d'état between 1814 and 1923.[25] One of the worst political possibilities occurs when officials abandon law and become tyrants. Another of the worst possibilities occurs when rivalry among factions descends into violence, as in India at independence or Rwanda in the 1990s.

The first goal of the constitution is to impose the rule of law and protect the liberty of citizens. Game theory provides a useful restatement of this goal. A player who follows the *minimax* strategy in a game minimizes the maximum harm that he can suffer.[26] The "minimax constitution," to coin a phrase,[27]

---

[23] The most influential version of economic positivism that expels policy values from science, with the possible exception of efficiency, is found in Robbins 1932 and Friedman 1953.

[24] Pigou 1950 is a classic in the economic tradition that the state should adjust the distribution of income produced by markets to alleviate poverty and increase equality. Dreze and Sen 1989 exemplifies this tradition.

[25] "A Survey of Spain," *The Economist*, 25 April 1992, p. 3.

[26] In a zero-sum game, minimizing the maximum harm is equivalent to maximizing the minimum payoff. Thus the minimax constitution can also be described as the maximin constitution.

[27] I introduce this phrase in Cooter 1992.

minimizes the harm when the worst political possibilities materialize. The minimax constitution pursues the classical political goals of security, legality, and liberty.

After providing security, legality, and liberty, a constitution can look to the prosperity of its citizens. To bring prosperity, the constitution must provide the legal framework for allocating resources efficiently to public and private goods. The legal framework includes competitive markets for private goods and competitive politics for public goods.

Perhaps the most discussed value in political theory is justice. Democracy provides a framework for alternative conceptions of justice to compete for the allegiance of citizens. Scholars try to influence politics by saying why one conception of justice is better or worse than another. This kind of scholarship, which I admire,[28] is normative and critical. My aim in this book, however, is different. I want to explain how constitutions can organize political competition to give citizens the laws and public goods that they want.

Now I turn from policy values to individual values. Politics attracts talented people with vast egos whose ambition brings vitality and danger to government. David Hume wrote, "In constraining any system of government, and fixing the several checks and controls of the constitution, each man ought to be supposed a knave, and to have no other end, in all his actions, than private interest."[29] Similarly, economists typically assume that individuals pursue their self-interest defined narrowly in terms of wealth and power.

Some models in this book assume that narrow self-interest exclusively motivates people. The facts justify this assumption insofar as political competition filters candidates for the single-minded pursuit of power. In other words, political candidates who constrain or deflect their pursuit of power by morality tend to lose elections. Conversely, the facts falsify this assumption insofar as political competition filters candidates for virtue, as some founders of the United States hoped when they envisioned voters electing a "natural aristocracy." Furthermore, people outside of politics, who escape electoral pressures, influence democratic government. For example, a citizen who votes in secret or an independent judge who decides a case can respond to his conscience instead of competition. An accurate model of voting by citizens or adjudication by judges must allow for a variety of individual values other than wealth and power, including self-expression.

Most models of electoral competition are driven by disagreement. The source of the disagreement, which might be self-interest or rival conceptions of the public interest, makes no difference to these models. I typically assume that people disagree over public choices, and leave the source of disagreement unspecified. This approach assumes difference in individual values without explaining their causes. To illustrate, under certain conditions majority rule tends toward

---

[28] I especially appreciate the attempt by Rawls to derive a theory of justice from Kantian ethics and his subsequent attempt to ground his theory of justice in politics. See Rawls 1971 and Rawls 1993.

[29] Hume 1987, p. 42.

the center of the distribution of political preferences. The central tendency of majority rule operates independently of the reason why citizens disagree with each other.

STRUCTURE AND CONTRIBUTION OF BOOK

I define democracy as competitive government and I assert that competition provides the best guarantee that government will satisfy the preferences of citizens. Most of this book uses strategic theory to predict the consequences of alternative forms of democratic organization. When the state commits to a constitution, it supplies the rules of the game of normal politics. I explain how to play under different rules.

I will describe briefly the book's parts. In part 1, chapters 2, 3, and 4 develop the theory of voting, bargaining, and administering, respectively. Taken together, these chapters develop general principles that I apply in the rest of the book. Students should work through these chapters carefully, whereas advanced scholars can skim much of this material. Chapter 2 explains the central tendency in majority voting (median rule) and the tendency of majority rule to spin its wheels (intransitivity). Chapter 3 explains the minimum winning coalition in a parliamentary system and the principles that govern lobbying. Chapter 4 uses the principal-agent relationship to analyze civil service bureaucracies, especially the trade-off among delegation of power, rules, and the diversion of purpose.

Turning to part 2, chapters 5 and 6 concern intergovernmental relations. The organization of relations among governments influences their ability to cooperate with each other. Chapter 5 analyzes the difference between unanimity rule and majority rule in intergovernmental relations. Chapter 6 analyzes the competitive mechanisms that cause successful governments to expand and unsuccessful governments to shrink. Chapter 7 concerns the relationship between government and administration. I explain how the organization of government determines the discretionary power of administrators to pursue their own purposes.

The same geographic area can have many governments or few governments. In democracies, decentralization multiplies elected governments and shrinks administration, whereas centralization deepens administration and reduces elected governments. Chapters 5, 6, and 7 address the problem of the optimal number of elections, or, equivalently, the optimal depth of state administration. Too many elections drain the reservoir of civic spirit that animates voters, and, conversely, too deep administration dilutes democratic purposes and gives excessive discretion to bureaucrats.

Whereas part 2 deals with governments externally, in part 3 I turn to the internal allocation of powers. Chapter 8 analyzes the special competency of the legislature, executive, and courts. The legislature represents the nation's political factions and interests, who make laws by making bargains. By enforcing the laws that embody political bargains, the courts facilitate political cooperation. Chapter 9 explains the interaction of the branches of government according to the extent of their separation. Separating powers causes government to proceed by bargains among the branches, not by orders from the executive. Separating powers also increases the minimum size required for a cartel to control the state.

In part 4 I turn from the powers of officials to the rights of citizens. Chapter 10 shows how to value rights by using economic theory. I contrast treating rights as commodities and treating rights as merit goods with distinctively social value. Chapter 11 relates the valuation of rights to competing traditions in political philosophy. Chapters 10 and 11 are more normative and philosophical than the rest of book, whereas chapters 12–14 return to predictive models. Chapters 12–14 concern three particular constitutional rights, specifically property, speech, and civil rights. I analyze the boundary between freedom and regulation of property, freedom and liability for speech, and discrimination and equality in competition. Finally, chapter 15 concludes the book by discussing the perspective of strategic theory on democracy.

Processes of Government:
Voting, Bargaining, Administering

IN A DEMOCRACY, candidates compete for office and the votes of citizens determine the winners. To win elections and form governments, politicians must bargain with each other and agree to cooperate. Once a government forms, it implements its policies through state bureaucracies. Thus, voting, bargaining, and administering are three basic government processes. I analyze these processes in chapters 2, 3, and 4, respectively, and I use these analyses throughout the book.

I will describe briefly some major themes in chapters 2, 3, and 4. When constitutions narrow voting to one dimension of choice, majority voting tends to settle toward the middle of the distribution of voters' preferences. Like a safe stock, one-dimensional choice has a modest, predictable yield. Alternatively, constitutions can allow voting to range freely over multiple dimensions of choice. Multiple dimensions of choice lower the transaction costs of political trades, with two possible results. First, politicians often bargain successfully and "roll logs." Just as people benefit most from trading widely in markets, so political factions benefit most from bargaining widely in politics. Second, bargaining among politicians may fail, with the consequence that majority voting spins its wheels. No one benefits from wheel-spinning. Like a risky stock, multidimensional choice can yield a lot or nothing, depending on political institutions and culture.

Politics has a large effect on citizens, whereas each individual citizen has a small effect on politics. Since ordinary citizens gain little for themselves by participating in democracy, few citizens invest the time and energy needed to obtain detailed information about electoral candidates and issues. When citizens remain rationally ignorant, politicians need costly campaigns to influence citizens and win votes. To finance campaigns, politicians trade political influence for money from lobbyists. Rational actors invest in an activity, including lobbying, when the profit equals or exceeds the return on alternative forms of investment. Since laws are general, lobbying tends to affect many people and interests. Displaced benefits prompt people to "free-ride" on lobbying by others. Lobbyists need to organize to overcome free-riding and solve the problem of collective action.

Elections ideally transmit the preferences of citizens to the politicians who head ministries or agencies. In implementing the government's program, however, each successive level of administration dilutes the political purpose transmitted by voters. To resist the dilution of purpose, rules must constrain the civil service. Constraint by rules, however, reduces the flexibility with which administrators respond to change. Consequently, rapid change favors relatively shallow administration and many elected governments, whereas slow change favors relatively deep administration and few elected governments. The next three chapters develop these principles of voting, bargaining, and administering in detail.

CHAPTER 2

Voting

> King [to his princes]. "I'll be your father and your brother too; Let me but bear
> your love, I'll bear your cares."
>
> —*Shakespeare's* Henry IV[1]

> If men were angels, no government would be necessary. If angels were to
> govern men, neither external nor internal controls on government would be
> necessary. In framing a government which is to be administered by men over
> men, the great difficulty lies in this: you must first enable the government to
> control the governed; and in the next place oblige it to control itself.
>
> —*James Madison*, The Federalist Papers[2]

SHAKESPEARE often depicts the nation as the king's family and the state as
the king's household. All is well in the nation so long as the king's relatives
and friends actually feel the love and affection that they proclaim toward each
other, but let them fall out and strife overtakes the state. In this warm and intimate account of government, politics resembles the family. Love and affection,
however, proved an unreliable foundation for politics. Most citizens these days
do not regard themselves as the government's children, and they want political
power restrained by something stronger than morality.

Eighteenth-century political theorists, including the founders of the United
States, treated government as more like a machine than a household. They
rejected the belief that politicians would act spontaneously in the public interest.
Instead of family government, they wanted to design something like a market
in which politicians would compete for votes, and this competition would direct
politicians to do good as by an invisible hand.[3] Just as efficiency requires economic competition, so responsive politics requires political competition.

The vision of democracy as a market for votes proved useful and enduring, but the techniques for analyzing a market for votes changed little until
recently, when economic theory was applied to politics. The basic techniques

---

[1] Henry IV, part 2, act 5, scene 2, ll. 57–58. Thanks to Robert Pearlman for this quote.

[2] Madison 1981b, p. 160. Thanks to David Lieberman for this quote.

[3] The relationship between public-choice theory and the political thought of Madison is discussed
in Eskridge and Frickey 1988, pp. 37–38, 40–56.

for analyzing voting, which this chapter develops, offer fresh insights into questions such as these:

Example 1: Some voters want government to be rich as fits the emblem of a great people, others want it starved into lethargy so it cannot hurt anyone, and most voters favor a position in between these extremes. Most politicians, however, just want to win elections. What political platform on government expenditure is most likely to command a majority of votes by citizens?

Example 2: Minorities sometimes feel excluded from political power, and majorities sometimes feel that pivotal minorities wield excessive political power. What determines the degree of responsiveness of democratic politics to minorities?

Example 3: When campaigning, some politicians are notoriously vague about their positions on particular policies. When does obfuscation help to win elections?

To begin to answer such questions, this chapter develops the economic theory of elections and applies it to the legislature and executive. The details of democratic institutions display as much variety as birdsong. To illustrate, elections are conducted by majority rule (winner receives at least half of votes), plurality rule (winner receives most votes), plurality run-off rule (two candidates receiving most votes in the primary stand against each other in the final election), super-majority rule (winner receives two-thirds of votes, as with constitutional amendments), sub-majority rule (party receiving, say, 10 percent of votes or more enjoys financial aid from state), pure proportional representation (parties receive seats in legislature in proportion to popular vote), and minimum proportional representation (parties receiving at least, say, 10 percent of the votes receive seats in legislature in proportion to popular vote). Citizens may elect the executive directly, as with presidents, or the legislature may elect the executive, as with a prime minister. Elections may occur at predetermined intervals or the executive may call elections at his discretion. Legislatures may have one house (unicameral) or two (bicameral). The legislature may amend bills proposed to it ("open rule"), or amendments may be forbidden ("closed rule"). The constitution may be explicitly written, with wide latitude for court interpretation, as in the United States, or the constitution may be unwritten, with little scope for court interpretation, as in Britain.

In spite of these differences, all elections share certain general features. This chapter abstracts from the differences and analyzes the general features of elections, proceeding along lines successfully applied to markets. Competition among firms seeking to satisfy consumers determines prices in a market. Similarly, competition among candidates seeking to satisfy voters determines public policies in a democracy. To develop this approach, I first explain how economics models the choice of voters among candidates (demand), and then I explain how candidates choose strategies to win elections (supply).

INDIVIDUAL VOTING

Citizens face several decisions in connection with voting. First I will assume that a rational person decides to participate in a vote and I will analyze how that person will vote. Second I will analyze how a rational citizen will decide whether to bother participating in a vote, and whether to abstain in voting on a particular issue. Third I will explain how to represent a voter's preferences by a utility function.

How to Vote: Self-Interest or Public Interest?

I like ice cream better than cabbage because of the taste, he likes San Diego better than Seattle because of the weather, and she likes the Republicans better than the Democrats because she is conservative. Among the many reasons that people have for their preferences, I will contrast two broad types. On the one hand, a citizen can vote based on material self-interest. A narrowly self-interested voter asks, "Which candidate will do more to increase my own wealth and power?"On the other hand, a public-interested voter asks, "Which candidate will benefit the country more according to my political philosophy?"

To supply efficient quantities of public goods, officials need information about the policy preferences of citizens. By supplying this information, self-interested voting sometimes promotes efficiency in the supply of public goods. All too often, however, citizens use politics to obtain advantages for themselves at the expense of others. The aim is redistribution, not efficiency. Thus banks want loan guarantees, farmers want price supports, unions want tariffs, artists want subsidies, taxis want fewer licenses for cabs, the elderly want property tax exemptions, and so forth. This kind of self-seeking wastes resources and oppresses the powerless. While people seldom criticize a consumer in the grocery store for following his self-interest when filling his shopping cart, people often criticize citizens for voting their self-interest.

Do most citizens vote their self-interest or the public interest? The determinants of voting behavior have been studied for many years. Survey research reveals that voters know little about issues or candidates, so they typically rely on guidance from political parties, ideology, and informed friends or associates. In spite of their ignorance, however, citizens tend to vote for candidates who promote the interests of the groups to which they belong. For example, farmers tend to vote for candidates who subsidize agriculture, ethnic groups tend to vote for candidates who benefit minorities, and investment bankers tend to vote for candidates who liberalize finance (Campbell et al. 1960).

Supporting candidates who advance a group's interests can benefit a person by showing solidarity with its members.[4] To illustrate, dairy farmers in a rural community may be more willing to cooperate with other dairy farmers who endorses milk subsidies. Conversely, an ethnic group may censor members who

---

[4] *Posner* forthcoming emphasizes this mechanism for creating social norms.

oppose preferential treatment for minorities.[5] In general, groups develop ideologies that advance a self-serving conception of the public interest, like the automobile worker who believes that "what's good for General Motors is good for America."

Assume that a political pollster asks me to rank three alternative political platforms by assigning the letter A to the platform that I like best, B to the middle platform, and C to the platform that I like least. Pollsters seldom ask whether self-interest or the public interest motivates my ranking. A utility function can represent a person's ranking of alternatives. The ability of a social scientist to represent preferences by a utility function has nothing to do with whether self-interest or a conception of the public interest generates the preferences. Later I will sketch a way to represent preferences by a utility function that applies to many types of voters.

Question: Machiavelli's book *The Prince* scandalized sixteenth-century Europeans by describing immoral methods by which princes can enhance their power. Similarly, collective-choice theory scandalizes some people today by explaining the logic of self-interest in democratic politics. Why do you think the assumption of self-interest in politics troubles people so much? Discuss some of the advantages and disadvantages of using this assumption about motivation to explain political behavior.

Why Vote?

Journalists often deplore the fact that only about half of the eligible citizens vote in major U.S. elections, and participation has fallen since the nineteenth century.[6] Voter participation rates are similar in other countries, except where democracy is new, the law compels citizens to vote as in Australia and Argentina, or the names of nonvoting citizens are posted in public as in some Italian towns. Unlike journalists, however, economists find voter participation rates mysteriously *high*. Models of self-interest predict much lower voter participation rates than actually occur, and here is why. A self-interested citizen will decide whether or not to vote by comparing the cost of voting and his expected benefit. Given current rates of voter participation, the probability is negligible that a single vote in a large election will effect the outcome. So the effort required to vote exceeds the expected benefit for voters in large elections.

Some notation clarifies this point. The value of the time required to vote usually measures its opportunity cost, which I denote C_i for citizen i. For simplicity, assume that the citizen cares about who wins the election, not the margin of victory. Let p_i denote the probability that citizen i's vote decides the election's outcome. Let B_i denote the increase in citizen i's wealth or power obtained by

---

[5] For the dynamics of "ethnification," see Kuran 1997.

[6] Bumper sticker on pickup truck in Berkeley: "If God had intended us to vote, He would have given us candidates."

getting his preferred outcome in the election.[7] Thus the expected benefit from voting equals p_iB_i. According to the *self-interested theory of voter participation*, a citizen votes when $p_iB_i \geq C_i$, and a citizen does not vote when $p_iB_i < C_i$. The self-interested theory of voting predicts that voter participation rates will fall until p_iB_i approximately equals C_i. The *paradox of voting* refers to the fact that current levels of voter participation far exceed the rate at which p_iB_i equals C_i. If the self-interested theory of voting accurately described the behavior of most citizens, voter participation rates would fall far below current levels.

To illustrate, assume that having your preferred candidate win the election is worth $1,000 to you. Assume that voting requires one hour of your time, which you value at $10. Self-interest prompts you to vote if $p_i\$1,000 \geq \$10$, which implies $p_i \geq 1/100$. In large elections, the probability of any one vote being decisive is *much* smaller than 1/100. Computing the subjective probability of being decisive p, which is called the *power of a vote*, depends on what the voter thinks other voters will do (Palfrey and Rosenthal 1985). According to one calculation, the power of a vote in a typical U.S. general election approximately equals 10^{-8}.[8] Under any reasonable assumptions, the power of a vote is so small in a large election that purely self-interested citizens would not bother to vote at current rates.

If narrow self-interest does not explain why people vote at current rates, what does? An important tradition in political theory dating from Aristotle holds that political participation appeals to the social nature of people. According to this tradition, people express themselves by performing civic duties, and self-expression is intrinsically satisfying.[9] Deliberative theories of democracy stress the satisfaction that people take in exercising the responsibilities of citizenship, such as voting.

By voting rather than not voting, I increase the probability that people who agree with my politics will like the election's results. So people who agree with my politics will say that I ought to vote. The fact that citizens often praise voters and criticize nonvoters indicates the existence of a social norm. Besides self-expression, people may vote to obtain praise or avoid criticism from others.

To represent the influence of civil duty, let v_i denote the value to i of fulfilling i's civic duty, where v_i is large for some people and small for others. According to the civic virtue theory, everyone votes whose value v_i outweighs the net cost $C_i - p_iB_i$. Thus citizens vote when $v_i \geq C - p_iB_p$.[10] This formula encapsulates

---

[7] To illustrate, in a vote between a Republican and Democratic candidate, the benefit B_i of a Republican voter i equals $u^i(x_r) - u^i(x_d)$, where "u" is willingness to pay.

[8] See discussion in Hasen 1996. Using a different method of calculation, Romer 1996 concludes that the probability of a tie in a U.S. presidential election in which fifty million people vote is approximately 10^{-4} (p. 200).

[9] Expressive voting theory is explored in Brennan and Lomasky 1993.

[10] Let $f(v, b)$ denote the density function representing the distribution of social value v and material benefit b among citizens. The total number of voters in an election, according to this theory, equals the sum of all the voters for whom v exceeds $C - pB$, or voter participation $= \int_{C-pB} f$.

a *mixed-motive theory of voting*, which combines self-interest and civic duty. The mixed-motive theory has testable implications.[11]

Questions

1. Use the concept of the "power of a vote" to explain why self-interested people would not allow voter participation rates to approach zero.

2. Predict the conditions under which a social norm requiring voter participation would be effective.

3. "By not voting I increase the power of everyone else's vote. Therefore, not voting is a kindness to others that should be encouraged. There is no civic duty to vote." Is anything wrong with this argument?

Ignorance and Abstention

Sometimes a rational person abstains from voting even though participation costs nothing. Rational abstention depends on who knows what. To understand rational abstention, assume that you are a member of a law faculty that must vote on whether or not to offer a job to a particular applicant. Your faculty follows a procedure of majority rule, with the chairman breaking ties. You ask yourself whether you should vote or abstain. If you vote, your vote will be either indecisive or decisive. If your vote will be indecisive, then voting or abstaining does not affect the outcome. For example, if six colleagues vote "yes" and four colleagues vote "no," then your vote will be indecisive.

If your vote will be decisive, then you will determine the outcome by voting, or, by abstaining you will allow the chairman to determine the outcome. For example, if five colleagues vote "yes" and five colleagues vote "no," then your vote will break the tie or your abstention will permit the chairman to break the tie. So you should decide whether to vote or abstain by asking whether you prefer to decide the outcome yourself or have the chairman decide it.

Two considerations should guide this decision: information and values. If you know more than your chairman knows about the issue, then you should vote. If your chairman knows more than you know about the issue, and if your chairman has the same values as you, then you should abstain. The hard choice comes when your chairman knows more than you know about the issue, and your chairman's values differ substantially from yours. Here you must balance information and values in deciding whether you prefer that the chairman or you determine the outcome of the vote.

To illustrate a hard choice, assume that your chairman can evaluate the job candidate's scholarship in constitutional law better than you. If the only issue

---

[11] As with self-interested theory, mixed-motive theory predicts that voter participation should increase when the power of a vote p increases, the private material benefit B_i from winning the election increases, or the opportunity cost of voting C_i decreases. In addition, the mixed-motive theory predicts that voter participation increases when the value of conforming to the social norm v_i increases. It might increase because more people internalize civic virtue, the social advantage from political participation increases, or the social cost from not voting decreases.

were constitutional scholarship, then you would abstain. Another issue, however, is ethnic diversity on the faculty. Everyone on the faculty has the same information about the ethnicity of job candidates, but colleagues disagree about its importance. Compared to the chairman, you put more weight on ethnic diversity and less weight on constitutional scholarship. If the only issue were ethnic diversity, then you would vote. Here you must balance the chairman's superior information against your disagreement with the chairman over values.

This analysis shows why ignorance about candidates or issues may cause rational voters not to participate in elections. The logic of nonparticipation follows the logic of abstention. If the citizen's vote will be indecisive, then voting or abstaining does not affect the outcome. If the citizen's vote will be decisive, then the citizen will determine the outcome by voting. Alternatively, by abstaining the citizens will make another voter decisive in determining the outcome. Call this person the *next decisive* voter. A rational citizen will decide whether or not to vote by asking whether he prefers to decide the outcome or have the next decisive voter decide.

The next-decisive-voter theory explains why rational, civic-minded citizens might not participate in elections. The case for rational nonparticipation by a citizen is strongest when the next decisive voter has similar values and better information. The next-decisive-voter theory predicts that participation rates will fall as values become more homogeneous (the distribution of values compacts) or information becomes more heterogeneous (the distribution of information spreads). The next-decisive-voter theory also predicts that people who abstain have less political information on average than people who vote.

In the past, many citizens could not choose to vote because incipient democracies restricted voting by gender, race, class, and property ownership. In modern democratic states, however, every adult citizen typically enjoys the right to vote. Outside of the state, voting restrictions remain important in some organizations. For example, corporations typically allocate votes to owners in proportion to their shares, cooperatives typically allow one vote per member, and homeowners associations or business improvement districts typically restrict voting to property owners (Ellickson 1998). I will develop a theory of elections that predicts outcomes from the preferences of voters, regardless of the extent of the franchise.

Questions

Feral cats prompt your town to elect a Cat-Catcher. When you come to vote in the general election, you scan the list of candidates for Cat-Catcher and realize that you know little about them. Describe how you might rationally decide whether to vote or abstain. Why might a rational citizen prefer to cast a *blank* ballot in an election instead of not participating?

Representing a Voter's Preferences

Imagine a simple electoral contest with two viable candidates, say, the nominees of the democratic and republican parties. In the election campaign, each candidate announces a platform that describes his position on the major issues. The platform encompasses the candidate's general ideology and specific policies on such matters as subsidies, tax relief, and regulations. In response, each citizen votes for the candidate whose platform conforms closest to his political preferences. The candidates understand these facts. Consequently, each candidate tries to find a platform that will command a majority of votes against the opposition's platform.

Some notation facilitates discussing this model. Specifically, let x_r denote the platform announced by the first candidate (republican), and let x_d denote the platform announced by the second candidate (democratic). Let n denote the number of citizens who will vote in the election. Each citizen ranks the possible platforms from best to worst. The ranking of platforms by any individual, say the ith individual, is indicated by a utility function. Higher values of the utility function indicate a higher ranking for the political platform. Thus, the utility value of platform x_1 to citizen i is $u^i(x_1)$, and the utility value of platform x_2 to citizen i is $u^i(x_2)$. If citizen i prefers x_1 to x_2, then the utility value of the former exceeds the utility value of the latter: $u^i(x_1) > u^i(x_2)$.

Each citizen is assumed to vote for the candidate with the preferred platform. To illustrate, many U.S. elections offer a choice between a Democratic and a Republican candidate. The utility $u^i(x_r)$ is the one that the ith citizen expects to enjoy by electing the Republican, and $u^i(x_d)$ is the utility that he expects from electing the Democrat. Here is the ith citizen's voting rule:

$$u^i(x_r) > u^i(x_d) \Rightarrow \text{citizen i votes Republican}$$
$$u^i(x_r) < u^i(x_d) \Rightarrow \text{citizen i votes Democratic}$$
$$u^i(x_r) = u^i(x_d) \Rightarrow \text{citizen i votes by flipping a coin.}$$

In deciding how to vote, all n citizens follow the same procedure as citizen i, except the utility functions are different for different people.

In this model, each side announces its program to the public and the winner in the election imposes its political platform upon everyone. In contrast, a consumer in the grocery store fills his shopping cart with goods for his own private use. Political platforms especially concern public goods such as expenditures on parks and the military, not private goods such as expenditures on ice cream and carrots. For public goods, the state supplies one quantity for everyone. This fact about public goods has consequences that I discuss several times in this book, especially in chapter 5.

A public good is indicated mathematically when the same variable enters the utility functions of different people. To illustrate, assume that two individuals, denoted i and j, have utilities u^i and u^j. If the variable x enters both their utility functions in the same quantity, as in $u^i(x)$ and $u^j(x)$, then x has the mathematical character of a public good. To illustrate, x might denote state expenditures on military defense. If, however, each person enjoys different quantities of the variable x, which can be denoted $u^i(x_i)$ and $u^j(x_j)$, then x has the mathematical character of a private good. To illustrate, $u^i(x_i)$ might denote person i's utility from consuming x_i pints of ice cream.

In this sketch of a voting model, political positions determine votes. In addition to political positions, a candidate's appearance, personality, or other personal attributes often sway voters. Furthermore, the candidates have to communicate with voters, which involves costly advertising and raises problems of credibility.[12] Besides positions on issues, the framing of issues also influences voting. To illustrate, framing affirmative action as a racial preference or nondiscrimination affects the response of Californians to it. Similarly, framing social security benefits as welfare or entitlement affects the response of citizens to it. These complications are best omitted in the initial stage of developing a theory of elections, which is my next topic.

AGGREGATING VOTES

Having analyzed how citizens decide whether to vote and how to vote, the next step is to explain how candidates choose their platforms to win elections. I begin with a simple, intuitive model of the central tendency in democratic elections.

Median Rule

Under certain conditions, electoral competition causes party platforms to converge toward the center of the distribution of political sentiment. To be more precise, the winning platform in certain conditions is the one favored by the citizen who is the median in the statistical distribution of political sentiment (Black 1958). This conclusion corresponds to the familiar fact that the candidates in U.S. presidential elections tend to adopt moderate positions on the political spectrum (Downs 1957).

The median tendency in democracy can be illustrated by using an example in which there are three voters, denoted A, B, and C. Figure 2-1 depicts their preferences, possibly as determined by a poll. Consider the change in A's utility, denoted $u^a(x)$, when moving from left to right in figure 2-1. A's utility increases when moving right in the direction of x_a^*. After passing x_a^*, A's utility decreases when moving further to the right. A prefers x_a^* the most because the utility curve $u^a(x)$ achieves its highest point when the platform is x_a^*. Similarly, the most preferred platform for voters A, B, and C are denoted x_a^*, x_b^*, and x_c^*, respectively.

Assume that two candidates compete for votes of the three citizens. To keep the analysis simple, I assume that no one abstains and all three voters have complete information. Each candidate must choose a political platform, and then each citizen votes for the candidate whose platform yields higher utility. It is not hard to see that in this three-voter example, the platform x_b^* will beat any other platform.

To see why, assume that x_b^* is chosen by the democrat and the republican chooses any platform located a little farther to the right. Voters A and B will get

---

[12] For an interesting model of political signaling through advertising, see Dharmapala 1998.

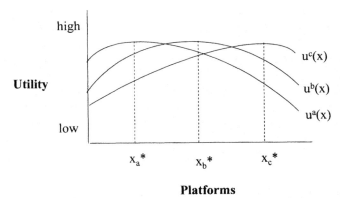

Platforms

Fig. 2-1 Platforms and Preferences

more utility from the democratic platform than from the republican platform, whereas C will get more utility from the republican platform, so the democrat will win by a 2 to 1 majority.

Reversing the example, assume that the republican chooses the platform x_b^* and the democrat chooses any platform a little further to the left. B and C will get more utility from the republican platform, whereas C will get more utility from the democratic platform, so the republican will win by a 2 to 1 majority. Thus, the party that discovers and announces platform x_b^* is unbeatable in the election.

In this three-person example, the winning platform x_b^* is the one most preferred by B. Notice that B is in the middle of the distribution of preferences in the sense that one voter's most preferred point lies to the right and one voter's most preferred point lies to the left. In general, when there are many individuals, rather than just three, the median is defined as the individual with an equal number above and below. For any odd number of n individuals, the median has $(n - 1)/2$ voters to the left and $(n - 1)/2$ voters to the right. When voters have preferences like those in figure 2-1, the winning platform is the one most preferred by the median voter. Since this platform defeats every alternative, it is the political equilibrium in the electoral competition. The actual winner in the election depends on which candidate has the information and opportunity to choose the equilibrium platform.[13]

The median rule explains the central tendency in some political systems. For example, many Americans can locate themselves along a simple left-right continuum, with "liberal Democrat" at one end and "conservative Republican" at

[13] If the candidates must commit to a platform with imperfect information, each one will make a guess about the dominant platform. If the candidates know the dominant platform and one candidate chooses the platform before the other (e.g., the incumbent chooses first), then the candidate who chooses first will win. If both candidates know the dominant platform and they choose simultaneously, both will choose the same platform, in which case voters will be indifferent over who wins.

the other. A common pattern in U.S. presidential campaigns is for the Republican candidate to take a position on the right wing in the primary elections when seeking the nomination and, once nominated, to move nearer to the middle of the political spectrum. The initial right-wing position appeals to the median voter in the Republican Party, as required to secure the party's nomination, and the moderate position appeals to the median voter among all the citizens, as required to win the general election. Similarly, Democratic Party candidates often start from the left in the primaries and move toward the middle after nomination.

Note that the median rule assumes that voters disagree, but it makes no assumptions about the cause of the disagreement. Some citizens try to advance their self-interest and others may try to advance a conception of the public interest. Their reasons for ranking political alternatives do not affect the scope of the median rule.

The median-voter model leaves out important features of real elections, such as party loyalty, voter ignorance, campaign spending, and personal appeal of candidates. Despite these omissions, the median rule is a useful starting point for a theory of electoral competition.

Questions

1. Suppose that left-wing voters become so filled with righteous anger at their political choices that they boycott a general election and do not vote. In which direction will their behavior shift the winning platform?

2. Explain why the median rule assumes disagreement, but not necessarily self-interested voting.

3. There are three voters (A, B, and C) and three alternatives (x_1, x_2, x_3). The voters rank the alternative from 1 to 3, with "3" indicating the most preferred alternative and "1" indicating the least preferred:

$$\text{person A: } 3 = u^a(x_1), \quad 2 = u^a(x_2), \quad 1 = u^a(x_3)$$
$$\text{person B: } 3 = u^b(x_2), \quad 2 = u^b(x_1), \quad 1 = u^b(x_3)$$
$$\text{person C: } 3 = u^c(x_3), \quad 2 = u^c(x_2), \quad 1 = u^c(x_1).$$

Which alternative wins a majority in paired voting against both of the others? Who is the median voter?

4. Three voters have the following utility functions:

$$\text{person A: } u^a = 2 + x$$
$$\text{person B: } u^b = 2 + 2x - x^2$$
$$\text{person C: } u^c = 3 - .5x.$$

Apply the median rule to find the value of x that represents a voting equilibrium.

5. Majority rule allegedly increases the government's legitimacy and intimidates a rebellious opposition by demonstrating publicly that more citizens support

the government's policies than oppose them. Defend or criticize this proposition by using the median rule.

Legislatures and Committees

The preceding analysis of political platforms concerns a general election in which candidates try to choose the winning platform. The analysis applies equally well to legislatures or committees that follow majority rule. In any such governing body, there will be some set of policies representing the status quo. From time to time a member will make a new proposal. After debate, the body will vote on the new proposal. If the new proposal fails to gain a majority, the status quo will persist. If the new proposal gains a majority, the group abandons the old status quo and the winning proposal becomes the new status quo. Future proposals may challenge the new status quo.

For purposes of formal analysis, there is an exact translation from platforms in a general election to proposals in a legislature or committee. Each proposal is pitted against the status quo. If the preferences of the legislators satisfy conditions prescribed in the median rule, the proposal most preferred by the median legislator will prevail.

Duverger's Law

In many countries like Britain and the United States, two major parties dominate important elected offices. In other countries, many parties win important offices. In addition to culture and history, the electoral procedure determines the number of parties. According to the "winner-take-all-plurality" procedure, the candidate who receives the most votes in a single election wins the office. To illustrate, if votes were divided among three candidates in the proportions 40 percent, 29 percent, and 31 percent, then the candidate receiving 40 percent wins the office. In plurality rule, there is no run-off between the two top contenders, no point voting, and no proportional representation.

Countries with the winner-take-all-plurality rule tend to have two dominant parties. This proposition is sufficiently true to be called a "law," although it is not an iron law.[14] "Duverger's Law" asserts that winner-take-all-plurality rule tends to eliminate small parties and create a two-party system. Collective-choice theory explains why rational voting produces this outcome (Riker 1982b). With several candidates, citizens vote strategically. To illustrate, if a voter's most preferred candidate has little chance of victory, the voter may opt for his second choice. Under the winner-take-all-plurality rule, citizens tend to vote for candidates whom they think others will vote for,[15] and this behavior compresses the number of viable parties to two. The equilibrium share of a third-party vote must be small in an election with many voters (Palfrey 1989).

---

[14] Canada and India are exceptions.

[15] Such an election resembles the beauty contest proposed by Keynes, in which the judges receive rewards for picking the winning contestant.

Coalition theory reaches the same conclusion. To see why, assume that the electorate falls into three groups of equal size called Left, Middle, and Right. If each group supports its own candidate, the probability of any one winning under the winner-take-all-plurality rule is one-third. However, if some Middle voters can be coaxed into the Left, then their combined strength will enable Left-Middle to win all the elections. Knowing this, Right will respond by coaxing some Middle voters into Right-Middle. At the end of this process, two large parties compete for the middle voters. Thus the winner-take-all-plurality rule tends to produce two dominant, evenly matched parties located near the center of the political spectrum.[16] Once established, this situation is very stable, because a vote for a third party has no probability of influencing the outcome, whereas a vote for one of the major parties could be decisive. In single-dimension voting, two parties will occupy the space of alternatives so as to preclude the entry of a successful third party (Palfrey 1984).

To make this argument precise, recall that the "power" of a vote equals the probability that it will be decisive. If the Republican and Democratic Parties are equally matched in a given election, then a change of one vote in either direction could tip the election. In contrast, a vote for a third party (say, the Libertarians or the Greens) has no prospect of changing the outcome. Thus a vote for one of the major parties has power, whereas a vote for a third party has no power.

I have explained how competition in winner-take-all elections tends to eliminate third parties. What keeps the two competing parties from merging into one grand coalition? If the parties remain separate, the winning party enjoys the spoils of power (offices, contracts, grants, etc.). If the parties merge, they must share the spoils of power with each other. Thus the desire to concentrate the spoils of power usually prevents mergers between the two dominant parties. The analysis of political coalitions in the next chapter develops this idea in detail.

In Japan, however, the desire to concentrate the spoils of power did not produce effective multiparty competition. Instead, one party (the Liberal Democratic Party or LDP) has held power during most of the second half of the twentieth century. This hegemonic party, however, contains powerful factions within it, which compete for power. The reasons why a single party dominates Japanese democracy are uncertain. Perhaps the citizens perceive that a single party can better impose political control on an exceptionally powerful administrative bureaucracy. Or perhaps a national coalition assuaged persistent fears of communism during the cold war. Or perhaps the explanation lies in Japan's special electoral rules.[17]

---

[16] My informal "proof" of Duverger's Law assumes the existence of a uniquely stable equilibrium in two-party competition. A sophisticated defense of Duverger's Law is found in Palfrey 1989. A discussion of the prospects of third parties in U.S. elections is in Gardner 1980.

[17] Until electoral changes were made in 1994, each electoral district in Japan returned several representatives to the House of Representatives, but the citizens could vote for only one of them. For example, if a district had three seats, the three candidates enjoying the most votes won, and each citizen residing in the district could vote for only one candidate. Instead of favoring a single hegemonic party, however, these rules seem to favor smaller parties. See Christensen 1994 and Cox 1994. Thanks to Tom Ginsburg for these facts and citations.

Questions

1. In the United States the two major parties choose a presidential candidate by primary elections in each state, which lead up to a national convention. The Democratic Party approximately follows the winner-take-all-plurality rule in each state, meaning the candidate who gets the most votes in the state's primary gets all the state's votes at the national convention. The Republican Party, in contrast, follows a rule closer to proportional representation, meaning that the votes at the national convention are divided in proportion to the votes the candidates received in the primary election. If you were a candidate with a small group of loyal followers who wanted to influence your party's nomination, but had little chance of actually winning it for yourself, would you rather be a Republican or Democrat?

2. In the United States, Duverger's Law seems to work at the national level but not at the local level. What might explain the ineffectiveness of Duverger's Law at the local level?

Alternative Voting Rules

Winner-take-all is one great family of voting rules used by democratic states. The other great family of voting rules is proportional representation, in which each political party receives seats in the legislature in proportion to the number of votes it receives in the election. Later I discuss proportional representation in detail. For now, note that winner-take-all consolidates parties and proportional representation fragments parties. Consolidation forces voters to choose the more preferred of the two parties, even if neither party closely reflects a voter's political preferences. In contrast, fragmentation permits each voter to choose a party closely matched to his own preferences. Conversely, consolidated parties tend toward stable government, whereas fragmented parties tend toward unstable government. Chapter 4 discusses this trade-off between representation and stability in more detail.

Besides these two great families of voting rules, a few governments and many private organizations use entirely different voting rules.[18] A survey by Jonathan Levin and Barry Nalebuff distinguishes sixteen types of voting rules, each with its own procedures, results, and intellectual champions (Levin and Nalebuff 1995). Examples are the single transferable vote,[19] various forms of

---

[18] For an empirical walkabout, see A. Wombat and I. Wallaby, "The Boomerang Effect in National Elections," *Central Australian Review of Law and Economics* 79 (1994): 114-647. Thanks to Geoff Brennan for this citation.

[19] With the single transferable vote, which is used to elect the Dail (Assembly) in Ireland and the Senate in Australia, each voter casts one vote and each candidate obtaining a prescribed quota of votes is elected. Votes in excess of the quota for a winning candidate are transferred to another candidate as designated by the voter. See Tideman 1995.

point voting inspired by Borda,[20] and approval voting.[21] What difference does the voting rule make to outcomes? Levin and Nalebuff conclude that different voting rules typically give the same results when a consensus exists among voters, whereas they give different results when a consensus does not exist.

Tinkering with voting rules can change the outcomes of close elections. Given that voting rules change outcomes, which voting rule is best? Scholars disagree widely about the standard for determining the best rule.[22] Chapter 4 briefly discusses several alternatives. As scholars identify the characteristics of different voting rules, some democratic organizations may take advantage of new knowledge to tailor their voting rules for desired results.

Questions

1. Why might African Americans benefit by changing U.S. electoral rules from plurality rule to proportional representation?

2. Compared to proportional representation, winner-take-all voting causes more corruption in drawing district boundaries ("gerrymandering"). Why?

EVALUATING EQUILIBRIA

The preceding section explained that under certain conditions, majority rule favors the platform preferred by the median voter. The location of the winning platform near the center of the political spectrum dampens the influence of extremists, which stabilizes democracy. Do other attributes make majority rule desirable? Economists evaluate public policies relative to a standard of efficiency. As defined in economic models, "efficiency" requires satisfying individual preferences. To satisfy preferences, governments supply public goods and the legal framework for markets to supply private goods. Is government efficient under the median rule?

The answer depends on the *type* of efficiency. I will distinguish among several types of efficiency that play a prominent role in policy analysis.

[20] A comparison of point voting based on Borda and plurality voting based on Condorcet is in Young 1995. Young favors plurality voting for two reasons, especially in a sophisticated form called maximum likelihood. First, given a right alternative and several wrong alternatives, plurality-type rules maximize the likelihood of a right decision. Second, plurality rules satisfy the independence of irrelevant alternatives (unlike Borda), as well as several other desirable axioms.

[21] In approval voting, each voter indicates on the ballot whether he "approves" or "disapproves" of each candidate. The candidate receiving the greatest number of approvals is the winner. When voters have good information about how others will vote, the outcome of approval voting captures all the information about the preferences of voters. See Weber 1995.

[22] One standard minimizes the probability that the collective choice will make factual errors in judgment. Another standard minimizes the error in representing the preferences of citizens in the legislature. Still another standard ensures that an alternative that can defeat any other alternative in paired voting will win the election. Yet another standard tries to reduce strategic voting in order to minimize the misrepresentation of preferences by voters.

Pareto Efficiency

Pareto efficiency is achieved when no change can make someone better-off without making someone else worse-off. For any Pareto-inefficient political platform, at least one alternative platform exists that some voters like better and no voter likes less. Given this fact, the Pareto-inefficient platform receives less votes than the alternative platform. Since the alternative platform defeats the Pareto-inefficient platform in a vote, the Pareto-inefficient platform is not a voting equilibrium.[23] Conversely, a voting equilibrium (if it exists) is normally Pareto efficient.

These conclusions apply to the median rule as depicted in figure 2-1. To find the set of Pareto-efficient points in figure 2-1, begin at the origin of the graph, which corresponds to an extreme left-wing program, and start moving to the right along the horizontal axis. At first, all three voters prefer the move to the right. However, once the point x_a^* is reached, which is the most preferred point by the most left-wing voter, any further moves to the right make voter A worse-off. Similarly, start from the extreme right side of the horizontal axis and start moving to the left. At first, all three voters prefer the move to the left; however, after reaching the point x_c^*, any further move to the left makes voter C worse-off. Thus the set of Pareto-efficient points contains all the platforms in the interval between x_a^* and x_c^*. The median platform necessarily lies in this interval, so the median rule is Pareto efficient.

Cost-Benefit Efficiency

Most laws make some people better-off and others worse-off. Pareto efficiency provides no basis for choosing among such laws. Guiding political choices requires a more definite and controversial standard. Unlike Pareto efficiency, cost-benefit analysis commends changes for which the gains to the winners exceed the losses to the losers.[24] For example, a move from x_a^* to x_b^* in figure 2-1 harms A and benefits B and C, so the change is not an improvement by the standard of Pareto efficiency. If, however, the harm to A is less than the sum of the benefit to B and C, then the change is an improvement by the cost-benefit standard.

The median rule is not generally efficient by the cost-benefit standard. To see why, assume that a three-person committee must decide a difficult issue by majority vote. The committee agrees that each person will write his or her vote on a slip of paper. When the slips of paper are collected, the chairman reports, "I have two slips marked 'Yes' and one marked 'No, No, oh please, please No!'"

---

[23] In complex models with strategic behavior, Pareto-inefficient voting equilibria can exist.

[24] Since the winners gain more than the losers lose, the former could compensate the latter in principle. Thus an improvement by the cost-benefit standard is also a "potential Pareto improvement." The change is not an actual Pareto improvement unless compensation is actually paid. The criterion of potential Pareto improvement is also called the "Kaldor-Hicks" criterion, after the two economists who developed the idea. For a discussion of these concepts with application to law and economics, see Coleman 1980.

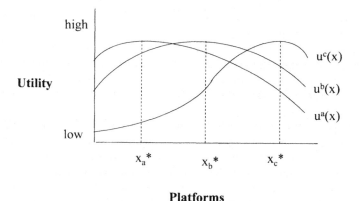

Platforms

Fig. 2-2 Intensity and Median Rule

Apparently two people favor the proposal and one person adamantly opposes it. In general, voting does not reflect the intensity voters feel toward issues. The intensity of feeling, however, influences the efficiency of the alternatives. The unresponsiveness of majority rule to the intensity of feeling about issues causes its inefficiency.

To illustrate the inefficiency graphically, assume that C's preferences in figure 2-1 shift down in the vicinity of x_a^* and x_b^* as depicted in figure 2-2. As a result of this change, C intensely dislikes left and moderate policies as depicted in figure 2-2. Unlike C, A and B have not changed their preferences. An efficient platform responds to shifts in sentiment, so efficiency requires the voter equilibrium to shift to the right.[25] However, the median platform, which commands a majority against any other platform, remains unchanged at x_b^* when passing from figure 2-1 to figure 2-2. Unlike the efficient platform, the median generally does not respond to changes in the intensity of sentiment in the wings of the distribution.

I have explained that the median rule is not generally cost-benefit efficient. Under a special assumption, however, it is. Majority rule counts voters, whereas cost-benefit analysis adds individual values. Counting voters gives the same result as adding individual values under the assumption of "strong symmetry." Under strong symmetry, each voter who gains from a change away from the

---

[25] This argument relies on the usual kind of marginalist reasoning found in economics. For an efficient platform, the benefits enjoyed by the winners from any small shift in the platform equals the harm suffered by the losers (marginal benefit = marginal cost). In comparing figures 2-1 and 2-2, the change in C's preferences, without any change in the sentiments of A and B, implies that the marginal benefit from shifting the platform a little to the right of x_b^* has increased, whereas the marginal cost remains unchanged. Therefore, the efficient platform must shift to the right as a result of the change in C's preferences. You can check this fact by sketching a curve equal to the sum of the utilities of the three people in figure 2-2.

median can be matched with at least one voter who loses, and the loser loses no less than the winner wins.[26]

To illustrate strong symmetry, consider a move from the median to the right. For each right-wing voter who gains, there must exist a left-wing voter who loses just as much. In figure 2-1, a move from x_b^* toward x_c^* benefits C and harms A. Strong symmetry implies that the loss to A is as large as the gain to C.

The requirement of symmetrical effects can be expressed in terms of the intensity of preferences. Democracy gives equal weight to all votes, regardless of how strongly the voters feel about the issues. From an efficiency perspective, however, more weight should be given to intensive preferences. When the distribution of political sentiment is strongly symmetrical, the intensity of right-wing feeling offsets the intensity of left-wing feeling, and vice versa.

Strong symmetry is rare in fact, but approximate symmetry is not so rare. To see why, consider the relationship between the total benefits and the mean benefits. By definition, the total benefits equal the mean benefits multiplied by the number of voters. Consequently, for a given number of voters, maximizing total benefits for all voters is equivalent to maximizing mean benefits.[27] In asymmetrical distributions, the mean and the median are different. In symmetrical distributions, such as the normal distribution, the mean and the median are identical. As the distribution of the voters' most preferred points becomes more symmetrical, the median approaches the mean. As the median approaches the mean, the voter equilibrium tends to become cost-benefit efficient. (Additional conditions are necessary to assure this result.[28])

Since many distributions are symmetrical, or nearly symmetrical, the mean and median are usually close together. Consequently, the winning platform in electoral competition is usually close to the efficient platform, at least in the stylized world discussed so far in this chapter. This fact provides a justification for majority rule as opposed to alternative procedures. *Super-majority rule* requires more than a majority—say, two-thirds—to enact a bill. Conversely, *sub-majority rule* requires less than a majority—say, one-third. Assuming symmetrical effects,

---

[26] In notation, let x_m^* denote the point most preferred by the median voter. Consider any alternative x^*. Let J denote the set of individuals who (strongly) prefer x_m^* to x^*, and let K denote the set of individuals who (weakly) prefer x^* to x_m^*. By strong symmetry, for each k in K there exists a j in J such that $u_j(x_m^*) - u_j(x^*) \geq u_k(x^*) - u_k(x_m^*)$. This fact implies

$$\sum_{i \in J \cup K} u_i(x_m^*) \geq \sum_{i \in J \cup K} u_i(x^*).$$

[27] Here we use the proposition that if continuously differentiable concave function $f(x)$ achieves its maximum at a value x^*, then the function $k \cdot f(x)$, where k is a constant, also achieves its maximum at the same point x^*. (If you know calculus, proof this proposition by taking the derivative and setting it equal to zero.)

[28] The "distribution" in this paragraph refers to the most preferred points of the voters. "Strong symmetry" concerns the utility functions of each individual. The "additional conditions" concern the relationship between utilities and most preferred points. Specifically, the representation of utilities must reduce to the representation of most preferred points.

majority rule is more efficient by the cost-benefit standard than rule by a super-majority or a sub-majority.

This discussion of efficiency measures costs and benefits relative to voters. Some citizens do not vote. How does voter participation affect this conclusion? What happens to the result when some people do not vote? If voters are a representative sample of all citizens, then the electoral outcome remains the same. To illustrate, Flemish and French speakers in Belgium often disagree about politics. If voter participation rates are the same in both language groups, then election results will be the same when 60 percent of the citizens vote as when 100 percent vote.

Conversely, if participants are a biased sample of all citizens, then voter participation rates change outcomes. To illustrate, if voter participation rates are 65 percent among the Flemish and 60 percent among the French, then election results in Belgium favor the Flemish compared to a situation where 100 percent of the citizens voted. Under median rule, biased participation causes inefficiency. To illustrate by an extreme example, North Carolinians cannot vote for the governor of Virginia, so a Virginia governor might benefit Virginians even at a large cost to North Carolinians. More generally, legislators vote on bills in representative democracy, but the benefits of the bills to legislators do not necessarily align with the benefits to citizens.

Questions

1. Compare attitudes of citizens toward military expenditure and abortion. In which case are preferences more likely to be strongly symmetrical?

2. According to contemporary surveys, a right-wing minority of American voters wants to outlaw abortion, and a left-wing a minority wants to outlaw the death penalty. Assume that each minority has very intense feelings. On cost-benefit grounds, would it be better for the minority to get its way on both issues or for the majority to get its way on both issues?

3. Among philosophers, "imperfect duty" means a duty to do an act some-times but not always. For example, a person with money may have the duty to give to some poor beggars but not to all poor beggars. Compared to 100 percent voter participation, participation by a representative sample of voters leaves the outcome unchanged and imposes the burden of voting on fewer people. From this fact, make an argument that voting is an imperfect duty of citizens.

4. Suppose that a beach that fills up with sunbathers on a warm Sunday afternoon. The sunbathers space themselves evenly such that the density of people is about the same everywhere on the beach. Two vendors with ice cream carts appear at the beach. The beach is one unit long and each vendor wants to choose a location for her cart that will maximize sales. The Parks Commission sets the price of ice cream. The hot sun makes people want ice cream and it also makes them reluctant to walk far to get it. If the vendors

are strictly competitive with each other and do not cooperate together, where will they locate? Why is this location inefficient by the cost-benefit standard?

5. Recall this question from above:
"Three voters have the following utility functions:

$$\text{person A}: u^a = 2 + x$$
$$\text{person B}: u^b = 2 + 2x - x^2$$
$$\text{person C}: u^c = 3 - .5x.$$

Apply the median rule to find the value of x that represents a voting equilibrium." Now suppose that C acquires an intensive dislike for large values of x, so that C's revised utility function becomes $u^c = 3 - x$. What is the voting equilibrium?

Welfare Analysis

Cost-benefit analysis gives equal weight to net benefits for everyone, regardless of income or wealth. Now I turn to another concept of efficiency that gives different weight to the net benefits of different people. When evaluating investment projects, the World Bank sometimes gives extra weight to the net benefits of very poor people. Weighting net benefits inversely by the income or wealth of the recipients is sometimes called "welfare analysis." The rationale underlying welfare analysis is that an extra dollar spent by the rich on opera tickets increases welfare by a smaller amount than an extra dollar spent by the poor on bread. (So why do many countries subsidize opera and not bread? I discuss the answer in chapter 10.)

The citizens in democratic countries vigorously debate whether or not the state should redistribute income from the rich to the poor. Libertarians typically oppose redistribution and socialists typically favor it. Consequently, libertarians often approve the policies favored by Pareto efficiency or cost-benefit analysis, whereas socialists often approve the policies favored by welfare analysis.

I characterized conditions under which majority rule maximizes the net benefits of voters. When does majority rule maximize the *welfare* of voters? I have no precise answer to this question. A democracy presumably creates a welfare state when the median voter believes that he will gain from it. Perhaps majority rule maximizes welfare when the median voter tries to maximize his welfare.

I distinguished three types of efficiency—Pareto, cost-benefit, and welfare. Applying each standard requires different amounts of information. Applying the standard of Pareto efficiency requires information about the preference orderings of individuals. Political polls provide reliable information of this kind. Cost-benefit analysis requires information about each person's willingness to pay for public goods. Cost-benefit techniques can often extract the necessary information from different kinds of data, but extraction is often difficult. Welfare analysis requires a set of weights for each class of people. Besides problems of information, choosing a set of weights provokes disputes about social values. I clarify these three differences in the appendix to this chapter where I explain three types of utility functions.

Questions

1. Economic efficiency can mean Pareto efficiency, maximizing net benefits, or maximizing welfare. Is one concept more scientific than the others, or are all three equally scientific?

2. There are three voters (A, B, C) and three alternatives (x_1, x_2, x_3). The voters rank the alternatives from 1 to 3, with "3" indicating the most preferred alternative and "1" indicating the least preferred:

$$\text{person A}: 3 = u^a(x_1), \quad 2 = u^a(x_2), \quad 1 = u^a(x_3)$$
$$\text{person B}: 3 = u^b(x_2), \quad 2 = u^b(x_1), \quad 1 = u^b(x_3)$$
$$\text{person C}: 3 = u^c(x_3), \quad 2 = u^c(x_1), \quad 1 = u^c(x_2).$$

   a. Which alternative is the voter equilibrium in paired voting?
   b. Which alternatives are Pareto efficient?
   c. Which alternative yields the highest sum of utilities?

3. Assume that B in the preceding problem acquires an intensive dislike for alternatives x_1 and x_2. To indicate this fact, rescale his utility as follows:

$$\text{person B}: 3 = u^b(x_2), \quad .2 = u^b(x_1), \quad .1 = u^b(x_3).$$

   a. Which alternative is the voter equilibrium?
   b. Which alternatives are Pareto efficient?
   c. Which alternative maximizes the sum of utilities?

No Equilibrium

My discussion of the median rule depicted electoral competition with a unique, stable equilibrium. A situation can arise, however, in which a political equilibrium does not exist. To appreciate intransitive cycles, the reader may recall a childhood game called "rock, paper, scissors." In this game, two players simultaneously thrust forward one hand in the shape of a rock (fist), a piece of paper (flat hand), or scissors (two fingers extended). The rules of the game are "rock breaks scissors," "scissors cut paper," and "paper covers rock." Each choice defeats one alternative and loses to the other. The best strategy for each player, assuming his opponent is fully rational, is to choose randomly among the three alternatives. Chance decides the game's outcome.

Like the child's game, there is sometimes no equilibrium in electoral competition. When there is no equilibrium, politics spins its wheels. Each time new officials are elected they undo the policies of their predecessors.

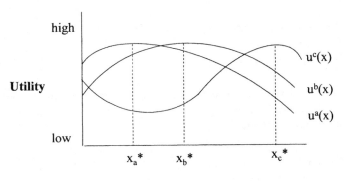

Platforms

Fig. 2-3 Intransitive Preferences

Spinning Wheels

To illustrate the absence of equilibrium, the preferences of C in figure 2-1 have been modified to yield figure 2-3. The preferences of A and B remain unchanged. The preferences of the three voters in figure 2-3 can be summarized as follows, where ">" means "preferred":

$$A: x_a > x_b > x_c$$
$$B: \quad x_b > x_c > x_a$$
$$C: \quad\quad x_c > x_a > x_b$$

Voting among these three alternatives yields the following outcomes:

$$x_a \text{ defeats } x_b$$
$$x_b \text{ defeats } x_c$$
$$x_c \text{ defeats } x_a.$$

Majority voting thus runs in a circle.

Examples of intransitive political preferences are easily constructed. To illustrate, consider these alternative levels of expenditures on public schools:

$$x_a^* = \text{low}$$
$$x_b^* = \text{moderate}$$
$$x_c^* = \text{high}.$$

There are three groups of voters of equal size. The conservative group prefers less expenditure on public schools rather than more. The moderate group prefers an intermediate level of expenditure. Finally, a third group of voters—call them the "aspiring-to-be rich" (known in the United States as yuppies, or young urban professionals)—have more complicated preferences. They would most prefer a high level of expenditure, in which case they will send their children to public school, but, if the level is not high, they would prefer it to be low, in which case they will send their children to private school. The worst alternative for them is a moderate level of expenditure on public schools. Letting ">" indicate "preferred," the preference rankings of the three groups are:

$$\begin{aligned}
\text{conservative:} \quad & x_a^* > x_b^* > x_c^* \\
\text{moderate:} \quad & x_b^* > x_c^* > x_a^* \\
\text{yuppy:} \quad & x_c^* > x_a^* > x_b^*.
\end{aligned}$$

In a majority vote, x_a^* defeats x_b^*, x_b^* defeats x_c^*, and x_c^* defeats x_a^*, so the outcome is intransitive.[29]

The cause of intransitivity can be clarified with the help of some technical terms. In figure 2-3, the conservative corresponds to A, the moderate corresponds to B, and the yuppies correspond to C. For the conservative and moderate, the graph forms a hill with a single peak. The preferences of the yuppy, however, resemble a valley with the bottom at x_b^* and with peaks at x_a^* and x_c^*. The sides of a valley are higher than its interior, so these preferences have a double peak. The median rule applies whenever preferences have a single peak, but not necessarily when they have a double peak. Strictly speaking, a sufficient condition for the most preferred point of the median voter to be a unique equilibrium in majority voting over paired alternatives is that everyone's preferences have a single peak, whereas a necessary condition for intransitivity is the presence of preferences with multiple peaks.

Consider the application of these results to elections for the legislature. Assume that two candidates for the same seat must pick a platform, and assume the preferences of voters form an intransitive cycle over platforms under majority rule. The two candidates are, in effect, playing rock, paper, and scissors. If they choose platforms simultaneously, luck determines the outcome. If one chooses before the other, the party who chooses second will always win. This fact can disadvantage the incumbent.[30]

---

[29] In this example, majority rule is "intranstive." A relation R is transitive by definition if, for any three variables x, y, and z, the following condition holds:

$$xRy \ \& \ yRz \Rightarrow xRz.$$

An intransitive relation is one that is not transitive, i.e., there exist three variables x, y, and z such that

$$xRy \ \& \ yRz \ \& \ zRx.$$

[30] The incumbent's platform may be known from his past acts. If preferences are intransitive, a platform exists that voters would prefer to the incumbent's platform. The challenger, who is free to make a fresh choice, can adopt one of these winning programs.

Questions

1. An election pits an incumbent against a challenger. Assume that the preferences of voters form an intransitive cycle under majority rule. Neither candidate is committed to a program at the commencement of the campaign. Would you advise your candidate to profess platitudes or take a firm stand on the issues?

2. Recall the beach example: A beach fills up with sunbathers on a warm Sunday afternoon. The sunbathers space themselves evenly such that the density of people is about the same everywhere on the beach. The hot sun makes people want ice cream and it also makes them reluctant to walk far to get it. Now suppose that three vendors with ice cream carts appear at the beach. The beach is one unit long and each vendor wants to choose a location that will maximize sales. If the vendors are strictly competitive with each other and do not cooperate together, where will they locate? (Hint: Intransitivity gives the answer.)

3. There are three voters (A, B, C) and three alternatives (x_1, x_2, x_3). The voters rank the alternatives from 1 to 3, with "3" indicating the most preferred alternative, and "1" indicating the least preferred alternative:

$$\text{person A: } 3 = u^a(x_1), \quad 2 = u^a(x_2), \quad 1 = u^a(x_3)$$
$$\text{person B: } 3 = u^b(x_2), \quad 2 = u^b(x_3), \quad 1 = u^b(x_1)$$
$$\text{person C: } 3 = u^c(x_3), \quad 2 = u^c(x_1), \quad 1 = u^c(x_2).$$

  a. Is there a voting equilibrium?
  b. Draw a bar graph with x_1, x_2, and x_3 arranged in that order on the horizontal axis and the preference ranking of each voter shown on the vertical axis. Which voter's preferences have two peaks?

Domination and the Core

Before proceeding, I want to restate the results about voting cycles in the language of cooperative game theory, which introduces concepts used later in this book. For given rules of collective choice, a *decisive* coalition gets its way when its members agree. To be precise, a coalition is *decisive* for a given pair of alternatives if, whenever everyone in the coalition prefers one alternative to the other alternative, the coalition can obtain its preference. Thus, when a state faces a choice between x and y, a coalition C is decisive over the choice if, when everyone in C prefers x to y, the state chooses x over y.

As explained, a decisive coalition gets its way when its members agree. If the members of a decisive coalition agree that they prefer one alternative over another, then the more preferred alternative *dominates* the less preferred alternative. To be precise, alternative x dominates alternative y if a decisive coalition C exists in which everyone prefers x to y.

Domination is important to stability. Whenever collective choice selects a dominated alternative, a coalition can form to replace it with the dominant alternative. A dominated alternative is, consequently, unstable. Intransitivity implies that *every* alternative is dominated by another alternative. Any alternative in an intransitive cycle is, consequently, unstable.

The phrase "Condorcet winner" refers to an alternative that can defeat any other alternative in paired voting.[31] A Condorcet winner is undominated, which means that no decisive coalition can form whose members prefer an alternative to a Condorcet winner. An undominated alternative is, consequently, stable.

Game theorists call the set of *un*dominated alternatives the game's *core*. When a game is formulated mathematically, theorists ascertain whether or not its core is "empty." An intransitive set has an empty core (no undominated alternative exists), whereas a Condorcet winner is "in the core" (undominated alternative), so the core is not empty when a Condorcet winner exists.

Questions

1. Explain why any point outside the game's core is unstable.

2. What does it mean to say that the equilibrium price in a perfectly competitive market is in the "core" of the game played by firms and consumers?

Is Intransitivity Bad?

Voting intransitivities often occur. Are they bad? It is easy to see why intransitive preferences are irrational for individuals. Suppose that a student takes his desk lamp—call it lamp A—to the flea market to trade for another. The student sees lamp B, which he prefers to lamp A, and he offers to trade lamp A and $5 for lamp B. The vendor accepts the offer. The student is carrying lamp B when he sees lamp C, which he prefers to lamp B, so he offers to trade lamp B and $5 for lamp C. The vendor accepts. Now the student turns to leave the flea market and on the way out he passes the stall where lamp A is being offered for resale. Since he has intransitive preferences, he likes lamp A better than lamp C, so he offers to swap lamp C and $5 for lamp A. The vendor accepts and the student goes home with lamp A (the same lamp he brought to the flea market) and he is $15 poorer. The intransitive buyer is a "money pump" for sellers.

There is a long philosophical tradition holding that a rational person can rank states of the world from bad to good.[32] Without such an ordering, a person has no concept of a better world to strive for. Intransitive preferences do not yield a ranking from bad to good because they run in a circle. The intransitive student did not have a vision of a better lamp. The objection to intransitive preferences is that they reveal no vision of a better world on the part of the actor.

---

[31] The term is named in honor of an eighteenth-century French mathematician and politician who defined the concept and used it in an early study of voting rules (Condorcet 1976).

[32] This requirement of rational ethics, which is implicit in the utilitarian tradition, was first formulated in a forceful, sustained argument in Sidgwick 1966.

This characterization of individuals also applies to the state. Given intransitive voting, the state lacks coherent goals. Instead of rejecting worse states of the world in favor of better states, intransitive voting goes in a circle. Circular politics does not reveal the goal of a better world to be achieved by collective choice.

Political philosophy typically justifies laws enacted in a democracy on the grounds that they represent the "will of the majority" or the "intent of the people's representatives." Given intransitive voting, however, these phrases make no sense. Intransitive voters have no collective "will" because they contradict themselves. Intransitive voting thus creates a problem in justifying democracy. The next chapter, which concerns bargaining, will explain the problem's solution.

Questions

1. If a person has intransitive preferences, would you rather trade with him or employ him in your company?

2. Contrast the "will of the majority" or the "intent of the legislature" under the median rule and intransitivity.

Impossibility

Students who first encounter voter intransitivity are inclined to minimize its importance. You might suppose, for example, that voter preferences are typically single-peaked like those in figure 2-1, which result in a voter equilibrium, and seldom double-peaked like those of voter C in figure 2-3, where no equilibrium exists. This supposition is a mistake. I have used figures depicting a single dimension of choice such as the size of total government expenditures. In a single dimension of choice, single-peaked preferences are apparently more common than double-peaked preferences. Collective choice, however, often involves multidimensional choices, such as expenditures on schools, police, and roads. Voter preferences often form intransitive cycles when political choices occur in multiple dimensions.

Voters' preferences may be single-peaked in one dimension of choice (x-axis), and also single-peaked in another dimension of choice (y-axis). The same voters' preferences, however, may be double-peaked on a curve in two-dimensional space. The voters with ordinary economic preferences ("convex indifference sets") often produce cyclical majorities in choices involving several dimensions.[33]

[33] To illustrate, consider an allocation of public funds to schools, roads, and police. Let x_a^* denote an allocation with large expenditures on schools, modest expenditures on roads, and little expenditures on police. Let x_b^* denote an allocation with large expenditures on roads, modest expenditures on police, and little expenditures on schools. Let x_c^* denote an allocation with large expenditures on police, modest expenditures on schools, and little expenditures on roads. Three voters with ordinary, convex preferences might rank the three possible allocations as follows:

person A (commuter with children): $x_a^* > x_b^* > x_c^*$.

person B (childless commuter): $x_b^* > x_c^* > x_a^*$

person C (fearful grandmother): $x_c^* > x_a^* > x_b^*$.

The three voters form an intransitive cycle under majority rule.

To state these facts more precisely, list all the logically possible ways to rank a small number of alternatives. Now consider the logically possible ways to assign these rankings to a small numbers of voters. Some assignments result in voting intransitivities and others result in Condorcet winners. The proportion of logically possible assignments that result in voting intransitivity increases with the number of alternatives and voters.[34] The so-called chaos theorem asserts that intransitivities are so frequent in multidimensional choice that almost any outcome could be reached by an appropriate sequence of votes (McKelvey 1979).[35]

Students often suppose that intransitive cycles result from particular voting procedures, such as voting over paired alternatives. Many variations in voting rules exist (run-off votes, point voting, super-majority rule, etc.). In a powerful generalization, Kenneth Arrow proved that no form of a democratic constitution can solve the problem of intransitivity in choosing public goods.[36] Tinkering with voting rules cannot solve the problem of intransitivities in democracy.

Agenda Setting

To prevent intransitive cycles from occurring, a democratic system must adopt specific rules and practices that have substantial costs. To illustrate, consider

[34] For example, the logically possible ways to rank the alternatives (x_1, x_2, x_3) are

$$R1: x_1 > x_2 > x_3$$
$$R2: x_2 > x_3 > x_1$$
$$R3: x_3 > x_1 > x_2$$
$$R4: x_1 > x_3 > x_2$$
$$R5: x_2 > x_1 > x_3$$
$$R6: x_3 > x_2 > x_1.$$

Let P_{123} denote the profile of preferences for three voters given by R_1, R_2, R_3. Some profiles yield voting cycles and other yield Condorcet winners. For example, P_{123} yields a voting cycle, whereas P_{124} yields the Condorcet winner x_1. As the number of alternatives increases and the number of voters increases, the proportion of logically possible profiles yielding voting cycles increases as a proportion of the total number of logically possible profiles (Riker 1982a). Riker remarks that political parties may reduce diversity in profiles, but politicians who want to manipulate outcomes may deliberately increase diversity (p. 122).

[35] Miller 1983 summarizes the relationship between diversity and intransitivity as follows:

The probabilistic literature on the paradox of voting has been concerned primarily with 1) calculating the likelihood that cyclical majorities arise in an impartial culture, i.e., a uniform distribution over all logically distinct individual orderings, and 2) determining how this likelihood changes as a culture deviates from impartiality. The basic conclusions are that the probability of cyclical majorities in an impartial culture increases as the number of alternatives, voters, or both increases. Moreover, as the number of alternatives increases, if majority rule fails to be transitive, the more likely it becomes that it will fail entirely and that one cycle will encompass all alternatives. Concerning departures from impartiality, the general thrust of conclusions is that greater social homogeneity (variously defined) with respect to preferences reduces the likelihood of cyclical majorities. (p. 126)

[36] This is just one interpretation of one of the most important theorems ever proven by an economist. See Arrow 1963, or chapters 3 and 3* of Sen 1970a.

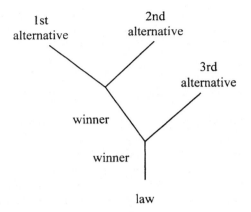

Fig. 2-4 Agenda

setting the legislative agenda. Voting in a legislature conforms to definite rules of procedure, often including a prohibition against reintroducing a defeated proposal. If defeated proposals cannot be reintroduced, an endless cycle of voting is impossible. Under these circumstances, the alternative that will prevail is the one that wins on the last vote. The alternative that will prevail on the last vote is usually predictable from the alternatives that prevail on the next-to-last vote. And the same relationship holds between the next-to-last vote and the vote preceding it. The agenda determines the order in which alternatives are considered. It is not hard to see that the final winner in the intransitive set can be determined by whoever sets the agenda. Thus, control of the legislative agenda avoids intransitivities by giving the agenda-setter the power to choose among intransitive alternatives.

To illustrate concretely, assume that the legislature considers three alternatives (x_a, x_b, x_c). The person controlling the agenda must fill in the "tree" in figure 2-4 that depicts the order of voting:

Assume that the three alternatives form the intransitive cycle,

$$x_a \text{ defeats } x_b$$
$$x_b \text{ defeats } x_c$$
$$x_c \text{ defeats } x_a.$$

Assume that the person who sets the agenda wants x_a to prevail. To assure the final victory of x_a, set the agenda so that the first vote pits x_c against x_b, and the final vote pits the winner of the first vote against x_a. Given this agenda, x_b defeats x_c in the first vote, and x_a defeats x_b in the final vote. Thus, the person who sets the agenda gets her most preferred outcome, as depicted in figure 2-5.

Alternatively, assume the person controlling the agenda wants x_b to prevail. To accomplish this end, set the agenda so that the first vote pits x_c against x_a, and the final vote pits the winner of the first vote against x_b. As a consequence, x_c defeats x_a in the first vote, and x_b defeats x_c in the final vote, as in figure 2-6.

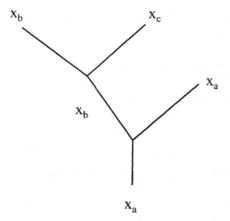

Fig. 2-5 Agenda Set for x_a to Win

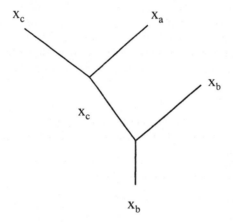

Fig. 2-6 Agenda Set for x_b to Win

In order for the person who sets the agenda to determine the outcome of voting over an intransitive cycle, he must think recursively. Specifically, he must figure out which alternative can be beaten by the one he most favors, pit them against each other in the last division, then repeat the same process of reasoning for the next-to-last division, and so forth back to the first division.

To avoid circular voting, legislatures characteristically adopt rules giving control over the agenda to particular officials, such as committee chairmen or the person presiding in the legislature. Empirical research concludes that the person who controls the agenda often determines the outcome in voting.[37] By choosing the agenda, the chairman in effect determines which majority will prevail. To

[37] Levine and Plott 1977.

illustrate by the preceding example, the chairman who sets the agenda determines whether the majority who prevails will be the one favoring x_a over x_b, x_b over x_c, or x_c over x_a.

Generalizing, democracy can avoid intransitive cycles by empowering someone to dictate which majority will prevail. Allowing a chairman to set the agenda achieves this end by one means. Other means also exist. Instead of giving control over the agenda to the chairman, the party leader can perform this role. To illustrate, the party of the British prime minister usually controls a majority of seats in Parliament. In important votes, the prime minister imposes strict discipline on members of the party. Consequently, the prime minister wins every important vote in Parliament. By dictating to the majority party, the British prime minister eliminates intransitive voting in the legislature. Unlike Britain, parliamentary systems without a majority party can cycle through coalitions, as has occurred in Italy in recent years.

Political commentators in the United States sometimes say that the president can use the media to "set the political agenda." To illustrate, assume the government must choose among x_a^*, x_b^*, and x_c^*, and the president wants x_b^* to win. To induce the majority of citizens to oppose the president, the opposition tries to frame the issue as a choice between x_a^* and x_b^*. The president, however, uses his command of the media to frame the issue as a choice between x_b^* and x_c^*, so that the majority of the public agrees with the president's choice.

Questions

1. To what extent can the following political actors set the agenda? (If you are not from the United States, substitute some similar offices from your country's government.)

Speaker of the House of Representatives

chief justice of the Supreme Court

president

committee chairmen in Congress

director of an agency (e.g., chairman of the Federal Trade Commission).

2. Discuss the advantages and disadvantages of choosing someone to set an agenda rather than allowing politics to cycle.

3. A legislature with three voters (A, B, C) chooses among three alternatives (x_1, x_2, x_3). The voters rank the alternatives from 1 to 3, with "3" indicating the most preferred alternative and "1" indicating the least preferred:

$$\text{person A}: 3 = u^a(x_1), \quad 2 = u^a(x_2), \quad 1 = u^a(x_3)$$
$$\text{person B}: 3 = u^b(x_2), \quad 2 = u^b(x_3), \quad 1 = u^b(x_1)$$
$$\text{person C}: 3 = u^c(x_3), \quad 2 = u^c(x_1), \quad 1 = u^c(x_2).$$

The alternatives are to be pitted against each other in majority voting, and a defeated alternative cannot be reintroduced. Assume that C determines the order in which the alternatives are to be considered (agenda-setter). If each person votes for her preferred alternative in paired voting, describe the agenda that enables C to get her most preferred outcome.

4. Repeat the preceding question, but instead of assuming that each person votes for his preferred alternative in paired voting, assume that each person votes strategically on the first vote. For example, if the first vote pits x_1 against x_2, A foresees that voting for x_1 in the first vote will cause x_3 to win in the second vote. Since x_3 is the worst outcome for A, he decides to vote for x_2 instead of x_1 on the first vote. When the parties vote strategically, C can assure that her most preferred alternative is the final winner by setting the agenda so that her most preferred alternative is introduced on the first vote. Explain why.

CONCLUSION

This chapter analyzes majority rule as a method for satisfying the preferences of citizens for collective action. With single-peaked preferences, majority voting over paired alternatives reaches an equilibrium most preferred by the median voter. The equilibrium is always Pareto efficient, and it approaches cost-benefit efficiency as preferences approach strong symmetry. With multipeaked preferences, however, voting may not have an equilibrium. When voting cycles, outcomes are irrational or arbitrary, and the "will of the majority" has no clear meaning.

"Why didn't the dog bark?" Sometimes Sherlock Holmes or Miss Marple solves a mystery by asking why something that should have occurred did not occur. I have explained why intransitive cycles should occur. Like Sherlock Holmes or Miss Marple, you should ask why cycles do not occur in particular political systems. As you will see, the means by which a democracy avoids intransitive cycles often marks its character.

I already described one such device—agenda setting. Setting an agenda stops cycling by giving the agenda-setter power to choose the outcome within the intransitive set. A powerful agenda-setter dominates some political systems.

Single-peaked preferences are probable (but not certain) in a single dimension of choice, whereas cycling is probable (but not certain) in multiple dimensions of choice. As explained in chapter 5, some political systems avoid intransitivity by narrowing political choices to a single dimension.

The next chapter explains how democracy provides a framework for efficient bargaining over public goods, much like markets provide a framework for efficient bargaining over private goods. Political bargaining is the most fundamental means to avoid voting intransitivity. Whereas majority voting can lead to inefficient or irrational results, bargaining theory supplies a more affirmative vision to support the liberal faith that democracy satisfies the political preferences of citizens better than any other form of government.

APPENDIX: THREE TYPES OF UTILITY FUNCTIONS

This appendix briefly explains the differences among ordinal utility, *von-Neumann-Morgenstern cardinal* utility, and interpersonal cardinal utility.

A pollster can ask a voter to rank three alternatives by using the letters A, B, and C. The ranking provides no information about how much more the voter likes one alternative than another. Since the distance between rankings has no meaning, the operation "B-C" is meaningless.

The pollster could obtain the same information by asking the voter to assign the numbers 3, 2, and 1 to the three alternatives, with a higher number indicating a higher preference.[38] As before, the ranking provides no information about how much more the voter likes one alternative than another. Since the distance between rankings has no meaning, the operation "2-1" is meaningless, even though using numbers rather than letters suggests that subtraction is meaningful.

Now assume the pollster wants more information. The pollster could ask the voter to assign a number between 0 and 5 to each candidate, with a higher number indicating a higher preference, and the gap between rankings indicating the extent of the difference. (Most voters would have difficulty responding, so an indirect method would get the same information more reliably, but my concern here is theoretical, not practical.[39]) A voter who performs this task provides information about how much more he likes one alternative than another. Assume the voter assigns "1" to the worst alternative, "2" to the middle alternative, and "4" to the best alternative. Since the distance between rankings has meaning, the operation "2-1" also has meaning. Specifically, the fall in the voter's satisfaction when changing from 4 to 2 exceeds the fall when changing from 2 to 1, as indicated by "4-2 > 2-1."

In the preceding example, the first voter gave the numbers (4, 2, 1) to the three alternatives. Now assume the pollster asks the same question of a second voter, who gives the numbers (5, 3, 0). The poll has not provided any information about how to compare the satisfaction of two different voters. Perhaps the first voter counts satisfaction in large units analogous to meters, whereas the second voter counts satisfaction in small units analogous to centimeters. We have no way to

---

[38] The particular numbers chosen do not matter so long as "larger" corresponds to "preferred." To illustrate, instead of the numbers 1, 2, and 3, the pollster could use the numbers -4, 8, and 10. Although the numbers differ, they convey the same information so long as higher numbers get assigned to more preferred alternatives.

[39] Distance between rankings can be measured by choices among gambles. To illustrate, the pollster might ask, "Assume that you face a gamble in which your third choice will win with probability .6 and your first choice will win with probability .4. Would you rather face this gamble or another gamble in which your third choice will win with probability .5 and your second choice will win with probability .5?" For a discussion of how to make public policy by using the preferences of people toward gambles, see Raiffa 1968.

compare the distance between the best and worst alternatives for the two voters. Perhaps 4-2 in units of satisfaction for the first voter exceeds 5-0 in units of satisfaction for the second voter, just as 2 meters exceeds 5 centimeters.

Scholars have long debated whether a method exists for making public policy by combining the satisfaction of different people.[40] Economists sometimes assume that such a method exists and then consider its consequences in formal models.[41] If such a method existed, then units of satisfaction could be standardized across people. If the answers of the two voters were given in standardized units, then an increase in satisfaction of 4-2 units for the first voter is less than an increase in satisfaction of 5-0 in units for the second voter, just as 2 meters is less than 5 meters.

Over a long history, economics has distinguished several types of utility functions.[42] The first type of utility function, in which utility differences have no meaning, is called *ordinal*. Pareto efficiency uses ordinal utility functions. The second type of utility function, in which utility differences have meaning for a single person, is called *cardinal* utility, or, more precisely, *von-Neumann-Morgenstern cardinal* utility. This type of utility is used to model individual choices under uncertainty. The third type of utility, which standardizes units for counting satisfaction of different people, is called *interpersonal cardinal* utility. This type of utility is used for welfare maximization.

Pareto efficiency clearly requires ordinal utility, and welfare maximization clearly requires interpersonal cardinal utility. What about cost-benefit efficiency? Cost-benefit efficiency can be regarded as welfare maximization under a special assumption about interpersonal cardinal utility. The special assumption is that utility increases by the same amount when an extra dollar is given to someone, regardless of who receives it. Under this assumption, the rich and the poor gain equal amounts of utility from an additional dollar. That is the method of cost-benefit analysis.

Alternatively, cost-benefit efficiency can be defended without reference to maximizing cardinal utility. To illustrate, if rational people were to bargain over the terms for organizing a state, they might agree to organize its politics to maximize the nation's wealth. This argument is a contractarian defense of cost-benefit analysis.[43]

---

[40] The method most discussed in economics is found in Harsanyi 1953 and Harsanyi 1955.

[41] The most famous example is the optimum income tax problem, as formulated in Mirrlees 1971.

[42] Besides an ordinal utility function, the other two primary types are von Neumann-Morgenstern utility, which applies to choice under uncertainty (von Neumann and Morgenstern 1944), and interpersonally comparable utilities, which apply to redistributive policies (Sen 1970a).

[43] For an exchange on this point, see Posner 1981 and Coleman 1980.

CHAPTER 3

Bargaining

> Bargaining is the art of persuading your opponent to take the nice shiny copper
> penny and give you the wrinkled old paper money.

TURN ON the television cameras and the U.S. Congress is a high-minded debating society. Turn off the television cameras and Congress resembles a bazaar. Similarly, the British Parliament debates in public, but private meetings of the cabinet can involve intensive bargaining among the ministers. In general, legislators orate in public and bargain in private. Despite public appearances, bargaining is the staple of legislative activity.

In legislatures as in markets, everyone can benefit from a good bargain. The exchange of commodities in markets and votes in legislatures can benefit society by giving people what they want. Political bargains, however, pass seamlessly from compromise to corruption without crossing a clear boundary. Many citizens who recognize the necessity of political deals still feel uneasy about politicians trading votes. Is the nation better-off when representatives bargain or vote their consciences?

This chapter clarifies the controversy over political bargaining by analyzing it. As developed in this chapter, the bargain theory of democracy covers trading votes, investing in politics, and forming coalitions. This theory gives fresh insights into questions such as these:

Example 1: What makes vote trading easier in the U.S. Senate than in the House of Representatives?

Example 2: Cold Rolled Industries, Inc., which manufactures steel and lobbies for tariff protection against imports, has $50 million to invest. How should it divide its investment between manufacturing and lobbying in order to maximize its profits?

Example 3: Assume that the largest party in Parliament lacks a majority, so it forms a coalition government with smaller parties. If the largest party maximizes its own power, which smaller parties will it invite to join the governing coalition?

The introduction in chapter 1 distinguished between price theory and game theory. The analysis of voting in chapter 2 mostly follows price theory by assuming that voters behave nonstrategically. The analysis of political bargains in this chapter mostly follows game theory by assuming that politicians behave strategically. So this chapter applies game theory to democracy.

TRADING VOTES

According to the model of perfect competition so beloved by economists, the exchange of private goods in perfectly competitive markets allocates resources efficiently. The exchange of votes in a legislature, however, never approximates perfect competition. Perfect competition cannot be established, even in principle, in a market for votes. To see why, consider how legislators bargain when they trade votes. Each legislator has an equal number of votes on each bill (exactly one vote). If the representative from Michigan cares especially about the automobile industry, whereas the representative from New York cares especially about banking, they can trade votes. The representative from Michigan will get two votes on automobile bills (his own and the New York representative's) and none on banking bills, whereas the representative from New York will get two votes on banking bills (his own and the Michigan representative's) and none on automobile bills.

When alternatives are equipoised, changing one vote tips the balance; each vote is decisive. In contrast, if the winner prevails by many votes, changing one vote does not influence the outcome. Insofar as voters care only about outcomes, the right to cast a decisive vote is valuable and the right to cast an indecisive vote has no value. As explained in chapter 2, the power of a vote equals the probability that it will be decisive. In a market for votes, each participant values a vote according to its power. Everyone, consequently, wants to trade their indecisive votes on one issue in order to obtain decisive votes on another issue. The decisiveness of one person's vote, however, depends on how other people vote. Interdependent values disrupt the trading of votes.

Here is a concrete example. Assume that persons A and B care intensely that a certain bill passes. Each one cares enough to trade votes on other issues in order to acquire a block of votes that includes the decisive vote on this issue. But A may hold back in the hope that B will shoulder the burden of trading for the needed block of votes, and B may do the same. A decisive block of votes may never be assembled because each player "free-rides." In general, the voters who are not involved in a trade have an interest in it because it affects the power of their votes. External effects prevent markets for votes from approximating perfect competition.

Questions

1. Legislatures typically have no formal mechanism to enforce the trading of votes. Suppose the chairman of the legislature had the power to "auction" votes, where the "price" would be votes on future legislation that the "buyer" transfers to the "seller." Explain how the free-rider problem would disrupt the auction.

2. Use the concept of the "power of a vote" to explain why U.S. labor organizations contribute heavily to those Democratic legislators with conservative constituencies (Stratmann 1994).

Coase Theorem

Although external effects prevent markets for votes from approximating perfect competition, bargaining can still achieve efficiency. To see why, I turn from the ideal of perfect competition to the ideal of perfect bargaining. Selling a used car, buying a corporation, making an international treaty, or drafting legislation requires negotiations. Bargaining theory ideally predicts the success and failure of negotiations. The inventiveness of people in developing strategies, however, makes prediction difficult.

In chapter 1 I mentioned a brilliant simplification to postpone analyzing strategy. Bargaining has various costs, such as renting a conference room, spending time in negotiations, and drafting an agreement. By expanding "transaction costs" to encompass all impediments to bargaining, Coase concluded that bargaining tends to succeed as transaction costs approach zero (Coase 1960; Regan 1972). Coase applied this idea to law and commentators formulated his conclusion as the Coase Theorem (Cooter 1982). The Coase Theorem asserts that private parties will bargain to an efficient allocation of legal entitlements provided that transaction costs do not impede the process.

The same proposition applies to legislators who trade votes. As the transaction costs of bargaining fall, the Coase Theorem implies that legislators will cooperate with each other and realize the surplus from political trades. *Assuming zero transaction costs of bargaining among politicians, the supply of private law and public goods by the state is efficient relative to the preferences of lawmakers.* I call this proposition the *political Coase Theorem.* In a democracy, lawmakers ideally represent the citizens. When this ideal is achieved, satisfying the preferences of lawmakers also satisfies the preferences of citizens. So we could say, *"Assuming zero transaction costs of political bargaining in a democracy, the supply of private law and public goods by the state is efficient relative to the preferences of the citizens."* I call this proposition the *democratic Coase Theorem.*

The Coase Theorem in its various forms resembles Galileo's proposition that objects moving on a frictionless plain will continue in the same direction at the same speed forever. Although friction is never zero, Galileo's proposition helps to design a ship's hull and a plane's wing. Similarly, although transaction costs are never zero, the Coase Theorem helps to design a constitution. By reducing the transaction costs of bargaining, the constitution increases the probability that political factions will cooperate with each other. Constitutions can be judged according to their ability to reduce the transaction costs of political bargaining.

Lacking enforceable contracts, politicians and chimpanzees follow the reciprocity maxim, "You scratch my back and I'll scratch yours." Reciprocity requires long-run relationships. As people form long-run relationships, transaction costs of bargaining decrease. Similarly, transaction costs decrease as fewer people must agree to the bargain. Thus a constitution promotes bargaining by promoting long-run relationships among political factions and keeping their representatives few in number.

In light of the Coase Theorem, political organization looks like a mechanism to lower the transaction costs of political bargaining. To illustrate, most legislatures are too large for all of the members to bargain directly with each other. The formation of parties, the creation of legislative committees, and the control of the legislative agenda reduce the transaction costs of bargaining. A theme in this book is that representative democracy can be justified as the constitutional form that minimizes the transaction costs of political bargaining among factions of citizens. In contrast, dictatorship precludes bargaining among citizens by excluding them from government.

Questions

1. Will bargaining succeed better in the U.S. Senate or House of Representatives?

2. Will close votes tend to occur more often in the Senate or the House?

3. Will Congress tend to cooperate better with a president who is newly elected or a president in his final year of office?

Sphere of Cooperation

Before the Second World War, the countries of Europe imposed tariffs on the flow of goods among them. Each tariff benefited some industries in the countries that imposed it, but, taken as a whole, tariffs harmed the economies of Europe. After the Second World War, the tariffs were gradually abolished to create a common market. Wider trading benefited all European countries. Underlying this fact is a theorem stating that narrow trading groups are (Pareto) inefficient in a competitive economy relative to wide trading groups.[1]

The advantage of wide trading in markets presumably applies to politics. Before the Second World War, the countries of Europe enacted national laws. Many of these laws benefited the enacting country and harmed other countries. In two world wars, the conflict escalated out of control. After the Second World War, Europeans formed a political union that facilitates political deals encompassing Europe, just as the common market facilitates economic deals encompassing Europe. Just as the common market brought many economic benefits, the European Union brought many political benefits to Europe, notably peace.

In economics and politics, the widest sphere of cooperation affords the greatest opportunity to satisfy peoples' preferences for private and public goods. This fact argues for world trade and world government. As a coalition grows, however, the transaction costs of government increase. World government, consequently, has higher transaction costs than national government. This book will often compare the gains from wider cooperation against the costs of political transactions with more people. I will show in part 2 that transaction costs explain

---

[1] The theorem states that the core shrinks to the set of competitive allocations as the economy grows larger. Theorems on the core are in Arrow and Hahn 1971.

the scope for governments in politics just as transaction costs explain the scope for firms in economics.

Consensus and Adversarial Voting

Complex legislation combines different issues that different legislators value differently. Legislators or their parties can negotiate with each other and trade votes so that each group gets its way on the issues it cares about the most, while conceding to others the issues that it cares about less. Perfect bargaining among legislators results in a Pareto-efficient bundle of laws relative to the preferences of legislators, which implies it is impossible to change the laws so as to increase the satisfaction of one legislator without reducing the satisfaction of another legislator.

If legislators have sufficient variety in their preferences, and if they exercise their preferences over a sufficiently large set of alternatives, then everyone has votes to trade with others. The most efficient bargain relative to the preferences of the legislators encompasses all of them. A bargain that encompasses everyone results in consensus legislation that passes without opposition. Unlike majority rule, a consensus does not suffer from intransitivity or inefficiency.

Democracy has advantages in creating a political consensus. Psychological studies have shown that individuals cooperate best when a focal point suggests a fair division of the surplus.[2] To illustrate, "fifty-fifty" (each gets half) is a focal point for dividing profits between two partners. Giving everyone the right to vote and allowing the majority to rule appeals to fairness. Majority rule thus provides a focal point for a fair division of the surplus from political cooperation.[3]

Some legislatures attain consensus on many bills. For example, much legislation enacted by the U.S. Congress consists in "private member bills" that effect few constituents, which Congress enacts with little or no dissent. The most important bills, however, typically divide Congress. When bargaining stops short of a consensus, the majority prevails. Instead of confirming a consensus, adversarial voting tests legislative strength.

Questions

1. Some organizations such as juries, the Security Council of the United Nations, and the Society of Friends (Quaker Church) require unanimity in order to act. These organizations are small. What would happen if they were large?

2. Pluralist democracy involves bargains struck among the representatives of *all* political factions (Dahl 1982). Use the Coase Theorem to discuss the conditions under which you expect democracy to be pluralist rather than majoritarian.

[2] Hoffman and Spitzer 1985a.

[3] The power of democracy to resolve difficult distributive problems is demonstrated in Oberholzer-Gee, Bohnet, and Frey 1997.

3. Interpret the phrase "the public good" or "the will of the people" in light of a political consensus.

4. In Japan, most legal disputes are settled out of court. Since the Second World War, Japan has been governed almost exclusively by one party that strives for consensus. Speculate on how these facts might be connected.

Bargaining in General: Used Cars

So far I have discussed the transaction costs of bargaining. Bargaining, however, involves strategy, which does not resemble the cost of toothpaste or soybean futures. To analyze strategy explicitly, I will abandon the simplification of treating strategy as a transaction cost and develop the elements of bargaining theory.

A bargain creates a surplus by agreement on its distribution. Consider this example of bargaining over a used car:

Adam, who lives in a small town, has a 1957 Chevy convertible in good repair. The pleasure of owning and driving the car is worth $3,000 to Adam. Blair, who has been coveting the car for years, inherits $5,000 and decides to try to buy the car from Adam. After inspecting the car, Blair decides that the pleasure of owning and driving it is worth $4,000 to her.

According to these facts, the potential seller values the car less than the potential buyer does, so there is scope for a bargain. Adam will not accept less than $3,000 for the car, and Blair will not pay more than $4,000, so the sale price will have to be somewhere in between. A reasonable sale price would be $3,500, which splits the difference.

The logic of the situation can be clarified by restating the facts in the language of bargaining theory. The *noncooperative* solution to the game occurs if Adam and Blair cannot agree on a price. If they cannot agree, Adam will keep the car and use it, which is worth $3,000 to him. Thus the noncooperative value of the game for Adam is $3,000. Blair will keep her money—$5,000—or spend it on something other than the car. For simplicity, assume that she values her money at its face value of $5,000. Thus the noncooperative value of the game for Blair is $5,000.

In the course of bargaining, the parties may assert facts ("The motor is mechanically perfect"), appeal to norms ("$3,700 is an unfair price"), and threaten ("I won't take less than $3,500"). In analyzing the art of bargaining, economic theory focuses on the credibility of threats. A credible threat asks for no more than the actor can obtain without the other's cooperation. Without Blair's cooperation, Adam can keep the car, the use of which he values at $3,000. The noncooperative value of the game to Adam, or his *threat value*, equals $3,000. So Adam can credibly threaten not to cooperate unless the price equals at least $3,000. Similarly, owning the car is worth $4,000 to Blair, so

Blair can credibly threaten not to cooperate unless she pays no more than $4,000 for the car.[4]

The parties to a bargaining game can both benefit from cooperating with each other. To be specific, they can move a resource (the car) from someone who values it less (Adam) to someone who values it more (Blair). Moving the resource from Adam, who values it at $3,000, to Blair, who values it at $4,000, will create $1,000 in value. The noncooperative value of the game is $3,000 in Adam's use-value and $5,000 in cash, thus totaling $8,000. The cooperative value of the game is $4,000 in Blair's use-value and $5,000 in cash, thus totaling $9,000. The *cooperative surplus* equals the amount by which the game's cooperative value exceeds its noncooperative value, specifically $1,000 in this case.

The distribution of the surplus from cooperation depends on the price at which the car is sold. For example, if Adam and Blair agree to a price of $3,500, then Adam gets $500 of the surplus and Blair also gets $500 of the surplus. Alternatively, if the price is set at $3,800, Adam gets $800 of the surplus and Blair gets $200. In general, the price affects the distribution of the surplus, but not the total amount of it.

Bargaining theory predicts that the price must fall in the interval between $3,000 and $4,000, but bargaining theory does not predict the *exact* price. Economists have long struggled with the fact that self-interested rationality alone does not determine the distribution of the cooperative surplus. Social norms help close the gap. A reasonable solution to the bargaining problem often gives each player his threat value plus an equal share of the cooperative surplus. Applied to this case, Blair should pay Adam $3,500 for the car. J. Nash was the first theorist to formalize the properties of the reasonable solution, so game theorists call it the *Nash bargaining solution* (Nash 1950). A long history of experimental economics concludes that people often reach a reasonable solution and split the surplus from cooperation.[5]

I have explained that economic theory divides the process of bargaining into three steps: establishing the threat values, determining the cooperative surplus, and agreeing on terms for distributing the surplus from cooperation. These steps will be used to analyze political bargaining.

Questions

1. In the example of Adam and Blair, how is the surplus distributed if the price equals $3,700?

2. In the example of Adam and Blair, explain why the price will not fall as low as $2,500.

---

[4] Without Adam's cooperation, Blair can use her $5,000 as she wishes. The noncooperative value of the game to Blair, or her *threat value*, equals the $5,000 that she keeps if she does not buy the car. If she buys it for $4,000, she gets $4,000 in use-value and she retains $1,000 in cash from her initial $5,000. Thus her total value equals her threat value of $5,000. Adam must sell the car to Blair for less the $4,000 in order for Blair to gain from the purchase.

[5] For example, see Bohnet 1998.

3. Suppose Adam receives a bid of $3,200 from a third party named Claire. How does Claire's bid change the threat values, the surplus from cooperation, and the reasonable solution in bargaining between Adam and Blair?

Democracy's Empty Core

When political bargaining succeeds, lawmakers cooperate rather than act on their threats. Their ability to threaten, however, determines the distribution of the surplus from cooperation. Thus a bargain in the legislature should reflect the relative strength of the parties. Sometimes, however, political bargaining fails. Failed political bargaining wastes resources in a contest for redistribution. Some additional concepts from game theory help explain contests for redistribution in democracies.

In a game of *pure conflict*, one player's win is another's loss. To illustrate, some poker players must lose whatever other players win, so wins and losses sum to zero (*zero-sum game*). Playing poker distributes wealth but does not produce it. Pure games of conflict are games of distribution, not production. The divergence of interests in a game of conflict makes the players adversaries, not allies or rivals.

Consider redistribution under majority rule. By assumption, any majority has the power to redistribute from the minority to itself. If players are symmetrical, the contest for distribution destabilizes every possible coalition. To see why, assume that three voters, denoted A, B, and C, must distribute $100 among them by majority rule. Initially, someone proposes to divide the money equally: (A, B, C) = ($33, $33, $33). A's counter-proposal is to share the surplus equally with B and give nothing to C: (A, B, C) = ($50, $50, $0). A and B can implement A's counter-proposal under majority rule, and A's counter-proposal makes A and B better-off than they would have been in the initial proposal. A coalition is *blocked* if another coalition can implement a distribution that is Pareto superior for its members.[6] So A's counter-proposal blocks the initial proposal.

It is not hard to see that *any* proposal is blocked by another proposal. Thus A's proposal is blocked by B's counter-proposal to distribute the surplus (A, B, C) = ($0, $75, $25), and B's proposal is blocked by C's counter-proposal to distribute the surplus (A, B, C) = ($50, $0, $50). By definition, the *core* of a game is the set of unblocked distributions. Since every proposal is blocked by an alternative, the game has an empty core. In general, *majority-rule games of distribution with symmetrical players have an empty core*. In this game, a majority coalition receives $100, but the payoff to the coalition falls to $0 if either member quits. Thus each member of the coalition can assert that his marginal contribution to the coalition is its full value. This demand is credible. However, not everyone in

---

[6] See the explanation of the core of a game in chapter 2.

the coalition can be paid the value of his marginal contribution.[7] Even though satisfying all the demands is infeasible, each of the demands may be credible.[8]

In chapter 2 I explained that games with an empty core are usually unstable. Redistribution by majority rule can cause intransitive voting cycles. Both Aristotle and Madison shared the opinion that poor people, if sufficiently numerous in a democracy, would use majority rule to redistribute wealth and destabilize the state.[9] Besides the obvious disadvantages, instability has an advantage: no group or faction can form a stable majority to exploit others. Any coalition that would like to enrich itself by using state power to exploit others knows that another coalition dominates it. Knowing this, the governing coalition may refrain from exploiting others for fear that its victims will be the next rulers.

To illustrate, in two-party competition, today's opposition is tomorrow's government. Knowing this, the party in power has reason to leave the courts independent. Conversely, when one party dominates politics, it has an incentive to exploit its power by politicizing courts. To illustrate, so long as elections regularly changed governments in Japan, historical data suggest that the government respected the independence of its courts. When governments no longer feared loss in elections, they exerted political influence over the courts (Ramseyer 1994). In contrast, persistent two-party competition in the United States preserved independent courts.

India provides another illustration. Western commentators often stress that stable democracies require educated and prosperous citizens. However, the world's largest democracy, India, is relatively stable despite much illiteracy and poverty. Theorists have proposed that Indian democracy endures because the country

---

[7] A member's marginal contribution to the coalition may be computed as the fall in the coalition's total value caused by the member's quitting. (I apply the *Shapely value* of a coalition member. See Luce and Raiffa 1967, p. 249.) With *increasing returns to scale* (super-additivity), however, cooperation does not create enough value for each member to receive the marginal product of membership, so paying the marginal product of membership to everyone is *infeasible*. To illustrate concretely, consider a coalition formed by A and B that distributes the surplus equally between them: $(A, B, C) = (\$50, \$50, \$0)$. If either member of the coalition were to leave it, the payoff to the coalition would fall from $100 to $0. By this logic, the marginal product of each of the two members of the coalition equals $100, but the total product of the coalition also equals $100. Consequently, paying $100 to each member of the coalition is infeasible.

[8] A threat by a member of a majority coalition is credible, according to one definition, if another coalition could satisfy the demand without worsening its own position. To illustrate by the preceding example, consider the coalition formed by A and B that distributes the surplus equally between them: $(A, B, C) = (\$50, \$50, \$0)$. If B were to withdraw from the coalition, the coalition's payoff would fall from $100 to $0. Noting this fact, assume that B demands a payoff of $75 to remain in the coalition. The threat is credible because B could leave the coalition and form a new coalition with C, distributing the surplus $(A, B, C) = (\$0, \$75, \$25)$, which makes B and C better-off. A, however, can also make the same demand as B; A and B can each make a credible demand for $75. Both demands cannot be satisfied, because there is only $100 to distribute. Thus, each demand is credible and both demands are infeasible.

[9] Aristotle wrote: "[W]here democracies have no middle class, and the poor are greatly superior in number, trouble ensues, and they are speedily ruined." See Aristotle 1962, book IV, chapter 9, section 14. Madson's concerns are discussed in Federalist 10 (Madison 1981a).

contains so many different kinds of people as distinguished by ethnicity, language, and religion, no one group can dominate the others. Whenever a cartel forms to control the state, a new coalition forms to oppose it. (James Madison made a similar argument for the stability of American representative democracy in *Federalist* No. 10.)

I explained that inefficiency and intransitivity are the price people must pay in a democracy when they cannot bargain together and cooperate. The empty core makes democracy look bad until it is compared to other political systems. Instead of eliminating threats, democracy limits them. Hostile parties in a democracy threaten to vote against each other. Better a hostile vote than a general strike, a car bomb, a shoot-out, or a coup d'état. Winston Churchill allegedly said, "The United Nations was not set up to get us to Heaven but to save us from Hell."[10] Better world democracy than world war. I call democracy the *minimax constitution* because it minimizes the loss from political noncooperation when the worst possibilities materialize.[11]

Pure Coordination

At the opposite pole from pure conflict stand pure *coordination games* in which the interests of different players converge perfectly (Lewis 1969; Schelling 1980). The best plan for anyone is best for everyone. Pure games of coordination are games of production, not distribution. A coordination game produces wealth without creating any conflict over distribution. Since interests converge, everyone who is fully informed agrees on the best plan of action.

In pure coordination games, imperfect information obstructs coordination. Allies must exchange information and search for the best plan. Discovering the best plan is easy for a coordination game with a uniquely stable equilibrium and harder for coordination games with multiple equilibria.

To illustrate, person A calls person B on the telephone and, in the middle of the conversation, the connection is broken unexpectedly. Both parties want to reestablish communications. If both call back immediately, however, each of them will get a busy signal. So there are two equilibria: A calls B, and B calls A. The problem is a lack of information about which solution to choose.

Coordination games with multiple equilibria are especially difficult to solve when local progress causes global regress. To illustrate by an analogy, mountain climbers in a fog might follow the rule, "Always go up." If the mountain slopes up to a single peak, following this rule will get the climbers to the summit. If, however, the mountain has two peaks, climbers following this rule may ascend a false summit, which takes them away from the true summit. Climbing the false summit is local progress and global regress.

[10] An able sleuth, Debby Kearney, found this quotation attributed to Churchill many times without a decisive reference. She also found it attributed to Henry Cabot Lodge and Dag Hammarskjöld.

[11] Minimizing the loss from noncooperation, or, equivalently, maximizing the noncooperative value of the game, has been called the "normative Hobbes Theorem." The Hobbes Theorem takes a far more pessimistic view about human cooperation than does the Coase Theorem. See chapter 4 of Cooter and Ulen 1999.

The surface of a single-peaked mountain is a convex set, whereas the surface of a twin-peaked mountain is a nonconvex set. A single-peaked mountain corresponds to a game with a uniquely stable equilibrium, and a twin-peaked mountain corresponds to a game with multiple equilibria. In general, *convex games of pure coordination are easier to solve than nonconvex games.*

To illustrate, drivers in Britain benefit from everyone's driving on the *same* side of the road, but drivers in Britain would benefit *more* from abandoning the practice of driving on the left side of the road and adopting the European practice of driving on the *right* side of the road. Driving on the left is a local maximum, and driving on the right is a global maximum. So far Britain has been unwilling to bear the conversion cost of changing from the local to the global maximum.

Producing by Distributing

I have discussed pure games of distribution and pure games of coordination. Most bargaining games are impure, involving cooperation and distribution. When bargaining, each party tries to secure the cooperation of others, which is productive. The productive aspect of bargaining causes the convergence of interests and promotes cooperation. When bargaining, each party also tries to secure the best terms, which is distributive. The distributive aspect of bargaining causes the divergence of interests and promotes conflict. In general, *cooperation produces and terms distribute.* In a bargaining game, the parties must agree on the terms for distributing the cooperative surplus in order to produce it. Agreement among the players in a bargaining game is easy to reach when production dominates distribution. Conversely, agreement is hard to reach when distribution dominates production.

In a zero-sum game, everyone is an enemy because one person's gains can only come through another's losses. In reality, however, politics is a bargaining game with a productive, creative dimension. By agreeing on distribution, people cooperate to mutual advantage. Focusing only on distribution misleads the observer into thinking that politics is a zero-sum game. The belief that political opponents are enemies, which Carl Schmitt developed into a political philosophy,[12] distorts the nature of politics.

The character of political bargaining identifies a trade-off in choosing between majority rule and unanimity rule. Unanimity rule requires the consent of everyone. The necessity of universal consent increases the costs of coordination and blocks involuntary redistribution. In contrast, majority rule overrides a dissenting minority. The power to override minorities decreases the costs of coordination and allows involuntary redistribution. The possibility of redistribution causes cycling and strategic behavior. The choice between unanimity rule and majority rule presents a trade-off between coordination costs and strategic costs.[13]

[12] See Dyzenhaus 1998.

[13] To illustrate, contrast a game with unanimity rule and majority rule. Under unanimity rule, the game has N players who can obtain a prize of $100 by agreeing on its division, and they get

In reality, unanimity rule often succeeds for small organizations and paralyzes large organizations. Recognizing this fact, a growing organization may begin with unanimity rule and later switch to majority rule. For example, as more countries join the European Union, the Council of Ministers increasingly replaces unanimity rule with majority rule for its decisions (see chapter 5). In general, *unanimity rule paralyzes large organizations and majority rule animates them.* Animation, however, comes at a cost. In general, *majority rule provokes contests for redistribution and unanimity rule eliminates contests for redistribution.* Majority rule creates the need for constitutional devices to dampen redistributive contests, such as a constitutional right to property. As discussed in chapter 12, a constitutional right to property diverts redistributive contests away from their most destructive forms, such as expropriating the property of political enemies, and channels them into milder forms, such the quest for tax breaks.

Enforceability and Incumbency

The ability of people to agree increases when they can bind their future actions. In markets, contracts bind future actions. In politics, however, limits on the ability of present officials to bind future officials restrict the deals they can strike.[14] To illustrate, when Congress enacts a bill, a future Congress remains free to repeal it. The sitting Congress cannot legally entrench legislation, say, by inserting a clause in a bill stipulating that its repeal requires a super-majority in a future Congress. This fact can obstruct bargaining with Congress. To illustrate concretely, President Reagan's plan for a "new federalism" called for reshuffling expenditures between the states and the federal government. The sitting Congress feared that after costs were shifted to the states, the president and a future Congress would not keep the federal government's side of the deal. The inability of the president and Congress to bind their future decisions apparently caused the deal to fail.[15]

---

nothing if they cannot agree. Under unanimity rule, the coalition of N people is in the core. As N becomes large, however, the costs of coordinating N people increases. Consider changing the rules of the game to majority rule. Under majority rule, any coalition of $1 + N/2$ players can obtain the prize of \$100 by agreeing on its distribution, provided that no one defects to another coalition. The reduction in coalition size from N to $1 + N/2$ reduces coordination costs among the players. Under majority rule, however, the core is empty. To diminish this problem, additional rules of the game could limit the scope of redistribution by a majority. For example, the rules of the game could prescribe that every coalition divide its payoff equally among its members.

[14] Levmore 1996 explores how candidates could precommit and why they usually do not.

[15] President Reagan wanted the states to assume responsibility for the cost of certain welfare programs (food stamps, Aid for Dependent Children) and sixty-one specific grant-in-aid programs. In exchange, the federal government would pick up all costs of certain medical programs (medicaid). In addition, the states could draw on federal funds from excise taxes and taxes on windfall profits in the oil industry. See Rochelle L. Stanfield, "A Neatly Wrapped Package with Explosives," *National Journal* 27 January 1982, pp. 356–62.

Constitutional amendment binds politicians by entrenching a law against legislative repeal. By amending the constitution, a political coalition makes a credible commitment whose strength depends on the difficulty of amendment. If amendment is too easy, the commitment is not credible. If amendment is too hard, the commitment is too difficult to make. The optimal process of constitutional appeal balances the strength and frequency of commitment. To illustrate this way of reasoning, Donald Boudreaux and A. C. Prichard (1993) argue that the burdensome process prescribed by Article 5 of the U.S. Constitution prevents political coalitions in the United States from making beneficial commitments. An easier amendment process would, in their view, provide better protection against political factions.

Without credible commitments, trust is critical to cooperation. Trust arises from past cooperation and future advantage from a continuing relationship. Thus, politicians who stay in office for a long time (repeat players) can make deals that brief officeholders (one-shot players) cannot make. To illustrate, the term of office is six years in the U.S. Senate and two years in the House of Representatives, so senators have an advantage over representatives in making deals.

Question: Compare the deal-making ability of a recently elected president and a president nearing the end of his final term ("lame-duck").

PROBLEM OF REPRESENTATION

In indirect democracy, the citizens elect the legislators and the legislators make the laws. The constitution should try to align the self-interest of legislators and the interests of citizens. Insofar as the constitution succeeds, the citizens are well represented by their legislators. If citizens are well represented, then bargains among the legislators satisfy the preferences of the citizens. If citizens are poorly represented, then bargains among the legislators satisfy the legislators and frustrate the citizens.

The theory called "pluralism" holds that different segments of society organize successfully to bargain with each other and influence politics (Dahl 1982). Pluralism presupposes that each group of citizens elects representatives to bargain for them. Representatives ideally enjoy political influence roughly in proportion to the number of people whom they represent. In reality, some citizens enjoy better representation than others, and some representatives enjoy disproportionate power. The bargain theory of democracy must explain these differences in the quality of representation and the power of representatives.

Unequal information can cause unequal representation. To illustrate how scarce political information is, assume that a committee of the U.S. Congress considers four proposals on educational expenditures. The National Organization of Women (NOW) makes the first proposal, the National Association for the Advancement of Colored People (NAACP) makes the second proposal, the National Union of Teachers (NUT) makes the third proposal, and the National Association of Manufacturers (NAM) makes the final proposal. Assume the committee follows the *king-of-the-hill* procedure, according to which the members vote "yes" or "no" on a series of alternatives, and the last alternative on the agenda to receive a majority of "yes" votes prevails. Following this procedure, the members can vote "yes" on all four proposals and the proposal by NAM wins. After the votes, a committee member who made speeches before each of these four organizations could report that he voted for each of their proposals. The report is true and utterly misleading.

In general, bargaining jeopardizes the accountability of legislators. To see why, assume that two bills, A and B, are pending in the legislature. Also assume the constituents of a certain district favor both bills, but passing A is more important to them than passing B. If the district's representative votes for both bills, her constituents will approve of her voting record. Assume, however, that both bills will be defeated unless she trades her vote on B to obtain a vote on A. Now the representative faces a dilemma. Her constituents care more about A than B, so they would presumably want her to trade votes in order to secure the passage of A. If, however, she does trade votes, she will go on record as voting against B. Since her constituents favor B, her opponent in the next election will tell the voters that she voted against B. Should she give her constituents their preferred legislation or their preferred symbols?

In general, sincere voting on each bill makes the legislator's voting record relatively easy to interpret and precludes the efficiency gains from vote trading. Conversely, vote trading obscures the information provided by a legislator's voting record and increases satisfaction with legislation.

What is the quality of the pickles inside a jar on the grocery shelf? Most people guess based on the brand. Similarly, when voters know little about candidates, party labels become important signals. So long as candidates adhere to the party's platform, party labels provide useful information. Thus the major political parties preserve the value of their "brand name" by disciplining their members and inducing ideological similarity.

Detailed political information comes from people in silk suits waiting in the lobby to talk to politicians when they emerge from their chambers. Professional "lobbyists" scrutinize the performance of politicians on details that go unnoticed by most voters, thus performing the valuable role of informing citizens about technical laws and regulations.[16] However, the citizens who get informed by lobbyists are mostly those who pay for it, and different groups of people pay lobbyists different amounts of money. Thus lobbyists increase the mean and the variance in political information known to citizens. The next section explains differential investment in lobbying.

Questions

1. A legislator who favors bills A and B may yet vote against B to secure passage of A. How could you measure the extent of strategic voting in a legislature?

---

[16] For a pure signaling model, in which contributions by interest groups signal information about the actual traits of political candidates, see Dharmapala 1998.

2. A well-known economist argued that fragmented power prevents Americans from holding officials accountable for failed policies thus paralyzing politics. He proposed abandoning the presidential system and adopting a British-style parliamentary system (Thurow 1980). Explain how fragmented power erodes accountability.

Investing in Politics

A rational investor channels money into the investments that yield the highest rate of return. When one investment has a higher expected rate of return than another investment with the same risk, funds will flow from the lower-yielding investment to the higher-yielding investment. This principle applies to investments in microprocessors, oil wells, and lobbying. For example, a computer company that earns 12 percent on keyboard production and 16 percent on lobbying for military contracts will shift funds from the former to the latter. (I assume that both investments are equally risky.)

After reallocating funds to reach equilibrium, every investment with the same risk earns the same rate of return. For example, in equilibrium the computer company that earns 10 percent on keyboard production also earns 10 percent on lobbying for military contracts. This proposition applies to investments in acquiring tax loopholes, import protection, monopoly restrictions, regulations limiting competition, and grants for research and development.

Since one form of investment easily substitutes for another, the supply of funds for lobbying is highly elastic in the long run. To appreciate the consequences of this fact, think of lobbyists as supplying legislation, and think of investors as demanding legislation. An increase in the price lobbyists charge for legislation should cause a large decrease in demand for legislation by investors. Furthermore, an increase in the price charged by lobbyists for legislation should cause a decrease in total expenditures on lobbying.

These predictions can be tested. The price charged by lobbyists for legislation should change with political organization. The division of powers in a democracy requires more officials to cooperate in making legislation. To illustrate, a bicameral legislature requires the cooperation of two houses to enact legislation, whereas a unicameral legislature only requires one house to enact legislation. Similarly, the fragmentation of offices among political parties makes cooperation among officials more difficult. More burdensome procedural rules in the legislature also increase the cost of "purchasing" legislation. Finally, public financing of campaigns or changes in information technology that decrease legislators' need for campaign funds should increase the cost of purchasing legislation. I conclude that the division of powers, the fragmentation of parties, more burdensome legislative procedures, and public financing of campaigns should increase the price charged by lobbyists for new legislation, thus substantially decreasing total expenditures by firms on lobbying in the long run.

Unlike firms, citizens seldom think of their donations to political causes as investments that must yield a competitive rate of return. Consequently, citizens are less likely to reduce their investments in lobbying when the price of legislation increases. The contribution of citizens to groups such as Greenpeace and the American Association of Retired Persons is presumably less elastic than the contributions of firms to lobbyists. If demand by citizens is inelastic, the division of powers, the fragmentation of parties, more burdensome legislative procedures, and public financing of campaigns, which increase the price charged by lobbyists for new legislation, should only moderately decrease total expenditures on lobbying by citizens' groups.

Profitability can explain the form of the legislation purchased by firms. To illustrate, assume that an industry must decide between lobbying for subsidies or lobbying to restrict competition by quotas and price controls. Subsidies will attract new firms to enter the industry and dissipate profits. Furthermore, the public can easily discover expenditures on subsidies. In contrast, quotas and price controls create monopoly profits while excluding entry, and the public has difficulty discovering their cost. So quotas and price controls are usually the first choice of the regulated industry.[17] To illustrate, airline regulations impose quotas and price controls on routes in many countries.

Questions

1 Assume that party label acts as a signal rather like a brand name on a commodity. Explain why this assumption might imply that parties will be more important in national elections than in local elections.

2. Explain why public financing of political campaigns might increase the cost of purchasing legislation through lobbying. Also explain why the American Association of Retired Persons might respond by spending more money on lobbying.

Free Rides and Costly Lobbying

The effects of new laws are spread among many people, but the costs of lobbying are concentrated. To illustrate, there are approximately 70,000 lawyers in California, so a regulation that benefits each of them by $100 creates $7 million in benefits for the profession. Assume that lobbyists could supply such a regulation at a cost of $140,000. If $2 could be collected from every lawyer in the state to pay for lobbying, each of them would receive a payoff of $100. This rate of return on investment exceeds Microsoft in its best years. But the self-interest of individual lawyers prompts each of them to free-ride on the contributions of others. Lobbying expenditures by a group depends on its ability to overcome the free-rider problem.

The free-rider problem is easier to overcome in a group with few members than in one with many. Monopoly and oligopoly concentrate production, whereas competition diffuses it. In many markets, a small number of producers

---

[17] For a detailed account of industry preferences for regulation, including historical data from the United States, see Stigler 1971.

sell to a large, diffuse group of consumers. The free-rider principle predicts that lobbying will be strong by corporations in concentrated industries, whereas lobbying will be weak by corporations in competitive industries and by consumers in all markets. Given asymmetrical lobbying, producers are more likely than consumers to "capture" an industry's regulator.[18]

A group can overcome the free-rider problem by finding a way to tax its members.[19] To illustrate, in order to practice medicine in most American hospitals, a doctor must belong to the American Medical Association (AMA). The dues that doctors pay to the AMA resemble a compulsory tax more than a voluntary contribution. The AMA uses the dues to finance lobbying on behalf of all doctors. In contrast, an ecology organization like the Sierra Club has no coercive hold on its members. Its dues resemble a voluntary contribution more than a compulsory tax. The Sierra Club must rely on idealism, not self-interest, to obtain lobbying funds. The free-rider principle predicts relatively strong lobbying by professional organizations and industrial unions and relatively weak lobbying by "public interest" groups.

A shortcoming of the free-rider principle is its exclusive focus on the supply of funds for lobbying and not their use. Politicians in a democracy are concerned with the number of votes that lobbyists can deliver. The lobbyists for a concentrated industry may have to spend a lot of money to deliver a modest number of votes, whereas the lobbyists for a popular organization may be able to deliver many votes at modest cost. Popular organizations are more efficient than industrial organizations at transforming money into votes. This observation predicts that the Sierra Club and the American Association of Retired Persons will obtain more political influence per dollar spent on lobbying than the National Association of Manufacturers.

The most powerful lobbyists solve the free-rider problem and efficiently transform money into votes. To illustrate, a small number of gun manufacturers donate substantial sums to the National Rifle Association (NRA), and many gun owners who belong to the NRA faithfully respond to its appeals with their votes. This fact explains why public opinion polls in some U.S. states consistently show the majority of voters favoring stricter controls on guns than legislators produce.

Theories of self-interest cannot explain the attachment of voters to idealistic causes. To illustrate, many people expect no direct return when they donate to lobbyists for the environment, poor people, or disadvantaged minorities. Political organizations with the skill to tap the altruism of people can enjoy financial support in contradiction of the free-rider principle. Economic theory so far has said little about altruistic impulses for lobbying.

Questions

1. A familiar list of U.S. organizations follows. First, rank them according to your guess about their ability to overcome the free-rider problem. Second,

---

[18] Kolko 1967; Stigler 1975; Spitzer 1988; and Elhauge 1991.
[19] See Olson 1965.

rank them according to your guess about their ability to attract idealistic donations.

Teamsters Union

Sierra Club

American Bankers Association

American Medical Association

American Association of Retired Persons

National Rifle Association

2. Give an example of a regulator that appears to be "captured" (controlled by the industry it regulates) and describe the political forces making capture possible.

Rent-Seeking

Investing in manufacturing facilities is wholly productive, whereas investing in lobbying is partly productive and partly redistributive. Investing in lobbying is productive insofar as it leads to more efficient laws. Rather than increasing efficiency, however, many laws redistribute government money or restrict competition. To illustrate, many of the deductions and exclusions in the federal tax code reduce its efficiency and redistribute the tax burden. Similarly, many regulations restrict competition in order to increase profits of the regulated firms.

Economists have developed useful language for describing wasteful political activities. In its technical meaning, "rent" refers to profits from passive ownership, as opposed to profits from productive activity. Scarce legal entitlements yield rent to their owners. To illustrate, a restaurateur who receives the exclusive right to operate a restaurant in a public park will enjoy monopoly profits. The concessionaire enjoys the "ordinary profits" that any competitive enterprise would enjoy, plus "excess profit" from being a monopoly. The excess profit is the "rent" from owning the concession.

Investing in lobbying to acquire scarce legal entitlements is called "rent-seeking." Although the phrase sounds invidious, economists apply it indiscriminately to behavior that ordinary people loath and admire. To illustrate, domestic steel manufacturers seek to exclude imports, airlines seek to prohibit discount fares, lawyers seek to exclude paralegals from supplying cheap legal advice, labor unions seek protection from nonunion workers, one ethnic group seeks protection from competition by workers belonging to another ethnic group, and media companies seek the exclusive right to supply cable television to small towns. Similarly, artists seek subsidies to paint pictures, universities seek subsidies for research, and sports teams seek subsidies to build stadiums.

Figure 3-1 elucidates the logic of rent-seeking. Assume that the government considers imposing a tax on one group of people and using the revenues to

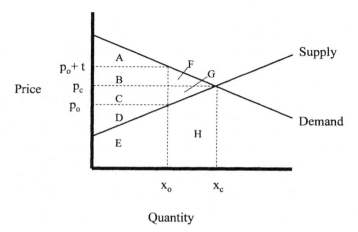

Fig. 3-1 Tax on Beverages

provide benefits to another group. To be specific, assume that a small town has many restaurants whose customers come from outside the area. The residents want to shift the burden of taxation from themselves to the customers of the restaurants. The local government proposes to reduce a poll tax on residents[20] and replace lost revenues with a new tax on consumption of beverages sold in restaurants.

The horizontal axis in figure 3-1 indicates the number of beverages purchased from restaurants in the town, and the vertical axis indicates the average price of a beverage. Without a tax, the quantity is x_c and the price is p_c.

Consider the effect of imposing a tax t, which is assessed for each beverage sold in restaurants, rather like a tax per package of cigarettes or a tax per liter of gasoline. The supply curve indicates the cost to producers of supplying the good to consumers. Consumers pay a price that equals the cost of supplying the good plus the tax. Thus the tax is a wedge between the supply curve of producers and the demand curve of consumers. The height of this wedge is the value of the tax t. To incorporate the wedge into figure 3-1, find the point where the vertical distance between the demand and supply curves equals the tax t, which is labeled x_o in figure 3-1. This is the new equilibrium, which occurs at the level of supply where the cost of supply plus the tax equals the amount consumers are willing to pay for the good.

If a tax t is imposed, the price paid by consumers will rise to $p_o + t$, of which p_o goes to the restaurants and t goes to the state. As a result of the beverage tax, the number of beverages purchased will fall to x_o. The total revenues raised by the tax equal $t \times x_o$, or the area B + C in figure 3-1. Since all the tax revenues go toward reducing the residential poll tax, residents would benefit from investing up to B + C in lobbying activities to ensure the enactment of the tax.

[20] A poll tax, which is a tax on each person, simplifies the example because poll taxes have little or no incentive effects.

The tax imposes a loss on restaurants and their customers. I will explain each loss in turn. The demand curve indicates the quantity that consumers will demand as the price varies. Equivalently, the demand curve indicates the price that consumers are willing to pay for the good as the quantity varies.[21] The consumers' surplus equals the difference between the prices consumers are willing to pay and the price that they actually pay. The loss imposed by the tax on the restaurant customers equals the decrease in consumers' surplus.

To compute this loss, notice that the consumer's surplus in the initial situation, before the tax is imposed, equals the area in between the demand curve and the horizontal price line through p_c. So the initial consumer's surplus equals $A + B + F$ in figure 3-1. After imposing the tax, the consumer's surplus equals the area in between the demand curve and the horizontal price line through $p_o + t$, which corresponds to area A. Thus the decrease in consumers' surplus equals $A + B + F - A = B + F$.

Now I turn from the customers to the restaurants. The supply curve indicates the quantity that sellers in a competitive market will supply as the price varies. Equivalently, the supply curve indicates the cost to sellers of supplying the good as the quantity varies. The difference between the price received by sellers and the cost of supplying it equals their profits. (Profits are also called "producer's surplus."[22]) Thus the loss imposed by the tax on restaurants equals the decrease in their profits. To compute this loss, notice that profits in the initial situation, before the tax is imposed, equal the area in between the horizontal price line through p_c and the supply curve. So the initial profits equal $C + D + G$ in figure 3-1. After imposing the tax, profits equal the area in between the horizontal price line through p_o and the supply curve, which corresponds to area D. Thus the decrease in consumers' surplus equals $C + D + G - D = C + G$.

I have explained that the tax imposes losses on consumers and restaurants equal to $B + F + C + G$ in figure 3-1. The tax, however, benefits residents by raising revenues that the state uses to offset reductions in the residential poll tax. A tax at rate t on x_o beverages raises total revenues equal to $t \times x_o$, which corresponds to $B + C$. The phrase "excess burden" refers to the difference between the burden imposed on the people who pay the tax, $B + F + C + G$, and the revenues raised by it, $B + C$. Thus the excess burden in figure 3-1 equals the small triangle $F + G$. (The excess burden is also called the "deadweight loss" from the tax, because it is the portion of the loss from the tax that is not offset by a gain.)

Since the loss to restaurants and their customers exceeds the gain to the beneficiaries of the tax in the form of tax revenues, the losers lose more than the winners gain. To be precise, the losers lose $F + G$ more than the winners

---

[21] These equivalencies are obtained mathematically by inverting the demand function. If the demand curve is written $x = f(p)$, then its inverse is written $p = f^{-1}(x)$. A one-to-one function can be inverted.

[22] Here I ignore a subtle difference of profits in the long and short run. The area between the price line and the short-run supply curve indicates the seller's profits excluding the cost of fixed factors of production. The area between the price line and the long-run supply curve indicates the owner's profits of factors inelastically supplied in the long run, such as the rent on owning land.

gain. In general, a tax or regulation imposed on a perfectly competitive market causes the losers to lose more than the winners gain. The justification for such a policy, if it has a justification, must rest on some grounds other than economic efficiency, such as distribution. In this example, the justification would have to rest on the desirability of redistributing wealth from restaurant owners and customers to the town's residents.

In lobbying against the tax, the maximum amount the losers would pay to defeat the tax is the full value of the loss the tax will impose upon them, which equals $B + C + F + G$. Similarly, in lobbying for the bill, the maximum amount the winners would pay equals the full value of the gain the tax creates for them, which equals $B + C$. An inefficient policy, by definition, imposes larger losses on losers than the gains it creates for winners. So the maximum amount the losers would pay to defeat the tax bill exceeds the maximum amount the winners would pay to enact it.

Legislators sometimes want to catch the attention of competing interests and test the strength of their sentiments. To illustrate, a legislator might propose new rules for dairy farms in order to "fetch" the farm lobbyists into his office for a private discussion. In Illinois such a proposal is called a "fetcher bill." Assume a politician "fetched" the parties affected by the proposed beverage tax and offered to "sell" the legislation to the highest bidder. In other words, imagine that a politician tells the residents, the restaurant owners and customers that he will either impose the tax or not impose it depending on which group is willing to pay more.

As explained, the potential losers are willing to spend more to block the tax than the potential winners are willing to pay to impose the tax. If the potential winners know this fact, then they might believe that they will lose a "lobbying war." Rather than losing the lobbying war, the potential winners from the tax may refuse to pay the politician anything. But if the potential winners refuse to pay the politician, the potential losers need not actually pay anything either. So nothing is spent on influencing the political process and the efficient outcome is achieved. This fortuitous outcome is rather like the two bull moose in mating season who take the measure of each other by displays and threats, and then the one who would lose the fight runs away.

Unfortunately, outcomes are not always so fortuitous in lobbying or mating. Bull moose sometimes kill each other, and political factions in a democracy sometimes waste large sums of money trying to outdo each other. A contest to acquire a legal right can dissipate the rents that a party enjoys from owning it. In our example, the homeowners might spend $B + C$ lobbying for the tax, and the consumers and restaurant owners might spend $B + C + F + G$ lobbying against the tax. The area $2B + 2C + F + G$ in figure 3-1 represents the maximum potential loss from dissipative rent-seeking, whereas the welfare triangle $F + G$ represents the loss from allocative inefficiency. In general, dissipative rent-seeking imposes much greater social losses than does allocative inefficiency.

As explained, $2B + 2C + F + G$ represents the maximum value that the parties would spend in lobbying, but they will not necessarily spend the maximum amount. The parties affected by this tax are classes of people—restaurateurs, customers, and homeowners. Lobbying may be in the interest of a class of people, but actually undertaking the lobbying may not be in the self-interest of any member of the class. To predict how much an individual will invest, it is necessary to predict his return on the investment. Spreading the benefit among many people dilutes the return, thus prompting free-riding.

Now I summarize the arguments about the complex role of money in politics. Investment in political influence provides voters with a way of expressing the intensity of their preferences, which increases the efficiency of politics. Furthermore, political advertising and lobbying increase the amount of information known to voters and may change their preferences as well. There are, however, several ways that money distorts the political representation of preferences. First, groups that cannot overcome the free-rider problem enjoy little influence. Second, unequal wealth results in unequal political influence. Instead of each person having the same threat value (the ability to withhold one vote), some citizens have far larger threat values than others (the ability to withhold contributions). Third, many investments in political influence aim to transfer wealth from politically favored groups to politically disfavored groups. These transfers are costly and unproductive. So the question of whether money invested in obtaining political influence improves or harms the workings of democracy is complicated. Chapter 13 returns to this question and discusses a novel reform proposal to limit the influence of money on politics.

Questions

1. Would you expect an increase in the elasticity of the demand and supply curves in figure 3-1 to result in more or less rent-seeking? Explain your answer.

2. Shoe manufacturers lobby for restrictions on imported shoes, and the Salvation Army lobbies for funds to support homeless alcoholics. Are both "seeking rents"?

3. To be sure that you understand figure 3-1, answer the following question about a similar graph in figure 3-2, which depicts the effects of a $.20 dollar beverage tax on the demand and supply of beverages by restaurants.

    a. Assume that the owners of restaurants and their customers do not enjoy any of the benefits from spending the tax revenues. How much would blocking the tax be worth to the owners of restaurants and their customers?

    b. Assume that the revenues from the beverage tax are used to reduce a residential poll tax. Also assume that the residents are neither owners nor customers of the restaurants. How much is the enactment of the tax worth to residents?

    c. Compare your answers to "a" and "b." Use efficiency to explain why one value exceeds the other.

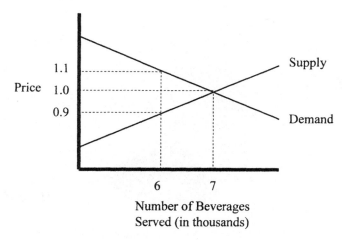

Fig. 3-2 Tax on Beverages

GOVERNMENT BY COALITION

Only two major parties exist in Britain and the United States, but other democracies have many political parties. To govern a country with multiple parties, a coalition must command a majority of votes in the legislature. In a highly fragmented political system, many different combinations of parties could form the government. The theory of rent-seeking predicts which coalition will actually form. A governing coalition must distribute the spoils of office among its members. Assume the party with the most seats in the legislature invites other parties to join in creating a government. The members of the governing coalition must share the spoils of power (offices, contracts, grants, etc.). The largest party that forms the coalition government wants to concentrate the spoils of power on its own members. To share the spoils of power as narrowly as possible, the largest party should form the smallest coalition that is large enough to govern.[23] The smallest coalition that is large enough to govern is called the *minimum winning coalition*.

To illustrate, assume that five parties, labeled A, B, C, D, and E, divide the seats in Parliament as depicted in figure 3-3. To form the minimum winning coalition, A will invite C to join in forming a government. The coalition of A and C will control 52 percent of the votes.

Notice that the theory of the minimum winning coalition predicts the relationship between the number of parties in the legislature and the size of the governing coalition. As the number of parties increases, wider choice among smaller parties permits the governing coalition to come closer to the minimum of 51 percent of the seats. So more parties implies fewer total seats on average in the governing coalition.

---

[23] This concept was first developed by Riker. See Riker 1962.

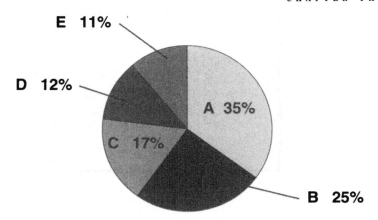

Fig. 3-3 Coalition Formation

In practice, a small majority has difficulty governing. To illustrate, a coalition with 52 percent of the seats could fall if a few legislators fail to turn up for a crucial vote. Given this fact, party A may choose to form a coalition with D and E, which gives the government 58 percent of the seats. The extra margin of safety may be worth the price of sharing the spoils of office with more people. Instead of the minimum winning coalition, government may be formed by the *minimum working coalition.*[24]

The role of ideology in politics is ignored by the prediction that the minimum winning coalition or the minimum working coalition forms the government. To illustrate the problem of ideology for these theories, assume the parties can be ranked on a left-right political scale depicted in figure 3-4. Parties are *connected* if they occupy adjoining positions on the left-right scale. Thus A is connected to B, and B is connected to C, but A is not connected to C. Ideological connection may increase the ability of parties to cooperate. Conversely, ideological distance may decrease the ability of parties to cooperate. A might have difficulties forming a coalition with C and even more difficulty forming a coalition with D or E. If ideological connection is necessary to form a coalition, then a government may form from the *minimum connected coalition.* The minimum connected coalition in figure 3-4 is B, C, and D, which together control 54 percent of the seats.

Like the median rule, the theory of the minimum connected coalition involves a single dimension on which parties can be ranked. Alternatively, assume that each party occupies a point in a multiattribute space of political choices. In politics as in markets, complementary tastes provide grounds for trade and cooperation. One party's preferences complement the preferences of another party when the first party cares the most about issues that the second party cares about the

---

[24] For a discussion contrasting minimum winning coalition and minimum working coalition, see Laver and Schofield 1990b, p. 94.

LEFT   CENTER   RIGHT

A	B	C	D	E
35%	25%	17%	12%	11%

Fig. 3-4 Connected Coalitions

least. This fact suggests that the largest party should look for coalition partners with complementary preferences. To illustrate, assume the largest Israeli party wants the key cabinet positions like defense, and some small religious parties want the state to enforce religious rules such as prohibiting commerce on the Sabbath. By forming a governing coalition among these parties, the government can give each party what it most wants. This reasoning suggests another principle for coalition formation, which could be called the *most complementary coalition*. The most complementary coalition maximizes the gains from trading votes.

Empirical research comparing various countries with coalition governments, especially in Europe, has shown that the minimum winning coalition and the minimum connected coalition have predictive value.[25] These theories do much better than chance in predicting the coalition that will form a government, although these theories are not necessarily right more often than they are wrong. Besides the logic of game theory, history and culture determine the composition of political parties in coalition governments.

Questions

1. In the following alignment of parties in figure 3-5 below, what is the minimum winning coalition? What is the minimum connected coalition?

2. Governments in the United States alternate between the Democratic and Republican Parties. What prevents one party from growing larger than the other and dominating most elections?

Unstable Coalitions

Coalition governments in some countries are notoriously unstable. For example, Italy had forty-three different coalition governments between 1945 and 1985.

LEFT   CENTER   RIGHT

A	B	C	D
14%	20%	35%	31%

Fig. 3-5 Winning v. Connected Coalitions

[25] Laver and Schofield 1990b.

Bargaining theory helps explain the instability. Earlier in this chapter I explained that a game of redistribution under majority rule with symmetrical voters has an empty core. Similarly, a game of coalition government with symmetrical parties has an empty core. An empty core causes instability.

To illustrate the similarity between majority rule redistribution and coalition government with symmetrical players, assume that three parties named A, B, and C have an equal number of seats in the legislature. Any two of the parties can form a coalition government. To keep the example simple, assume that the governing coalition can distribute 100 units of political payoffs (offices, contracts, honors, etc.), and a party excluded from the governing coalition receives a political payoff of 0. To begin bargaining, someone proposes to form a coalition of all three parties and distribute the payoffs equally: $(A, B, C) = (33, 33, 33)$.[26] A counters with the proposal to form a coalition with B and give nothing to C, thus yielding the payoffs $(A, B, C) = (50, 50, 0)$. A's proposal makes A and B better-off, and they can implement it under majority rule, so A's proposal blocks the initial proposal. Now C counters with a proposal to form a coalition with B and distribute the payoffs $(A, B, C) = (0, 75, 25)$. C's proposal blocks A's proposal. As in the majority-rule redistribution game, *any* proposal in the coalition game is blocked by another proposal, so the game has an empty core. The same instability afflicts coalitions to form a government and trading of votes in a legislature.

Questions

1. Explain the possible instability in the minimum winning coalition in figure 3-3.

2. In 1994 Italy changed its electoral law in an attempt to increase the stability of coalitions. If the goal is to increase stability, what constitutional rules would you endorse?

Coalitions in Two-Party Systems

Nikita Khrushchev, who was dictator of the Soviet Union in the late 1950s and early 1960s, said to Germany's foreign minister, "Tell me, what is the 'opposition'?" The foreign minister answered, "The opposition is the government of tomorrow."[27] The alternation of successive governments creates a kind of dialogue that invigorates politics. Recognizing this fact, some tribal people divide themselves into two halves or moieties for purposes of government. For example, one pueblo in the southwestern United States traditionally divides the tribe into "winter people," who are associated with hunting and govern during the winter months, and "summer people," who are associated with agriculture and govern during the summer months.

---

[26] In experiments, people often solve this game by an equal division of the stakes, even though this solution is not in the core.

[27] Quoted in Fikentscher 1993, p. 10.

Two-party politics eliminates legislative bargaining or changes its character. Most people in Britain support the Labor Party or the Conservative Party. Since the 1930s elections have vacillated, with one party holding a majority for a while and then the other party obtaining a majority. In Britain, the party that has a majority in Parliament governs. The majority party can enact any legislation that it wishes, and it has no need to form a coalition that encompasses minority parties. Instead of forming a coalition, governing parties exclude others from a share in the spoils of government.

Bargaining in Britain takes place within the governing party, or between its members and citizens who are outside of Parliament, not between political parties. The British prime minister is a member of the legislature and she exercises firm discipline over her party. In fact, the prime minister requires all members of her party who sit in Parliament to vote the same way that she does on every important issue. The most important bargaining occurs within the ruling party before a bill goes to Parliament. Legislation in Britain should not be regarded as a bargain struck by regional representatives. Rather, legislation is the means by which the governing party implements its program. The need to win elections disciplines the party's program. Competition presumably compels the two parties in Britain to search for a program that is a Condorcet winner in general elections.

The United States also has two-party politics, with the Democratic and Republican Parties vying for office. However, one party seldom holds the presidency and also a majority in both houses of Congress. Consequently, one party seldom has the power to enact legislation by relying exclusively on its members. In addition, party discipline is not so strict in the United States as it is in Britain. Consequently, the president's party, which forms the government, cannot enact all the legislation that it wants. Legislating in the United States often requires bargaining between the president and the Congress, or between leaders in the two parties.

The Game of State

So far my analysis has assumed a secure democratic framework of government. In many states, however, the constitution does not command much respect or obedience. Political officials in these countries violate or suspend the constitution to benefit themselves. I will briefly discuss political bargaining without an effective constitution.

The *game of state* refers to the problem of creating a large state from competition among smaller units of government. Modern weapons and bureaucratic organization enable a large state to supply law and order at lower cost and higher quality than can small competing states. Once people stop fighting with each other, the creation of a unified state yields a large peace dividend, as illustrated by comparing western Europe before and after 1945.

A *natural* monopoly exists when one large firm can produce at lower cost than can several small firms. A large state has a natural monopoly on force. In the game of state, the potential gains from peace exert pressure to end factional violence and create a unified state. The coalition of the whole, in which each faction renounces force, dominates any smaller coalition. No smaller coalition can block the coalition of the whole, so the coalition of the whole fills the core in the game of state. The theory of natural monopoly predicts continuing pressure to end factional violence and create large, peaceful states. In this book, I focus on the consequences of stable constitutions, not their pre-conditions, so I do not analyze the causes of persistent factional violence.

The game of creating the state differs from the game of governing it. A unified state must have a particular constitution. In a democracy, popular competition for office determines who will govern the state. The strength of democracy comes from institutionalizing competition to control the state's monopoly powers. However, the choice of one governing coalition over another redistributes the spoils of office. This game of redistribution has an empty core, which destabilizes politics. A democratic constitution cannot guarantee the elimination of this instability.[28]

CONCLUSION

Chapters 2 and 3 concern two fundamental processes of government, specifically voting and bargaining. When constitutions narrow voting to a single dimension of choice, majority rule tends to yield a result in the middle of the distribution of voters' preferences (median rule). In these circumstances, transaction costs typically block bargaining across issues. Alternatively, constitutions can allow voting to range freely over multiple dimensions of choice. Multiple dimensions of choice lower the transaction costs of political trades, thus increasing the potential surplus from political cooperation. However, multiple dimensions of choice also increase the risk that bargaining will fail. When bargaining fails, majority rule in multiple dimensions can provoke an unstable game of redistribution. In part 2 I will discuss in detail alternative forms of organization by which democracies choose between median rule and bargaining.

---

[28] An analogy between economics and politics clarifies this point. As the number of participants in the market increases, they lose their power to bargain over prices. When carried to its logical extreme, this expansion in the market leads to perfect competition, in which everyone trades at the market price. These facts form the basis of the proof that the core of an economy shrinks to the perfectly competitive allocation as the economy grows by replication (Arrow and Hahn 1971). This result, however, is not obtained in the presence of a natural monopoly. As an economy expands, a natural monopoly does not disappear. Similarly, as the state expands by unifying smaller jurisdictions, natural monopoly persists, which creates the problem of distributing the peace dividend.

CHAPTER 4

Administering

The heaviest element known to science was recently discovered ... tentatively
named administratium.... Since it has no electrons, administratium is inert.
However, it can be detected chemically as it impedes every reaction it contacts.
According to the discoverers, a minute amount of administratium
causes one reaction to take over four days to complete when it would have
normally occurred in less than a second.

—*Internet joke*[1]

GOVERNMENT BUREAUCRACY is usually good for a laugh, as the preceding Internet joke indicates, but the stakes are no joke. In the developed countries, taxes take half or more of the marginal earnings from the typical citizen and government expenditures (not counting transfers) account for more than one-third of the economy. Given the stakes, laughter should yield to analysis.

Having analyzed voting and bargaining in the two previous chapters, I turn to administering, which is the third fundamental process of government. Elections ideally transmit the preferences of citizens to politicians, who bargain and translate preferences into programs. Implementing programs in a modern state depends on an array of ministries, departments, and agencies. A democratic state should try to organize its bureaucracies to pursue explicit ends by efficient means.

[1] Here is the complete joke as transmitted to me by Geoffrey Miller.

News Flash: New Chemical Element Discovered

The heaviest element known to science was recently discovered by investigators at a major U.S. research university. The element, tentatively named administratium, has no protons or electrons and thus has an atomic number of 0, but does have one neutron, 125 assistant neutrons, 75 vice neutrons and 111 assistant vice neutrons, which gives it an atomic mass of 312. These 312 particles are held together by a force that involves the continuous exchange of meson-like particles called morons. Since it has no electrons, administratium is inert. However, it can be detected chemically as it impedes every reaction it contacts. According to the discoverers, a minute amount of administratium causes one reaction to take over four days to complete when it would have normally occurred in less than a second. Administratium has a normal half-life of approximately three years, at which time it does not decay, but instead undergoes a reorganization in which assistant neutrons, vice neutrons and assistant vice neutrons exchange places. Some studies have shown that the atomic mass actually increases after reorganization. Attempts are being made to determine how administratium can be controlled to prevent irreversible damage, but results to date are not promising.

Administration follows a hierarchical chain of command stretching from major politicians at the top to minor civil servants at the bottom. Administration proceeds primarily by orders from superiors to inferiors. Each link in the chain of command tries to impose its will on the next link. The interests of superior and inferior administrators, however, align imperfectly. Consequently, each link in the chain dilutes the purpose transmitted from the preceding link. The dilution of purposes gives each ministry and agency its own life and will.

In this chapter I develop a general theory of administration and predict the response of state agencies to law. I especially focus on the delegation of authority and the imposition of rules. I will consider the consequences of constitutional obstacles to delegating authority ("nondelegation doctrine") and constitutional requirements to follow rules ("legality"). After analyzing administrative processes in this chapter, I will consider the overall behavior of ministries and agencies in chapter 7.

Here are some examples of questions addressed in this chapter:

Example 1: In a typical state bureaucracy, the minister and assistants at the top are political appointees, whereas the workers below them are nonpolitical civil servants. If a minister replaces some top civil servants with political appointees, how will the ministry's behavior change? Where should politics end and administration begin?

Example 2: A ministry uses its discretionary power to harm someone, who sues for relief. At the trial's conclusion, the court orders the ministry to promulgate rules and follow them. How will replacing discretionary power with rules influence the ministry's objectives?

Example 3: Some administrators have discretion and others must follow explicit rules. If the pace of innovation accelerates in a regulated industry, should discretion or legality increase?

PARABLES OF ADMINISTRATION

Implementing government policy involves a chain of authority in which superiors delegate to subordinates. Thus the prime minister chooses a foreign minister to direct the foreign office, the foreign minister chooses an assistant to handle administration, and the assistant selects a civil servant to oversee daily operations. Economics models the delegation of authority as a *game* between a *principal* and an *agent*. The principal is the superior who sets policy and the agent is the subordinate who implements it. I will refer to all state organizations that implement policies as "agencies," regardless of whether they are technically agencies, ministries, departments, commissions, or some other type of organization.

When discharging their responsibilities, the officials in a bureaucracy face two kinds of fundamental decisions that I model in two different games. First, an official can exercise power directly or delegate it to a subordinate.[2] The *delegation game* shows how a rational principal makes this decision. The constitution and other fundamental laws sometimes require or prohibit the delegation of authority. The delegation game predicts some consequences of requirements or prohibitions on delegation.

Second, an official who delegates power can allow the subordinate full discretion in its exercise or constrain its exercise by imposing rules. The *rule game* shows how a rational principal makes this decision. Imposing a rule decreases flexibility and increases legality. Fundamental laws such as the constitution sometimes require officials to promulgate rules and follow them. The rule game predicts some consequences of discretion and legality in administration.

Delegation Game

Now I develop the delegation game. When a principal delegates power, a loyal agent uses the power to implement the principal's policy. In reality, however, many agents fall short of this ideal, especially when their interests diverge from the principal's interests. Factors affecting the fidelity of agents include their character, their willingness to take risks, the principal's ability to monitor the agent's behavior, and the future need of the principal and agent for each other. Instead of discussing many factors, I will reduce the problem of delegation to its simplest elements and analyze one fundamental trade-off.

A rational, amoral agent will divert resources to his advantage when the probability of detection by the principal is low. When the project enjoys good luck, a high level of productivity disguises the agent's diversion of resources. Thus, the agent will divert resources when the project enjoys good luck with sufficiently high probability to disguise diversion. Knowing this, the principal in charge of such a project will exercise power directly. Conversely, the principal will delegate power to the agent when the project will suffer bad luck with sufficiently high probability to reveal diversion. Knowing this, the principal in charge of such a project will delegate power to the agent.

Figure 4-1 concretely embodies these facts in a game tree. In the first branching of the tree, the principal decides whether to exercise power directly or delegate it. If the principal delegates power, the agent can either implement the principal's policy (*loyal agent*) or divert resources to his own advantage (*disloyal agent*). After the agent chooses an action, random events result in a good state or a bad state of the world. To illustrate, most state administrators cannot predict or control elections or the stock market. For convenience, I describe such random events as *nature's choosing* between a good or bad state. Finally, in the right side of figure 4-1, the game tree ends in the payoffs to the principal and agent, which I explain later.

Having described what the principal and agent do, now I describe what they know. The parties know the structure of the game as depicted in figure 4-1, but each player may or may not know the details. The principal who delegates

[2] Mashaw 1985.

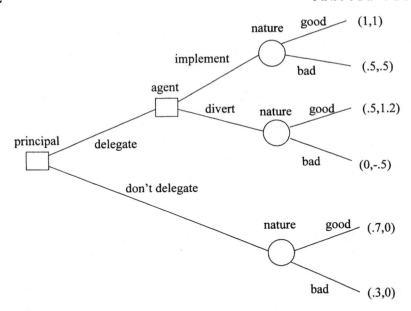

Fig. 4-1 Delegation Game

knows fewer details than the principal who exercises power directly. To stylize this difference, I assume that the principal who exercises power directly can observe the state of nature, whereas the principal who delegates power cannot observe the state of nature.

Now I relate these assumptions to the right side of figure 4-1 where the game tree ends in payoffs. At each terminal point on the right side of figure 4-1, the principal's payoff is first in the parentheses and the agent's payoff is second. The absolute values of the payoffs signify nothing, but the relative magnitudes depict important facts. First consider the payoffs from delegating power. After delegation, the principal does not observe the agent's choice of an action or nature's choice of a state. If the principal's payoff is *very high*, as indicated by the number 1 in figure 4-1, then the principal can infer that the agent was loyal and lucky. If the payoff is *very low*, as indicated by 0, the principal infers that the agent was disloyal and unlucky. If, however, the payoff is modest, indicated by .5, the principal cannot infer whether the agent was loyal and unlucky, or disloyal and lucky.

The summary of the payoffs in figure 4-2 shows what the principal can infer from what he observes. The values 1 and 0 are unique payoffs that appear only once in figure 4-2, so the principal can infer the agent's action and nature's state from these payoffs. Good luck reveals loyalty and bad luck reveals disloyalty. In contrast, .5 appears in two of the cells in figure 4-2. This nonunique payoff does not support an inference about the agent's act or nature's state. Bad luck disguises loyalty and good luck disguises disloyalty.

		Agent	
		implement (loyal)	divert (disloyal)
Nature	good (lucky)	1 (reveal)	.5 (hide)
	bad (unlucky)	.5 (hide)	0 (reveal)

Fig. 4-2 Principal's Payoff From Delegating

Instead of delegating power, the principal can exercise it directly. By exercising power directly, the principal in figure 4-1 receives .7 in a good state and .3 in a bad state. For a given state of nature in figure 4-1, the principal who exercises power directly receives less than he would receive from delegating authority to a *loyal* agent. The principal gains from delegating to a loyal agent by saving time and effort. Conversely, the principal who exercises power directly receives more than he would receive from delegating authority to a *disloyal* agent. The time and effort spent by the principal on the direct exercise of power is less than the resources diverted by a disloyal agent.

When the principal exercises power directly, the agent receives his basic payoff, which I designate as 0. Delegating authority to the agent increases his responsibility and opportunities. After delegation, the agent who is loyal or lucky receives more than his basic payoff. Specifically, the loyal and lucky agent receives 1, the loyal and unlucky agent receives .5, and the disloyal and lucky agent receives .5. In contrast, the agent whose bad luck reveals his disloyalty receives less than his basic payoff, specifically $-.5$.

SOLUTION

The delegation game's solution is a pair of strategies that maximize each player's expected payoff, given the strategy of the other player. To find the game's solution, proceed recursively (backward in time) from the last decision to the first decision. Assuming the principal delegates, the last decision is the agent's choice between implementing and diverting. The agent's payoff from diverting exceeds his payoff from implementing in a good state of nature, whereas the opposite is true in a bad state.[3] So the agent's best strategy depends on the relative probability of a good state and a bad state of nature. To be precise, the rational agent diverts when the probability of a good state exceeds $\frac{5}{6}$, and implements otherwise.[4]

[3] The following table summarizes the agent's payoffs.

		Agent's Act	
		implement (loyal)	divert (disloyal)
State of	good	1	1.2
Nature	bad	.5	$-.5$

[4] Let p denote the probability that the state of nature is good, and let $1 - p$ denote the probability that the state of nature is bad. Implementing yields the agent's expected payoff of $1p + .5(1 - p)$. Diverting yields the agent's expected payoff $1.2p - .5(1 - p)$. Implementing and diverting yield the same expected payoff to the agent when p solves the following equation:

Now consider the principal's best strategy. When the agent diverts, the principal's best strategy is "don't delegate."[5] Conversely, when the agent implements, the principal's best strategy is "delegate."[6] So the rational principal exercises power directly or delegates depending on the probability that nature will disguise or reveal the agent's act. In this example, the rational principal exercises power directly when the probability of a good state exceeds $\frac{5}{6}$, and delegates otherwise. The game's solution can be summarized as follows:

$$p \geq \tfrac{5}{6} \Rightarrow \text{principal exercises power directly}$$

$$p < \tfrac{5}{6} \Rightarrow \text{principal delegates, agent implements.}$$

Note that this "solution" assumes a contract between the principal and agent with invariable terms. Civil service rules and union rules severely constrain contracts within government. Computing the optimal contract without constraint on the terms poses a different, more complicated problem from the one I solved.[7]

GRAPH

Figure 4-3 graphs the trade-off characterized by the delegation game. The horizontal axis represents the proportion of power directly exercised by the principal. Moving from left to right on the horizontal axis, the principal's direct exercise of power increases from 0 percent to 100 percent, and, conversely, the principal's delegation of power decreases from 100 percent to 0 percent. The

---

$$1p + .5(1 - p) = 1.2p - .5(1 - p).$$

implement	divert
(loyal)	(disloyal)

Solving this equation yields $p = \frac{5}{6}$, which is the tipping point discussed in the text.

[5] This conclusion follows immediately from the agent's payoffs as depicted in the following table.

		Principal's Act	
		delegate	don't delegate
State of	good	.5	.7
Nature	bad	0	.3

[6] This conclusion follows immediately from the agent's payoffs as depicted in the following table.

		Principal	
		delegate	don't delegate
State of	good	1	.7
Nature	bad	.5	.3

[7] In a general game of contracting, the parties could adjust the payoffs by making side payments, which could improve their incentives. To illustrate by using figure 4-1, the principal and agent both prefer a contract in which the principal promises to pay the agent a bonus of .3 conditional on the agent's receiving a payoff of 1. This contract is optimal because it always induces the agent to implement as required for efficiency, rather than divert. State bureaucracies, however, contain many rigidities and nontransferable benefits that preclude optimal contracting. In general, the typical obstacles to an optimal contract include the principal's limited information and the agent's risk aversion or inability to borrow (Shavell 1979).

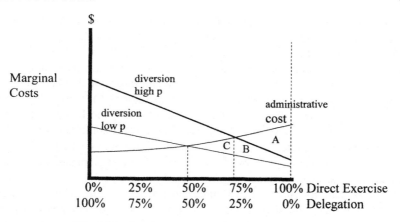

Fig. 4-3 Administrative Cost-Diversion Trade-Off

vertical axis in figure 4-3 represents two kinds of marginal cost. Moving from left to right, the principal devotes more time to supervising the project, so total and marginal administrative costs typically increase, whereas total and marginal diversion costs typically decrease.[8]

A principal who wants to minimize total costs equates the marginal cost of administrative and diversion. Such a principal prefers the level of delegation indicated by the intersection of the administrative cost curve and the diversion cost curve in figure 4-3.

As the probability p of a good state of nature increases, good luck disguises disloyalty and agents divert more resources. Figure 4-3 represents this fact by shifting up the diversion cost curve as the probability of good luck increases from p_{low} to p_{high}. Notice that an increase in the probability of a good state of nature from p_{low} to p_{high} causes the principal's optimal level of delegation to shift down from 50 percent to 25 percent. In general, *luck that disguises the behavior of agents makes delegation less attractive to principals.*

EXAMPLE

Here is a concrete example of the delegation game. Assume that the minister of health (principal) develops a plan to maximize the number of kidney transplants obtained by spending a given sum of money. The plan's success depends on cooperation by the nurses. If the nurses cooperate (good state), the plan will succeed. If the nurses resist (bad state), the plan will fail. The minister cannot control or predict the response of the nurses (nature).

The minister can implement the plan directly or delegate power to her chief administrator (agent). If the minister directly implements the program, she receives a high payoff if she is lucky (.7) and a low payoff if she is unlucky (.3). Alternatively, the minister can delegate power to the administrator, which saves

---

[8] *Marginal* diversion costs typically decrease, and *marginal* administration costs typically increase, because the principal typically supervises first those activities where diversion is worst and administrative costs are least. These facts justify the standard assumption of convexity.

the minister's valuable time. The administrator, however, would prefer to divert some funds from kidney transplants to his special field of emergency care. After delegating power, the minister is too remote from daily operations to observe the behavior of the administrator and nurses. If the program fails badly (0), the minister will infer correctly that the unlucky administrator diverted funds, and so the minister will punish the disloyal administrator (-5). If the program succeeds highly (1), the minister will correctly infer that the lucky administrator implemented the program loyally and reward the loyal administrator (1). If the program succeeds modestly (.5), the minister will not know whether the administrator diverted funds and enjoyed good luck (1.2) or implemented the program and suffered bad luck (.5).

If the probability is sufficiently high that good luck will disguise diversion, the self-interested administrator prefers to divert funds, so, anticipating this fact, the minister will implement the program directly. Conversely, if the probability is sufficiently high that bad luck will reveal diversion, the self-interested administrator will implement the minister's plan, so, anticipating this fact, the minister will delegate power to the administrator.

Another example concerns monitoring the behavior of state agencies by courts. If the probability is sufficiently high that bad luck will reveal wrongdoing by the state agency, courts may prefer to give wide discretion to the agency. To give wide discretion, courts will defer to the agency and dismiss most suits alleging wrongdoing. If, however, the probability is low that bad luck will reveal wrongdoing, courts may prefer to monitor carefully the behavior of an agency. To monitor the agency, courts will allow most suits alleging wrongdoing by the agency to proceed to trial.

SIGNIFICANCE OF DELEGATION GAME

Having developed a model to analyze delegation, I next consider its legal significance. Constitutions and other fundamental laws usually allow officials to delegate power and sometimes require officials to exercise powers directly. A *nondelegable* power has consequences predicted by the delegation game. With unrestricted delegation, the principal balances diversion costs and the opportunity cost of his time spent on administration, as indicated in figure 4-3. With a prohibition against delegation, the principal may not strike this balance. A binding prohibition forces him to use time on administration whose value to him exceeds the cost of the precluded diversion. Prohibiting delegation imposes a larger loss on the principal when he wants to delegate more power, and he wants to delegate more power when the fear of bad luck deters agents from diverting resources.

Figure 4-3 illustrates these facts. To be concrete, assume that the probability of good luck equals p_{high}, so the principal's preferred level of delegation equals 25 percent. Now assume that laws prohibit the official from delegating power, so delegation falls from 25 percent to 0 percent. The prohibition against delegation imposes a total loss on the principal indicated by area A in figure 4-3. If the probability of good luck falls from p_{high} to p_{low}, the prohibition against delegation imposes additional costs on the principal. With p_{low}, the principal prefers to delegate 50 percent of his power. Thus an effective prohibition against delegation imposes costs on the principal equal to the area A+B+C in figure 4-3.

I used figure 4-3 to depict the cost imposed on the principal by a nondelegation rule. As explained, the costs rise with the value of the principal's time and the probability that bad luck will reveal diversion of resources. To illustrate, the constitution may require a high court to decide appeals or certain kinds of cases, rather than refer them to a lower court. For example, in the U.S. federal system, the circuit courts must accept all appeals on questions of law, not delegate the decision to the lowest-level courts.[9] The circuit court's loss from such a requirement increases with its load of cases, which increases the opportunity cost of its time. Similarly, civil courts in European countries often have to refer constitutional questions to the constitutional court, and the constitutional court cannot delegate constitutional questions to lower courts. The constitutional court's loss from such a requirement increases with its load of cases.

The executive's responsibility provides another example of nondelegation. If the constitution imposes on the executive the duty to execute the laws, as with Article 2 of the U.S. Constitution, then the executive cannot delegate power in a way that would undermine this duty.[10] As the extent of delegation increases, the constitution may impose limits.[11] The executive's loss from such restrictions increases with the opportunity cost of its time and its ability to monitor lower levels of administration. In general, the nondelegation doctrine imposes larger costs on the principal when diversion by the agent is less likely.

Many constitutions give the legislature exclusive power to tax, so administrators cannot impose new taxes. The courts may rule that the legislature cannot delegate its taxation powers to administrators. Circumstances sometimes arise, however, in which administrators make decisions about fees that resemble taxes. The courts may decide that new fees are in fact new taxes, thus prohibiting administrators from imposing the new fees. Instead of the administrators setting the new fees, the legislature must set them. As before, the legislature's loss from this restriction on delegation increases with the opportunity cost of its time and its ability to monitor fee-setting by administrators.

---

[9] U.S. federal courts have three levels: trial (district courts), appeals (circuit courts), and the Supreme Court. The courts of appeal (circuit courts) must accept all appeals from trial courts with a justiciable issue. In principle, trial courts decide the facts and appeals courts decide the law. In practice, however, the federal courts of appeal achieve some control over their dockets by declaring issues appealed to them as "matters of fact" rather than "matters of law," thus assigning the issue to the trial court. Unlike the appeals courts, the Supreme Court has full control over its docket of cases. The Supreme Court accepts approximately 1.5 percent of appeals to it, thus delegating the rest of the decisions to an intermediate court. (Each year the November issue of the *Harvard Law Review* provides data on appeals and acceptances for the U.S. Supreme Court.)

[10] This issue is explored in *Industrial Union Dept., American Petroleum Institute*, 448 US 607, 100 SCt 2844, 65 LEd2d 1010 (1980).

[11] Excessive delegation of power by statute is explored in *Commodity Futures Trading Commission v Schor*, 478 US 833, 106 SCt 3245, 92 Led2d 675 (1986).

In another example, this one from Germany, the "statute against literature threatening the youth" (mainly directed against free advertisement for pornography and positive descriptions of violence) must contain exact provisions regarding how the members of the censoring body are selected. The legislature cannot delegate the task of specifying these provisions.[12] On the other hand, the legislature can delegate choice of the orthography of the German language taught in schools.[13]

I have explained the loss imposed on an official by a rule prohibiting delegation. Sometimes, however, society gains from the such a restriction. Now I turn from the costs of nondelegation borne by officials to possible public benefits.[14]

So far I have interpreted "diversion" in the delegation game as the agent's following his preferences rather than implementing the principal's policy. A more sinister interpretation concerns corrupt officials diverting resources for personal gain. Corruption has a long tradition in state administration. In Europe and the United States in the past, many state officials received bribes, not wages, for their work. To illustrate, in seventeenth-century England, Pepys, whose reform of the admiralty allegedly created Britain's first modern civil service, was told that the pay for his first admiralty job was what he could make of it.[15]

Corrupt officials, who occupy some offices in all countries and most offices in some countries, break laws and distort policies in exchange for bribes. By diffusing and obscuring responsibility, delegation increases opportunities for corruption. Bribe-taking by an agent may harm the public more than it harms the principal. Consequently, the public might benefit from more direct administration by the principal than he would voluntarily choose. (Later in this chapter I analyze a more important mechanism for reducing corruption, specifically, replacing individualized decisions with rules.)

Now I turn to a different kind of public gain from nondelegation. Delegation of power can occur within a branch of government or between branches of government. Intrabranch delegation preserves the constitutional separation of powers, whereas interbranch delegation may violate the constitutional separation

---

[12] *Entscheidungen des Bundesverfassungsgerichts* (Constitutional Court decisions), vol. 83, 130.

[13] Constitutional court file 1 BvR 1640/97. Thanks to Georg von Wagenheim for this and the preceding citations.

[14] Thanks to Dan Rodriguez for help on this section.

[15] "This morning my Lord [Sandwich] carried me by coach to Mr Crews, in the way talking how good he did hope my place would be to me and, in general, speaking that it was not the salary of any place that did make a man rich, but the opportunities for making money while he is in the place" (Latham and Matthews; 1970, p. 222). Thanks to Peter Hacker for this citation.
Here is a popular joke in Mexico.

> 1st boy: What do you want to be when you grow up?
> 2nd boy: President of Mexico.
> 1st boy: Then I want to be your brother.

of powers.[16] To illustrate, if the constitution separates courts and legislature, a high court can remand a decision to a lower court, but a high court cannot remand a legal decision to the legislature, and the legislature cannot assign a political decision to a court.

Disputes over interbranch delegation often involve ambiguity in the definition of constitutional powers. To illustrate, Article 1 of the U.S. Constitution gives the legislature the exclusive power to make laws, and the legislature cannot delegate this power to the executive. Does the executive "make laws" for purposes of the Constitution by imposing wage and price controls on the economy, or by imposing burdensome regulations on employers?[17] Does the comptroller general "make laws" by imposing limits on government expenditures to reduce the deficit?[18]

Similarly, the German government or Parliament must decide on disputes that are "political," whereas the German constitutional court must decide disputes that are "constitutional." Thus the question of who must decide whether or not nuclear medium-range missiles may be deployed in Germany turns on whether it is a political or legal question.[19]

In effect, interbranch delegation revises the constitution without following the procedures prescribed for a constitutional amendment. The theory of cartels explains the resulting harm. Like vertical mergers in industry, intrabranch delegation typically does not affect the concentration of state powers. Like horizontal mergers in industry, *interbranch* delegation can concentrate state powers.[20] Concentrating powers removes obstacles to a political cartel. To illustrate, courts would destroy the rule of law by delegating their power over legal disputes to the executive. Prohibiting interbranch delegation helps maintain competitive government, which defines democracy.

Just a the members of an economic cartel favor restraining trade, the officials who want to form a political cartel will favor interbranch delegation of power. For example, if the president's party enjoys a majority of seats in the legislature, then the legislature may eagerly vote to give some of its power to the president.

---

[16] Note that constitutions sometimes separate powers within the same branch, in which case interbranch delegation can undermine the constitutional separation of powers. To illustrate, if the constitution creates a bicameral legislation, then one chamber may be unable to relinquish some of its power to the other chamber. See *Immigration and Naturalization Service v. Chadha*, 462 US 919, 103 SCt 2764.

[17] *Industrial Union Dept. v American Petroleum Institute: Mistretta v US*, 488 US 361, 109 SCt 647, 102 Led2d 714 (1989).

[18] *Bowsher v Synar*, 478 US 714, 106 SCt 3181, 92 LEd2d 583 (1986).

[19] *Entscheidungen des Bundesverfassungsgerichts* (Constitutional Court decisions), vol. 68, p. 1: "[T]he constitutional court must not review foreign and defense policy unless the policy is obviously arbitrary. Further, the court decided that the government may decide on foreign and defense policy on its own, unless binding treaties are concluded." Thanks to Georg von Wagenheim for this information.

[20] Note that interbranch delegation can disperse powers rather than concentrate them. For example, a relatively powerful executive might delegate powers to a relatively weak legislature. The usual case, however, goes in the opposite direction.

By reducing competition, interbranch delegation of power benefits politicians in the ruling party for the same reason that it harms the public. The fact that officials in the legislature and executive both want to concentrate power without formally revising the constitution is no reason for the constitutional court to allow it. Courts do not require a disagreement between the executive and legislature to justify policing the separation of their power.[21]

The "separation of powers" means separate institutions sharing powers (Neustadt 1986). When separate institutions share powers, action requires cooperation among them. Cooperation often proceeds through bargains. By separating powers, the constitution makes government proceed through bargains rather than orders. By policing the separation of powers, the courts maintain the bargaining strength of each branch against the others. According to the bargain theory of democracy, the courts should aim to preserve bargaining power, but not obstruct cooperation.

Questions

1. Explain how good luck in a project disguises diversion of resources.

2. Explain why prohibiting delegation costs the principal more when good luck becomes less likely.

3. Figure 4-1 assumes a fixed penalty for detected diversion. Assume the penalty increases. Does the "tipping value" p increase or decrease?

4. Figure 4-1 assumes that the principal who delegates cannot observe the agent or nature. Discuss alternative ways of monitoring the agent, such as periodic observations of the state of nature or random observations of the agent's decisions.

5. Footnote 4 computes the probability of a good state at which a rational agents tips between implementing and diverting. Assume that the agent's highest possible payoff for undetected diversion of resources rises from 1.2 to 1.4. Compute the new tipping value of p.

6. An economic cartel reduces the supply of private goods to increase profits, whereas a political cartel often increases the supply of public goods to enlarge the state. Economists have a long history of estimating the economic costs of private monopolies, whereas no accepted methodology exists for estimating the economic costs of political cartels. Discuss some ways to measure the economic costs of reducing political competition by interbranch delegation of power.

Rule Game

After delegating responsibility for implementing a policy, should the principal give the agent discretion or require the agent to follow a rule? Principals

---

[21] In contrast, Choper 1980 argues that disagreement between branches typically justifies intervention by courts.

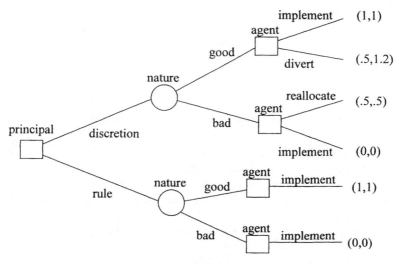

Fig. 4-4 Rule Game

impose rules on agents for a variety of reasons, such as reducing transaction costs, improving coordination, increasing predictability, reducing disparity, and facilitating transparency. Instead of discussing many reasons, I will reduce the problem of imposing rules to its simplest elements and analyze one fundamental trade-off. Imposing rules on agents reduces their opportunities to divert resources, whereas giving discretion to agents allows them to respond flexibly to changing circumstances. Diversion of resources is the cost of flexibility in an organization.

I will formulate the rule game to analyze the trade-off between diversion and flexibility. In the delegation game, the agent acts and then nature chooses a state of the world. The rule game reverses the order: nature chooses a state and then the agent acts. Knowing nature's state, the agent who enjoys discretionary power can respond flexibly to events as they develop. The principal wants the agent to reallocate resources when unexpected events occur, and the principal does not want the agent to divert resources when events occur as expected. Discretion gives the agent control over the decision, whereas a rule requires the agent to implement the principal's plan in all circumstances. The principal must decide whether to give the agent discretion or impose a rule.

Figure 4-4 depicts the rule game concretely as a tree. First, the principal decides whether to give the agent discretion or impose a rule. Second, nature chooses a good or bad state. Third, if the agent has discretion, the agent decides whether to follow the principal's plan or divert resources. Alternatively, if the principal imposes a rule, the agent must follow the principal's plan, regardless of the state of nature.

The payoffs from different paths in the game tree appear in parentheses at the right side of figure 4-4, with the principal's payoff given first and the agent's

		Agent	
		implement	reallocate
Nature	good (lucky)	1.0 (reveal)	.5 (hide)
	bad (unlucky)	0 (hide)	.5 (hide)

Fig. 4-5 Principal's Payoff From Giving Discretion to Agent

payoff second. As with the delegation game, relative payoffs illustrate important facts, whereas absolute payoffs signify nothing. The principal's plan is designed for a good state. If a good state materializes, the payoff to the principal is higher when the agent implements the principal's plan (1), instead of diverting resources to an alternative project (.5). If a bad state materializes, however, the payoff to the principal is higher when the agent reallocates some resources to the alternative project (.5) instead of implementing the principal's plan (0). Thus, a loyal agent with discretion implements the principal's plan in a good state and reallocates resources to an alternative project in a bad state.

The agent's interests do not coincide perfectly with those of the principal. In a good state, the agent's payoff is higher when he diverts resources to his preferred project (1.2) instead of implementing the principal's plan (1). In a bad state, the agent's payoff is also higher when he reallocates resources to his preferred project (.5) instead of implementing the principal's plan (0). The agent's dominant strategy is to divert resources, which serves the principal in a good state and disserves the principal in a bad state.

Now I turn from what the actors do to what they know. As in the delegation game, the rule game assumes that the principal who delegates a task to the agent knows the entire payoff matrix and observes his own payoff, but he does not observe the state of nature or the agent's act. Figure 4-5 summarizes what the principal can infer from what he observes. When his payoff equals 1, the principal can infer both the state of nature (good) and the agent's act (implement). Similarly, when his payoff equals 0, the principal can infer the state of nature (bad) and the agent's act (implement). When his payoff equals .5, however, the principal cannot infer whether the agent's reallocation was loyal (bad state) or disloyal (good state).

SOLUTION

The rule game's solution is a pair of strategies that maximize each player's expected payoff, given the strategy of the other player. As before, I solve the game recursively. Assuming the principal gives discretion to the agent, the last decision in time is the agent's choice between implementing the principal's policy or reallocating resources. As depicted in figure 4-4, the agent's payoff from reallocating exceeds his payoff from implementing, regardless of the state of nature, so the agent has a dominant strategy.[22] Knowing this, the principal computes his best strategy by assuming that the agent will use discretion to reallocate resources. As depicted in figure 4-4, imposing a rule on the agent

[22] The following table summarizes the agent's payoffs.

yields a higher payoff to the principal in a good state, whereas giving discretion to the agent yields a higher payoff to the principal in a bad state. In this example, the rational principal imposes a rule when the probability of a good state exceeds $\frac{1}{2}$, and, otherwise, the rational principal gives the agent discretion.[23] The game's solution can be summarized as follows:

$$p > .5 \Rightarrow \text{principal imposes rule, agent implements}$$
$$p < .5 \Rightarrow \text{principal gives agent discretion, agent diverts.}$$

I mention in passing several more special assumptions in my formulation of the rule game. First, my "solution" solves the problem of delegating power for a given contract between the principal and agent. Computing the optimal contract for the principal and agent requires another formulation of the problem.[24] Second, I computed the game's solution when rationally self-interested actors play it once. In reality, the actors may repeat the game, which gives the agent more reason to cooperate. Third, I implicitly assumed that the principal cannot invest in monitoring the agent. In reality, monitoring increases the risk of punishment, which deters diversion by agents. Finally, I assume that agents are self-interested, whereas some agents may remain loyal due to moral commitment.

GRAPH

Figure 4-6 graphs the trade-off between diversion and flexibility characterized by the rule game. The horizontal axis represents constraint of the agent by rules, which increases when moving to the right. The rule of law implies that officials follow rules, instead of exercising discretion. Consequently, the horizontal axis characterizes more constraint by rules as an increase in "legality." Conversely, the horizontal axis represents the agent's discretionary power, which increases when moving to the left.

The vertical axis of figure 4-6 depicts the principal's marginal costs. Moving from left to right, the principal imposes more rules and allows less discretion

		Agent's Act	
		implement	reallocate
State of	good	1	1.2
Nature	bad	0	.5

[23] If p denotes the probability that the state of nature is good, imposing a rule and giving discretion to the agent yield the same expected payoff to the principal when p solves the following equation:

$$1p + 0(1 - p) = .5p + .5(1 - p).$$
$$\text{rule} \qquad \text{discretion}$$

Solving this equation yields p = .5, which is the tipping point.

[24] In a general game of contracting, the parties could adjust the payoffs by making side payments, which could improve their incentives. To illustrate, if $p < .5$, instead of retaining the contract resulting in the payoffs in figure 4-4, the principal and agent both prefer a contract in which the principal promises to pay the agent a bonus of .3 conditional on the agent's receiving a payoff of 1. This contract, like any optimal contract, induces the agent to maximize the joint payoffs.

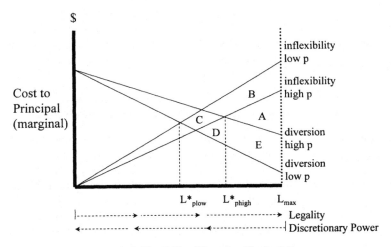

Fig. 4-6 Flexibility-Diversion Trade-Off

to the agent, so diversion costs typically decrease and inflexibility costs typically increase at the margin.[25] The intersection of the marginal cost curves corresponds to the level of legality that minimizes the principal's total costs.

The costs of inflexibility and diversion depend on the environment's predictability. Good luck reduces the cost of inflexibility, so an increase in the probably p of a good state causes the "inflexibility curve" to shift down in figure 4-6. Conversely, good luck increases the diversion of resources by agents, so an increase in p causes the "diversion" curve to shift up. Combining these effects, an increase in the probability of good luck from p_{low} to p_{high} causes the principal's preferred level of legality to shift up from $L^*_{p_{low}}$ to $L^*_{p_{high}}$.

In general, *predictability makes rules more attractive to principals, whereas unpredictability makes discretionary power more necessary.*

EXAMPLES

To illustrate the rule game, I will modify the example in which the minister of health constructs a plan to maximize the number of kidney transplants. Implementation of the plan requires the work of an administrator and cooperation from the nurses. If the nurses cooperate, the minister's highest payoff (1) comes from the administrator's implementing the plan. If the nurses resist, however, the minister's highest payoff is higher when, instead of implementing the plan (0), the administrator reallocates some funds to another program (.5). The minister must decide whether to impose rules that enforce the plan or give the administrator discretionary power.

---

[25] *Marginal* diversion costs typically decrease, and marginal inflexibility costs typically increase, because the principal typically imposes rules first on those activities where diversion cost most and inflexibility costs least.

The minister cannot observe the behavior of the nurses or the administrator. A high payoff (1) enables the minister to infer that the administrator implemented the plan and the nurses assisted, and a low payoff (0) enables the minister to infer that the administrator implemented the plan and the nurses resisted. In contrast, with an intermediate payoff (.5), the minister cannot infer whether the administrator reallocated funds in response to the nurses' resistance or diverted funds even though the nurses cooperated. If the nurses are more likely to cooperate than resist, the minister's payoff is higher from imposing the rule. Conversely, if the nurses are more likely to resist than cooperate, the minister's payoff is higher from giving discretion to the administrator.

A second example concerns procurement by the state. In many state universities a professor who wants to purchase a computer must follow prescribed procedures that constrain the choice of sellers and the terms of the contract. Procurement rules typically reduce purchasers' discretion in order to avoid kickbacks or bribes.

A third example concerns challenges to the legality of actions by state agencies. Assume the court interprets a statute and imposes a rule on a state agency. Individuals harmed by departures from the rule have the right to sue the agency, thus alerting the court concerning the agency's misbehavior. To illustrate concretely, federal courts interpreted the U.S. Constitution as requiring the police to recite a list of procedural rights when charging a person with a crime ("Miranda warnings"). If police obtain evidence about a crime by failing to recite these procedural rights, the courts exclude the illegally obtained evidence from trial. Like all rules, the procedures do not fit every case. Even so, the courts apparently prefer to prescribe the rules for all cases rather than give discretion to the police.

SIGNIFICANCE OF RULE GAME

Having developed the model of rules, I next consider its significance. The constitution or other fundamental laws sometimes require officials to make rules and follow them. The rule game predicts some consequences of the *constraints of legality*. Requiring more legality than the principal prefers imposes costs on him. Specifically, the principal loses to the extent that the cost of an agent's inflexibility exceeds the reduction in diversion costs. The magnitude of the principal's loss depends on the environment's predictability. The harm from enforced legality is greater when the environment becomes less predictable.

Figure 4-6 illustrates these facts. To be concrete, assume the probability of good luck equals p_{low}, so the principal prefers $L^*_{p_{low}}$. Now assume that the principal is forced to increase legality to L_{max}. The resulting loss to the principal equals the amount by which the cost of inflexibility exceeds the marginal cost of diversion in the interval $[L^*_{p_{low}}, L_{max}]$, as indicated by the area $A + B + C + D + E$. If the probability of a good state rises from plow to p_{high}, the principal's loss from a requirement of maximum legality L_{max} shrinks from the area ABCDE to the area A.

POLITICS, CIVIL SERVICE, AND COURTS

In many state bureaucracies, politicians occupy the top offices and civil servants occupy the subordinate offices. To illustrate, the U.S. president appoints the head of most agencies, each head chooses a personal staff, and the civil service fills most jobs below the head's personal staff. Alternatively, political appointment can go deep into administration. In a patronage system, the winners in the game of politics distribute state jobs to loyal followers as the spoils of victory. To illustrate, patronage operates deep in administration in the city of Chicago and many developing countries.

Administration by civil servants suffers from inflexibility, whereas administration by political appointees suffers from corruption. The best system apparently provides for political appointment at the top level in the bureaucracy and civil service control below the top. The rule game can explain why patronage produces more efficient government at high levels of administration and civil service rules produce more efficient government at low levels of administration.

Think of the state as a chain of relationships in which each official is an agent relative to those above him. In the typical state bureaucracy, civil servants are agents relative to the political appointees heading the organization, political appointees heading the organization are agents relative to elected officials, and elected officials are agents relative to the citizens who vote. In each of the chain's links, a combination of discretion and legality orders the relationship with the agent. Now I explain why efficiency requires discretion to dominate legality at the top of the chain and legality to dominate discretion at the bottom of the chain.

The closer to the top of the chain, the more citizens know about officials. To illustrate using U.S. foreign affairs, the communications media scrutinize the president, monitor the secretary of state, occasionally notice an ambassador, and mostly ignore civil servants in the State Department. When the principal has more information, the agent has less scope for undetected diversion of resources. In terms of figure 4-6, more information for the principal causes diversion costs to rise more slowly as the agent receives more discretion.

Although voters have good information about top officials, the environment of high politics is unpredictable. In terms of figure 4-6, low predictability increases the costs of inflexibility. To illustrate, unpredictable diplomatic crises require a flexible response by the secretary of state.

Extensive monitoring and an unpredictable environment tip the balance in favor of giving broad discretion to officials at the top of agencies. Broad discretion requires politics, not the civil service. Instead of imposing rules, voters communicate goals to top officials. Thus, efficient administration in a democracy requires political control over top officials in state agencies.

Conversely, the public cannot scrutinize lower levels of administration. Consequently, the public holds top officials responsible for any diversion of resources detected in the lower levels of administration. To discharge their responsibility, high officials impose rules to reduce diversion by low officials.

In terms of figure 4-6, less information for the principal causes diversion costs to rise more quickly as the agent receives more discretion. Rules constrain such abuses. So efficiency in a democracy requires civil service rules to control employment at less visible levels of administration. (High officials also have other reasons to make rules for a complex bureaucracy.[26])

The problem of monitoring also arises in a judicial hierarchy. When faced with disputes, courts sometimes can choose between deciding each case on its own merits or developing general rules that apply to all cases. Case-by-case adjudication retains flexibility for lower courts and permits them to diverge from the preferences of higher courts. In contrast, rules reduce flexibility in lower courts and compel them to conform more to the preferences of higher courts.[27]

My discussion of politics, administration, and courts suggests three vague boundaries that demarcate significant changes in discretionary power. First, officials enjoy *strong* discretion when law leaves them free to pursue political goals. To illustrate, legislators have strong discretion in proposing legislation, and the executive has strong discretion when selecting the cabinet. Second, officials enjoy *weak* discretion when the law prescribes goals and leaves officials free to choose the means. To illustrate, a civil engineer in the ministry of roads can decide how to build a road required by an executive order, and the ministry of education can design a program to improve literacy as prescribed by legislation. Third, *pure legality* leaves officials without any discretion, which results in mechanical decision making. To illustrate, a table that prescribes an exact punishment for each crime or the exact division of assets on divorce leaves little discretion to judges.

Legislators and the executive typically have political discretion, and civil servants typically have technical discretion. The situation of judges is more complicated. Common-law systems give judges discretion to make some kinds of law, whereas civil-law systems sometimes aspire to eliminate the discretionary power of judges. Philosophers of law disagree about the ideal mix of politics, technique, and legality in judging.[28] In any case, pure legality, or the mechanical application of law, fails for most decisions. British unions periodi-

---

[26] As the state bureaucracy grows, regulatory agencies pose obstacles to citizens, who turn to elected officials for help. Providing help requires knowledge that increases by interacting with the state bureaucracy over many years. In doing such "casework" for constituents (Fiorina 1977), the incumbent in the legislature has the advantage of experience over a challenger. Following the principle, "The best guide to a maze is its architect," legislators have an incentive to create a bureaucratic maze so that voters reject challengers and rely on incumbents as guides. Thus, incumbent politicians sometimes seek an electoral advantage by increasing the complexity of administration faced by citizens and retaining control over it.

[27] In common-law systems, trial courts decide facts and appeals courts decide law. In these systems, case-by-case adjudication allows lower courts to control more outcomes by making them turn on facts. Conversely, general rules allow higher courts to control more outcomes by making them turn on law.

[28] Thus Ronald Dworkin, who is among the most celebrated Anglo-American philosophers, argued early in his career that each legal dispute has one right answer, thus suggesting that judges have little discretion (Dworkin 1977). Subsequently he revised his views and allowed the political vision

cally paralyzed the railways by a tactic called "work-to-rule," which means that the workers implemented all rules literally. Like the railroads, courts that apply rules mechanically cannot do justice.

Questions

1. Explain why principals give agents discretion rather than rules when the best policy depends on unpredictable contingencies.

2. The worst payoff in figure 4-4 equals 0. Assume that it rises to .25. If $p = \frac{1}{3}$, then imposing a rule yields the same expected payoff to the principal as giving discretion to the agent. Prove it.

3. Assume that the principal in the rule game in figure 4-4 attaches a reward r to a loyal agent who implements the principal's plan in a good state of nature. What is the smallest value of r that would induce the rational agent to claim the reward?

4. Courts can decide disputes by general rules or case by case based on particular facts. Discuss the difference between adjudication by rules and case-by-case adjudication as means by which courts can control state agencies.

Summary and Conclusion

Parties propose programs to voters, voters choose among programs in elections, and ministers or heads of agencies direct administrators to implement the programs. Each link in the chain of authority consists of a principal and an agent. Time constrains each principal to delegate power to agents. Delegating power to agents saves administrative costs for principals and gives agents more opportunity to divert resources. So each successive delegation of power permits each successive level of administration to dilute the political purpose received from voters.

A principal delegates more power to those agents with less incentive to divert resources. Agents have less incentive to divert resources when they run a higher risk that events will reveal diversion. Thus, principals prefer to delegate power when their opportunity costs are high and when they have a high probability of discovering diversion by agents. The delegation game models these facts.

By imposing rules on agents, principals can reduce the diversion of resources. Rules, however, reduce the flexibility of agents in responding to changing situations. Agents need more flexibility when the environment is less predictable. The rule game models these facts.

The constitution or fundamental laws may constrain officials by restricting delegation. If the constraint is effective, the official must devote more time than

---

of a judge to influence decisions (Dworkin 1986). Note that empirical studies often conclude that judges on high courts implement their own political philosophies (Brenner 1982).

he prefers to the task in question, thus raising administrative costs. Effective restrictions also reduce the diversion of resources by agents. Nondelegation makes sense when the public interest favors the administrator's attending to a particular task beyond the level dictated by his self-interest. Nondelegation across branches helps preserve the separation of powers and promote political competition.

In addition to constraining delegation, the constitution or fundamental laws may also require legality. If the legality constraint binds, officials lose flexibility. Agents need more flexibility to respond to unpredictable changes. Thus, when the pace of change accelerates, officials need fewer rules.

The three chapters in part 1 analyze voting, bargaining, and administering. The rest of the book uses these analyses. Part 2 concerns relations between governments, part 3 concerns relations of the branches within a government, and part 4 concerns individual rights.

The Optimal Number of Governments

ACCORDING TO THE usual economic formulation, corporations are hierarchies bounded by markets (Coase 1937; Williamson 1995). Small firms require less hierarchy and more markets, whereas large firms require more hierarchy and fewer markets. For example, an automobile manufacturer can buy tires for its cars from another corporation or make tires in a subsidiary. Buying tires involves two firms using a market, whereas making tires involves one firm using hierarchical organization. The relative efficiency of buying or making a private good depends on the relative efficiency of markets and hierarchies. The optimal hierarchy in firms and the optimal number of markets pose the same problem.

Just as the private sector consists of markets and hierarchies, so the public sector consists of governments and hierarchies. In democracy, the citizens elect their government, so democratic states are hierarchies bounded by elections. Centralized states require fewer governments and more hierarchy, whereas decentralized states require more governments and less hierarchy. For example, the national assembly can direct the ministry of education to provide schools for all localities (centralized), or boards elected in each locality can provide local schools (decentralized). The relative efficiency of centralized and decentralized states depends on the relative efficiency of hierarchies and elections. The optimal depth of hierarchy and the optimal number of governments pose the same problem.

Part 2 applies the principles of voting, bargaining, and administering to the problem of the optimal number of governments. Chapter 5 concerns relations among governments. In theory governments facing zero transaction costs will bargain to efficient agreements. This is true regardless of the organization of intergovernmental relations. In reality the organization of associated governments affects the outcomes of bargaining among them. Governments can associate on the basis of unanimity rule or majority rule. Unanimity rule causes holdouts, which weaken the bargaining position of governments that gain most from collective action. Conversely, majority rule enables a majority to shift costs to the minority, which weakens the bargaining position of governments excluded from the governing coalition.

The consequences of majority rule depend on the scope of elected government. The constitution can prescribe separate governments for separate purposes, or the constitution can prescribe multipurpose governments with broad purposes. To illustrate, a constitution can separate the school board from the town council, or the constitution can merge them. Narrowing the scope of each government tends to replace bargaining over multiple issues with majority rule over each issue (median rule).

Having discussed unanimity rule, majority rule, and the scope of each government in chapter 5, we turn to chapter 6, which concerns competition among governments. For local public goods, a legal framework of free mobility causes governments to compete for residents, which can promote efficient government. Even without mobility, the right of communities to contract freely with governments ideally increases the efficiency by making governments compete with each other. The ability of citizens to correct the legislature by ballot initiatives and referenda can also increase the pressure for efficient administration. As electronics reduce the transaction costs of conducting elections, direct democracy will become an increasingly attractive supplement to legislatures.

Chapter 7 turns to administration. Whereas equals negotiate, subordinates follow orders. Specifically, governments in an association negotiate, whereas subordinates in a unitary state obey. An association of governments requires multiple elections, whereas a unitary state requires a steep hierarchy and few elections. Too deep administration dilutes democratic purposes and gives too much discretion to administrators, in which case the constitution should replace hierarchies with elected governments. Conversely, too many elections can drain the reservoir of civic spirit that animates voters, in which case the constitution should replace governments with hierarchies.

Intergovernmental Relations

> The [U.S.] federal system was created with the intention
> of combining the different advantages which result from the
> magnitude and the littleness of nations.
>
> —*Alexis de Tocqueville*[1]

LIKE A BACH FUGUE, states develop, dissolve, and reorganize around persistent themes. Western European nations fuse into the European Union, while ethnic groups within these nations try to secede. In the Americas, Mercosur in the south and NAFTA in the north emulate Europe's common market, while French nationalists struggle to secede from Canada. In eastern Europe, new nations emerge as the communist bloc shatters. While these events grab headlines, novel governments with particular responsibilities quietly flourish, such as the World Trade Organization or a special district supplying water to several U.S. counties.

Different states offer different models for answering positive and normative questions about allocating power among levels of government. Centralized states like France and Japan subordinate regions and localities to the national government, federal systems such as the United States and Switzerland reserve powers for the states or cantons, and confederations like the British Commonwealth and the Commonwealth of Independent States (former Soviet Union) provide a loose framework for cooperation.

I will approach the problem of "the magnitude and the littleness of nations" much like economists analyze corporations. As explained in the introduction to part 2, corporations are hierarchies bounded by markets, and democratic governments are hierarchies bounded by elections. Decentralized states require more governments and less hierarchy, whereas centralized states require fewer governments and more hierarchy. The relative efficiency of centralized and decentralized states depends upon the relative efficiency of governments and hierarchies.

Figure 5-1 summarizes the problem of the optimal number of governments. On the vertical dimension, government can be deep in hierarchy with few elections, as in a unitary state, or shallow in hierarchy with many elections, as in a federal system. On the horizontal dimension, government can be broad with many functions combined under a single government, or government can be narrow with each separate function under a special government. The optimal number of governments is the point in the space where citizens enjoy the greatest satisfaction of their preferences.

[1] Tocqueville 1945, p. 168, quoted in Oates 1990.

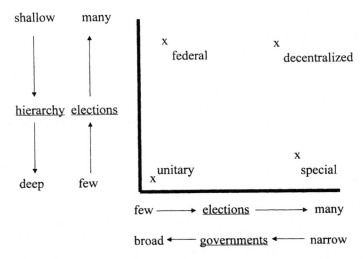

Fig. 5-1 Optimal Number of Governments

In market economies, successful firms expand and unsuccessful firms contract, so competition ideally produces the most efficient combination of small and large firms. In democratic politics, candidates and parties compete vigorously for office, but successful states do not automatically expand and unsuccessful states do not automatically shrink. To illustrate, if German federalism outperforms French centralism, relatively few French citizens become German citizens, nor does the boundary between these nations automatically move west. Under current conditions, democracy produces intensive competition for office, but competition does not automatically adjust jurisdictional boundaries to secure what de Tocqueville called the "different advantages which result from the magnitude and the littleness of nations."

When competition sorts winners from losers, institutions can evolve and improve by trial and error. Weak competition among jurisdictions, however, blunts competitive processes, so states must improve by design. This chapter analyzes the consequences of alternative designs for intergovernmental relations, including unanimity versus majority rule, single-purpose versus multipurpose government, and redistributive transfers. My approach uses the technical character of public goods as the starting point for analyzing strategic behavior. I will address such problems as the following:

Example 1: In most countries, the central government provides the nation's military defense and local governments provide city parks. What characteristics of "defense" and "city parks" help explain this fact?

Example 2: A town holds a referendum to decide whether to govern local schools by the town council or a separately elected school board. What difference does the organization make to the supply of public goods?

Example 3: Some member-states want the European Union to remain a loose confederation, whereas others favor relatively strong central government. Which alternative is more likely to give people the public goods that they prefer?

CHARACTER OF STATE GOODS

The state directly supplies some goods and regulates the supply of others. I will relate the technical characteristics of goods to the best level of government for supplying them. Technical characteristics of goods can cause markets to fail (Arrow and Hahn 1971). Market failure provides the conventional economic justification for state supply and regulation of goods. Economic theory has analyzed the forms of market failure and proposed remedies for them (Breyer 1982; Schultze 1977). Following this line of analysis, I will develop and criticize a conventional prescription for the best level of government to supply public goods.

Pure Public Goods

To develop the theory of public goods, first recall their definition. *Pure* public goods are *nonrivalrous*, meaning that one person's enjoyment does not detract from another's enjoyment. For example, military expenditures can provide security from invasion, and the security enjoyed by one citizen does not detract from the security enjoyed by another citizen.

Besides being nonrivalrous, pure public goods are *nonexcludable*, which means that it is infeasible or uneconomic to exclude individuals from enjoying their benefits. For example, no resident of the United States during the cold war was excluded from the benefit of deterring a Soviet missile attack. Similarly, no one is excluded from driving on local streets, presumably because collecting access fees is uneconomic.

When exclusion is infeasible or uneconomic, individuals have an incentive to free-ride by not paying for public goods. Free-riding prevents suppliers from earning a profit, thus precluding the private supply of public goods. The state can prevent free-riding by collecting taxes to finance public goods. To prevent free-riding completely, the state must tax everyone who benefits from the public good.

Everyone in the nation benefits from *pure* public goods. The central government can tax everyone in the nation more effectively than state or local governments can. These facts imply a prescription: *When a public good is pure or nearly pure, the central government should provide for it.* In other words, the central government should raise the revenues and use them to supply the public good, either directly by state production or indirectly by purchasing the good from a supplier. This prescription is the beginning of the conventional theory of federalism, but not the end. I will explain this theory and then criticize it.

Congestable Public Goods

Instead of being pure, however, many public goods have local characteristics that influence the spread of benefits and the scope of free-riding. Like Hyde Park in London or the Great Salt Sea in Utah, some public goods have a location. Public goods with a location are often afflicted by congestion. To illustrate, as a park becomes crowded, one person's enjoyment of it detracts from another person's enjoyment. Similarly, one more commuter on a congested road slows down other commuters.

Supplying efficient quantities of congestable public goods requires information about their use. A local government usually has more information about local congestion of public goods than does the central government. In addition, local residents can effectively monitor and discipline local officials. Local officials, consequently, have more information and better incentives than do central officials for supplying many congestable public goods. These facts imply a second prescription in the conventional theory of public goods: *When a public good suffers local congestion, local government should provide it.*

To illustrate, assume that a city neighborhood needs a small park for local residents. The local residents have the information to balance costs and benefits in siting and scaling the park. Local residents also have strong incentives to monitor the officials responsible for creating and maintaining local parks. These facts favor assigning power over city parks to local governments. In contrast, assume that people from all over a nation could benefit from establishing a large park in the mountains. Responsibility for this park should fall on officials who have a national political perspective.

Spillovers

As explained, the distinction between pure public goods and congestable public goods motivates the conventional economic prescription for allocating responsibility between national and local government. Some public goods, however, do not fit into either of these categories. Water and air pose a special problem because they circulate in regions formed by natural contours such as rivers and mountains, which correspond imperfectly to political boundaries. Pollution, consequently, spills over from one government jurisdiction to another. Spillovers create an incentive for each government to free-ride on pollution abatement by others.

To avoid free-riding by localities, the government with primary responsibility for abatement should encompass the natural region affected by pollution. For example, a special district for controlling the pollution of a river basin may encompass all residents living along the river, regardless of their town, county, or state. These facts imply a third conventional prescription: *When the effects of a public good or bad spill over jurisdictions, a special district should provide the good or control the bad.* For example, a special district might provide clean water to several counties, or a special district might impose liability on local governments that pollute.

Special districts are more important than visible. For example, few residents of California know that their state contains over five thousand special governments such as water districts, school districts, park districts, and transportation districts. The residents of a California special district typically elect a board of directors with the power to propose taxes for approval by the voters and spend revenues to pursue the special district's purpose. Later I discuss the proposal of two economists who envision special districts creating a European *market for governments* (Frey and Eichenberger 1995).

Conventional Prescription

Table 5.1 summarizes the three conventional prescriptions connecting the technical character of public goods to the best jurisdiction for supplying them. These three prescriptions reduce to one: *Assign power over public goods to the smallest unit of government that internalizes the effects of its exercise.* I call this proposition the *internalization prescription for government jurisdiction.* [2]

Questions

1. Make a list of five goods provided by different levels of government in a country of your choice. Use table 5.1 to predict the level of government that will provide each good most efficiently. Compare your predictions to reality.

2. Assume that government *must* set standards for building offices and wiring toasters. Argue that local government should set construction standards and central government should set wiring standards.

3. In the 1980s, the U.S. federal government imposed water pollution standards on reluctant states, whereas the government of Europe allowed the European national governments more freedom to develop their own policies toward water pollution. Use table 5.1 to explain why water pollution on major rivers was typically worse in Europe than in the United States at the time.

TABLE 5.1
Internalization Prescription for Government Jurisdiction

Good	Character	Market Failure	Best Jurisdiction
Pure Public good	Nonrivalrous and nonexcludable	Individuals free-ride on taxes	Central government
Local public good	Congestable	Localized congestion	Local government
Spillover	Externality	Localities free-ride on abatement	Special district

[2] Mancur Olson (Olson 1969) proposed the "principle of fiscal equivalence," according to which the reach of government for finance should be equivalent to the effects of the public good.

4. Discuss the difference between the central government's pricing a spillover and regulating it (Revesz 1996).

5. Germany is privatizing telephone services and taking the lead in creating a European currency. Make an economic argument for decentralizing telephones and centralizing currency.

BARGAINING AND THE CHARACTER OF STATE GOODS

According to the internalization prescription, the jurisdiction of government should extend as far, and no farther, than the effects of the public goods it supplies. To illustrate the principle, if the government in jurisdiction A produces a public good x that affects its own residents and also affects residents of neighboring jurisdiction B, then governments A and B should merge for the purpose of producing x. This prescription makes no more sense than the proposition that if corporation A trades with corporation B, then the two corporation should merge to form a single corporation. In general, the fact that one organization affects another is insufficient reason to merge them.

Different organizations typically deal with their effects on each other through bargains. Recall that the *Coase Theorem* asserts that players will bargain to an efficient allocation of resources provided that transaction costs do not impede the process (see chapter 3 for details). Applied to intergovernmental relations, the Coase Theorem asserts that when transaction costs are low, bargaining will correct the oversupply or undersupply of public goods. The organization of relations among governments does not matter to the efficiency of the outcome. *Assuming zero transaction costs of bargaining, the supply of public goods is efficient regardless of the number of governments.*[3] For example, when local governments can bargain costlessly with each other, the central government need not supply pure public goods and special districts are not required to respond to spillovers.

In reality, the organization of bargaining affects its outcomes. In this chapter I discuss how to organize bargaining among different governments that supply local public goods. The internalization prescription for allocating power to different levels of government seems antiseptic compared to the dirt and danger of politics. In reality the supply of public goods in a democracy responds less to efficiency and more to politics. The bargaining theory that I develop is more realistic and more political than the internalization prescription.

Externality and Internality

I begin by relating the technical character of public goods to the problem of bargaining among governments. The *internality* of an act refers to the cost or

[3] Here is the equivalent proposition for the private sector: *With zero transaction costs of bargaining, the supply of private goods is efficient regardless of the number of markets.* The choice between markets and hierarchies only matters to efficiency because of transaction costs

		externality	
		positive	negative
internality	positive	too little	too much
	negative	too little	too much

Fig. 5-2 Spillovers and Incentives

benefit enjoyed by the actor, whereas the *externality* refers to the cost or benefit conveyed by the act to others (Schelling 1978a). Internalities and externalities can be positive (good) or negative (bad). Figure 5-2 depicts the four possibilities.

Because this chapter concerns intergovernmental relations, I will interpret "internalities" in figure 5-2 as effects of an act of government on the people residing within its jurisdiction, and I will interpret "externalities" as *spillovers* from one jurisdiction to another. Under this interpretation, I will explain the cells in figure 5-2.

Researchers in a state university may discover new ideas that profit the state (positive internality), and other states may profit from borrowing these ideas (positive externality). New ideas are a *boon* to everyone. Self-interested actors tend to undersupply boons that benefit themselves and spill over to benefit others.

When supplying water to residents (positive internality), a local government may degrade the water available in other localities (negative externality). Pollution is a harmful *by-product*. Self-interested actors tend to oversupply products that benefit the actors and incidentally harm others.

Sometimes a rugged coastline without harbors requires a lighthouse. A local government that maintains a lighthouse bears its costs. If no ships dock within its jurisdiction, the residents of the local government gain little or nothing from the lighthouse. In such circumstances, maintaining a lighthouse is a beneficence. Self-interested actors undersupply a beneficence that costs them (negative internality) and benefits others (positive externality).

If an act produces negative internalities and negative externalities, a self-interested actor will curtail the act to reduce the negative internalities. A self-interested actor, however, will not curtail the activity as much as required when taking account of the negative externalities. For example, a local government that removes water from a river for drinking probably considers the harm to local fishing within its jurisdiction (negative internality) more than the harm downstream in other jurisdictions (negative externality). Consequently, the southeast cell of figure 5-2 is labeled "too much."

Spontaneity and Organization

According to this interpretation of figure 5-2, a government tends to supply too little of a public good whose benefits spill over to other jurisdictions (a boon or beneficence), and a government tends to supply too much of a public bad whose costs spill over to other jurisdictions (harmful by-product). In this context, government "supply" refers to production directly by the state and to state regulation of private activity by its citizens.

When public goods or bads spill across jurisdictions and cause inefficiencies, everyone can benefit in principle from a remedy. The best remedy depends on incentives created by the technical character of the public good or bad. Boons create coordination problems that people often solve spontaneously with little or no government organization. In contrast, by-products and beneficence often create problems of cooperation whose solution requires organization or sometimes coercion. I will discuss coordination, cooperation, and coercion as alternative remedies to externalities.

COORDINATION

Conflicting interests provide the usual obstacle to cooperation. In chapter 3, however, I characterized pure *coordination games* in which the interests of the players converge perfectly. When interests converge perfectly, everyone who possesses the necessary information agrees about the best action. In pure coordination games, imperfect information provides the only obstacle to cooperation.

To illustrate, consider adhering to a common standard. As their economies entwine, adjacent towns benefit from adopting the same standard for weights ("metric system") and time ("Paris time"). Similarly, a firm that adopts a common industrial standard may increase its profits (positive internality) and also increase the profits of other firms supplying peripheral products (positive externality). In these examples, coordination increases the internality, so a common standard is a boon to everyone.

If coordination increases the internality, then behavior will tend to converge toward closer coordination. Convergence is spontaneous in the sense that unorganized actors voluntarily adopt the same behavior for their own advantage. Spontaneous convergence goes to the best result when the problem has a uniquely stable solution. When coordination games have multiple equilibria, however, spontaneity may converge on an inferior result. Obtaining a superior result may require organization and planning. Also, actors may disagree over the preferred standard because the one who must change will bear transition costs, or because someone owns the preferred standard and can charge its users.

To illustrate, the users of personal computers would benefit from adopting the same operating system, but obstacles to coordination include technical disagreements, transition costs, and ownership rights. Similarly, everyone in Europe would benefit from driving on the same side of the road, but Britain and the rest of Europe settled into different equilibria. A uniform standard requires someone (presumably Britain) to pay the costs of transition. The same argument applies to the different gauge of railroad track in France and Spain, or Russia and most of western Europe.

When coordination games have multiple equilibria, converging to the best equilibrium may require creating private or public organizations to exchange information. Thus countries and companies often organize conventions to promulgate international standards for products in world trade. Similarly, the Commonwealth of Independent States (former Soviet Union) provides a framework for exchanging information among members without coercing them. In spite of obstacles, actors usually solve coordination games spontaneously or with noncoercive organizations (Sykes 1995; Sykes 1996).

COOPERATION

I discussed boons in which the interests of different actors converge. For by-products and beneficence, however, the interests of different actors diverge. Correcting the oversupply of harmful by-products or the undersupply of beneficence requires cooperation, not just coordination. Cooperation typically requires bargaining among people whose interests partly converge and partly diverge. When bargaining, each party tries to secure the cooperation of others, which is productive, on terms favorable to himself, which is distributive. In bargaining problems, distribution is the obstacle to production.

Bargaining typically involves costly negotiations. In bargaining among governments, the transaction cost of negotiating and the bargaining power of the parties depend partly on the constitution. For example, unanimity rule creates different incentives from majority rule, as I will explain.

COERCION

Unlike unanimity rule, majority rule introduces the possibility of coercion. Collective action is coercive when one or more rational actors do not agree to it. Coercion often occurs because the collective action makes an actor worse-off than no collective action. Coercion, although dangerous, sometimes becomes necessary to solve a failure in bargaining such as holdouts or free-riding, as I explain in the next section.

Unanimity or Majority Rule?

Laws made by the majority bind everyone in a typical democracy, whereas international treaties bind only those states that sign them. Unanimity rule is the strongest form of super-majority rule. So majority rule and unanimity rule define two poles of intergovernmental relations.

I apply the phrase *pure centralization* to a political system in which a *national majority* of citizens or their representatives, and no one else, can make laws. By "centralization," I mean that a national majority can dictate to the states or regions. Unitary states like France, Japan, and New Zealand approach pure centralization. I apply the phrase *pure decentralization* to a political system requiring *unanimity* among separate states to make a law. Examples of pure decentralization include the European Union when operating under its original rules as applied in the Council of Ministers.

Unlike the two pure types, *federalism* often mixes unanimity and majority rule, depending on the type of law. To illustrate, the U.S. Constitution reserves some powers for the states, so harmonization of laws in these areas requires unanimous agreement, whereas a majority in the federal legislature can impose laws on the states in other areas. To use another illustration, when Canada "repatriated" its constitution in 1992, it sought unsuccessfully the agreement of all its provinces, whereas the federal legislature follows majority rule.[4]

Assuming zero transaction costs of political bargaining, the Coase Theorem predicts an efficient supply of public goods under decentralized or centralized politics.[5] The Coase Theorem, however, is the beginning and not the end of analysis. Political bargaining consumes time and provokes strategic behavior, so transaction costs are high. A realistic analysis concerns the effects of centralization and decentralization on the transaction costs of bargaining.

Unanimity and Holdouts

In chapter 3 I asserted that a switch from unanimity to majority rule reduces transaction costs of collective action. The transaction costs of bargaining increase geometrically with the number of bargainers. So unanimity rule *paralyzes large organizations and majority rule animates them.*

As an organization grows, it may switch from unanimity to majority rule in order to avoid paralysis. For example, as more countries join the European Union, the Council of Ministers increasingly follows majority rule rather than its original unanimity rule (see chapter 9). Similarly, switching from unanimity to majority rule may make an organization more willing to accept new members. For example, the shift toward majority rule makes the Council of Ministers more willing to accept new countries into the European Union.

A successful federal system with unanimity rule must have few members, whereas a successful federal system with majority rule can have many members.[6] In general, *a shift from unanimity rule to majority rule increases the optimal number of governments in a federal system.* I explained in chapter 1 that the Coase Theorem simplifies reality by treating strategy as part of the transaction costs of interaction, whereas a more satisfactory approach explicitly models

---

[4] Until 1982, the Canadian constitution was merely an 1867 act of the British Parliament that defined the respective rights of, and the division of powers between, the Canadian federal and provincial governments. It was binding on the federal government and Canadian provinces. The constitution was repatriated in 1992 by acts of the British Parliament and Canadian federal government. All of the Canadian provinces and the federal government agreed to the repatriation expect for the province of Quebec, which has still not given its formal consent to the repatriation or to the Canadian Charter of Rights and Freedoms. Although Quebec's formal consent was not required, and Quebec is subject to the Canadian Constitution Act of 1982 and the Charter of Rights and Freedoms, attempts to persuade Quebec to agree to a further amended new constitution have been ongoing since then. My thanks to Bradley J. Freedman for this information.

[5] Technical qualification: Given weak "income effects," substitute "same" for "efficient" in this prediction. For details, see Cooter 1982.

[6] Perhaps the only institution of modern Western government that formally operates by a unanimity rule is the jury. However, some Japanese say that their government proceeds by consensus, some Poles cherish memories of its tradition "liberum veto" system, and some business of the United Nations is conducted by a consensus technique under the direction of the secretary general (so-called consensus resolutions under Article 10 of the U.N. charter).

strategy. Now I will use strategic theory to explain why unanimity rule paralyzes a large organization.

As a coalition grows, each player who joins demands a fraction of the resulting increase in the coalition's value as the price of cooperation. With increasing returns to the scale of a coalition, the last member to join increases the coalition's value more than previous members, so the last member to join can demand the best terms. Everyone who recognizes this fact has an incentive to hold out in order to join the coalition last.

This proposition applies to bargaining among governments under unanimity rule. Unanimity rule makes each government decisive for collective action. Assume that collective action is more efficient than individual action, so returns to the scale of a coalition increase sharply as the last government joins. Each government who recognizes this fact has an incentive to hold out and join the coalition last, in order to extract the best terms. *In general, increasing returns to the scale of cooperation among regional or local governments creates a problem of holdouts.*

To illustrate, assume that five local governments have jurisdiction over segments of a lake's shore. The five governments want to use the lake for recreational swimming, which requires all of them to stop polluting. The governments negotiate to distribute abatement costs. An agreement among any four governments is worthless without participation by the fifth government, so returns to the scale of cooperation increase sharply when the fifth member joins the coalition. If any four governments reach a tentative agreement, the fifth government can refuse to cooperate unless the others pay most of its abatement costs. Any government, however, could be the fifth government to agree. Recognizing this fact, all five governments may hold out, which paralyzes abatement efforts, and so the lake remains polluted.

In reality, small groups solve the problem of holdouts under unanimity rule, whereas large groups cannot solve it.

MAJORITY AND STAMPEDES

Having explained why unanimity rule paralyzes large organizations, I now will explain why majority rule animates them. Majority rule creates competition to become the decisive member in a majority coalition. To illustrate, in an assembly of 101 persons, a coalition of 51 members forms a majority. To form a majority coalition, a minority coalition of 50 members must attract one additional member. Instead of holding out and risking exclusion, many of the 50 outsiders may hasten to join the majority coalition. In general in a democratic assembly with $1 + n$ seats, people compete to join a coalition of $n/2$ members in order to share in the advantages of power.

To illustrate by the preceding example, assume that five local governments form a council with the power to impose a pollution abatement program on its members by majority vote. A coalition of three local governments can impose an abatement plan on the other two, including making the outsiders pay a disproportionate share of abatement costs. A minority coalition with two members must attract an additional member to create a majority coalition. The three players outside this coalition may want to join in order to avoid being excluded from power. Competition to become the decisive member of the majority coalition can prevent holdouts and sometimes provoke a stampede.

The switch from unanimity to majority rule typically solves the problem of holdouts in a large organization and creates many new problems. By facilitating collective action, majority rule enables the governing coalition to do more good or more bad. Contests over distribution exemplify the bad. The members of the governing coalition may provide local public goods for themselves and tax nonmembers disproportionately. In general, *central provision of local public goods creates opportunities for rent-seeking that increase with the size of the state* (Persson and Tabellini 1994).[7]

Rent-seeking is stable when a persistent majority redistributes wealth to itself. Conversely, rent-seeking is unstable when majorities cycle. I explained in chapter 3 that majority-rule games of distribution with symmetrical players have an empty core. The practical implication of this fact is that rent-seeking can undo itself and cycle.

To illustrate, consider the example of a council of five local governments that can impose a pollution abatement program on its members by majority vote. Assume that a coalition of three local governments makes a plan requiring the other two local governments to pay most of the abatement costs. Each of the three local governments in the majority coalition can credibly threaten to quit if it does not receive a disproportionate share of the coalition's value. These considerations may destabilize any potential coalition. Overcoming the instabilities of majority rule requires natural affinities and specific institutions discussed in previous chapters, such as political parties.

TERMS OF AGREEMENT

I have discussed how centralization and decentralization affect the likelihood of successful bargaining. Now I consider how centralization and decentralization affect the terms of an agreement. The terms of an agreement depend on the bargaining power of the parties. Bargaining power depends on the consequences of bargaining failure. If bargaining fails, each party must do its best without cooperation from the others. The parties who benefit least from cooperation have the most bargaining power. (See the discussion of the Nash bargaining solution in chapter 3.)

How well each party can do on its own without the cooperation of others depends on the collective-action rule. First consider unanimity rule. Failed bargaining under unanimity rule paralyzes collective action. Consequently, *when bargaining under unanimity rule, the regions and localities with least need for cooperation can demand the best terms.* To illustrate, upstream jurisdictions

[7] This is one reason why Buchanan and Tullock (1962 [1967]) stress the advantages of unanimity rule in their classic book that revived contractarianism.

have less need for cooperation in controlling water pollution than downstream jurisdictions. When bargaining under unanimity rule, the upstream jurisdictions can extract favorable terms of cooperation from the downstream jurisdictions. In a regional plan to abate pollution, unanimity rule causes the downstream jurisdictions to pay a disproportionate share of abatement costs.

Now consider a change from unanimity rule to majority rule. With centralization, a national majority can impose its will on the minority. Bargaining strength lies with the potential members of a majority coalition. When *bargaining under majority rule, the regions and localities inside the national coalition can demand the best terms of cooperation from outsiders.*

To illustrate, return to the example of bargaining over a regional plan to abate pollution. Assume that downstream jurisdictions, which outnumber upstream jurisdictions, form a majority coalition. Under these assumptions, the downstream jurisdictions can extract very favorable terms from the upstream jurisdictions. The final agreement will require the upstream jurisdictions to pay a disproportionate share of abatement costs. In this example, the downstream jurisdictions benefit from majority rule, whereas the upstream jurisdictions benefit from unanimity rule.

In general, *a change from unanimity to majority rule transfers bargaining power from the parties who need collective action least to the parties inside the national coalition.*

Questions

1. Predict some consequences of changing from unanimity rule to majority rule in Europe's government.

2. Assume that a federal government consists of five peripheral governments that border on the ocean and ten peripheral governments without coastline. Contrast the consequences of majority rule and unanimity rule for the number of lighthouses and their financing.

3. Explain why computer software flourishes without government standards to assure the compatibility of different products.

4. The central government or peripheral governments can provide social insurance in federal systems. A recent study concluded that centralized social insurance chosen by voting provides overinsurance relative to the standard of economic efficiency, whereas an intergovernmental transfer scheme chosen by bargaining provides underinsurance (Persson and Tabellini 1996). What might cause this result?

Instruments of Central Control

I have contrasted centralized decisions subject to national majorities and decentralized decisions requiring regional or local unanimity. Now I will discuss how

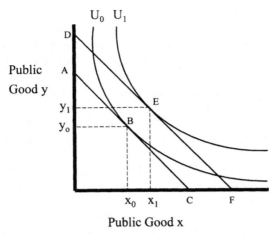

Fig. 5-3 Block Grant

central governments can influence peripheral governments through money grants and orders.

BLOCK GRANTS, TIED GRANTS, MATCHING GRANTS

Central governments collect taxes and allocate some funds for peripheral governments to spend, possibly with "strings attached." *Block grants* are funds given to peripheral governments to spend in any way they wish, with no strings attached, thus giving the recipient discretion in using the funds. In contrast, strings are attached when the central government makes the grant's amount dependent on its use. Strings may take the form of *tied grants* that require the recipient to spend funds for a particular purpose, or *matching grants* (subsidies) that augment the recipient's own expenditures on specific items.

What difference do strings make to the actual pattern of expenditures by recipients? Economics provides a simple answer, which I explain with figures. Assume that a peripheral government has consistent preferences over public goods x and y, as depicted by the indifference curves U_0 and U_1 in figure 5-3. Initially, the peripheral government, which receives no funds from the central government, faces a budget constraint indicated by line AC. The peripheral government initially chooses the combination of public goods corresponding to point B, where AC is tangent to U_0. At point B, the combination of goods is (x_0, y_0).

Now consider the consequences of a block grant from the central government to the government depicted in figure 5-3. A block grant, which the peripheral government can spend as it wishes, shifts the budget line up from AC to DF. The slope of the budget line does not change because the block grant does not change the relative prices of goods x and y. Given the budget line DF, the peripheral government chooses point E, where DF is tangent to U_1 and the combination of

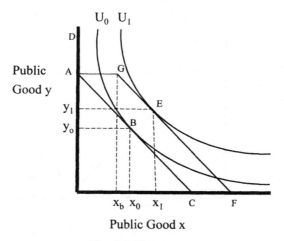

Fig. 5-4 Tied Grant

goods is denoted (x_1, y_1). Thus a block grant causes the consumption of public goods to shift from (x_0, y_0) to (x_1, y_1). In general, *block grants to peripheral governments change their expenditures on public goods.*[8]

Instead of a block grant, assume that the central government ties the grant to the purchase of public good x. Tying requires the peripheral government to use all the grant money to purchase good x. The horizontal line segment AG in figure 5-4 represents the tied grant, which must be spent to purchase good x in the quantity x_b. After exhausting the grant, the peripheral government can use its own funds to buy more of good x or good y. The line segment GF represents combinations of x and y from which to choose. Thus the tied grant creates a budget line with a kink, as given by line AGF.

Given the kink in the budget line AGF, the peripheral government chooses point E, where AGF is tangent to U_1 and the combination of goods is denoted (x_1, y_1). Thus the tied grant in figure 5-4 causes the same consumption of public goods as the block grant in figure 5-4. Tying funds is ineffective in figure 5-4 so long as the budget line is tangent to an indifference curve at a point beyond the kink. Beyond the kink, the peripheral government supplements the tied grant with its own funds to purchase more of the tied good. In general, *tied grants have the same effect as block grants of equal value so long as the peripheral government uses some of its own funds to purchase the good to which the grant is tied.*

Instead of a block grant or a tied grant, assume that the central government gives a matching grant to purchase good x. In other words, the central government uses its funds to match a given percentage of the peripheral government's expenditure on good x. In contrast to good x, the peripheral government must

---

[8] Block grants can also stimulate reductions in local taxes, with no change in expenditure on public goods. This outcome, however, is unlikely in practice.

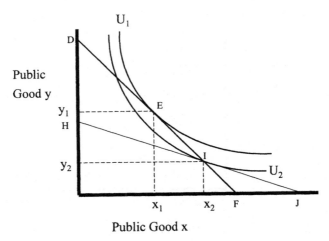

Fig. 5-5 Matching Grant

use only its own funds to purchase good y. Thus, a matching grant lowers the relative price of the matched good for the recipient. The fall in price causes the peripheral government to purchase more of the matched good. In general, *matching grants increase consumption of the matched good more than block grants or tied grants of the same magnitude do* (Oates 1972).

With a matching grant, the central government conditions the size of the subsidy on the amount of the peripheral government's own money that it spends on the matched good. The peripheral government would prefer to have money unconditionally rather than conditionally. In general, *block grants satisfy the preferences of the recipient more than matching grants of the same magnitude do.*

To illustrate, figure 5-5 compares a block grant and a matching grant, holding constant the total subsidy paid by the central government to the peripheral government. The peripheral government's budget line is DF under the block grant, which causes the peripheral government to choose point E. Now consider the consequence of changing from a block grant to a matching grant. The slope of DF indicates the relative price to the peripheral government of buying the two public goods. A matching grant changes relative prices. Let HJ indicate the peripheral government's budget line under the matching grant, which causes the peripheral government to choose point I. Thus, a shift from block grant to matching grant causes the peripheral government to shift from point E to point I.

Notice that points I and E are on the budget line DF, so the total subsidy paid by the central government is the same for the block grant and the matching grant. However, the shift from block grant to matching grant causes an increase in the matched good from x_1 to x_2, and a decrease in the unmatched good from y_1 to y_2. Also, the shift from block grant to matching grant causes a fall in the peripheral government's utility from U_1 to U_2. In general, matching grants cause more consumption of the matched good and less satisfaction by the recipient government than do block grants of equal value.[9]

STABILITY

I distinguished pure centralization under majority rule and decentralization under unanimity rule. In practice, intergovernmental relations typically employ, unanimity rule for some decisions and majority rule for others. Mixed systems provide room for dispute over centralization and decentralization. The same group of people may form a permanent minority in a federal system and a permanent majority in a peripheral government. In general, *a permanent minority in a federal government with a permanent majority in a peripheral government typically exerts pressure for decentralization.*

To illustrate, French speakers are a minority in Canada and a majority in Quebec. Independence from Canada for Quebec would increase the power of its officials, who press for decentralization. (Better to be prime minister of a country than governor of a province.) Similarly, the Flemish induced Belgium to create regional Parliaments corresponding to the major ethnic divisions.[10] (Better to be a leader in the Flemish Parliament than a follower in the Belgian Parliament.)

Conversely, if a majority coalition emerges as a stable winner at the national level, it can use central government authority to redistribute power and wealth toward its members. Thus, a stable national majority coalition stands to gain by centralizing power. In general, *a stable national coalition exerts pressure for centralization in a mixed system.*

To illustrate, for many years the Democratic and Republican Parties have alternated in controlling the U.S. federal government. The predictable success of these parties creates pressure from their leadership for centralization. Thus, the U.S. Constitution gives federal authorities the power to regulate interstate commerce (Article I, Section 8). Over the years, federal authorities have increased their control by expanding the interpretation of this clause from the channels of interstate commerce (e.g., rivers for steamboats, railway lines), to goods in interstate commerce (e.g., wheat, automobiles, lottery tickets), and finally to whatever affects interstate commerce (e.g., farming, manufacturing).[11] Resistance to centralization of power in the United States especially comes from the southern states that historically formed a permanent minority in the federal system.

[9] In technical terms, this result occurs because a block grant has a "pure income effect," whereas a matching grant has a "price effect" as well as an income effect. Note, however, that it is possible for a matching grant to result in a decline in expenditures on the matched good, just as it is possible for a fall in the price of bread to cause a fall in its consumption.

[10] Belgium has four parliaments representing the nation, Brussels, Wallonie (French), and Flanders (Flemish). French speakers traditionally dominated in national government. Now, however, the Flemish are a majority. Even so, Flemish nationalists prefer to govern a Flemish nation than govern Belgium.

[11] The steady expansion of the definition of interstate commerce was stopped, at least temporarily, in *U.S. v Lopez*, 115 SCt 1624 (1995), which held that regulating guns near schools is not a proper exercise of the commerce clause.

The European Union is committed by treaty to the "principle of subsidiarity," according to which higher levels of government should not perform tasks that lower levels of government can perform (Bergh 1997). Thus the European government in Brussels should restrict its intrusions on national governments to the minimum necessary to unify Europe. For example, whenever possible the European government should use a directive that specifies ends and leaves the means of implementation open to national governments to decide, rather than create a European regulation that specifies the means every nation must use to achieve a given end.

Questions

1. Predict differences in the effects of tied grants and matching grants for improving public transportation such as subways.

2. A central government agency that wants to increase automobile safety must choose between a design standard and a performance standard for brakes. The design standard requires installing antilock disk brakes on all new cars, whereas the performance standard requires all new cars to pass a test of braking effectiveness. Compare the efficiency of these two kinds of regulations.

3. Try to formulate the principle of subsidiarity in economic terms by using the concept of efficiency.

COMPREHENSIVE OR SINGLE-PURPOSE GOVERNMENT? HORIZONTAL DIVISIONS

Centralizing and decentralizing concerns the vertical allocation of power among governments at different levels. Now I turn to the horizontal allocation of power among governments at the same level. Decisions can be made in one government with broad jurisdiction or in several governments with narrow jurisdiction. For example, the town council can control police and schools, or the town council can control police and a separately elected school board can control schools. Changes can be dramatic, as in New Zealand where 466 local authorities were amalgamated into seven in 1989 (Memon 1993). I will contrast multipurpose government and single-purpose government.

Splicing and Factoring

Broad jurisdiction *splices* independent issues together like the strands of a rope. In contrast, narrow jurisdiction *factors* politics into independent issues like a mathematician dividing a large number into prime numbers. What difference does it make whether jurisdiction is spliced or factored? I answer this question using the analysis from chapter 2 that contrasts voting on single and multiple dimensions.

Splicing widens the scope for bargaining by lowering the transaction costs of political trades. Politicians often bargain successfully by combining issues and "rolling logs." Just as people benefit most from trading widely in markets, so political factions benefit most from bargaining widely in politics. Splicing has the advantage of increasing the surplus realized by political cooperation.

Splicing also has a disadvantage. Assume that voters' preferences are single-peaked in one dimension of choice (x-axis), and also single-peaked in another dimension of choice (y-axis). Given these assumptions, voting separately on each issue gives the median as the unique winner on each dimension of choice. The same voters' preferences, however, may be double-peaked on a curve in two-dimensional space. Given this assumption, voting in two dimensions cycles. In this example, factoring yields the median rule and splicing yields intransitivity. In general, splicing increases the probability of cyclical voting. Avoiding cyclical voting in the legislature requires an undemocratic mechanism like agenda control.

To conclude, splicing facilitates bargaining across issues, and successful bargaining across issues satisfies the preferences of voters more completely than allowing the median voter to prevail on separate dimensions of choice. But, if bargaining fails, splicing increases the probability of cycling and the need for agenda control, whereas factoring allows the median voter to prevail on separate dimensions of choice. Median rule on separate dimensions of choice often satisfies the preferences of voters more efficiently than an unstable contest of distribution. Single-purpose government is like a safe stock with a modest yield, whereas multipurpose government is like a risky stock that pays a lot or nothing.

Example: City Council and School Board

To illustrate these facts, assume that expenditure on police and schools are the two major political issues in a small town. First, consider a town council that decides both issues (spliced). The council provides a forum for bargaining and cooperating. If bargaining succeeds, council members who care intensely about police may trade votes with council members who care intensely about schools, so that each one gets what it wants most. If bargaining fails, the council members may waste resources in an unstable contest of distribution.

Second, consider a town council that controls police and a separately elected school board that controls schools (factored).[12] Factoring denies a forum for bargaining and cooperating over the two issues. With single-peaked preferences, the median voter prevails on each dimension of choice.

Table 5.2 sharpens the example with numbers. Assume that voters in a town are divided into equal numbers of liberals, conservatives, and moderates. Expenditure can be high or low for schools and police, with the resulting net benefits for each group of voters indicated in table 5.2.[13] The liberals intensely prefer high expenditures on schools and mildly prefer the savings in taxes from low

[12] Another way to factor is by allowing the citizens to vote directly on expenditures for schools and police, with the two issues separated on the ballot.

[13] Table 5.2 implicitly assumes additive separable utility functions for each group, so any group's total utility equals the sum of its utility on each of the two issues.

TABLE 5.2
Voter's Net Benefits

| | School Expenditures | | Police Expenditures | |
	low	high	low	high
liberal	0	11	1	0
conservative	1	0	0	11
moderate	2	0	3	0
total	3	11	4	11

expenditures on police. The opposite is true of conservatives, who intensely prefer high expenditures on police and mildly prefer the savings in taxes from low expenditures on schools. The moderates mildly prefer the tax savings from low expenditures on police and schools. The row labeled "total" indicates the sum of net benefits to the three groups.

Assuming majority rule, contrast the consequences of splicing and factoring issues in table 5.2. If the issues are factored, then two out of three voters (conservatives and moderates) vote for low expenditures on schools, so factoring results in low expenditures on schools. Furthermore, two out of three voters (liberals and moderates) also vote for low expenditures on police, so factoring results in low expenditures on police. Thus, factoring results in low expenditures on schools and police.

If issues are spliced, the voters must choose among four combinations of public goods depicted in the columns of table 5.3. The net benefits to voters depicted in table 5.3 are calculated from the numbers in table 5.2. For example, (low,high) indicates low expenditures on schools and high expenditures on police, which result in a payoff of 0 for liberals, 12 for conservatives, and 2 for moderates.

TABLE 5.3
Voter Net Benefits from Combinations of Public Goods

| | Expenditures on Schools and Police, Respectively | | | |
	(high,high)	(low,low)	(high,low)	(low,high)
liberal	11	1	12	0
conservative	11	1	0	12
moderate	0	5	3	2
total	22	7	15	14

The numbers in table 5.3 can be used to deduce the winner in a vote between any two alternatives. If voters simply vote their preferences in table 5.3, without bargaining or trading, then an intransitive cycle results. Specifically, two of three voters (liberal and conservative) prefer (high,high) rather than (low,low). Two of three voters (conservative and moderate) prefer (low,low) rather than (high,low). Two of three voters (liberal and moderate) prefer (high,low) rather than (low,high). And, finally, two of three voters (conservative and moderate) prefer (low,high) rather than (high,high). Thus voting in table 5.3 results in an intransitive cycle.

Tables 5.2 and 5.3 illustrate the general principle that splicing dimensions of choice can cause intransitivity where none exists on any single dimension of choice. With spliced choices, avoiding intransitivity requires a nondemocratic mechanism like agenda control, or, alternatively, splicing may cause the voters to bargain with each other and cooperate. Since liberals care more about schools than police, whereas conservatives care more about police than schools, they could profitably trade votes. A platform calling for high expenditures on schools and police allows the liberals and conservatives to get what they want on the issue that each one cares about the most, as required for efficiency. [14] Stabilizing such an agreement requires the parties to abandon the majority-rule game of distribution, which has no core,[15] and cooperate with each other.

Whether a comprehensive government or many single-purpose governments satisfy the preferences of political factions better depends on the ability of politicians to cooperate. In general, *splicing increases the gains from cooperation and factoring decreases the losses from conflict.* Finding the optimal number of governments requires balancing these considerations. These facts suggest the prescription, "Splice when cooperation is likely and factor when conflict is likely."

Applications

Sometimes a constitution factors, as when a town's constitution establishes an elected council and a separately elected school board. Alternatively, a constitution may allow for factoring without requiring it. For example, the constitutions of the U.S. states prescribe procedures for establishing special governments for parks, transportation, and water. Citizens can establish or abolish special governments by following the prescribed procedures. Alternatively, the constitution

---

[14] Cost-benefit efficiency requires choosing the level of expenditures that maximizes the sum of net benefits, which occurs with high expenditures on both schools and police.

[15] Since the voters' preferences form an intransitive cycle, any coalition formed simply by trading votes in table 5.4 is dominated by another coalition (empty core). For example, a liberal-conservative coalition to obtain (high,high) is dominated by a liberal-moderate coalition to obtain (high,low); a liberal-moderate coalition to obtain (high,low) is dominated by a conservative-moderate coalition to obtain (low,low); and so on. Thus the liberal-conservative coalition might not prove stable. To guarantee its stability, the parties would need the ability to make side payments. With side payments, the liberal-conservative coalition dominates other possible coalitions, and no possible coalition dominates the liberal-conservative coalition.

may limit or forbid factoring, as when it prevents a branch from delegating authority or a government from ceding authority.[16]

I have discussed clear-cut cases of factoring, but unclear cases often occur. To illustrate using the European Union, the ministers forming the Council of Ministers differ on certain issues. Thus the Council may consist of the national ministers of agriculture to decide a question about farm subsidies, whereas the Council may consist of the national ministers of transportation to decide a question about railroads. The changes in membership presumably impede bargaining across issues. How serious the impediment is remains an unanswered empirical question.[17] In reality, the national ministers of finance often dictate to other national ministers, so the finance ministers can often bargain across issues. To resolve whether the organization of the Council of Ministers factors issues requires empirical research on logrolling.

Questions

1. Suppose the population of a town is heterogeneous, consisting of several distinct cultures and ethnic groups. When does heterogeneity commend factoring jurisdictions, and when does heterogeneity commend splicing jurisdictions?

2. Assume that the legislature faces a choice in its rules. The whole legislature can either decide all issues or delegate decisions on specific issues to specific committees. Apply the analysis of factoring and splicing to determine the optimal committee structure.

3. An empirical study by Eugenia Toma on U.S. data found that schools provide more net benefits for families and fewer net benefits for educators when state school boards are elected rather than appointed (Toma 1983). How might the theory developed above explain this fact?

SUMMARY AND CONCLUSION

I have approached intergovernmental relations as a problem of bargaining among governments. If political bargaining were costless and always succeeded, then governments would always cooperate to supply efficient quantities of public goods. With zero transaction costs, any number of governments is optimal. In reality, however, political bargaining is costly and sometimes fails. Consequently, the optimal number of governments minimizes the transaction costs of political bargaining required to secure cooperation in supplying public goods.

[16] See the discussion of the nondelegation doctrine in chapter 4 and the discussion of secession in chapter 6.

[17] Presumably each minister with a specific portfolio must respond to the finance minister on all issues involving expenditures, and every minister must respond to the prime minister. The question is how far these communications go toward removing impediments to bargaining across issues.

According to the conventional prescription, power over public goods should be assigned to the smallest unit of government that internalizes the effects of its exercise. In contrast, a strategic approach emphasizes the politics of bargaining. A unanimity rule creates a problem of holdouts in large organizations and gives bargaining power to the parties who need collective action least, whereas majority rule can create a contest of distribution and gives bargaining power to the majority coalition. Multipurpose government facilitates comprehensive bargaining, whereas single-purpose government prompts median rule.

Central governments use various instruments to influence peripheral governments. Tied grants and block grants have much the same effect, whereas matching grants cause relatively more consumption of the subsidized good. Central laws that dictate ends and not means (directives) allow peripheral governments to use local information when implementing policy, whereas central laws that dictate means (regulations) require central authorities to possess extensive local information.

Centralizing creates one government with deep bureaucracies, whereas decentralizing creates many governments with shallow bureaucracies. Trends toward privitization and decentralization suggest that the future will bring less government and more governments. The result, I hope, will be federalism and not feudalism. This chapter has analyzed cooperation between governments; the next chapter turns to competition between governments.

Government Competition

> Think globally, act locally.
>
> —*popular bumper sticker on cars in Berkeley, California*

IN HIS magisterial book *A Theory of Justice*, John Rawls asserts that a just state gains support from citizens when placed in competition with other states.[1] Similarly, an efficient stàte gains support from citizens when placed in competition with other states. Competition among governments comes from people moving to governments and governments moving to people. This chapter canvasses theories of intergovernmental competition, including mobility, choice of private laws, and contracting for public goods. I will explore the global consequences of local government actions and address such questions as:

Example 1: By lavish spending on its state school, a suburb attracts rich, intellectual families. This school has its own computer network, whereas another state school in a poor city neighborhood struggles to afford books. Does residential mobility increase the efficiency of local government by clustering people together who have similar tastes, such as intellectuals? Or does mobility merely exacerbate inequality by clustering people together with similar incomes, such as the rich?

Example 2: An ethnic minority occupies a neighborhood in a large city. The neighborhood council enacts an ordinance requiring neighborhood signs to use only the minority's language. A court must decide whether the ordinance violates the constitutional rights of advertisers. Will a decision in favor of the neighborhood council increase or diminish diversity among neighborhoods?

Example 3: The European Union issues directives requiring the European nations to harmonize their laws. Under what circumstances does harmonization reduce competition among governments and make them less responsive to citizens?

Example 4: In Switzerland, 50,000 signatures by citizens create a referendum on any law enacted by the federal legislature. Is this requirement a good way to filter good proposals and separate them from bad proposals? Or is this requirement a waste of resources?

Instead of benefiting citizens, political competition sometimes harms them. In extreme cases, competition among governments spills over into conflict.

[1] See Rawls 1971, p. 177, 496–503.

The detritus of territorial wars litters the history of states. In addition to wars, even mild competition sometimes harms the public. In a celebrated example, Albert Hirschman observed that monopoly power by a Nigerian railroad forced aggrieved buyers to "voice" their complaints through politics. The development of competition from trucks, however, permitted buyers to "exit," which caused railway services to deteriorate (Hirschman 1970). Applied to legal regimes, Hirschman's theory predicts that political voices are sometimes more efficient than market choices. Similarly, decline in racial discrimination has allegedly caused talented African Americans to exit poor neighborhoods, thus causing deterioration in ghetto institutions (Wilson 1987). Using another example, lawyers sometimes argue that different regulations in different jurisdictions provoke a "race to laxity." For example, decentralized environmental law can cause jurisdictions to compete for business by allowing more pollution.

The complexity of history falsifies most universal statements about social life, including the proposition that citizens always benefit from more competition in politics. Lacking universals, social science must rely on generalizations. A theme of this book is that democracy achieves superiority over other forms of government by harnessing political competition. The superiority of democracy over other forms of government rests on the generalization that competition is better than monopoly in government. Facilitating competition carries the promise of greater satisfaction of citizens with government, whereas abandoning competition in favor of monopoly serves the interests of political cartels.

In markets, greater efficiency automatically results in more customers, but in politics better government does not automatically result in wider jurisdiction. To repeat an illustration, if German federalism outperforms French centralism, few French citizens become German citizens, nor does the border separating these nations automatically move west. Centuries of territorial warfare testify that politicians crave the power that comes from expanded jurisdiction. If this motive were harnessed for creation rather than destruction, people could benefit dramatically. To create pressures for improvement, good governments must automatically expand and bad governments must automatically shrink.

Under current conditions, some people and firms move to successful governments or opt to come under their laws. Competition among governments, however, stops far short of automatic flux in response to performance. Most democratic constitutions amplify competition among candidates and mute competition among governments. To illustrate, most democracies strictly regulate the entry of immigrants, and many nations have legal impediments to internal mobility, such as immobile pensions or housing benefits. Furthermore, many countries have no laws on how to create special governments or contract with them. Transferring powers from one government to another can violate constitutional provisions on sovereignty. Finally, many national courts resist enforcing the terms in a contract that designate a foreign court to resolve disputes.

State officials often enrich themselves at the expense of citizens and suffocate enterprise under a blanket of bureaucracy. Sometimes direct democracy can correct failures of indirect democracy. In unusual cases such as Switzerland

and California, the constitution facilitates ballot initiatives enabling citizens to hold a referendum. Ballot initiatives compete with governments to make laws. Most democratic constitutions, however, inhibit referenda by imposing costly procedures for ballot initiatives or making no provision for them.

Increasing political competition carries the hope of improving alignment between the interests of politicians and the preferences of citizens. With good organization, competition among governments can produce a race to quality and efficiency. Realizing that hope requires improving the legal framework for competition among governments. I will analyze that framework as applied to mobility, choice of private laws, public goods, and direct democracy.

MOBILITY

Different people have different preferences with respect to public goods. For example, one person may value parks more than safe streets, and another person may value safe streets more than parks. Since local public goods are supplied to everyone in a jurisdiction, efficiency requires clustering together people with similar preferences. The people who especially prefer parks should live in a locality that devotes its resources especially to parks, and the people who especially prefer safe streets should live in a locality that devotes its resources especially to safe streets. In other words, sorting diverse populations into groups with relatively homogeneous tastes can give each of them their preferred public goods. The optimal number of jurisdictions thus increases with population diversity (Alesina and Spolaore 1997).

Clusters and Tiebout

People with similar tastes voluntarily cluster together in order to enjoy their preferred combination of local public goods. Consequently, mobility contributes to efficiency in local public goods. To refine thinking about clustering, I will extend the concepts of equilibrium and efficiency to mobility. Define *location equilibrium* as a situation in which no one prefers to move from one jurisdiction to another. If relocating people cannot increase anyone's satisfaction without decreasing someone else's satisfaction, then the location equilibrium is Pareto efficient.

Scholars have extensively studied the question, "What conditions make a location equilibrium Pareto efficient?"[2] I reduce their answers to two unrealistic

---

[2] The first formulation of this problem is Tiebout 1956. A recent, more complete statement in Inman and Rubinfeld 1997 identifies these five necessary and sufficient conditions:

(T1)   Publicly provided goods and services are produced with a congestable technology
(T2)   There is a perfectly elastic supply of jurisdictions, each capable of replicating all attractive economic features of its competitors
(T3)   Mobility of households among jurisdictions is costless
(T4)   Households are fully informed about the fiscal attributes of each jurisdiction
(T5)   There are no interjurisdictional externalities

Also see Stiglitz 1982.

conditions, whose logical purity helps explain clustering. First, people must enjoy "free mobility," which means no legal or economic obstacles to moving. Legal obstacles include residence permits or exclusionary zoning, and economic obstacles include the cost of moving from one place to another. Second, jurisdictions must be sufficiently numerous to accommodate differences in taste among different types of people. To be precise, the highest order of efficiency requires as many jurisdictions as types of people. Given free mobility and many jurisdictions, people with similar tastes will voluntarily cluster together to obtain the highest order of efficiency in the supply of local public goods.

In reality, however, mobility is costly and jurisdictions are limited in number. Like transaction costs, mobility costs obstruct movements toward efficiency. Like uniformity in mass production, too few jurisdictions cause too much similarity in jurisdictions relative to differences in people. With costly mobility and few jurisdictions, people with similar tastes still cluster together to obtain more of their preferred combination of local public goods, but the result falls short of the highest order of efficiency.

The contribution of free mobility to the efficient supply of local public goods provides an economic justification for guaranteeing mobility as an individual right in a federal system. For example, the European Union guarantees the right of workers to compete for jobs throughout Europe. To implement this right, the European Union now tries to dismantle the economic obstacles to mobility, notably the incompatibility of housing, health, and pension benefits in different localities and nations. As obstacles diminish, the economic model predicts that people with similar preferences for local public goods will cluster together more in the future than they did in the past.

Notice that this prediction of clustering by tastes contradicts the conventional prediction that mobility homogenizes culture. To illustrate, the historical district in many cities attracts people who especially value culture, whereas many suburbs attract families who want to raise children in safety and convenience. Mobility can accentuate the difference between childless families in the historical district and families with children in the suburbs. Similarly, a university town draws together an international population united by their love for learning. Mobility can also facilitate the clustering of ethnic or religious groups who prefer proximity to each other.

Restrictions

Now I turn to the paradox that restraint can increase freedom. As explained, free mobility contributes to clustering and efficiency. Restrictions on freedom within jurisdictions, however, can increase choice among jurisdictions. To see why, consider architectural regulations. Restricting neighborhood architecture to a uniform style appeals to residents who like architectural purity. To be concrete, some residents of London prefer a neighborhood consisting purely of Georgian houses. Private mechanisms such as restrictive covenants usually fall short of producing uniform architecture. In practice, keeping buildings purely in one style requires the state to prohibit building in another style.

This proposition generalizes beyond architecture to other choices of local government. A community of people who cluster together in a neighborhood to perpetuate a culture may want to exclude other practices and people. To illustrate, when given the choice, some religious communities will forbid commerce on the Sabbath and require schools to display religious symbols, some family neighborhoods will prohibit the sale of pornography, and some ethnic groups will impose restrictions on using foreign languages. Given enough jurisdictions and free mobility, imposing restrictions on the activities of individuals in some jurisdictions does not harm anyone. People who prefer diversity will cluster in mixed neighborhoods that develop in unrestricted jurisdictions and people who prefer similarity will cluster in pure neighborhoods that develop in restricted jurisdictions. For example, permitting restrictions on where to buy pornography creates the option to live where it is *not* sold.

Some urban areas approximate the assumptions of free mobility and many jurisdictions. In most places, however, costly moving and scarce jurisdictions create a trade-off between uniformity and diversity. Local restrictions can produce some neighborhoods without Sabbath commerce, pornography, or signs in foreign languages, whereas the absence of local restrictions will often result in commerce on the Sabbath, the sale of pornography, and the mixing of languages.

Local restrictions bring nonconforming individuals into legal conflict with their neighbors. For example, a fashionable person tries to build a postmodern house in a Georgian neighborhood, an agnostic opens his store on the Sabbath, a magazine store sells pornography in a family neighborhood, or an Anglophone operates a school in Quebec. In these circumstances, the individual may allege that the local restrictions violate his individual rights, whereas the neighbors may claim that enforcing community values preserves the distinctiveness of neighborhoods.

Government must respond to this trade-off, especially when courts adjudicate individual rights. Central governments can require, forbid, or permit local governments to enforce community values. By *requiring* local governments to enforce community values, central governments induce many pure neighborhoods. By *forbidding* local governments to enforce community values, central governments induce many mixed neighborhoods. By *permitting* neighborhoods to enforce certain community values, central governments typically induce some mixed and some pure neighborhoods. Insofar as the social goal is diversity among neighborhoods, central governments should permit local governments to enforce community values. Insofar as the social goal is diversity within each neighborhood, central governments should forbid local governments to enforce community values.

Notice that the costs of mobility determine the severity of the trade-off between individual rights and community values. Local restrictions are not oppressive when nonconforming individuals can easily move to unrestricted communities. Low relocation costs are a reason to allow local communities to develop different interpretations of individual rights. Conversely, local restrictions are oppressive when costs preclude nonconforming individuals from moving. High relocation costs are a reason for imposing the same respect for individual rights on different local governments. The strength of the right to be different should depend partly on the cost of leaving a community. *In general, parochial rights fit mobile societies and universal rights fit immobile societies.*

If local governments have power over these decisions, how will they use it? In practice, particular institutions and facts of history determine the answer. A simple theory, however, provides a useful benchmark for analysis. Property owners often care intensely about property values. As a jurisdiction becomes more popular, people bid up the value of its land. Assume that residents induce local governments to adjust taxes and local public goods in order to maximize the value of land (Brueckner 1983; Scotchmer 1994). Under this assumption, local governments compete with each other to maximize land values.

To increase demand by mobile citizens, some jurisdictions will impose restrictions, such as requiring uniform architecture. These restrictions appeal to people who prefer similarity rather than diversity within a neighborhood. Other jurisdictions, however, will retain individual freedom, such as allowing mixed architecture, thus appealing to people who prefer diversity within a neighborhood. Local governments that maximize land values will adjust the mixture of restricted and free neighborhoods to respond to the preferences of citizens.

Exclusion

Do tastes for local public goods predict the actual way that people sort themselves into jurisdictions? Examples confirming the prediction easily come to mind. Connoisseurs cluster near restaurants, critics live near theaters, equestrians move to the green belt, religious enclaves try to exclude the world, and ethnic communities use local ordinances to sustain their traditions.

Besides clustering by taste, however, people also cluster by income. Neighborhoods often sort by class because the rich exclude the middle class and the middle class excludes the lower class. The logic of taxation partly explains why relatively rich people try to exclude relatively poor people. Everyone in a jurisdiction receives the same local public goods, but not everyone has the same ability to pay taxes. When local taxes finance local public goods, attracting people with high income enables the residents of a particular jurisdiction to enjoy a high level of local public goods with a low rate of taxation. Conversely, a concentration of poor people requires a high rate of taxation to finance a modest level of local public goods. If local taxation finances local public goods, relatively rich neighborhoods will seek legal devices to exclude relatively poor people.

Within countries where citizens can move freely, local governments especially rely on zoning to keep out poor people (Ellickson 1977; Fischel 1985).

Zoning controls the size of lots, the height of buildings, and the types of economic activities. To illustrate, exclusionary zoning in U.S. suburbs typically confines poor people to the cities, where the poorest people remain homeless and cause baffling social problems (Ellickson 1996). Reversing this pattern, historical preservation and other laws keep downtown Paris expensive and confine relatively poor Parisians to the suburbs.

Economics provide a theoretical basis for distinguishing restrictive zoning, which clusters people with similar tastes, and exclusionary zoning, which excludes relatively poor people. *Zoning is exclusionary if it keeps people out of a neighborhood who share the residents' tastes in local public goods but not their income.*

Some courts have taken dramatic measures to address inequalities caused by exclusionary zoning. For example, some state courts in the United States have required affluent suburbs to rezone in order to allow public housing for poor people.[3] In another example, California courts ordered the reorganization of school finance. Public schools in California were traditionally financed by local property taxes, which caused rich neighborhoods to spend more money on public schools than poor neighborhoods could. The courts required California to equalize school expenditures in different localities by replacing local property taxes with statewide taxes (Inman and Rubinfeld 1979). The result is more equality in public schools and more flight to private schools. Instead of clustering in localities with excellent public schools, Californians who want to spend more than the state average on educating their children increasingly turn to private schools.

Whereas exclusionary zoning keeps poor people out, social welfare programs draw them in. Given mobile poverty, a government with relatively generous welfare programs draws the poor from jurisdictions with relatively grudging welfare programs. Localities might respond to this fact by reducing welfare programs in order to discourage poor immigrants, thus producing a race to the bottom. A strong effect in this direction could justify the federal government's imposing a minimum welfare standard on local governments.

Alternatively, the concentration of poor people in a locality increases the block of voters who favor generous welfare programs. Poor migrants attracted to high welfare jurisdictions could tip the electoral balance in favor of still higher welfare payments, thus increasing the gap between high and low welfare jurisdictions. Proof that states "race apart" would presumably undermine the case for the federal government's imposing a minimum welfare standard on local governments. Given the controversial politics of welfare, empirical studies inevitably disagree about the extent to which high welfare jurisdictions attract poor migrants and the extent to which migration causes a race to the bottom or a race apart.[4]

---

[3] *Southern Burlington County NAACP v Township of Mt. Laurel*, 336 A 2d 713 (NJ 1975), 456 A 2d 390 (NJ 1983); *Mt. Laurel III: Hills Development Co. v Bernards*, 103 NJ1, 510 A 2d 621(1986).

[4] Brinig and Buckley 1997 find that high welfare states in the United States attract welfare migrants, and the presence of welfare migrants creates a political lobby that tends to increase

During the last decade, mobility of labor and capital has increased, while state welfare programs have retrenched or declined in many nations. Some proponents of redistribution despair for its future. Eighteenth-century legal scholar Blackstone said, "[M]ankind will not be reasoned out of the feelings of humanity."[5] Instead of giving up on redistribution, perhaps more mobility requires people to pursue income redistribution with less coercion. Instead of thinking in terms of a welfare state, perhaps people should think in terms of a welfare society.[6]

Immigration

Vast migrations of people through history created the different peoples of the world (Cavalli-Sforza 1995; Cavalli-Sforza and Cavalli-Sforza 1995). Over centuries, territories became nations and nations enacted laws to restrict the movements of foreigners. In recent years, falling transportation costs and large differences in wages between countries have intensified pressures for migration (Hollifield 1994). According to a recent survey, "There are about 100 million persons living and often working outside their countries of citizenship, making this 'nation of migrants' equivalent in size to the world's tenth most populous country."[7]

Relatively rich countries attempt to control immigration by imposing quotas of various kinds. For example, the U.S. quota system admits a relatively high proportion of poor, uneducated immigrants, who begin at the bottom of the socioeconomic scale and often work their way up. In contrast, Canada's point system restricts immigrants by wealth and education, so many immigrants enter Canada at the middle of the socioeconomic scale or higher (Buckley 1995). Unlike the United States and Canada, Japan allows almost no immigration.

Economic theory evaluates quotas for immigrants much as it evaluates quotas for goods (Chang 1996). Quotas on immigrants obstruct the exchange of labor, just as quotas on imports obstruct the exchange of goods. Conversely, free mobility of labor has the same advantages in terms of economic efficiency as free trade in goods. So economic efficiency requires free trade and free immigration.

Immigration, however, impacts many issues other than economic efficiency, such as distribution, culture, religion, and the environment. Passionate feelings

---

welfare payments. Their observations explain why differences in welfare payments across states have persisted or even increased with time. They see no case for imposing a federal minimum welfare standard and they see a possible case for a federal maximum welfare standard. Peterson and Rom 1990, however, find that poor migrants respond to economic opportunities created by expanding economies much more than they respond to welfare payments. They deny the existence of a welfare magnet.

[5] Blackstone 1765 [1992], p. 238.

[6] "[I]t may better to think in general terms of a Welfare Society rather than specifically of a Welfare State" (Casson 1991, p. 254).

[7] Martin 1994, p. 1.

of people on these issues guarantees the persistence of immigration quotas in relatively rich countries.

What are the consequences of immigration quotas? Just as restriction of trade creates a black market, the persistence of quotas creates illegal immigration. To understand this phenomenon, consider an economic parable that focuses narrowly on wages. High wages provide an incentive to migrate from one country to another. Migration away from the low-wage country bids up its wages, and immigration into the high-wage country bids down its wages, thus reducing the difference in wages between the two countries. As the cost of mobility approaches zero, the location equilibrium requires equal wages everywhere. In brief, wage differences between nations create a disequilibrium that migration corrects.

In this parable, "wages" should be interpreted as "relative net wages." Thus, *relatively* high wages attract illegal immigrants from Bangladesh to India, even though both countries suffer from low *absolute* wages. *Net wage* equals pay for work minus essential costs, such as the cost of housing and medical care. For illegal immigrants, essential costs include the costs of exclusion from social insurance, fear of arrest and deportation, and legal costs.

If quotas restrict legal immigration, then the "marginal" migrant who makes the location equilibrium is an illegal immigrant. To illustrate, the equilibrium model predicts that illegal immigration from Mexico to Los Angeles will continue so long as the net wage of an *illegal* factory worker in Los Angeles exceeds the net wage of a *legal* factory worker in Mexico. Equivalently, the model predicts that *illegal* immigration from Guatemala to Mexico will continue so long as the net wage of an *illegal* worker on a coffee plantation in Mexico exceeds the net wage of a *legal* worker on a coffee plantation in Guatemala.

According to this model, reducing differences in net wages reduces the amount of immigration required for equilibrium. For example, illegal immigration will slow if free trade causes wages to grow faster in the relatively poor country.[8] The model also predicts that illiberal or inhumane measures will retard illegal immigration, such as denying illegal aliens social services and the protection of law.

Questions

1. Explain the problem of clustering people of similar tastes when the types of people outnumber government jurisdictions.

2. How can restrictive zoning increase freedom?

3. Characterize the illegal migration equilibrium between Spain and Morocco.

4. In the United States, each state government can decide whether or not to provide the poor with "stamps" redeemable for food at grocery stores. A state that decides to have such a program, however, cannot exclude striking workers from receiving the stamps. Excluding striking workers is an "unconstitutional

---

[8] For a review of data on wage conversion between rich and poor countries, see Bardhan 1996.

condition" for such programs.[9] How does the doctrine of unconstitutional conditions affect the location equilibrium?

CHOICE OF PRIVATE LAWS

Having discussed the movement of people to jurisdictions, now I discuss the movement of jurisdictions to people. The place where goods are made, sold, or used determines jurisdiction over most disputes in private law. Sometimes, however, people can choose the jurisdiction to resolve a dispute. For example, if buyer and seller reside in different countries, their contract may specify which jurisdiction controls disputes. Similarly, many contracts stipulate the resolution of disputes through arbitration, thus replacing public courts with private courts. Finally, firms exert some control over jurisdiction of their disputes by choosing where to incorporate. I will discuss the mechanisms and conditions under which the choice of jurisdiction enables people to obtain the laws that they prefer.

Bargained Contracts

When is contracting for jurisdiction efficient? A full answer requires a theory of contract, which I cannot develop here.[10] A brief answer uses the Coase Theorem, which reduces strategic behavior to transaction costs.

Information enables people to perceive their interests accurately, and bargaining enables people to advance their perceived interests. A contract, consequently, tends to advance the interests of the parties as fully as possible when they bargain together and they are informed. In general, bargained contracts between informed parties tend toward pair-wise Pareto efficiency. Absent "third-party effects," which fall on noncontracting parties, bargained contracts between informed parties are socially efficient.

This proposition extends to contract terms stipulating how to resolve disputes or designating the court or arbitrator with jurisdiction over the dispute. *Absent third-party effects, bargaining between informed parties results in socially efficient terms stipulating jurisdiction over disputes.* To illustrate, if a bargained contract between informed parties stipulates adjudication according to Japanese law, then applying Japanese law to such a contract creates value. Similarly, if a bargained contract between informed parties stipulates adjudication by the International Chamber of Commerce (ICC), then applying ICC law creates value.

Facilitating Contracts for Jurisdiction

The preceding principle gives a reason why law should facilitate contracts for jurisdiction. Facilitation has two aspects. First, courts must enforce the terms of

---

[9] *Lyng v International Union, UAW*, 485 US 360 (1988), as discussed in Epstein, Eskridge, and Frickey 1988.

[10] See Cooter and Ulen 1999, chapter 6 and 7.

contracts that stipulate jurisdiction. Uniform principles of enforceability increase the confidence of the parties in the effectiveness of contract terms stipulating jurisdiction. Second, courts must enforce judgments by other courts. If the defendant's assets are located in a different jurisdiction than the jurisdiction stipulated for deciding disputes, then the dispute must be tried in one jurisdiction and enforced in another. A domestic court must enforce the judgment of a foreign court. Enforcing the judgment of a foreign court requires an international agreement or a practice of mutual recognition between courts.

To illustrate by arbitration clauses, many countries have enacted the United Nations Commission on International Trade Law (UNCITRAL) model law of international arbitration, which narrowly specifies the legal grounds for challenging contract terms stipulating the resolution of disputes by arbitration.[11] Similarly, most nations have joined the New York Convention of 1958 requiring national courts to enforce arbitration clauses in international contracts. Domestic courts often enforce foreign arbitral judgments more readily than foreign court judgments. This legal framework has created a vigorous competition among arbitration courts, especially in Paris, London, and New York.

Harmonizing Law

Competition causes more successful jurisdictions to innovate and less successful jurisdictions to emulate. To illustrate, the trust, which is unknown in civil law, developed into a flexible instrument for investing and transferring wealth in Britain. This fact gave London an advantage over Paris in competing for funds in the 1980s. France responded by adapting instruments of the civil law to resemble the trust more closely (Hansmann and Mattei 1994). In this example, innovation differentiated common law from civil law, and emulation harmonized civil law with common law. *When competition drives legal evolution, innovation differentiates and emulation harmonizes.*

In principle, competing jurisdictions can supply optimal innovation and harmonization in contract law, just as competing firms can supply optimal innovation and uniformity in the design of automobiles and computers. In practice, many obstacles impede competition among jurisdictions. Model laws and restatements can speed up the process of innovation and diffusion by focusing the best legal minds on concrete problems and publicizing superior rules.

Unlike model rules or restatements, harmonization by treaty, convention, or federal law typically binds governments to uniform laws. I refer to such agreements as "obligatory harmonization." Obligatory harmonization diminishes jurisdictional competition and reduces the scope of bargaining over jurisdiction between the parties to a contract. Do the gains from standardization exceed the losses from blunting competition among jurisdictions? When treaty, convention, or federal law binds several governments, innovation must proceed by agreement

---

[11] Article 34 of the UNCITRAL model law of international arbitration specifies six conditions under which a court can set aside an award of an arbitral tribunal (United Nations Commission on International Trade Law 1985).

among all of them. Revisions to treaties, conventions, or federal laws often lag behind changes in economy and society. I believe that jurisdictional competition is typically more efficient for contract law than is obligatory harmonization.[12]

Voluntary Transactions and Relationships

I have explained that informed parties who bargain for jurisdiction can create competition among jurisdictions to supply efficient contract laws. Can competition among jurisdictions succeed when the parties to contracts remain uninformed or do not bargain over the terms that stipulate jurisdiction? Furthermore, can competition among jurisdictions succeed when the affected parties do not have a contract? I can only sketch an answer.

Standard form contracts, which offer a package of terms without possibility of modification ("take-it-or-leave-it"), preclude bargaining. Even so, these contracts do not necessarily indicate market failure or inefficiency (Koetz 1997). Instead, standard forms can lower transaction costs. Sellers compete by offering different contracts and different prices, not by bargaining over the terms in contracts. In these circumstances, standard forms facilitate competition, not indicate its absence.

Similarly, the purchaser of stock cannot ordinarily bargain with the issuer over jurisdiction for disputes, but competition among jurisdictions can increase the efficiency of corporate law. The states in the United States compete vigorously to supply corporate charters, with Delaware being the most successful. Some evidence indicates that competition among states contributes to improvements in corporate charters.[13] Furthermore, legal protection influences the extent of stock financing by corporations in different countries (La Porta, Lopez-de-Silanes, and Shleifer 1997). Proposals exist to extend jurisdictional competition to securities laws.[14]

I have explained that jurisdictional competition can sometimes work without bargains. In addition, jurisdictional competition can sometimes work with little information. To illustrate, a buyer who knows little about computers often takes price as a signal for quality. Price accurately signals quality in markets so long as informed buyers make the market. Similarly, contracts for jurisdiction

[12] See Koetz 1996, who cautions against harmonization of European private law, including contracts, at least in the immediate future. Note that European directives that overlap national law can create complexity by adding new regulations without repealing old statutes. To illustrate using an example from Koetz 1997, the scope, process, and substance of the British Unfair Contract Terms Act of 1977 differ from the European Union's directive on Unfair Terms in Consumer Contracts. To achieve consistency, the British need to repeal the 1977 act and replace it with a new statute. Instead of following this difficult and time-consuming process, the British government responded to the directive by adopting new regulations and leaving the 1977 act in place. The resulting combination of new regulations and old statute complicates and confuses contract law.

[13] Romano 1987. See Bebchuk 1992 for an account of some limits of competition among jurisdictions in increasing the efficiency of corporate law.

[14] Choi 1998 would allow issuers of securities to choose a regulatory regime and jurisdiction. Thus U.S. issuers could choose German securities law and German courts, or German courts could choose U.S. securities law and U.S. courts.

might work with many ignorant parties, provided that informed parties make the market. In general, competition for contracts with asymmetrical information can produce a variety of results, some efficient and some inefficient.[15]

Now I consider third-party effects. In general, the advantages of jurisdictional competition do not extend to third-party effects. For example, assume that a borrower approaching bankruptcy promises to repay a new loan before compensating the victims of a past accident. The lender and the borrower are the first and second parties, and the accident victims are third parties. The loan agreement benefits the first and second parties at the expense of the third parties. Such a contract can be pair-wise Pareto efficient, but it is typically socially inefficient.

Visionary mechanisms could sweep third parties into contracts and extend jurisdictional competition in novel directions (Cooter 1989). I will describe briefly an example from the law of accidents. A right is *contingent* if it matures when an uncertain event occurs. To illustrate, tort rights are contingent on an accident occurring. A contingent right offered for sale in a market is a *contingent commodity*. To illustrate, a call option is a right to buy stock if the market price reaches the price stipulated in the contract. The mechanisms for extending contracts into accident law treat tort rights as contingent commodities. The basic idea is to buy and sell rights to recover damages before accidents occur, much like buying and selling options before the market reaches the strike price. In principle, competitive markets for liability rights can solve some perplexing problems that baffle tort reform, such as combining optimal insurance for victims and efficient deterrence of injurers.[16]

Contracts for unmatured tort claims could stipulate the jurisdiction to adjudicate disputes. By this means, jurisdictions would compete over these novel contracts just as jurisdictions currently compete over conventional contracts.

These possibilities, however, are visionary. So long as courts prohibit the sale of liability rights, markets cannot form. Besides these visionary mechanisms, social norms assigning responsibility for harm might evolve toward efficiency. If common-law courts enforce such norms, or if civil-law courts use such norms to interpret statutes, the law made by judges can evolve toward efficiency (see discussion in chapter 8). Whether competition among jurisdictions would enhance or retard the evolution of social norms toward efficiency remains unanalyzed by scholars.

---

[15] An early, influential paper on the topic is Schwartz and Wilde 1979. Recent papers include Emons 1996 and Emons 1998 or 1999.

[16] Many potential accident victims have adequate private insurance to cover their losses. With the insurance market providing compensation, the remaining task for liability law is to deter accidents efficiently. One way to deter accidents efficiently is to extract the full value of the harm from the injurer at low transaction costs. Think of the injurer who pays a court judgment as acquiring the victim's liability right. The transaction costs of transferring liability rights are much higher in courts than in markets. To get the right to recover damages out of court, allow the potential victim to sell the right at any time, including before an accident occurs. A description of how a market for unmatured tort rights might improve the efficiency of accident law is found in Cooter 1989.

COMPETITION TO SUPPLY PUBLIC GOODS

Now I turn from jurisdictional competition over private law to jurisdictional competition over public goods. Competition in supplying local public goods requires people to move to more efficient jurisdictions or more efficient jurisdictions to move to people. Having discussed mobile people, I now discuss mobile jurisdictions.

The Fifth Freedom

States often supply goods like education that have the basic characteristics of private goods. Competition in the supply of these goods merely requires some adjustments in the law. For example, with appropriate revision in the law, a citizen of France who resides in Alsace might attend a school across the border in Germany and pay using a voucher. This example concerns competition among states that produce goods. In addition to producing goods, states buy private inputs for public goods, such as rifles used by the military to defend the country. Designing new ways for the state to produce less and buy more is a frontier of privatization.[17]

Unlike prices for private goods, however, taxes for public goods are compulsory. Years of research by economists have not produced a workable mechanism to overcome free-riding on the supply of most public goods.[18] Since no way exists to replace compulsory taxes with voluntary prices, the supply of truly public goods must rest on collective choice, not individual choice. In a democracy, collective choice usually means voting.

In principle, a community could vote to contract with a government to supply a local public good. For example, the members of a small community could entertain bids from several larger governments or special districts to supply water or collect garbage. Almost everyone agrees that democratic states should provide citizens with a right of free mobility, thus allowing people to move to more efficient jurisdictions. In time almost everyone may agree that democratic states should provide local governments with a right of free contract with other governments, thus allowing jurisdictions to move to people.

Bruno Frey and Reiner Eichenberger propose that the European Union guarantee its citizens the right to replace all-purpose inclusive governments with governments formed for specific functions.[19] This "fifth freedom" would ideally give European citizens choice over governments, not merely choice over candidates. Citizens and localities could choose from a menu of special governments,

---

[17] See Libecap 1989. George Stigler allegedly said that identifying a market failure and recommending government intervention is like awarding the prize in a music competition to the second contestant after listening to the first contestant. The second contestant may prove worse than the first, and state intervention may prove worse than the market failure.

[18] The old problem of "preference revelation" in public finance developed into the new problem of "mechanisms design" in mathematical economics. The basic problem is to avoid free-riding in paying for public goods. For some attempted solutions, see Wilson 1987 and Emons 1994.

[19] Frey and Eichenberger 1995 and Frey 1996). Also see Breton 1996.

each offering to provide public goods and collect taxes. This proposal would implement the strand in contractarian philosophy that advocates actual contracts for government, as opposed to hypothetical contracts (Simmons 1997).

In my earlier discussion of mobility, I explained that mobile people cluster together for efficiency and distribution. Similarly, laws regulating the formation of special districts must consider the politics of redistribution as well as the economics of efficiency. To illustrate, if rich people can separate themselves from poor people by forming a special district for public schools, the rich can lower their taxes and increase their expenditures per pupil on schools. Given the right legal framework, however, competition among special governments can increase the efficiency of public goods, not create enclaves for the rich.

Secession

In a democracy, individuals typically have the right to leave a jurisdiction, but groups seldom have the right to secede. Many constitutions make no provisions for secession, just as many marriages make no provisions for divorce. Sometimes secession occurs peacefully, as illustrated by Estonia and Czechoslovakia. Sometimes secession provokes bloody civil wars as in Bangladesh, Nigeria, and the United States. Uncertainty about the right of secession and the absence of accepted procedures presumably contributes to civil wars of secession. Conversely, stipulating procedures can provoke a group to threaten secession in order to gain an advantage in bargaining over distribution.[20]

Unfortunately, systematic writing by social scientists about secession is rare (A. Buchanan 1991; Bolton and Roland 1997). I will briefly consider the economic logic of secession and its implications for constitutions. Among the many reasons for secession, efficiency and distribution are two on which economic theory focuses. I consider each in turn.

The cost of government often increases with diversity among citizens. To illustrate, empirical research shows that successful cooperatives reduce the transaction costs of making collective decisions by keeping membership homogeneous (Hansmann 1990; Hansmann 1998). When citizens perceive themselves as too different, they may prefer to separate and lower the cost of governance, as illustrated by the division of Czechoslovakia into a Czech nation and a Slovak nation. Reducing the transaction costs of shared governance can motivate secession, although the zealots who lead secessionist movements use more colorful language.[21] Given mutual agreement to secede, constitutional provision for an orderly process can reduce costly uncertainties.

Sometimes, however, majoritarian politics enables a majority to exploit the minority. In these circumstances, secession concerns ending exploitation, not lowering transaction costs. Instead of mutual agreement, the majority may resist

---

[20] From this fact, some theorists conclude that secession is a moral right but not a legal right (Sunstein 1991).

[21] Even economists would not go to the barricades under the banner, "Zero transaction costs or death!"

the minority's attempts to secede. In these circumstances, constitutional provisions for secession strengthen the position of the exploited minority.

A secessionist group may also want to lay claim to national wealth. A compelling example comes from the Independent Nation of Papua New Guinea, where the small island of Bougainville contains one of the world's richest copper and gold mines. If Bougainville's attempted secession succeeds, a small group of islanders will divide the wealth that once supplied 44 percent of Papua New Guinea's exports (Young 1997). In these circumstances, constitutional provisions for secession strengthen the position of the minority wanting to expropriate national wealth.

Transition costs of secession depend on entanglement of assets and intermingling of populations. When populations and assets are relatively separate as in the former Czechoslovakia, transition costs of secession are modest. Conversely, when populations get mixed together, separating them for purposes of secession can have tragic and inhumane consequences, as in the former Yugoslavia.

I discussed lowering transaction costs, ending majority exploitation, and expropriating wealth as economic motives for secession, which must be weighed against the transition costs. In reality, however, economic motives typically mix with atavistic nationalism. No easy solution exists for hostile passions. In a future world, however, competition among governments might raise problems of secession for economic reasons, as when a town secedes from a county. In anticipation of these cases, Frey and Eichenberger propose that special governments created in the future should contain explicit provisions on the general principles for dividing assets, possibly including a price paid for exit. Such a constitutional provision resembles a prenuptial agreement on the terms of a possible divorce. Declaring in advance general principles for dividing assets can avoid secession by reducing the incentive for the dominant group to exploit the subordinate group, or for one group to secede as a means of expropriating national wealth.

Questions

1. Explain the conditions under which efficiency requires enforcing contract terms that stipulate jurisdiction.

2. Discuss the case for standardizing civil procedure internationally.

3. Kaiser Permanente, a large corporation that sells comprehensive health care services to Americans, requires consumers to submit all disputes over medical malpractice to compulsory arbitration. Discuss whether public courts should recognize and enforce the contract term containing this requirement.

4. Discuss whether the seller of a consumer good should be able to choose German liability law for a product sold in Italy.

5. How does the technical character of public goods create an obstacle to allowing individuals to choose governments?

6. Discuss how competition among jurisdictions affects the following:

workplace safety

automobile safety standards (design or performance)

standard weights and measurements

licensing lawyers

chartering corporations

DIRECT AND INDIRECT DEMOCRACY

Most democracies hold direct votes by citizens from time to time on major issues, such as whether Quebec should secede from Canada or whether Denmark should join the European currency union. In most countries, legal obstacles assure that referenda are rare. For example, Italian voters can organize an "abrogative referendum" (a referendum to repeal a statute), but not a "positive referendum" (a referendum to create a statute).

A few governments, however, routinely decide many issues by direct vote of the citizens. The Swiss hold direct votes on such issues as whether to increase the salaries of officials or whether to retain compulsory military service for adult males. In addition, most important legislation in Switzerland must survive a yes-or-no vote by the citizens to become law. Californians hold direct votes on everything of interest to them, from constructing prisons to affirmative action. Direct voting has created some of California's most important laws, such as "Proposition Thirteen," which capped property taxes and sparked a nationwide "revolt of the tax payers" in the 1970s (Wildermuth 1998). Over half of the state constitutions in the United States provide for some form of ballot initiative, and other states seem to be following California in using this process more frequently (Verhovek 1998).

In addition to the legal obstacles, costs limit the frequency of referenda. Gathering signatures from citizens is expensive and exhausting, and holding an election is costly for the state. In the future, however, technological developments such as electronic voting and collection of signatures over the Internet could dramatically lower the transactions cost of direct democracy. With costs falling, direct democracy could become a new frontier of decentralization. In this section I analyze the consequences of direct democracy, especially drawing on the experience of Switzerland and California.

Procedures and Effects

Procedures for direct democracy differ by place and issue. To illustrate, the collection of 50,000 signatures in Switzerland creates a referendum on any law enacted by the federal legislature. In a referendum, the legislation is accepted or rejected by a simple majority of votes. In contrast, the collection of 100,000 signatures in Switzerland creates a referendum to amend the federal constitution. To succeed, the referendum must win a majority of the votes in the nation and also a majority of votes in a majority of the cantons (Frey and Bohnet 1994).

Like Switzerland, California requires the accumulation of signatures to bring issues directly to the voters, but the organization of the process differs dramatically. In California, direct democracy is a big business. To illustrate the scope of activity, the seventeen initiatives on the ballot in 1996 lured $141.3 million in contributions, which exceeded the total of $105.7 million spent by several hundred candidates who ran for the California legislature that year (Howe 1998).[22] California referenda resemble commercial products with a development cycle.[23]

Many observers wonder whether the state should facilitate or impede direct democracy. To answer this question, I first ask whether direct democracy produces different results from indirect democracy. In Switzerland, the results in 39 percent of recent referenda contradict the outcome that representative government would have produced.[24] Tax rates are lower in Swiss jurisdictions where citizens directly decide on public goods (Pommerehne 1990). In referenda Swiss citizens seem to prefer lower taxes and lower government salaries than legislators prefer. Referenda undermine the exclusive power of elected officials to set the political agenda.[25]

Most important, as Frey argues, direct democracy in Switzerland increases the morale of citizens and improves their intrinsic motivation to support government. The process of direct democracy is relatively transparent. Each side must appeal directly to the citizens, who understand more fully why the political process yields one result rather than another. The morale of citizens apparently improves because they feel informed and empowered. To support this argument, Frey offers evidence that direct democracy in Switzerland makes citizens more willing to pay taxes and inform themselves about politics.[26]

Commentators sometimes assume that referenda slant outcomes toward the right or the left. However, a survey of California ballot initiatives does not indicate any bias in favor of liberal or conservative causes (Verhovek 1998). Instead favoring the left or the right, California ballot initiatives are all over the political spectrum. In California, ballot initiatives cost their supporters more than lobbying the legislature. Californians apparently pursue the more costly

---

[22] Note, however, that this comparison is potentially misleading. In direct democracy, all the money is spent on issues. In contrast, political expenditures in indirect democracy include money spent on electoral campaigns plus money spent on lobbying activities.

[23] See Howe 1998 and Wildermuth 1998.

[24] "[I]n 39 percent of the 250 obligatory and optional referenda held in Switzerland between 1948 and 1990, the will of the majority of the voters differed from the opinion of Parliament"(Frey and Bohnet 1994 p. 153).

[25] "Popular referenda have proven to be very successful in Switzerland for fighting restraints on competition in the political market .... Referenda and initiatives are means to break the politicians' coalition against the voters .... they take the agenda-setting monopoly away from the politicians and enable outsiders to propose issues for democratic decision, including those that many elected officials might have preferred to exclude from the agenda" (Frey and Bohnet 1994 p. 151.

[26] Frey 1997a; Frey 1997b, and Kirchgassner and Frey 1990 as cited in Voigt 1997b.

alternative because they believe that ballot initiatives mostly create laws that the legislature would not enact. In the next section I explain why referenda and legislation yield different laws.

Factoring by Referenda, Splicing by Legislation

Most constitutions restrict referenda and initiatives to a yes-or-no vote on a single issue.[27] To illustrate, Californians might be asked to vote "yes or no" on restricting abortions and "yes or no" on capital punishment, but the law precludes Californians from being asked to vote "yes or no" on restricting-abortion-and-restricting-capital-punishment.

A practical reason compels restricting each ballot initiative to a single issue. Logrolling, which combines issues in a single vote, requires bargaining. Bargaining among different groups requires representation. Ballot initiatives bypass elected representatives. Thus a multiple-purpose ballot initiative invites bargaining without bargaining agents. With agents, bargaining among many people inevitably fails.

In legislatures the members often bargain, compromise, and draft a single bill that combines different issues. In contrast, rules restricting ballot initiatives to a single issue prevent logrolling, so different groups have little incentive to bargain or vote strategically. When citizens vote their preferences on a single dimension of choice, the median usually prevails. In general, *direct democracy factors the issues, so the median voter should prevail*. In contrast, members of legislatures bargain, compromise, and roll logs. If bargaining fails, legislatures must try to avoid an unstable redistributive contest by undemocratic means such as agenda control. In general, *indirect democracy splices issues, which should result in bargains or cycles*.

The contrast between splicing and factoring predicts some consequences of a shift from indirect to direct democracy. A change from indirect to direct democracy often replaces bargains among representatives with the preference of the median voter on each dimension of choice. Is this change better or worse? That depends on how well indirect democracy works. Given informed voters and competitive elections, indirect democracy produces effective representation of political interests. If representatives bargain successfully and cooperate with each other, then citizens get their way on their preferred issues. In these circumstances, indirect democracy satisfies the preferences of voters better than direct democracy.

Indirect democracy, however, can create a political cartel whose members conspire to blunt electoral competition. For example, the spectacular disclosure of corruption among leading Italian politicians in the 1990s suggests that citizens had little influence over deals struck by their representatives. An opaque political process and proportional representation made Italian electoral competition relatively ineffective. In these circumstances, a change to direct democracy can break the political cartel. In addition, indirect democracy can cause an unstable

[27] See California Constitution, art. 2 sec. 8d.

contest of redistribution among interest groups. Changing to direct democracy can increase stability, which should increase the satisfaction of citizens with politics.

I have explained that direct democracy causes the median voter to prevail on each dimension of choice, which is better than a cycle or a political cartel and worse than perfect bargaining by elected representatives. This proposition summarizes the main difference in theory between direct and indirect democracy. Besides this large difference, some small differences are sometimes important.

First, direct democracy gives more weight to those citizens who actually vote, whereas indirect democracy gives more weight to the number of citizens living in a district. To illustrate, assume that poor people, who vote at relatively low rates, live in poor districts. Indirect democracy apportions representatives by population, so the number of representatives from poor districts reflects the number of poor citizens, including those who do not vote. In contrast, direct democracy responds to the citizens who actually vote. Thus, in the preceding example where rich people vote at higher rates than poor people do, direct democracy gives more weight to the opinions of rich people. This phenomenon tilts California ballot initiatives in favor of older, conservative, white citizens.

Second, critics of direct democracy allege that the majority of citizens will vote to redistribute wealth from the few to the many. For example, if most citizens buy auto insurance, they will vote to cap its price. Or if most citizens rent houses, they will vote for rent control. More generally, critics of direct democracy allege that the majority of citizens will vote to undermine the rights of the minority.

This criticism, however, has a weak foundation in theory. From the viewpoint of theory, direct democracy factors voting, which does not necessarily harm minorities more than spliced voting. Spliced voting encourages citizens to coalesce into blocks to bargain with each other. A system of proportional representation can guarantee representation in political bargaining to every minority group. Two-party competition, however, contains no such guarantees. When groups coalesce, some minorities may suffer permanent exclusion from the ruling coalition.

In contrast, after factoring the issues, the minority on one dimension of choice is seldom the same group of people as the minority on another dimension of choice. Any single person with complicated political views wins on some dimensions of choice and loses on others. In general, factoring issues can dissolve large blocks of citizens and ensure that everyone wins some of the time. In addition, all the nonmedian voters participate in determining the median voter. Thus, everyone's preferences have an effect on the voter equilibrium. Under these conditions, majorities do not exploit minorities more under direct democracy than they do under indirect democracy.

Any democratic system of politics, whether direct or indirect, requires protection of minorities, such as ethnic groups and wealthy people. Later I discuss various forms of protection, such as bicameralism and constitutional rights. For now, note that Bill of Rights in the U.S. Constitution constrains the states, so a federal judge would nullify a California referendum that violates the U.S. Bill of Rights. This fact imposes an essential constraint on California's referenda.

Notice that the comparison of direct and indirect democracy parallels the comparison between single-purpose and multipurpose governments in chapter 5. In indirect democracy the constitution can prescribe separate governments for separate purposes, or the constitution can prescribe multipurpose governments. Similarly, in direct democracy the constitution can limit each popular referendum to a single purpose, or the constitution can permit multipurpose referenda. Narrowing the scope of each government or election creates obstacles to bargaining across issues by political factions, so the median rule determines the outcome.

Bonding Ballot Initiatives

In addition to the legal obstacles, transaction costs currently limit the frequency of referenda. Specifically, the cost of gathering signatures currently limits the number of referenda placed on the ballot. In the future, however, technological developments such as collection of signatures over the Internet and electronic voting could dramatically lower the transactions cost of direct democracy. With lower costs, the pace of referenda could accelerate, thus forcing citizens to vote on a barrage of hopeless proposals and to decide close votes over and over again.

Is there a better means to ration referenda than collecting signatures? Bonding offers an attractive alternative. According to this approach, supporters could place a proposition on the ballot by posting money bond with the electoral commission. If the proposition performed well in the election, the bond would be returned. Conversely, if the proposition performed poorly in the election, the state would confiscate the bond. For example, in lieu of 100,000 signatures, supporters of an initiative might post $100,000, which they would forfeit unless the initiative won, say, at least 45 percent of the votes.

Compared to collecting signatures, bonding reduces the transaction costs of direct democracy. Compared to cheap collection of signatures over the Internet, bonding discourages frivolous or previously defeated initiatives. By bonding ballot initiatives, constitutional law could reduce the velocity of direct democracy without stopping it or imposing unnecessary costs. Note that some countries, notably New Zealand and the United Kingdom, already require candidates for Parliament to post bond, which they forfeit for poor performance in elections.

Also note that people accused of crimes in the United States must post bail to escape jail while awaiting trial. The person who appears for trial recovers the bail, whereas the person who fails to appear for trial forfeits the bail. In reality, most people borrow money for bail from a professional bail bondsman, who charges a rate based on his assessment of the risk. Similarly, with ballot initiatives a market should develop allowing supporters to borrow the bond.

Lenders would charge low rates for promising ballot initiatives that carry low risk and high rates for unpromising initiatives that carry high risk.

CONCLUSION

Why do democratic governments so often fail to satisfy the political preferences of citizens? Incomplete political competition partly explains the shortfall. Democratic constitutions organize competition among candidates for office and blunt competition among governments for jurisdiction over people and money. In this chapter I analyzed the legal framework for mobility, choice of private laws, contracting for public goods, and direct democracy.

Mobility promotes efficiency by clustering people with similar preferences for local public goods. Contracting for jurisdiction promotes efficiency by allowing people to choose the best jurisdiction to resolve future disputes. Visionary schemes might some day extend competition among jurisdictions to encompass liability for accidents and the supply of local public goods. Ballot initiatives allow citizens to substitute median rule for failed legislative bargains. In general, improving the legal framework for political competition carries the promise of greater satisfaction of citizens with government.

Ministries and Agencies

The decisive reason for the advance of bureaucratic organization has always been its purely technical superiority over any other form of organization. The fully developed bureaucratic mechanism compares with other organizations exactly as does the machine with the non-mechanical modes of production.

—*Max Weber*[1]

We [state officials] are humble subordinates who can scarcely find our way through a legal document and have nothing to do with your case except to stand guard over you for ten hours a day and draw our pay for it.

—The Trial *by Franz Kafka*[2]

THE POWER of state bureaucracy awes us when we peer over the sheer wall of an enormous dam or look up at a battleship bristling with sailors. As the preceding quotation indicates, the German sociologist Max Weber believed that modern state administration embodies instrumental rationality, defined as the pursuit of explicit ends through efficient means. Governments, however, also construct unneeded dams to enrich cement manufacturers and dispatch battleships to perform tasks requiring a rowboat. Focusing on these facts, another famous writer in German, Franz Kafka, described state bureaucracy as a labyrinth where condemned citizens wander without hope of escape. Kafka apparently believed that government bureaucracy embodies irrationality, defined as the pursuit of contradictory ends by inefficient means.

A democratic state should try to organize its bureaucracies to pursue explicit ends by efficient means, as envisioned by Weber. Motivating and controlling bureaucracy raises fundamental questions of law, which must be solved to avoid the irrationality envisioned by Kafka. This chapter develops a framework to analyze the interplay of politics and administration. I will analyze political

---

[1] Weber 1974, p. 214. Weber described how a perfect bureaucracy operates: "Precision, speed, unambiguity, knowledge of the files, continuity, discretion, unity, strict subordination, reduction of friction and of material and personal costs—these are raised to the optimum point in the strictly bureaucratic administration . . . . Bureaucratization offers above all the optimum possibility for carrying through the principle of specializing administrative functions according to purely objective considerations."

[2] Kafka 1956, p. 9–10.

and judicial oversight of administrators. Here are some examples of questions addressed in this chapter:

Example 1: Assume the constitution separates the executive and the legislature. Do administrators in the state bureaucracy have more discretionary power when they are subject to review by the executive, the legislature, or both?

Example 2: A court or similar outside body imposes a tedious process on state administrators who wish to engage in environmentally sensitive activities. Administrators respond by reducing these activities. Will ministries or agencies with broad powers reduce these activities more or less than ministries or agencies with narrow powers?

Example 3: The constitution of a certain country empowers the president to appoint the supervisor of banks with confirmation by the legislature. Before the appointee's five-year term of office expires, the president wants to remove the supervisor of banks. The courts must decide whether the constitution allows the president to remove the supervisor of banks unilaterally, or whether removal requires the consent of the legislature. How will the court's decision affect the discretionary power of the supervisor of banks?

Example 4: The ministry of aviation, which regulates airline schedules, is financed from general tax revenues. If financing from a tax on aviation fuel replaces financing from general tax revenues, how will the ministry's behavior change?

GENERAL FEATURES OF STATE ADMINISTRATION

The legislature, judiciary, and executive make decisions whose implementation in a modern state depends on an array of ministries, departments, and agencies. Each of these organizations has its own history and character. To illustrate using the United States, the Department of State is old and the Environmental Protection Agency is new, the Department of Defense is large and the Federal Reserve Board is small, the Comptroller of the Currency deals with banks and the Occupational Health and Safety Administration deals with employers. In addition to differences, however, all of these organizations share some common characteristics by virtue of being government bureaucracies. I will mention four common characteristics that form the basis for the models in this chapter.

First, politicians fund, oversee, and appoint the leadership of most government bureaucracies. For example, the U.S. president appoints and removes the secretary of agriculture, and the Department of Agriculture receives most of its funds from appropriations by Congress. Politicians can usually influence a ministry or state agency by appointing or removing its leaders, adjusting its budget, reviewing its performance, and imposing rules upon its behavior. Political control at the top forces bureaucracies to respond to politics. In exceptional cases, however, the law insulates a state organization from political influence. To illustrate, the U.S. central bank (Federal Reserve Bank) finances itself from profits, not congressional appropriations, and the president appoints the members of its governing board to fourteen-year terms of office. Organizations like the central bank are exceptions proving the rule that elected officials directly control most ministries or state agencies in a democracy.

Second, in state administration, an official's income and power increase with the size of the administrative unit under his control. Promotions come quickly to administrators when their organization grows, and promotions come slowly to administrators when their organization shrinks. Thus, administrators typically value size and growth of their organization. Given discretionary power, civil servants press to expand administration. An amusing example from the 1920s charts the steady increase in employees of the British admiralty simultaneously with the steady decrease in British naval ships.[3]

Third, hierarchical organizations adopt rules for making decisions. As modeled in chapter 4, rules reduce the ability of lower-level officials to divert resources from the purposes imposed by higher-level officials. Without rules, the bureaucracy spins out of control and diverts public resources for its own benefit. However, rules also reduce the flexibility of officials in responding to change. With excessive rules, the inflexibility of state administrators stifles the citizens.

Fourth, many government organizations regulate the private economy, which responds by influencing the regulators. Regulator and regulatee relate to each other intimately and strategically. The regulatees' interest in the behavior of the regulator is focused, whereas the general public's interest is diffuse. Consequently, the regulatees usually enjoy disproportionate influence with the regulator. In the extreme case, the regulatees capture the regulator and use the state to extract monopoly profits or subsidies (Elhauge 1991; Stigler 1975).

The common characteristics of state administration are political control from above, pressures to expand from within, pressures from organized interests outside, and the need to follow rules. These common characteristics suggest the possibility of a general theory of state administration, as opposed to particular theories based on the unique history of each organization. In chapter 4, the delegation game and the rule game analyzed how each link in the chain of authority dilutes purposes imposed from the top. In this chapter, I build on dilution effects to predict the response of state bureaucracies to law.

ADMINISTRATION AS BUREAUCRACY

State agencies typically use tax revenues to supply a service or produce public goods. To depict these facts, the horizontal axis in figure 7-1 indicates the size

---

[3] See the chart titled "Admiralty Statistics" on p. 8 of Parkinson 1957. The capital ships in commission declined from 62 in 1914 to 20 in 1928, while dockyard officials and clerks increased by 40 percent and admiralty officials increased by 78. One version of "Parkinson's Law" asserts that the size of a bureaucracy varies inversely with amount of work that it has to do.

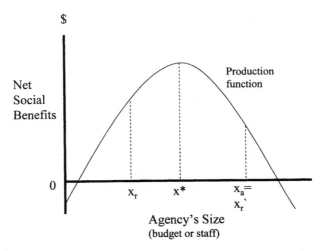

Fig. 7-1 Agency Size

of the ministry or agency as measured by budget or staff. As the organization grows, it supplies more public goods at higher total costs. The vertical axis indicates the benefits to society, or net social benefits, which equal the value of the public goods minus the cost of supplying them. Starting from the origin in figure 7-1, net social benefits increase as the ministry or agency expands. Net social benefits reach their maximum when the agency's size equals x*, which is the agency's most efficient size. Beyond x*, further expansion of the organization costs more than the value of the additional public goods, so net social benefits decrease as the organization's size increases.

Many informed citizens will presumably prefer the ministry or agency's size to equal x*, which maximizes net social benefits. If administrators, interest groups, and politicians pursued the public interest as defined by the efficient allocation of resources, they would also aim for a ministry or agency of size x*. In fact, each group has its own distinct interests, which I will sketch.

As a state organization expands, administrators in it gain more responsibilities and more pay. Administrators thus typically favor expansion beyond the size required for allocative efficiency. The *engorgement principle* is the hypothesis that administrators in a ministry or agency strive to maximize its size as measured by budget and staff (Niskanen 1971). In terms of figure 7-1, state administrators want to go as far to the right on the horizontal axis as possible, say to point x_a.[4]

While administrators seek to expand each state bureaucracy, interest groups may pursue other ends. For example, many ministries or agencies provide valuable services to industries and also impose burdensome regulations. A regulated industry prefers a state regulator whose size maximizes the industry's profits. As

---

[4] I implicitly assume that constraints bind as the agency expands, so that x_a is a finite number.

the state bureaucracy grows in size, valuable services and burdensome regulations increase at different rates. The rate at which each increases determines the size of the state bureaucracy that maximizes the industry's profits. Figure 7-1 depicts a typical result in which the regulatee prefers a smaller regulator, say the point x_r, rather than the social optimum x^*.

Figure 7-1 depicts the interests of regulators and administrators, as well as the social optimum. As depicted, the administrators prefer a large organization x_a and the regulatees prefer a small organization x_r. Whereas regulatees and administrators have a concentrated interest in a particular ministry or agency, most citizens have a diffuse interest. Consequently, regulatees and administrators typically organize better than citizens. Better organization results in better information and more influence. Since many citizens remain unorganized and rationally ignorant, the persuasive power of regulatees and administrators disproportionately influences electoral competition. Sometimes results follow the median rule, which can yield the cost-benefit optimum as explained in chapter 2, and sometimes regulatees or administrators alter the outcome. If electoral competition favors the regulatees over the administrators in figure 7-1, then the winning politicians will prefer a small ministry or agency.[5] Conversely, if electoral competition favors the administrators over the regulatee, then the winning politicians will prefer a large agency.

As explained, the point x_r in figure 7-1 depicts regulatees who want to shrink their regulator. In many situations, however, the regulatees capture the regulator and use the state to extract monopoly profits or subsidies (Elhauge 1991; Stigler 1975). To illustrate, many airlines apparently prefer for the state aviation agency to choke entry and enforce high fares. Similarly, many farmers prefer large agricultural subsidies and many retirees prefer large social security benefits. In these circumstances, the regulatees and other beneficiaries may favor a large agency, as indicated by x_r' in figure 7-1. Under these conditions, the combined influence of regulatees and regulators creates strong pressure for a large state bureaucracy.

According to this sketch of a behavioral theory of ministries or agencies, the interests of the administrators and regulatees typically conflict with the interests of the general public. In the next section I will explain how agencies react when politicians and judges try to control them.

Question: Assume that politicians determine the size of state agencies, and assume that politicians respond more to state administrators and regulatees than to the general public. Describe the configuration of interests of these groups that will result in a larger state agency than required for allocative efficiency. Next, describe the configuration of interests that will result in a smaller state agency than efficiency requires.

---

[5] Assuming effective electoral competition, indifference curves for politicians in figure 7-1 would be isoquants for votes.

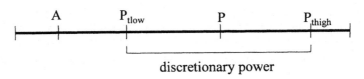

discretionary power

Fig. 7-2 Ministry or Agency Power and Transaction Costs

MONITORING MINISTRIES AND AGENCIES

The constitution and other fundamental laws allocate the powers to oversee the state bureaucracy. To illustrate, in a typical presidential system, the executive can issue orders to civil servants, the legislature can hold hearings and adjust appropriations of ministries or agencies, and the courts can adjudicate complaints against administrators. I will analyze how the separation of powers affects discretionary power in administration. My analysis introduces a spatial model of discretionary power that reappears in chapter 9.[6]

Unilateral Oversight

I begin by formalizing the idea that a civil servant's discretionary power ends where an act triggers effective oversight. The policy choices of a civil servant typically trigger oversight by departing too far from the preferences of a politician or judge. Figure 7-2 depicts a single dimension of choice for public policy. The dimension of choice could be any policy represented by a variable, such as expenditure on a particular program or the ideological location of a policy from right to left.

I assume that an administrator directly controls the variable in figure 7-2, and a politician or judge has the power to oversee the administrator. Consequently, I call the administrator the "agent" and the overseer the "principal." Point A represents the agent's most preferred value for the variable. If unconstrained, the agent would choose point A. The preferences of the principal, however, constrain the agent. Point P represents the most preferred value of the principal. The principal's dissatisfaction with the agent's policy increases with the distance between P and the agent's choice. I assume that by exercising oversight, the principal can force the agent to choose point P. Exercising oversight, however, imposes transaction costs t upon the principal. Consequently, the principal will not exercise oversight unless the resulting reduction in dissatisfaction exceeds the transaction costs t.

To characterize this behavior mathematically, let P_t indicate the point where the principal's dissatisfaction with the agent equals the transaction costs of oversight. P_{tlow} denotes the lower value of P_t, and P_{thigh} indicates the upper value of P_t. Any choice of a point *inside* the set $[P_{tlow}, P_{thigh}]$ will *not* trigger oversight. Conversely, any choice of a point *outside* the set $[P_{tlow}, P_{thigh}]$ *will* trigger oversight.

[6] For a recent contribution to the spatial model of agency discretion, see Spitzer 1990.

The agent's discretionary power in figure 7-2 equals the set of points that do not trigger oversight: $[P_{tlow}, P_{thigh}]$. A rational agent will choose the point closest to his most preferred point, subject to the constraint of not triggering oversight. To illustrate, a rational agent will choose point P_{tlow}, which is the closest value to A inside $[P_{tlow}, P_{thigh}]$.

Requiring the agent to follow rules and not make individualized decisions often lowers the transaction cost of oversight by the principal. As depicted in figure 7-2, lowering the transaction costs of oversight reduces the agent's discretionary power by decreasing the distance between P_{thigh} and P_{tlow}. (Recall the rule game in chapter 4 where imposing rules reduces the agent's discretionary power.) Rules pervade bureaucracies in order to lower monitoring costs and reduce the diversion of resources. To illustrate, the Swiss usually apply a formula for dividing federal resources among the nation's three major language groups. Federal administrators who depart from this conventional rule risk scrutiny and reprimand.[7] The formula lowers the transaction cost of monitoring administrators by narrowing the class of cases receiving scrutiny.

When rules give rights to individuals, the agent who breaks the rules causes the victim to appeal for redress. By appealing for redress, victims alert the principal to the fact that the agent has broken the rules. So principals promulgate rules in order to obtain the information needed to control agents. Monitoring by responding to complaints has been described as "putting out fires."

To illustrate, assume that an administrator must follow a prescribed process for deciding whether to grant or deny a permit. If the administrator violates the process and denies a permit to someone, the victim may appeal to a court or administrative tribunal. In conducting its inquiry, the court or administrative tribunal will inform the administrator's superior about the allegations against the administrator. Conversely, if, instead of a rule, an administrator has discretion to vary the process when deciding on an application for a permit, then the applicant who is denied a permit may have no grounds for appeal. Without an appeal, the court or administrative tribunal will not alert the administrator's superior about the administrator's behavior.

High political officials, such as legislators and ministers, require feedback from constituents concerning the performance of administrators.[8] Discovering better means to alert political officials about the actions of administrators lowers the transaction costs of oversight and reduces the discretionary power of the state bureaucracy.

Administrative Procedures Act

According to figure 7-2, reducing the transaction costs of oversight increases control over administrators. To reduce the transaction costs of oversight, many

[7] The conventional formula gives 10/15 of resources to German speakers, 3/15 to French speakers, and 2/15 to Italian speakers.

[8] "Our results indicate that lobbying can help reduce information asymmetries between Congress and the bureaucracy, and that the mere threat of sounding a 'fire alarm' can result in policy concessions for interest groups" (Epstein and O'Halloran 1995).

nations have laws imposing uniform procedures on administrators.[9] The prescribed procedures often differ depending on the issue to be decided. One kind of procedure is used to decide individual rights, as when issuing or denying a building permit. Another kind of procedure is used to promulgate regulations for a class of people, as when making a safety standard for constructing buildings. The law often holds administrators to a higher standard of legality when deciding individual rights than when making regulations. As a result, an administrative procedure to decide individual rights often resembles a court proceeding, whereas making a regulation often resembles legislation.

To illustrate, every U.S. agency must follow the decision-making procedures prescribed in the Administrative Procedures Act, except when specific legislation stipulates alternate procedures. Courts have interpreted this law to require quasi-judicial procedures ("formal procedures") for deciding individual rights and quasi-legislative procedures ("informal procedures") for making regulations. Quasi-judicial procedures involve a hearing, the right to give evidence, and a decision based on the record of the proceedings. For example, if a firm applies for a permit, the administrators typically must have a hearing to decide whether to grant the permit and must decide based on the record of the hearing. If administrators refuse the application for a permit and the applicant appeals, a review of the process will consider whether the record of the hearing justifies the administrator's decision.

In contrast, quasi-legislative decisions must follow a less burdensome procedure involving a proposal by the administrators, publishing the proposal, inviting comments, considering the comments, and announcing the decision. After following the prescribed procedures to obtain information, the administrators can use their own discretion in making a decision. Promulgating a new regulatory standard does not require a hearing and a decision on the record of the hearing. If someone challenges the legality of the new regulatory standard, the tribunal will not demand that the administrators produce a written record of the information forming the basis of the decision.

U.S. federal courts decide whether to classify decisions by agencies as quasi-judicial or quasi-legislative under the Administrative Procedures Act. Classifying a decision as quasi-judicial creates strong rights in individuals to appeal an agency's decision to the courts. Conversely, classifying a decision as quasi-legislative gives more discretionary power to the agency.

To illustrate from an actual case,[10] assume that the nuclear agency grants an operating permit to a particular power plant without considering the environmental consequences of reprocessing spent nuclear fuel from this plant. The nuclear agency decrees that the environmental impact of reprocessing spent nuclear fuel is a general problem of all nuclear power plants. Consequently, an application to operate a particular nuclear power plant need not address the issue of reprocessing spent nuclear fuel from this particular plant.

[9] A comparison between uniform administration in the United States and more diverse procedures in Germany is in Rose-Ackerman 1994.

[10] *Vermont Yankee Nuclear Power Corp. v Natural Resources Defense Council*, 435 US 519, 985 SCt 1197, 55 LEd2d 460 (1978).

When an environmental organization sues the nuclear agency for violating the Administrative Procedures Act, the court could deem the decision to omit spent fuel from the environmental impact statement as quasi-judicial or quasi-legislative. If courts deem the decision quasi-judicial, the nuclear agency must follow a relatively burdensome procedure each time it issues an operating permit. The quasi-judicial procedure includes the right of the environmental organization to present testimony at a hearing and the obligation of the agency to reach a decision based on the record of the hearing. Affected parties who disagree with the agency's decision in a particular case can easily find a legal issue over which to sue. Alternatively, if courts deem the decision quasi-legislative, the nuclear agency can follow a less burdensome procedure and create a regulation applicable to every case. Affected parties who disagree with the agency's decision in a particular case cannot so easily find a justiciable issue.

To interpret this example using figure 7-2, identify the "principal" P with a powerful political figure who wants to control the nuclear agency, such as the president or the chairman of a congressional committee. If courts classify the nuclear agency's decision as quasi-judicial, groups that disagree with the nuclear agency, such as aggrieved environmentalists, will tend to sue. The suit will alert the president or the committee chairman that the nuclear agency has run afoul of a political constituency. The president or the committee chairman may respond by pressuring the nuclear agency to change its behavior. Thus, feedback from the lawsuit lowers the transaction costs of oversight for the principal, which reduces the discretionary power of the agent.

If the preferences P of the president or committee chairman diverge from the preferences A of the nuclear agency, the principal will distrust the agent and thus welcome court monitoring of the agent. Conversely, if the preferences P of the president or committee chairman converge with the preferences A of the nuclear agency, the principal will trust the agent and thus want the court to give discretionary power to the agent. (Recall the delegation game in chapter 4, according to which delegating discretionary power to the agent saves scarce time for the principal.)

"Sovereign immunity" once referred to the doctrine that the English king could not be sued in his own court. American law absorbed this principle as an aspect of the separation of powers. To keep the executive and judiciary separate, it is said, no one can sue the government in its own court. If, however, administrators cannot be sued, then the executive is deprived of information about the behavior of administrators that court proceedings would disclose. Enforcing sovereign immunity eliminates a tool for disciplining administrators.

To illustrate this doctrine, exposure to radiation during atmospheric tests of atomic bombs between 1946 and 1963 caused disease or death to some American soldiers and civilians. Statutes and judicial decisions on sovereign immunity protect the U.S. government from resulting suits.[11] However, civilian contractors who supplied equipment for the tests or helped conduct them were not shielded from legal liability until passage of the "Warner Amendment," a rider

[11] For protection against suits from soldiers, see *Feres v United States*, 340 US 135 (1950). For protection against suits by civilians, see Federal Tort Claims Act, 28 U.S.C.A. 2680(a).

to a defense appropriation bill enacted in 1984. This statute allows the U.S. government to be substituted as a defendant for private contractors in suits arising out of atomic weapons testing. After substitution, the government asserts its sovereign immunity. Two federal circuit courts have upheld the Warner Amendment's constitutionality and the Supreme Court refused to hear the appeals.[12] Apparently the government and private contractors are sometimes shielded from the consequences of their negligent practices with regard to radiation.[13]

The threat of liability deters everyone—individuals, businesses, and the state—from exposing people to danger. The doctrine of sovereign immunity thus deprives citizens of an essential mechanism for disciplining the state. Perhaps that is why U.S. courts have deeply eroded the doctrine of sovereign immunity in recent years by allowing more suits against the government.

Questions

1. Assume that transaction costs of oversight increase in figure 7-2. Describe the resulting change in $[P_{tlow}, P_{thigh}]$. Explain how the resulting change in behavior by administrators depends on whether A is inside or outside $[P_{tlow}, P_{thigh}]$.

2. Assume that the chief executive appoints the minister of housing, who directs the civil servants in the ministry of housing. Why might the chief executive and the minister of housing want citizens to have the right to appeal decisions by the ministry of housing to a tribunal?

Multiple Principals

Figure 7-2 depicts a single principal with powers of oversight. Sometimes, however, multiple principals have powers of oversight over a single event. This situation is called the common agency problem. To illustrate, when the constitution separates powers, more than one branch of government may have the power to oversee administrators in the state bureaucracy. The consequences for the agent differ depending on whether the principals exercise oversight unilaterally or cooperatively.

By *unilateral* I mean that a principal can exercise the particular power of oversight on its own. For example, the executive and legislative may have unilateral power to investigate an agency's behavior. By *cooperative* I mean that one principal cannot exercise oversight without agreement by the other principal or principals. For example, effective discipline of administrators may require the legislature to hold hearings resulting in findings and the executive to respond to the findings by issuing orders to the administrators. Or the executive may remove an official from office and nominate a successor and the legislature may

[12] Atmospheric Testing Litig., 820 F2d 982 (Ath Cir. 1987); *Hammong v United States*, 786 F2d 8 (1st Cir. 1986).

[13] Fletcher 1990.

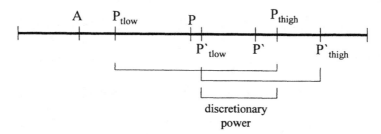

Fig. 7-3 Unilateral Oversight by Two Principals

have to confirm the nomination. Or the executive may issue a new order to the agency and the court may have to review the order's legality.

I will extend figure 7-2 to represent unilateral and cooperative oversight, respectively. In figure 7-2, the principal will not review the agent unless the resulting reduction in the principal's dissatisfaction exceeds the transaction cost of the review. Adding an additional principal with power of unilateral oversight increases the probability that a given behavior by the agency will trigger review by one of the principals. Figure 7-3 depicts these facts by adding a second principal to figure 7-2. $P^{\backprime}$ denotes the most preferred point of the second principal, and the set $[P^{\backprime}_{tlow}, P^{\backprime}_{thigh}]$ denotes the range of points that will *not* trigger review by the second principal. With power of unilateral review by two principals, the agent's discretionary power in figure 7-3 equals the intersection of the set of points that will not trigger review by the first or second principal:

$$\text{agent's discretionary power} = [P_{tlow}, P_{thigh}] \cap [P^{\backprime}_{tlow}, P^{\backprime}_{thigh}]$$

$$= [P^{\backprime}_{tlow}, P_{thigh}].$$

Rather than choosing P_{tlow} as in figure 7-2, the rational agent in figure 7-3 will choose $P^{\backprime}_{tlow}$. In general, adding another principal with unilateral oversight usually decreases, and cannot increase, the agent's discretionary power.[14]

I have shown that adding a second principal with unilateral power of review *de*creases the agent's discretion. Next I show that adding another principal with *cooperative* oversight *in*creases the agent's discretionary power. With cooperative oversight, each principal can veto oversight by another principal. To be specific, assume that reviewing and changing an administrative decision requires the cooperation of the executive and legislature. Figure 7-4 depicts the most preferred point of the executive, E, and legislature L, on a dimension in policy space. Starting from the left side of figure 7-4, the executive and the legislature prefer moving to the right. Once the point E is reached, however, the executive opposes and the legislature favors moving further to the right.

Similarly, starting from the right side, the executive and the legislature prefer moving to the left. Once the point L is reached, however, the legislature

---

[14] In principle, the intersection $[P_{tlow}, P_{thigh}] \cap [P^{\backprime}_{tlow}, P^{\backprime}_{thigh}]$ could be empty, in which case the agent is paralyzed unless the principals cooperate and bargain to an agreement.

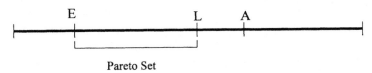

Fig. 7-4 Agency's Discretionary Power

opposes and the executive favors moving further to the left. Thus the set of points between E and L, denoted [E,L], defines the Pareto set relative to the preferences of the executive and legislature.

If the agent chooses its policy from any point outside the Pareto set, the executive or the legislature both prefer some point inside the Pareto set. They are, consequently, prepared to cooperate in reviewing the agent and directing a change in its policy. Whether E and L actually review A depends on transaction costs. If transaction costs of review are zero, E and L will cooperate in conducting a review whenever the agent chooses a point outside of [E,L]. If transactions costs of review are positive, E and L will cooperate in conducting a review whenever the agent chooses a point far enough outside of [E,L] such that the benefit to the executive and legislature from a change exceeds their transaction costs from conducting the review.

Conversely, if the agent chooses its policy anywhere inside the Pareto set, the executive or the legislature will block any attempt to change the policy by not cooperating in conducting the review. This is true even when the transaction costs of review equal zero. Assuming review is costless, the set [E,L] defines the agent's discretionary power. To illustrate by figure 7-4, the agent most prefers point A, and L is the closest point in the Pareto set to A, so the rational agent that faces costless review chooses point L. By choosing point L, the agent guarantees that the legislature will veto any attempt by the executive to review the agent. Assuming oversight is costless, the agent's discretionary power equals the Pareto set for the principals who can veto oversight. In general, adding another principal to those who must cooperate in order to review the agent usually increases, and cannot decrease, the agent's discretionary power.

Notice that in figure 7-2, where I assume unilateral oversight, the discretionary power of the agent shrinks and disappears as the cost of oversight by the principal falls toward zero. In other words, transaction costs of oversight create the discretionary power of administrators. The situation is different in figure 7-4, where I assume cooperative oversight. As the cost of oversight by the principals falls toward zero in figure 7-4, the discretionary power of the agent approaches the Pareto set for the principals. In other words, disagreement among principals creates the discretionary power of administrators.

Questions

1. Assume the executive appoints and removes ministers. Consequently, the executive can review the ministry. Assume that courts initially refuse to review

the legality of a certain class of actions by the ministry, and, subsequently, the courts change and assert this power. In other words, the courts initially defer to the executive and subsequently stop deferring. Do the new facts constitute "unilateral" or "cooperative" review as defined above? Predict how the change in the court's behavior will affect the discretionary power of the minister.

2. The comptroller general of the United States, who runs the General Accounting Office, is appointed by the president. The courts determined that the president can remove the comptroller general without the consent of Congress. Adapt figure 7-4 to show how the comptroller general's discretionary power would increase if removal required the consent of Congress.

3. The U.S. president appoints some administrators and nominates others whom the Senate must confirm. Predict how the difference between appointment and nomination by the executive changes the discretionary power of the president. Also predict how the difference affects the behavior of an agency's directors.

INFLUENCING STATE AGENCIES

I will now consider some instruments that principals use to influence agencies. When the state supplies some kinds of public or private goods, many decisions must be made about individuals, such as determining coverage of a regulation or eligibility for a benefit. Such decisions can be made retail or wholesale. The retail procedure uses individualized decision making. The wholesale procedure promulgates a rule and applies it to everyone.

The two procedures differ with respect to transaction costs. The transaction costs of individualized decision making increase rapidly as the state supplies more of the good. In contrast, promulgating a general rule requires an initial expenditure, but once the rule is promulgated, the cost of applying it to additional decisions is relatively low.

Figure 7-5 depicts the difference in transaction costs between retail and wholesale decisions. The horizontal axis represents the quantity of the good supplied by a ministry or agency, and the vertical axis represents the ministry or agency's total transaction costs of supplying the good. The transaction cost of individualized decision making increases rapidly as the supply of goods increases, as indicated by the steep line labeled "individualized decisions." The wholesale procedure requires promulgating a general rule, which requires an initial expenditure indicated by c. Once the rule is promulgated, however, the cost of applying it to additional decisions is relatively low, as indicated by the modest slope of the line labeled "general rules."

The intersection of the total cost curves, which occurs at $z^`$, is a tipping point. Individualized decision making is cheaper when supplying less than $z^`$ of the good, whereas promulgating a general rule is cheaper when supplying more than $z^`$ of the good. Thus, general rules are more efficient than individualized

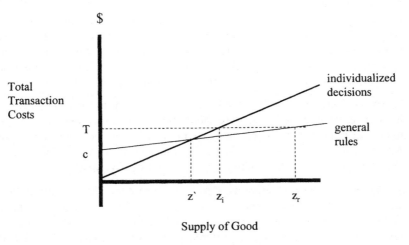

Fig. 7.5 Production Function

decisions for supplying large quantities of goods. For example, transaction costs T will produce z_r goods by general rules or z_i goods by individualized decision making.

To illustrate the contrast in procedures, consider two examples modeled on actual U.S. legal cases.[15] Open land is scarce in urban areas, so new roads are sometimes built through parks. Decisions about locating new roads, which require comparing the value of transportation and parks, can be made retail or wholesale. Retail requires the transportation department to hold hearings and weigh all the factors that could influence the unique value of each parcel of parkland. Wholesale requires the transportation department to promulgate rules specifying the criteria to use when purchasing parkland for roads. Rules restrict the scope of issues for consideration. Once the transportation department promulgates rules, it must follow them instead of considering the unique value of each parcel of land.

Given these facts, the horizontal axis in figure 7-5 can be interpreted as miles of roads built through parks by the transportation department. When building few roads, the retail procedure that uses individualized decision making is cheaper. When building many roads, the wholesale procedure that uses rules saves transaction costs for the transportation department.

As a second example, consider the construction of nuclear power plants. Assume that the nuclear agency decides whether to license the operation of a nuclear power plant.[16] For this example, interpret the horizontal axis in figure 7-5 as the number of nuclear power plants licensed for operation by the nuclear

[15] This hypothetical is based on *Citizens to Preserve Overton Park, Inc. v Volpe*, 401 US 402, 91 SCt 814, 28 LEd2d, 136 (1971).

[16] This hypothetical is suggested by *Vermont Yankee Nuclear Power Corp. v Natural Resources Defense Council*.

agency. "Individualized decision making" means that before making a decision, the nuclear agency holds hearings or otherwise consults with the affected parties. At these hearings, the nuclear agency decides what to do in light of the particular features of each case. "General rules" means that the nuclear agency promulgates rules that specify the criterion to use in making these decisions, and then the nuclear agency restricts its deliberations to the criteria specified in the rules. When licensing few nuclear plants, the retail procedure that uses individualized decision making is cheaper. When licensing many nuclear plants, the wholesale procedure that uses rules saves transaction costs for the nuclear agency.

As a third example, I apply the retail-wholesale distinction to the decisions of courts. Recall the preceding discussion in which the court had to decide whether the licensing of nuclear power plants by the nuclear agency is "quasi-judicial" or "quasi-legislative." If courts classify the nuclear agency's decision as quasi-judicial, the court can decide these disputes case by case, which gives intensive control to the court. Conversely, if courts classify the nuclear agency's decision as quasi-legislative, the court can decide a case about the general rules followed by the nuclear agency. To illustrate concretely, interpret the horizontal axis in figure 7-5 as the number of suits heard by the court, and interpret the vertical axis as the court's costs in hearing suits. According to this interpretation of figure 7-5, if few nuclear plants must be licensed in the future, the court can decide case by case at low transaction costs. In these circumstances, the court obtains intensive control over the nuclear agency at low transaction costs. If, however, many nuclear plants must be licensed in the future, the court will pay high transaction costs for case-by-case adjudication. Instead, the court may prefer making a general rule, which sacrifices some of its control over the nuclear agency and lowers its transaction costs.

In general, if the court finds itself beyond z in figure 7-5, then it must trade off transaction costs and control over administrators. A rational court will make this trade-off by comparing its preferences and the preferences of administrators. If the court's preferences diverge from the administrators' preferences, the court will tend to favor the high level of control obtained through case-by-case decision making. Conversely, if the preferences of the court converge with the preferences of the administrators, the court will tend to favor saving transaction costs by making general rules.[17]

Questions

1. The ministry of forests must decide which state forests to license for harvesting and which to preserve. So far the ministry of forests has made such decisions case by case. Discuss when the ministry of forests will change its procedures, abandon case-by-case decisions, and make a general rule.

2. In licensing nuclear power plants, assume the court must decide whether the nuclear agency must follow a quasi-judicial procedure or a quasi-legislative

---

[17] I implicitly assume constant opportunity cost of the court's time. As the opportunity cost of the court's time increases, the court will tend to favor general rules over case-by-case decisions.

procedure with respect to the environmental impact of spent nuclear fuel. Also assume the executive who appoints the head of the nuclear agency is pro–nuclear power, whereas the court is anti–nuclear power. Describe how a rational court might make this decision.

How Procedures Affect Results

Politicians and courts often try to affect administrators by imposing procedures for making decisions. For example, the executive tries to reign in the environmental agency by imposing procedures for issuing logging permits, or a court tries to reduce police abuse by requiring policemen to record interrogations of prisoners. When will imposing burdensome procedures on administrators produce different results, instead of yielding the same results at higher cost?

To answer this question, I will apply the distinction between retail and wholesale decisions to agents. Assume that an agent produces z_r goods in figure 7-5 by applying a wholesale rule. The number of decisions made by the agency exceeds $z^`$, so the wholesale rule is cheaper than case-by-case decisions. Now assume that a principal, who might be a political official or a court, wants to reduce the agent's supply of this good. To do so, the principal requires the agent to switch from wholesale to retail decisions. The switch in procedure increases the agency's cost of supplying this public good.

Will the agent respond by decreasing its supply of this public good? For private firms, an increase in the cost of supply causes a reduction in the quantity supplied (supply curve shifts up). Applying price theory to the state reaches the same conclusion about ministries and agencies. If the democratic process works, politicians reward administrators for supplying goods, not wasting resources. An increase in the cost of supplying one good causes administrators to produce less of it and to produce more of another good.

The extent of the decrease usually depends on the administrators' ability to substitute another good in place of the one burdened by more costly procedures. When substitution is easy politically and technically, imposing a more costly procedure causes a *large* decrease in the supply of the good in question. To illustrate, if the agency is responsible for producing a large number of public goods that require similar technology, then the agency can easily shift resources from producing one good to another.

Conversely, when substitution is difficult politically or technically, imposing a more costly procedure causes a *small* decrease in the agency's supply of the public good in question. To illustrate, if the agency is responsible for producing a small number of public goods that require dissimilar technologies, then the agency has difficulty shifting resources from producing one good to another.

To illustrate concretely, contrast the effects of courts' imposing burdensome procedures on building roads through parks and licensing nuclear power plants. Requiring individualized hearings before building roads through parks will presumably cause the transportation department to build fewer roads through parks. Similarly, requiring the nuclear agency to conduct individualized hearings before licensing nuclear power plants will presumably cause the nuclear agency to license fewer nuclear plants. Although the effect goes in the same direction in both cases, its size presumably differs. The transportation department presumably builds a small fraction of its roads in parks so it can build roads elsewhere. Instead of resisting the court's decision, the transportation department will probably avoid burdensome procedures by locating new roads away from parks.

The nuclear agency, however, is situated differently. Assume that the nuclear agency has no jurisdiction over coal or hydroelectric power. If courts impose burdensome procedures on building nuclear power plants, the nuclear agency cannot shift its activities to supplying another good. To sustain its employment and appropriations, the nuclear agency needs to build or license *nuclear* power plants. Consequently, administrators in the nuclear agency will resist decreases in nuclear power plants. Under this assumption, imposing higher transaction costs on licensing nuclear power plants will increase the cost of nuclear power without causing the nuclear agency to shift resources to supplying another good.

Politicians and courts often try to influence administrators by imposing procedures for making decisions. Administrators respond to external controls by adjusting their product mix in order to protect their organization's employment and appropriations. Administrators accept external direction when doing so does not jeopardize the size of their organization, whereas administrators resist external directions that jeopardize future size and growth. In general, *politicians and courts that impose burdensome procedures to change outcomes will have the most effect on administrators who can easily substitute against the burdened good.* (The appendix to this chapter analyzes substitution effects more formally.)

These facts point to an advantage of large, broad, state bureaucracies. A large, broad organization produces many different products, so it can shift from producing one to another by an internal transfer of workers. Since substitution is relatively easy, it responds to external attempts to change its output. To illustrate, in Germany the administration for each state has broad responsibility to implement federal projects, so substitution is relatively easy between federal projects within the administration of a state. In contrast, a relatively small, narrow organization produces a few products, so shifting to another product may require laying off workers or transferring them to another organization. Since substitution is relatively difficult, a small, narrow organization resists external attempts to change its output. In the next section, however, I explain an offsetting advantage of a relatively narrow organization with few products.

STRATEGIC POLICY

The response of administrators to external controls depends in part on financing. General tax revenues typically finance ministries and state agencies, so these organizations have an incentive to lobby the legislature for higher appropriations.

Alternative financing can improve the organization's incentives. A better incentive system automatically provides more revenues to an organization that produces public goods more efficiently. To illustrate, with *user fees* the state organization collects more revenues by supplying more of the public good for people to use. To be concrete, a public swimming pool that finances itself from an entry fee will enjoy more revenue by making the pool more attractive to more people.

The same result can be achieved by financing from a tax on a private good that complements the public good. To illustrate, if gasoline taxes go to road construction, then the transportation ministry gains more revenues by building roads that drivers will use intensively, as required for efficiency, instead of building unneeded roads. Similarly, if a percentage tax on the value of the catch of fish finances the department of fisheries, then the department of fisheries has an incentive to adopt regulations that maximize the value of the catch in the long run. In general, financing the supply of a public good by a tax on its private complements will create an incentive for the state organization to maximize the supply of the public good.

In general, *incentives for state administrators improve by replacing general tax revenues with financing from user fees or a tax on a private good that complements the public good produced by the state organization.* The public sector needs more *incentive-compatible financing*, by which I mean financing that automatically rewards the efficient production of public goods.

Questions

1. In a presidential system, the legislature's committee structure often parallels the structure of the executive. To illustrate, the U.S. House Committee on Defense parallels the Department of Defense. Discuss some possible effects of parallel organization on the monitoring and behavior of administrative agencies.

2. Discuss ways to finance the Department of Commerce and the ministry of science by taxing private goods that complement the public goods supplied by these agencies.

SUMMARY AND CONCLUSION

Instead of being slaves that meticulously execute orders, ministries and state agencies exert independent influence in government. Administrators typically try to expand their organization beyond the size that maximizes net benefits to the public. Regulatees encourage or resist this expansion depending on whether they can control the ministry or state agency. Consequently, citizens, administrators, and regulatees disagree over the preferred size of state administration. In competitive democracy, politicians respond to the public, administrators, or regulatees depending on the strategy that maximizes votes.

Law and policy provide some means for controlling ministries and state agencies. Effective organization reduces the transaction costs of oversight, thus reducing the discretionary power of administrators. The discretionary power of administrators also shrinks when the constitution grants unilateral power of oversight to multiple principals, whereas the discretionary power of administrators expands when the constitution requires cooperation among multiple principals to exercise oversight.

Sometimes principals impose burdensome procedures on administrators engaging in activities disfavored by the principals. If the administrators can substitute a favored activity for the disfavored activity without jeopardizing appropriations, then increasing the transaction costs of one activity effectively diverts the agency's efforts to the other activity. Otherwise, the agency will continue engaging in the disfavored activity and absorb the additional transaction costs.

The behavior of ministries and state agencies forms part of the larger problem of the optimal number of governments. Elections ideally transmit the preferences of citizens to politicians, who translate preferences into programs implemented by ministries or agencies. To impede diversion and dilution by administrators, the fundamental laws can reduce the height and breadth of bureaucracy, which requires increasing the number of elections. Conversely, too many elections drain the reservoir of civic spirit that animates voters, leaving them uninformed and unmotivated. When too many elections alienate voters and make elected officials inconspicuous, the fundamental laws can reduce the number of elections by replacing governments with broader, deeper bureaucracies. In general, the constitution should splinter unmanageable bureaucracies by organizing more elections, and, conversely, the constitution should consolidate inconspicuous governments by increasing the depth of administration.

An Englishman allegedly kept a diary of the things he saw each day for use by scientists as "empirical evidence." Such a diary may interest historians, but it has little value for science. Scientific theories separate causes from background noise. Similarly, the stylized models in this chapter provide parables of administration to sort causes from background noise in the behavior of state agencies.[18] A better understanding of state agencies can help democracy make administration resemble Weber's instrumental rationality rather than Kafka's irrational malevolence.[19]

APPENDIX: PRICE EFFECTS AND THE
PREFERENCES OF ADMINISTRATORS

The appendix uses the theory of consumer demand to explain more precisely how administrators respond to the transaction costs of supplying a particular

[18] For examples of using alternative theories to test the textured, historical facts of government decisions, see Ackerman 1972 and Allison 1971.

[19] Specific reform proposals to improve administration in the United States are in Pildes and Sunstein 1995.

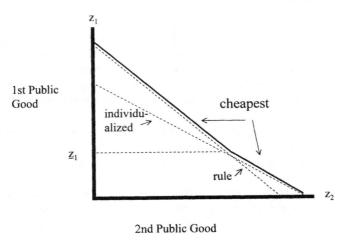

Fig. 7-6 Agency's Production Possibilities

public good. Assume that the state organization can supply public good z_1, which is depicted on the vertical axis in figure 7-6, or public good z_2, which is depicted on the horizontal axis. The lines in figure 7-6 represent combinations of the two goods that can be produced with given resources and procedures. At low levels of production of good z_1 that fall below $\underline{z}_1$, individualized decision making reduces the cost of producing z_1. At high levels of production of good z_1 that rise above $\underline{z}_1$, applying a rule reduces the cost of producing z_1. Unlike z_1, I assume for simplicity that applying a rule is always cheaper for supplying z_2. The line labeled "cheapest" uses the cheaper alternative between individualized decisions and rules for z_1 to produce a given combination of goods, while holding the agency's budget constant.

To be concrete, z_1 might indicate "roads built through parks" and z_2 might indicate "roads built outside parks." As depicted in figure 7-6, the requirement of individualized decision making for roads built through parks increases their relative cost when their quantity exceeds $\underline{z}_1$.

Alternatively, z_1 might indicate "licensed nuclear power stations" and z_2 might indicate "licensed nuclear reactors for medical research." As depicted in figure 7-6, the requirement of individualized decision making for licensing nuclear power stations increases their relative cost when their quantity exceeds $\underline{z}_1$.

If the principal requires the agency in figure 7-6 to adopt individualized decision making for z_1, the agency will presumably respond to the increase in cost by switching resources from production of z_1 to production of z_2. To depict the extent of the switch, I have added the agency's indifference curves in figure 7-7. These curves indicate the agency's preferences for supplying the two public goods. The agency maximizes utility by moving along the production possibility curve to the point of tangency with an indifference curve. If the agency

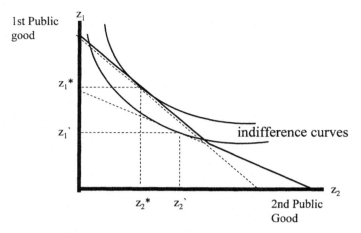

Fig. 7-7 Substitution and Agency's Preferences

can choose procedures freely, it maximizes utility by producing (z_1^*, z_2^*). If the agency must use individualized decision making for z_1, it maximizes utility by producing $(z_1^`, z_2^`)$. Notice that an increase in the cost of producing z_1 causes its quantity to fall to $z_1^`$, whereas the quantity of $z_2$ increases to $z_2^`$. Thus the agency substitutes production of z_2 for z_1.

The ease of substituting z_2 for z_1 depends on the agency's preferences, which determine the shape of the indifference curves. The agency presumably prefers a larger budget and staff. Some uses of funds win the approval of politicians, who will reward the agency with higher appropriations in the future. Thus the agency's preferences in figure 7-7 depend on its strategy for winning political approval.

Question: Modify the agency's utility curves in figure 7-7 to indicate the change when z_2 becomes harder to substitute for z_1.

PART THREE

Optimal Division of Powers

HAVING DISCUSSED the optimal number of governments in part 2, I now turn to the optimal organization of a government. The constitution organizes a government by distinguishing its branches and allocating powers among them. By convention, the executive, legislature, and courts form the branches of government. Chapter 8 analyzes the special competency of each branch of government, which I summarize. The executive branch forms a hierarchy whose members interact primarily through orders. In contrast, the legislature forms a house whose members interact primarily through bargains. The allocation of powers between executive and legislature determines the mixture of orders and bargains that animate the state. An independent judiciary guarantees the enforcement of bargains embedded in laws.

Without organization, legislative bargains often fail. Political parties organize the legislature and discipline legislators. Within a party, legislators interact relatively more by orders. Between parties, legislators interact relatively more by bargains. Government, consequently, proceeds in a state with few parties relatively more by orders, whereas government proceeds in a state with many parties relatively more by bargains. By giving more power to the executive and fostering large parties, a constitution favors government by orders. Conversely, by giving less power to the executive and fostering small parties, a constitution favors government by bargains.

The special competence of each branch, which I analyze in chapter 8, suggests the consequences of different ways to allocate powers among them, as analyzed in chapter 9, which I summarize. The executive implements legislation and provides leadership in making law, whereas the legislature provides a forum for bargaining among the nation's factions. Focusing on the transaction costs of bargaining answers many questions about the size and organization of the legislature. The optimal legislature minimizes the transaction costs of bargaining among the nation's factions. Bargaining is easier when agreements are enforceable. Independent courts enforce agreements by interpreting legislation in light of the underlying bargain. Focusing on the court's role in lubricating political bargains answers many questions about the theory of interpretation and the role of courts in making law.

In markets and politics, cartels destabilize as their size increases. By separating political powers, constitutions increase the size of the cartel required to monopolize state power. Thus, separating powers reduces the likelihood that a person or party gains political hegemony. Besides sustaining competition, the separation of powers channels their interaction. To explain interaction among separate powers, I identify and use repeatedly two different models of interaction among the branches of government.

First, one group of officials may have the exclusive power to initiate and revise bills, whereas another group of officials may have the power to enact the bills into legislation. The first group of officials, called the "gatekeepers," can make all-or-nothing offers to the second group of officials called the lawmakers. For example, the European Commission has exclusive power to initiate proposals to the Council of Ministers. The Council of Ministers must either enact the proposal or retain the status quo.[1] Similarly, under certain procedural rules, committees in the U.S. House of Representatives can propose a bill to the whole House, which the House can enact or defeat, but not revise. As another example, the Council of Legislation in Japan's ministry of law allegedly has exclusive power to propose changes in civil and business law. In general, when faced with an all-or-nothing choice, rational legislators will vote for any bill that they prefer to the status quo. Consequently, the gatekeepers have discretionary power to choose any proposal satisfying the constraint that lawmakers prefer it to the status quo.

Second, assume that a court or administrator has the power to interpret law. Also assume that undoing the interpretation requires fresh lawmaking. For example, undoing a court's interpretation of a statute often requires enacting new legislation, and undoing a civil servant's interpretation of a regulation often requires promulgating a new regulation. With the separation of powers, several lawmakers must agree in order to make a fresh law. To make agreement possible, each of the separate powers must prefer the fresh law to the old law. The interpreters of law such as judges and civil servants can exercise power for themselves by exploiting potential disagreements among lawmakers. In general, interpreters of law have the discretionary power to choose any interpretation such that no alternative exists that everyone prefers who must cooperate to make fresh law.

---

[1] I greatly simplify the actual bargaining that occurs between the Commission and Council. See chapter 9.

CHAPTER 8

Specialization

LIKE THE architect's blueprint for a building, a constitution describes the legal foundations of the state. Every constitution defines offices and allocates powers to them, and a good constitution allocates powers to the branch and level of government that exercises them the best. A conventional formula distinguishes among the legislative, executive, and judicial branches of government. By convention, law should be made by the legislature, enforced by the executive, and interpreted by the courts. Reality is much more complicated than this simple formula. Each of the three branches of government performs all three activities, although not to an equal extent.

In this chapter I describe the branches of government and the functions that they perform in economic terms. I will go beyond description by applying models of voting and bargaining to the branches of government. My analysis will explain the special competence and vulnerability of each branch of government. This chapter will answer such questions as these:

Example 1: Many legislatures have an upper chamber (the senate) and a lower chamber (the house). How does a second chamber protect the majority of citizens against lawmaking by a minority?

Example 2: In some countries, the citizens directly elect the executive (president), and in other countries the legislature elects the executive (prime minister). What difference does this make to legislative bargains? How does the separation of powers affect bargaining power in the legislature?

Example 3: Majority rule can cause cycling in legislatures. What about cycling in judicial panels? What problems does the possibility of cycling create for judicial interpretation of statutes?

RATIONALES AND SHORTCOMINGS OF CONVENTIONAL FORMULA

According to the conventional formula, law should be made by the legislature, enforced by the executive, and interpreted by the courts. This formula has a simple rationale. Electoral competition ideally aligns the goals of legislators and their constituents. The legislature provides a forum for bargaining among a society's political factions. Making laws requires bargaining and deliberation, which the legislature does best. To organize legislative bargaining, legislators form parties and submit to the executive's leadership. The executive brokers deals and implements agreements. Enforcing laws requires decisive action, and the executive, with its hierarchical organization, can act decisively. Interpreting laws accurately requires independence from politics and money, and the courts are ideally the most independent branch of government. In brief, the legislature provides the best forum for bargaining over laws, the executive can act decisively to implement law, and independent courts can interpret law.

These roles can be restated in more economic language. The legislature provides a forum for political bargaining with low transaction costs. Successful bargaining requires credible commitment to agreements. Commitments are more credible given low-cost implementation by the executive and neutral interpretation by the judiciary. Hierarchy in the executive lowers the cost of implementation, and independence of the judiciary increases the likelihood of neutral interpretation.

In reality, each of the three branches of government performs all three activities, although not to an equal extent. In every country the executive agencies make laws by creating regulations and interpreting them. For example, the U.S. president appoints the director of the Environmental Protection Agency, who creates, interprets, and enforces environmental regulations. Similarly, the legislature has some power to interpret and enforce statutes. For example, committees of the U.S. Congress hold hearings to investigate the behavior of officials. During these hearings, committees often interpret law for officials and enforce it upon them. Finally, courts in most countries have some power to make law and enforce it. A law is conventionally defined as an obligation backed by a state sanction. By this definition, judges make a new law whenever they interpret a statute and find that it imposes a new obligation upon people. Courts also enforce law by issuing injunctions and other coercive orders, such as garnishing the defendant's wages in order to repay a debt.

Besides being too simple, the conventional formula distorts a fundamental fact about the state. In chapter 1 I argued that democracy promotes efficiency by reducing the transaction costs of political bargaining. An unorganized legislature, however, cannot bargain successfully and enact needed legislation. Organization and leadership of the legislature comes especially from the executive. In parliamentary systems, the executive provides leadership and organization directly as a member of the legislature, while in presidential systems the executive provides leadership and organization indirectly to the legislature as leader of a large party. Unlike the simple formula, the strategic theory of democracy recognizes the executive's role in legislative bargains. I will use strategic theory to analyze each branch of government.

Legislature

Understanding legislative activity requires understanding legislative incentives. Competition quickly eliminates from office the few legislators who do not want to be reelected. Reelection is, consequently, the inevitable goal of most legislators.[1] How legislators get reelected depends on electoral rules and party organization, which vary from place to place. Elections can be at-large or by

---

[1] Mayhew 1974 and Fiorina 1977.

district,[2] and districts can be historical or equal in size.[3] Electoral districts can elect representatives by plurality rule, majority rule, or proportional representation. The party leadership can designate the party's nominee or the members of the party can vote for its nominee in a primary election.

Regardless of the electoral rules and party organization, however, candidates or their parties must appeal to voters in order to win. When voters are well informed, winning elections requires giving the voters what they want. To get what the voters want, legislators must bargain and strike deals. The legislature reduces the transaction costs of political bargaining by providing a forum for the representation of parties, factions, and interests. This is the legislature's special competence.

I will analyze how different ways of organizing a legislature affect its specia competence. My analysis encompasses the size of the legislature, party composition, electoral rules (plurality rule v. proportional representation), and bicameralism.

Transaction Costs and Legislature's Optimal Size

Suppose that a constitutional convention must decide the size of the legislature. The legislature could consist of every citizen, a single person, or any number in between. What is the best size? The interplay between representation and bargaining provides the answer. The constitutional convention must balance two considerations. First, legislation requires costly negotiation. (A colleague grumbled as he left a faculty meeting, "I can't think this slowly.") The cost of negotiating tends to fall as the number of negotiators falls. Taken to its logical limit, a legislature consisting of a single representative minimizes the transaction costs of negotiating to make legislation.

Second, a larger legislature has a higher ratio of representatives to citizens. As the ratio increases, the citizens are more likely to know their representatives, so citizens can demand better representation. As the ratio increases, the legislators are more likely to know their constituents, so legislators are able to represent citizens better. More information permits and requires legislators to represents citizens better. Taken to its logical limit, these facts imply that citizens receive the best representation from a legislature consisting of all the citizens, like New England town meetings. Aristotle wrote that the many do better than the few "just as a feast to which many contribute is better than a dinner provided out of a single purse."[4]

---

[2] To illustrate, until recently the city of Berkeley, California, had a council of nine members. At each election, three council seats were contested. Citizens throughout the city could vote for three candidates for the council. The electoral rules were recently changed. Now the city of Berkeley is divided into electoral districts, with each district electing one counselor.

[3] To illustrate, the U.S. states are divided into electoral districts with equal population for electing the House of Representatives, whereas each state elects two senators. Thus California, with more than thirty million inhabitants, has many more representatives and the same numbers of senators as North Dakota, which has fewer than one million inhabitants.

[4] "[T]he many, of whom each individual is but an ordinary person, when they meet together may very likely be better than the few good, if regarded not individually but collectively, just as a feast

Besides reducing errors in representation, a larger legislature makes fewer errors in making laws for two reasons. First, the "Law of Large Numbers" asserts that random errors tend to cancel each other as the sample size grows. This principle implies that under certain conditions, aggregation cancels the errors in factual judgments made by individual legislators. As the legislature increases in size, the probability diminishes that the majority will make a mistake in factual judgement.[5]

The application of this principal to government has several versions, notably by Condorcet.[6] When the probability of each legislator's making the right decision exceeds .5, adding an additional legislator decreases the probability of a mistake by the majority.[7] Another formulation emphasizes the median rule. Assume that each member of the legislature observes the facts with purely random error (normal distribution with a mean of zero). The expected error in the median voter's judgment falls as the size of the legislature increases. More generally, it can be shown that among all group decision rules on two alternatives (one of which is in fact correct), simple-majority rule is most likely to identify the correct outcome.[8]

Second, in addition to making errors in objective facts, legislatures make errors in representing the subjective values of citizens. Differences in subjective values, which economists describe as differences in preferences, create scope for political bargains. In a town meeting attended by all the citizens, each person can bargain for himself. In a representative assembly, however, each legislator must represent different citizens with different preferences. As the ratio of citizens to representatives increases, legislators make more mistakes in representing the preferences of citizens. These mistakes prevent legislatures from exhausting the gains from political bargains.

I have explained that a smaller legislature lowers the transaction costs of lawmaking, whereas a larger legislature makes fewer mistakes of fact and representation. A trade-off apparently exists between transaction costs and mistakes in legislation. If the only aim were minimizing transaction costs of making

---

to which many contribute is better than a dinner provided out of a single purse" (Aristotle, *Politics III*, ll. 1281a–1281b).

[5] This logic assumes independent judgment by each legislator. In reality, debating precedes voting. In debate people learn new information that can change their judgment. The exchange of information may become more efficient as the size of the legislature falls. The proofs of the superiority of a large legislature typically neglect the role of debate in reaching decisions. A more complex model would allow the legislators to exchange information and influence each other and would acknowledge that increasing the size of the legislature increases the transaction costs of its members' exchanging information with each other.

[6] For Condorcet's "jury theorems," see Condorcet 1976. Explanations are in Young 1995 pp. 51–52 and Goldman 1999.

[7] Alternatively, assume that legislators are drawn at random, some of whom make errors with probability greater than .5. If the *expected* probability of an additional legislator's making the right decision exceeds .5, adding an additional legislator decreases the *expected* probability of a mistake by the majority.

[8] Nitzan and Paroush 1982; Shapley and Grofman 1984 as cited in Young 1995, p. 52.

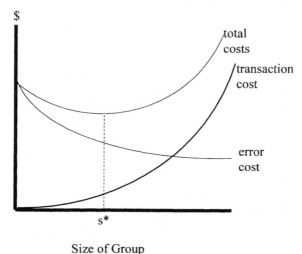

Fig. 8-1 Costs of Decisions as Function of Group's Size

legislation, the legislature should consist of a single person. If errors in factual judgments and representing preferences were the only considerations, the legislature should consist of the entire nation. Taking both factors into account, the legislature's size is optimal when one more member improves the accuracy of the decision by an amount equal to the resulting increase in transaction costs.

To illustrate the optimum, the horizontal axis in figure 8-1 indicates the size of the group making the decision, and the vertical axis indicates costs. According to the graph, transaction costs increase with the group's size, whereas error costs diminish, at least up to a point. The total costs, which equal the sum of transaction costs and error costs, decrease at first and subsequently increase with the group's size. The minimum point on the total cost curve, denoted s*, indicates the optimal size of the decision-making group.

Optimal Party Composition

A similar logic applies to the legislature's composition by political party. Consider the difference between two systems of proportional representation. Pure proportional representation, as in Israel, exists when citizens vote for parties and the seats in the legislature are allocated strictly in proportion to votes received. Minimum proportional representation exists when citizens vote for parties, and the seats in the legislature are allocated in proportion to the votes received by all parties enjoying a minimum proportion of votes. To illustrate, in Germany the seats in the legislature are divided in proportion to votes among all the parties receiving at least 5 percent of the popular vote.[9]

---

[9] German parties must receive a smaller minimum proportion of votes (1 percent to .5 percent) to receive government funds for conducting political campaigns.

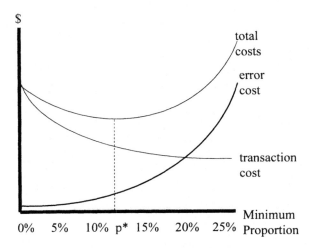

Fig. 8-2 Costs of Decisions with Minimum Proportional Representation

Suppose you were designing a constitution incorporating minimum proportional representation, and you had to select the minimum proportion. A lower minimum allows the representation of more parties in the legislature. By opening the legislature to small parties, the legislature represents more diverse political views. As discussed above, more diversity in political views reduces the probability of errors of representation. As parties fragment, however, the transaction costs increase for creating a coalition to enact legislation. Finding the best level at which to set the minimum proportion requires balancing error costs and transaction costs, much like finding the optimal size of the legislature.

Figure 8-2 depicts the balancing of costs, with the minimum proportion shown on the horizontal axis. Figure 8-2 resembles figure 8-1 with the curves labeled "transaction cost" and "error cost" reversed. The optimum in figure 8-2 occurs at the point p* where the reduction in transaction costs from raising the minimum proportion exactly offsets the increase in error costs. So computing the minimum proportion of votes for representation in the legislature is much the same as computing the legislature's optimal size.

Plurality Rule v. Proportional Representation

In chapter 3 I described the two great families of voting rules as plurality rule and proportional representation. The discussion of Duverger's Law in chapter 3 explained that plurality rule tends to consolidate factions into two centrist parties. Parties consolidate because citizens throw away their votes by voting for minority parties. By reversing the order of argument, it is easy to see why proportional representation tends to create a system with many political parties. Under proportional representation, each citizen tends to vote for the party whose preferences most closely resemble his own. In a parliamentary system, each party in the legislature can bargain to join the governing coalition, and in a presidential system each party in the legislature can bargain to obtain the chairmanship of an important committee. A citizen does not throw away a vote by voting for a small party so long as it has some bargaining power. Proportional representation thus fragments parties by empowering all parties, whereas plurality rule consolidates parties by stripping power from minority parties.

ERRORS IN REPRESENTATION

Under proportional representation, the difference between a party's fraction of votes and its fraction of seats represents a kind of error in representing the citizens. To formalize this idea, define the *error in representing a party* as the absolute value of the difference between the party's fraction of the popular vote and the fraction of its seats in the legislature. To illustrate, assume that the fraction of the popular vote for the legislature equals .6 for the Christian democratic party, .3 for the socialist party, and .1 for the green party. To keep the example simple, assume that every electoral district mirrors the nation as a whole, so the vote in each district equals .6 for the Christian democratic party, .3 for the socialist party, and .1 for the green party.

Now compare plurality rule and proportional representation. In a system of plurality rule by district, the Christian democrats receive all of the seats, so the error in over-representing the Christian democrats equals $|1 - .6|$. Similarly, the error in under representing the socialists and the greens equals $|0 - .3|$ and $|0 - .1|$, respectively. The total error under plurality rule equals $|1 - .6| + |0 - .3| + |0 - .1| = .8$. In contrast, a system of pure proportional representation assigns .6 of the seats to the Christian democratic party, .3 to the socialist party, and .1 to the green party. With perfect proportional representation, the error in representation equals $|.6 - .6| + |.3 - .3| + |.1 - .1| = 0$.

Under plurality rule, the voters for minority parties have no representation and the officials in minority parties have no public offices. To correct the error in representation and obtain public offices for party officials, the socialist party and the green party will probably consolidate in time, or one of them will disappear. In general, underrepresentation of parties drives their consolidation. Consequently, the system with the greatest error in representation creates the strongest force for consolidating parties. Conversely, perfect proportional representation eliminates error in representing parties, which fragments parties and destabilizes governments. This general pattern is confirmed in comparing many nations.[10]

BUNDLING CANDIDATES

With majority rule in district elections, the voters can pick and choose among candidates. In contrast, under many systems of proportional representation, each party designates a list of candidates and the voters choose among alternative lists. On any party's list, a voter may like some candidates and dislike others. In drawing up a party's list, the leadership typically balances the intrinsic appeal of

[10] Rae 1995, p. 70, citing Powell 1982.

candidates to voters and the loyalty of candidates to the party. The party leaders will sacrifice some popularity to increase loyalty. Thus proportional representation tends to strengthen party loyalty.

A market analogy clarifies the logic of party leadership. Assume that you own the only restaurant on a popular vacation spot where you serve two foods: hamburgers and fried potatoes. To make the most money, should you sell hamburgers and potatoes separately, or should you only sell a combination plate? The answer depends on the structure of demand.

Omnivores like hamburgers and potatoes, vegetarians like potatoes and not hamburgers, and carnivores like hamburgers and not potatoes. Consider a vegetarian's response to alternative menus. If you sell each item separately, most vegetarians will spend a little to buy potatoes. If you bundle the two items, some vegetarians will spend a lot to buy the combination plate, and some vegetarians will not buy anything. The profitability of bundling versus unbundling depends on the elasticity of demand by different groups of consumers.[11] In general, bundling the two goods is more profitable when doing so causes a small reduction in total sales, and unbundling is more profitable when doing so causes a large increase in total sales.

The party leadership faces an optimal bundling problem similar to that of the restaurateur. As in markets, a political party facing inelastic "demand" by voters has more power to name loyal candidates, rather than name popular candidates. Theory predicts that other things equal, parties facing the least elastic demand from voters will demand the greatest loyalty from candidates. Thus, monopoly power of a party increases the demand of its leaders for loyalty. Conversely, monopoly power by a party causes a decrease in the popularity of legislators with voters in a system of proportional representation.

DISTRICT MAGNITUDE

Instead of being perfect, systems of proportional representation often contain imperfections designed to shrink the number of parties. I already discussed the example of minimum proportional representation. Another device allocates seats to parties by weighting the proportion of the votes that they receive so as to increase the representation of larger parties. For example, a party that receives 40 percent of the vote may receive 60 percent of the seats, whereas a party receiving 15 percent may only receive 5 percent of the seats. A Belgian mathematician devised such a weighting rule that Spain adopted for its Parliament (the "D'hondt" rule). Another approach adopted by Italy in recent electoral reforms allocates 25 percent of the seats in Parliament to the parties by proportional representation and fills the remainder of the seats by winner-take-all elections in districts.

A frequent imperfection in proportional representation concerns the size of electoral districts. The *district magnitude* refers to the number of legislative seats assigned to each electoral district. For example, the U.S. House of

---

[11] Commodity bundling in markets is explained in Adams and Yellen 1976. No simple formula expresses the optimum.

Representatives has a district magnitude of 1, with 435 seats in as many districts. In general, plurality rule has a district magnitude of 1. In contrast, Israel elects its entire legislature in one national district, so that magnitude equals several hundred. Worldwide, most magnitudes fall somewhere between 1 and 20.[12]

When the district magnitude is small, proportional representation makes errors. To illustrate, if a district has 3 seats and 5 parties, at least 2 parties must go without representation. Conversely, if a district has 10 seats and 5 parties, all parties may have representation. As the magnitude of the district rises, a system of proportional representation makes smaller errors in representation.[13] Generalizing Duverger's Law, I conclude that a reduction in district magnitude tends to reduce the number of parties.

DIRTY TRICKS WITH DISTRICTS

A reduction in district magnitude also provides an incentive to "gerrymander" the boundaries of electoral districts in order to maximize a party's seats in the legislature. To illustrate gerrymandering, assume that an official must divide a certain area into two districts, each represented by one legislator. Also, assume that 51 percent of the citizens in the area vote Left and 49 percent vote Right. If the boundaries are drawn so that each of the two districts contains 51 percent Left voters and 49 percent Right voters, then Left will win both seats. Alternatively, if the boundaries are drawn so that most Left voters are in one district and most Right voters are in the other district, then each party will win one seat. The boundaries decisively change the representation of the two parties in the legislature.

Theory predicts an increase in gerrymandering with low-magnitude districts and plurality rule. As predicted, accusations of gerrymandering frequently occur in the U.S. The U.S. Constitution allocates seats in the House of Representatives to states in proportion to their population.[14] Shifts in population as revealed by the census provide an occasion to redraw the boundaries of the electoral districts, which are usually drawn by the state legislature, possibly subject to veto by the governor. The Democratic Party in the U.S., which has controlled most state legislatures in recent years, has been accused of gerrymandering to produce a Democratic majority in Congress.

Is this belief justified? The error in representation provides a very simple test for gerrymandering. If Democrats win about 50 percent of the popular vote, and if districts are not gerrymandered, then Democrats should also win about 50 percent of the seats in Congress on average. On the other hand, if Democrats win about 50 percent of the popular vote and Democrats win much more than 50 percent of the seats in Congress, then the Democrats probably gerrymandered the districts.

[12] Rae 1995, p. 65.

[13] Rae 1995, p. 68, citing Rae 1971 and Lijphart 1994.

[14] There is, in fact, a tricky problem in the arithmetic. Dividing seats in the House by the proportion of people in a state usually leaves a remainder. The rule for allocating the remainder is apparently biased against large states. See Steen 1982.

Applying this simple test to U.S. congressional districts detects little gerrymandering.[15] The self-interest of politicians explains this finding. When drawing boundaries for electoral districts, a party maximizes its seats by spreading its faithful voters in order to create a small majority in each electoral district. Senior legislators, however, want safe seats. To create safe seats, the senior legislators want to concentrate the party's faithful voters in a few districts. Thus the interests of the party as a whole favor gerrymandering to win many seats by narrow margins, and the interests of the party's senior legislators favor gerrymandering to win few seats by wide margins.

Sometimes gerrymandering follows the interests of the party, and sometimes gerrymandering follows the interests of senior legislators. In aggregate these effects apparently cancel each other in the United States. Insofar as this result holds generally, the legal mechanism for redrawing electoral boundaries affects individual elections but not the aggregate composition of the legislature by party. Self-interest solves the aggregate problem of gerrymandering by parties, without resorting to proportional representation or at-large elections.

In the United States, especially troublesome charges of gerrymandering involve race. In 1998, 9 percent of the seats in the U.S. House of Representatives (39 out of the 435) were held by African Americans, whereas 12 percent of Americans identified their race as African American in the 1990 census. Thus, the proportion of African Americans in the U.S. population exceeds the proportion of African Americans in Congress. Parties have sometimes gerrymandered districts to reduce black representation, and courts have sometimes ordered the redrawing of district lines to increase black representation. To illustrate, responding to a court order to create a black district in North Carolina, Democrats drew distorted boundaries, apparently to ensure that the Republicans would lose the seat. The district, whose shape was so unnatural that it became known as the "ugly district," provoked a national debate among legal scholars.[16]

CONDORCET WINNERS

Having discussed representation, transaction costs, and error costs, I turn to another consideration in evaluating legislative performance. Recall from chapter 2 that a Condorcet winner is an alternative that can defeat any other alternative in paired voting. One standard for judging the organization of a legislature is whether or not it picks out Condorcet winners. In other words, if a Condorcet winner exists, will the legislature find and enact it? I will explain why plurality rule tends to find and pick Condorcet winners, whereas proportional representation does not.

In three-party competition, the winner of the election is not necessarily a Condorcet winner under most voting rules. To illustrate, assume a three-way

[15] "Virtually all the political science evidence to date indicates that the electoral system has little or no systematic partisan bias, and that the net partisan gains nationally from redistricting are very small" (Cain and Butler 1991).

[16] See Polsby and Popper 1993 for a discussion of this case and other cases on racial gerrymandering.

contest in which the Right party wins 45 percent, the Left party wins 40 percent, and the Green party wins 15 percent. To keep the example simple, assume that these proportions obtain in every district, as well as in the nation as a whole. If the election is conducted under plurality rule, the Right wins in every district. If the election is conducted under proportional representation in a parliamentary system, the Right is usually invited to form a government. So the Right wins in a three-party contest.

Now assume that the Green party is eliminated, so the voters must choose between the Right and the Left. If Green loyalists vote Left, the results are 45 percent for the Right and 55 percent for the Left. In two-party voting, the Left can defeat the Right. So the Left wins in a two-party contest. A Condorcet winner, by definition, prevails in paired voting, so the Left is a Condorcet winner. Notice that in this example, the Condorcet winner (the Left) prevails in voting between two parties, and another party (the Right) prevails in voting among three parties.

Under most voting rules, third-party alternatives are relevant to which of the two largest parties wins.[17] Consequently, a Condorcet winner can lose in an election involving three parties. According to Duverger's Law, plurality rule typically eliminates third parties. Given only two parties, the party that can defeat any other party in paired voting always wins. Thus, Condorcet winners tend to prevail in plurality rule in the long run, but not in proportional representation.

PREFERENCE REVELATION

The preceding examples with three parties implicitly assume that citizens vote their true party preferences. Instead of revealing their true party preferences, citizens sometimes vote strategically. To illustrate, under plurality rule with three parties, members of the Green party observe that voting Green causes the Right to win, so they might switch and vote Left. As another example of strategic voting, even after the Left absorbs the Green party, some members of the Green party might announce that they will vote Right until the Left government adopts stronger policies to protect the environment. Similarly, under proportional representation some Greens might vote against their party, say to prevent their leaders from forming a coalition with the Right.

In general, no democratic voting rule based on the ranking of candidates by citizens can motivate voters to respond truthfully in all circumstances.[18] However, some voting rules induce strategic behavior in circumstances where other rules do not. As the preceding example suggests, strategic voting by citizens especially occurs when several parties (more than two and less than, say, five) compete for office. With a small number of parties, citizens can make the necessary calculations to determine when strategic voting pays off. When proportional representation results in many parties, however, small parties can have power

---

[17] Thus, collective choice with three parties usually violates the assumption of the independence of irrelevant alternatives, which figures in Arrow's Impossibility Theorem. For a discussion, see chapter 3 of Sen 1970a.

[18] This proposition is formulated as a theorem in Gibbard 1973 and Satterthwaite 1975.

in government equal to or exceeding their proportion of seats. In these circumstances, citizens can often advance their political values most by voting for the party that they most prefer, even if it is a small party. Conversely, when plurality rule results in two-party competition, citizens usually advance their political values most by voting for the major party that they most prefer, even if they do not like the major parties very much.

ORGANIZATIONS OR BARGAINS?

My discussion of Duverger's Law suggests a fundamental way to change the transaction costs of legislation. Orders and bargains are two different ways by which people cooperate with each other. Superiors give orders to subordinates, and equals bargain. Within parties, hierarchy and discipline enable the party leadership to give orders to party members. Between parties, however, the absence of hierarchy or discipline requires party leaders to bargain with each other. According to Duverger's Law, plurality rule consolidates parties, whereas proportional representation fragments parties. Thus plurality rule channels political transactions into organizations, whereas proportional representation channels political transactions into bargains. *In general, plurality voting favors organization over bargains in the legislature, whereas proportional representation favors bargains over organization.*[19] Organizations bring stability to politics at the cost of not representing the preferences of some citizens. In contrast, bargaining among multiple parties represents preferences more fully at the cost of instability.

The advantage of one system over the other depends partly on history. If the worst danger to a democracy is legislative paralysis, then proportional representation aggravates the problem. Introducing imperfections in representation can energize such a system. Alternatively, if the worst danger to a democracy is abuse of power by a political cartel, then a move toward proportional representation can destabilize the cartel by destabilizing government. More perfect representation can open the system to more diverse influences. Next I consider another way to destabilize political cartels: bicameralism.

Questions

1. Suppose that immigration diversifies the population of a country. Predict the resulting shift, if any, in the curves in figure 8-1.

2. What difference would it make in the United States if retired judges, rather than politicians, chose the boundaries of electoral districts?

3. Contrast the objectives of minimizing error in representation and creating stability in government.

4. Analyze the proposition, "Proportional representation is better in principle than in fact because it disorganizes electoral competition."

---

[19] For a discussion of the difference between hierarchies and bargains in private business, see Williamson 1975.

Bicameralism

Constitutions often create two chambers of the legislature with different principles of representation. The lower chamber typically represents people. To illustrate, the House of Representatives in the U.S. Congress consists of 435 representatives elected from districts with almost equal numbers of voters. Similarly, the European Parliament consists of 626 representatives elected by the people in each country according to the country's electoral laws.

The upper chamber, in contrast, may represent people, states, or something else. To illustrate, the U.S. Senate consists of two representatives elected from each of the fifty states, and Europe's Council of Ministers consists of one representative of the government of each nation in the European Union. Representation by states implies disproportionate representation of people. To illustrate, California and North Dakota each have two senators, even though North Dakota's population in 1990 was 2 percent of California's population.[20] Similarly, Germany and Denmark each send one minister to Europe's Council of Ministers, even though Germany has many more people than Denmark.[21]

In addition to differing in composition, the two chambers differ in power from one country to another. A strong upper chamber has roughly the same powers as the lower chamber to initiate and veto legislation. A weak upper chamber, in contrast, can discuss, advise, or even delay legislation but cannot initiate legislation or veto it. In some countries, such as the United States and Australia, the upper chamber's power roughly equals the lower chamber's power. In other countries, such as Spain, the upper chamber is relatively weak. Britain's House of Lords, which formerly represented aristocratic birth and possessed power, now possesses no power and represents outstanding achievement.

Are two chambers better than one? To address this question, I want to analyze some hidden consequences of bicameralism. To keep the analysis simple, I will focus on the strong form of bicameralism in which both chambers must concur to create new legislation. (My conclusions apply to some weaker forms of bicameralism and not to others.) If enacting legislation requires the concurrence of two chambers, then they must bargain with each other explicitly or implicitly. The necessity of bargaining increases the transaction costs of legislation. Higher transaction costs reduce the speed and quantity of new legislation. Conversely, higher transaction costs of change privilege the status quo. So the first effect of bicameralism is to privilege the status quo over alternatives.

Recall from chapter 3 that majority-rule games of distribution with symmetrical players have no core. This fact can create an unstable pursuit of advantage by legislators. The core is empty in a unicameral legislature when, for any possible initial situation, a proposal for fresh legislation to redistribute wealth will command a majority of votes. Thus any initial distribution of wealth is

---

[20] The U.S. Senate disproportionately represents rural states with small populations, and this fact partly explains the persistence of government subsidies to agriculture.

[21] In chapter 5 I explain that the Council of Ministers decides some issues by weighting the votes of ministers according to the size of their country. Weighted voting moves the representation of states in the direction of the representation of people.

vulnerable to a proposal for redistribution. Adding a second chamber to the legislature, however, can sometimes remedy this instability. The reason is easy to see. In a bicameral system, a majority in the first chamber may prefer a new proposal for redistribution to the status quo, whereas a majority in the second chamber may prefer the status quo. If the second chamber blocks any feasible proposal to change the status quo, the status quo is in the game's core. In general, adding a second chamber often stabilizes the game of legislation by privileging the status quo.[22]

Privileging the status quo is especially important in a system of district elections with majority rule. In such a system, unicameralism allows a minority of citizens to impose its rule on the majority of citizens. To illustrate by a concrete example, assume that a nation has a unicameral legislature where each district elects one representative by majority rule. A party that wins 51 percent of the vote in 51 percent of the districts has a majority of the seats in the legislature, even though the party only wins slightly more than one-fourth of the votes in the nation as a whole. With a unicameral legislature, the party representing one-fourth of the population could enact extensive legislature opposed by most citizens. Adding a second chamber to the legislature protects against this possibility. A party with 51 percent of the popular vote in 51 percent of the districts for the first chamber is unlikely to win a majority of seats in the second chamber.

Figure 8-3 depicts these facts. Assume that a nation consists of three states, labeled A, B, and C. Assume there are two parties, named Left and Right. In figure 8-3, the shaded area represents the number of Right voters, and the blank area represents the number of Left voters. To consider unicameralism, focus on the *bottom half* of the figure. According to figure 8-3, 51 percent of the voters are Right in districts 1, 3, and 5, whereas 0 percent of the voters are Right in districts 2 and 4. Under unicameralism, each district elects one representative to the legislature. Consequently, Right controls three seats and Left controls two seats, even though Right's percentage of the popular vote in the nation as a whole equals approximately 30 percent. Thus, the Right minority can rule over the Left majority in a unicameral legislature.

Bicameralism typically changes this result. Assume the second chamber represents states, where districts 1 and 2 constitute State A, districts 2 and 3 constitute

[22] Miller, Hammond, and Kile 1996; Miller and Hammond 1990; and Hammond and Miller 1987. To illustrate, consider this variation in the majority-rule game of dividing $100. Assume the first chamber consists of five districts denoted (A,B,C,D,E), each with one vote. Assume the division (33,0,33,33,0) is the status quo. Assume the only alternative proposal is (0,30,40,0,30). The majority coalition (B,C,E) prefers the alternative proposal, so the status quo is unstable in the first chamber. Now add a second chamber to the legislature that consists of three states denoted (I,II,III). State I encompasses districts A and B in the first chamber. State II is identical to district C. State III encompasses districts D and E. Thus (I, II, III) = (A + B, C, D + E). Use this formula to convert payoffs in districts to payoffs in states. Thus the status quo yields (33,33,33) in the second chamber, whereas the proposed alternative yields (30,40,30). States I and II prefer the status quo, and state III prefers the new proposal. I have shown that a majority coalition in the first chamber will enact a particular redistributive proposal and a majority coalition in the second chamber will block it. Given two feasible alternatives, the status quo is unstable in a unicameral legislature and stable in a bicameral legislature.

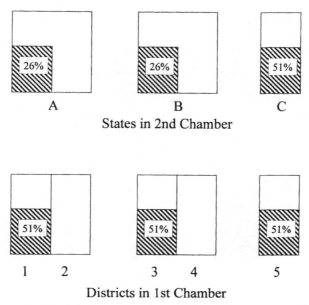

States in 2nd Chamber

Districts in 1st Chamber

Fig. 8-3 Bicameralism Protects Majority against Minority and Vice Versa

State B, and district 3 constitutes State C. The *top half* of figure 8-3 represents these facts. Each state elects one representative to the second chamber, so Right controls one seat and Left controls two seats. In figure 8-3 the popular minority controls the first chamber and the popular majority controls the second chamber. In these circumstances, successful legislation requires bargaining between the Right in the first chamber and the Left in the second chamber.

The preceding discussion began by considering a unicameral legislature consisting of the first chamber depicted in the bottom half of figure 8-3. Next I added a second chamber depicted in the top half of figure 8-3. Adding the second chamber blocks minority rule and forces bargaining between the Left and Right. Alternatively, adding a second chamber can also block majority rule. To see why, reverse the example and begin with a unicameral legislature consisting of the second chamber as depicted in the top half of figure 8-3. A unicameral legislature consisting of the second chamber in figure 8-3 permits the Left majority to rule. Now add another chamber as depicted in the bottom half of figure 8-3. The move to a bicameral legislature permits the Right minority in the additional chamber to block the Left majority in the original chamber. Under this interpretation of figure 8-3, adding another chamber blocks majority rule and forces bargaining between the Left and Right.

In general, bicameralism can protect the majority against minority, and bicameralism can also protect the minority against the majority. Instead of minority rule or majority rule, bicameralism makes the majority and the minority cooperate in order to rule. The two groups must cooperate to rule so long as one group

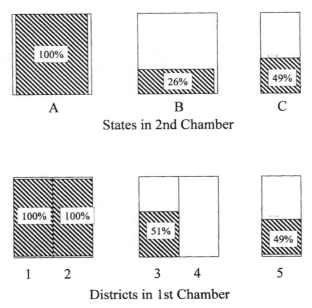

controls one chamber of the legislature and the other group controls the other chamber. (Later I explain how, by increasing the transaction costs of legislation, bicameralism shifts power from legislature to courts.)

I have explained that bicameralism can protect majorities against minorities, and vice versa. A more conventional approach protects by entrenching rights in the constitution. Between these alternatives, bicameralism has a distinct advantage over constitutional rights. Specifically, bicameralism protects existing rights without blocking consensus legislation.[23]

Question: Consider the distribution of voters depicted in figure 8-4, where the shaded area represents the number of Right voters and the blank area represents the number of Left voters.

1. Which party governs in a unicameral system with the second chamber in figure 8-4 as the only legislative body?

2. Which party governs in a unicameral system with the first chamber in figure 8-4 as the only legislative body?

3. Can either party govern by itself without the other's cooperation in a bicameral system?

4. Suppose the legislature in figure 8-4 were expanded from two chambers to three. Predict the consequences for Condorcet winners and minority rights.

[23] Buchanan and Tullock 1962 (1967) makes a similar argument in chapter 16. Similarly, Levmore 1992 argues that bicameralism protects minorities without blocking Condorcet winners.

5. Australia and the United States have bicameralism–the lower chamber represents people and the upper chamber represents states. In the United States, however, people elect the president directly (presidential system), whereas in Australia the lower chamber selects the executive from among its members (parliamentary system). Predict which system provides greater protection of the majority against a minority and vice versa.

EXECUTIVE

The executive differs from the legislature in its perspective on politics. In a presidential system, the presidential candidates have an incentive to identify their party's platform with the median voter. In a parliamentary system, this mechanism does not operate directly because the prime minister is not directly elected. In either system, however, the executive has an incentive to develop a national program and make legislators adhere to it. A national perspective drives the executive toward the center in the nation's distribution of political preferences.

To implement a national program, the executive must provide leadership and organization to the legislature. I will contrast two general types of leadership by using a market analogy. According to the usual economic formulation discussed in the introduction to part 2, corporations are hierarchies bounded by markets. Small firms require less hierarchy and more markets, whereas large firms require more hierarchy and fewer markets. The members of a hierarchy interact especially through orders, whereas the participants in a market interact especially through bargains.

Similarly, legislative bargaining resembles a market and parties resemble firms. A disciplined political party forms a hierarchy whose members interact especially through orders. In contrast, legislators from different parties interact especially through bargains. Larger parties imply more orders and fewer bargains. Conversely, smaller parties imply fewer orders and more bargains. The optimal number of parties depends on the relative efficiency of orders and bargains.

Like markets, legislative bargaining can succeed in principle with little organization or formal structure. In practice, however, bargaining fails in unorganized legislatures for three reasons discussed in chapter 3. First, the value of a legislator's vote depends on how other legislators vote, and this externality disrupts the trading of votes. Second, most legislatures contain too many members for each one to bargain with everyone else. Third, legislators may refrain from deals to preserve the purity of their voting record as a signal to their constituents.

To overcome these obstacles and to secure the gains from cooperation, a legislature must organize its members politically through parties and legally through its internal rules. Much party structure and discipline in the legislature comes from the executive. A strong executive supplies more orders and fewer bargains, whereas a weak executive supplies more bargains and fewer orders.

The strength of the executive depends especially on his ability to reward and punish legislators. The power to reward and punish differs according to the method for choosing the executive. In a presidential system like the United States, direct election by citizens for a fixed term of office creates an independent executive, who controls the administrative agencies. Legislators often need to help their constituents by securing favorable treatment from administrators. The executive's power over legislators comes especially from delivering, or withholding, favorable treatment by administrative agencies.

In a parliamentary system, in contrast, the government is formed by the party that wins a majority of seats in parliament, or, if no party wins a majority, by the party that can assemble a coalition commanding a majority of votes. The prime minister can reward legislators by including them in the government, and the leading legislators compete to ascend the hierarchy of cabinet posts. Minimizing the size of the winning coalition maximizes the rewards available to its members. (In chapter 3 I explained that this way of reasoning leads to the minimum winning coalition, the minimum working coalition, the minimum connected coalition, or the minimum complementary coalition.)

In a parliamentary system, a government persists in office so long as it commands a majority in parliament, or until it reaches the maximum number of years allowed by law between general elections. (The actual rules and conditions for dissolving Parliament differ from one country to another.[24]) In order to remain in power, a government usually must win a majority on all major bills. To ensure a majority, the party leadership must exercise tight discipline over votes by junior members. The senior members of a governing coalition receive cabinet posts and then distribute lesser offices among their followers. If the leaders of a party cannot reliably deliver the votes of its members, that party cannot sustain a government. An undisciplined party, consequently, is an undesirable partner in coalition government. Successful parties acquire the discipline needed to participate in parliamentary government. In addition, proportional representation in some parliaments typically strengthens discipline by allowing the party's leadership to designate who will fill the seats apportioned to the party. In general, parliamentary systems create strong incentives for political parties to acquire discipline.[25]

I have contrasted government by orders in a democracy with a few large parties and a strong executive, and government by bargains in a democracy with many small parties and a weak executive. Now I will summarize the characteristics of constitutions that tend toward one result or the other. Plurality rule

---

[24] For variations across twenty European countries, see table 4.1 p. 64 of Laver and Schofield 1990a. In many countries, the government "falls" when it commits itself to a bill that loses in the legislature. In these circumstances, the prime minister usually resigns and another party tries to form a governing coalition or a general election is declared. From time to time, people retire from parliament or die, and a "by-election" fills the vacancy, so the power of the parties can shift without a general election.

[25] In an unusual permutation, Switzerland has proportional representation and weak party discipline. The explanation may lie in the shared executive power in the federal council and the referendum system.

merges parties and proportional representation multiplies parties. Parliamentary government strengthens party discipline and a presidential system weakens it. Bicameralism weakens the executive and unicameralism strengthens the executive. So a unicameral parliamentary system with plurality rule in many districts favors a strong executive and a small number of disciplined parties. Interaction by officials in such a government relies relatively more on orders and relatively less on bargains. To illustrate, two well-disciplined parties dominate government in the United Kingdom, and the governing party does not need to bargain.

Conversely, a bicameral presidential system with proportional representation in few districts favors a weak executive and a large number of undisciplined parties. Interaction by officials in such a government relies relatively more on bargains and relatively less on orders. I know of no constitution with all of these characteristics. Note, however, that Italy, which possessed some of these characteristics, averaged almost one new government per year in the forty years from 1948 to 1988.

The Budgetary Bramble Bush

A difficult procedural problem in any democracy, which illustrates executive leadership, concerns the budget. Many legislatures enact bills that require expenditures for particular purposes like building bridges, performing operas, or treating injured veterans. Such bills, however, seldom specify how to pay for the expenditures, such as collecting bridge tolls, selling opera tickets, or charging for medical care. Rather, the funds are usually drawn from general revenues provided by broad taxes on income, property, and sales. Every state faces a tricky problem of aligning the sum of particular expenditures authorized by the legislature with the available tax revenues.

In a democracy, the legislators ideally respond to the preferences of their constituents for public goods. Responsiveness to citizens requires the legislature to consider the value of each item in the budget. Sound macroeconomics, however, requires aggregate expenditures to align with tax revenues.[26] If the legislature freely decides on expenditures item by item, then aggregate expenditure may not align with tax revenues. Conversely, if the legislature commits to aligning expenditures with tax revenues, then the legislature is not free to decide on expenditures item by item.

Different countries have different budgetary processes to handle the conflict between politically responsive expenditures and sound macroeconomics. Centralized budgeting typically reduces responsiveness and increases macroeconomic control. For example, expenditure legislation in the European Union must begin with a proposal from the Commission to the Council of Ministers. The Council can accept or reject the proposal, but not modify it.[27] Thus the

---

[26] I say "align," not "equal," to keep my discussion neutral on the question disputed among economists of the conditions under which the budget should exactly balance.

[27] For details, see chapter 9.

Commission controls aggregate expenditures by controlling individual expenditures. This centralized process reduces the scope for the ministers to evaluate each item on its merits. Similarly, parliamentary systems with strict party discipline often concentrate control over the budget in the prime minister.

In contrast, the U.S. Congress follows more decentralized budgeting procedures. Bills that authorize expenditures usually originate with specialized committees of Congress. The members of these committees usually represent the special interests benefited by the bills. For example, a congressman from New York, which has many large banks, will ask for appointment to the committee that originates banking bills, and a congressman from Michigan, which has many automobile factories, will ask for appointment to the committee that originates highway bills.

When committees report these bills to Congress for action, the resulting legislation "authorizes" expenditure but does not "appropriate" the funds. Authorized expenditures cannot be made until the funds are appropriated. Appropriating the funds for a project requires a separate bill that follows a different procedure from the bill that authorized the expenditures. Bills to appropriate funds normally originate in the Appropriations Committee of the House of Representatives. Unlike the committees on banking or highways, the Appropriations Committee views expenditures as a whole. The Appropriations Committee is supposed to align total appropriations and total revenues. Thus the decentralized process of authorization responds more to political preferences and the centralized process of appropriation responds more to macroeconomics.

A Fiscal Constitution?

In reality, decentralized budgeting often produces excessive deficits. For example, the Appropriations Committee, in cooperation with the Rules Committee, has the power to manipulate the congressional agenda in the United States. Until the 1970s, conservative Southern Democrats dominated these committees and restrained federal spending. Subsequently, the role of seniority diminished in making committee assignments, Southerners lost much of their control, the Appropriations Committee's power weakened, and budget deficits increased.

To understand why decentralized budgeting often produces excessive deficits, imagine that five economists decide to have lunch together and split the check. Each one pays 20 percent of the cost of ordering additional food, so everyone orders too much and overeats. Similarly, individuals who can obtain benefits from the government pay a fraction of the costs that fall upon all taxpayers. Specific expenditures benefit small groups a lot and broad taxes hurt everyone a little. The small groups of beneficiaries hire lobbyists to press the legislature to enact many expenditure bills, with little regard for aggregate expenditures. In general, legislatures often produce budget deficits because individual legislators bargain harder for expenditures to benefit their supporters than anyone bargains to restrain expenditures by others.[28]

At the end of the twentieth century, a buoyant U.S. economy has lifted tax revenues and produced budget surpluses, but many conservatives believe the structural causes of excessive deficits persist. A "fiscal constitution" could correct the structural problem by precommitting the legal process to budgetary restraint. In a potentially dramatic move toward centralization, the U.S. Congress recently enacted a version of the president's "line-item veto," which allows the president to eliminate individual expenditures contained in comprehensive bills while leaving other expenditures unaffected.[29] Furthermore, many leading conservatives would amend the U.S. Constitution to require a balanced budget.[30] If such an amendment passes, however, no one knows how Congress would reorganize to comply.

In the United States, the President can serve only two terms in office, but no such limits apply to most other offices.[31] With congressional seniority comes power, especially the best committee appointments. The most senior representatives in Congress and state legislatures use their power for costly projects to benefit their own districts. Observing this fact, many citizens advocate term limits for all elected officials. By eliminating seniority, the supporters of term limits hope to reduce pork-barrel projects that contribute to deficits. Without term limits, some citizens feel compelled to reelect an official whose seniority gains special advantages for their district, even though such advantages harm the nation as a whole.[32]

[28] The logic of bargaining is developed formally in Dharmapala 1996. Notice that the preceding argument applies to state expenditures with concentrated benefits, not to state expenditures with diffuse benefits. Public goods with diffuse benefits, such as parks and clean air, reach the opposite conclusion. To understand the problem of diffuse benefits, imagine that someone takes contributions from five economists to buy lunch for everyone. For each $1 that each one of them contributes, he expects to receive $.20 in food, so everyone contributes too little and no one gets enough to eat. Like the economists at the group lunch, each member of an interest group who contributes to political lobbying receives a fraction of the total benefit. In chapter 3 I explained that the ability of an industry or group to overcome free-riding determines the level of its lobbying efforts. Diffuse benefits and concentrated costs cause insufficient expenditures in a decentralized system of budgeting. Many legislatures around the world succumb to this problem and produce too few public goods such as parks and clean air.

[29] For details, see chapter 9, pp. 221–223.

[30] For example, Niskanen 1992 proposes the following constitutional amendment:

> Section 1. Congress may increase the limit on the public debt of the United States only by the approval of two-thirds of the members of each Chamber.
> Section 2. Any bill to levy a new tax or increase the rate or base of an existing tax shall become law only by the approval of two-thirds of the members of each Chamber.

[31] The U.S. Supreme Court has found that, although the Constitution explicitly imposes a term limit on the president, it implicitly forbids term limits for Congress and other federal offices. However, the Constitution apparently does not forbid term limits for state offices, including the legislatures of the states (Elhauge 1997). Some states, including California, have imposed term limits on state legislators.

[32] Elhauge 1995 observes that the voters in each district could get the same result as term limits would provide by not reelecting their representatives to Congress. However, voters do not want to

In addition to obtaining "pork" for their own districts, senior legislators restrain expenditures by other legislators. For this reason, more rapid turnover in the legislature may not reduce aggregate expenditures. In a wolf pack, killing the alpha male disorganizes the pack and provokes a struggle for power. Similarly, term limits disorganize the legislature and provoke a struggle for power. Disorganization is unlikely to produce a closer alignment of government expenditures and revenues.

As explained, states usually align income and expenditures by centralizing budgetary power so the controlling officials have a national perspective. (Mancur Olson stresses the importance of an "encompassing interest."[33]) In principle, economists should have a lot to say about designing decentralized decision-making processes that preserve incentives to align expenditures and income. So far, however, the ingenuity of economic theorists has found little application to budgeting.

An exception is an interesting proposal by Susan Rose-Ackerman (Rose-Ackerman 1992). Legislation often begins with a preamble stating a high-minded purpose and then proceeds with pork-barrel provisions in the main body of the law. Thus the general purposes stated in the preamble have no real connection to the legislation's substance. Rose-Ackerman would allow judges to void legislation whose financial provisions could not advance their stated purpose. To illustrate, judges might void legislation that declares the youth deserve the best possible education and then reduces expenditures on school science laboratories, or judges might void legislation that declares the nation needs to increase the competitiveness of its industry and then appropriates subsidies for obsolete technologies. The kind of judicial review proposed by Rose-Ackerman would not tolerate wide discrepancies between the stated ends and the chosen means in legislation. Requiring a closer match between stated ends and means in bills would raise the quality of legislative speech. Higher quality legislative speech would increase the information available to citizens who elect the legislators.

Questions

1. Explain why a shift from plurality rule to proportional representation tends to cause government to rely more on bargains and less on orders.

2. Politicians who remain in office for five or ten years often authorize the state to issue bonds that mature in twenty years. Describe ways to align the time horizon of politicians and bond markets.

---

give up special privileges unless everyone gives them up. The advocates of term limits are willing to sacrifice the seniority of their own representatives in order to eliminate the seniority of the representatives from other districts. Elhauge argues that term limits are "pro-democratic" because voters in each district can express their true preferences over candidates, rather than feel compelled to return a senior representative with whom they disagree (Elhauge 1997).

[33] Olson 1993 stresses the role in economic development of politicians with an encompassing interest.

3. Consider the statement, "Allowing legislators to attach unrelated appropriation riders to bills is a Pareto-inferior budgetary process." What does this mean?

4. In 1994, more than 90 percent of incumbents won reelection to the U.S. Congress. At the same time, voters in many states agitated to impose limits on the terms of office in order to prevent politicians from being reelected repeatedly. Explain why these two facts do not necessarily demonstrate that voters are irrational.

5. At the Constitutional Convention, the founders of the United States debated whether to cap the number of terms of office that a president can serve. Some delegates feared that a president who served many terms might effectively become a king. Others argued that a cap might cause a president in his last term of office to pursue private advantage or his own eccentric vision of the public good.[34] In 1951 presidents were limited to two terms in office by passage of the twenty-second Amendment to the U.S. Constitution. Can you identify any evidence that presidents behave differently in the first term of office as opposed to the last term?

JUDICIARY

Having discussed the role of the legislature and executive, I turn to the judiciary. Economists usually want to arrange incentives so that material self-interest converges with the public interest. Given perfect convergence, self-interested people are guided by an "invisible hand" to do what is best for society. Convergence is the strategy in constitutional design for the executive and the legislature in a democracy, but not for the judiciary. The material self-interest of a person concerns power and wealth. Judges are not supposed to decide cases that influence their own power or wealth. Furthermore, judges are shielded from political and economic influences. The aim of constitutional design for the judiciary is independence, not convergence. By definition, the material welfare of a *perfectly independent* judge is not affected by the way he decides cases.

To understand how independence affects judges, consider their intrinsic values. Most judges have a moral and political vision that guides their understanding of the law. Combined with the facts and law, this vision usually implies a right way to decide a case. Judges express their moral and political vision by deciding cases according to their conception of what is right.[35] For a perfectly independent judge, doing what he thinks is right costs him nothing. Judges presumably do what they think is right when it costs them nothing. Thus independence prompts judges to express their moral and political vision in their

[34] See Madison's record of remarks of Gouverneur Morris in *Notes of Debates in the Federal Convention of 1787, Reported by Jones Madison*, (Athens: Ohio University Press, 1966), p. 323. Thanks to Paul Edwards for this footnote.

[35] Recall the discussion of expressive voting in chapter 2.

decisions. In general, as a decision maker's independence increases and the effect of his decisions on his self-interest diminishes, his decisions increasingly express his intrinsic beliefs about right and wrong. To illustrate empirically, regression analysis shows the predictability of opinions of U.S. Supreme Court justices based on their underlying political philosophies (Brenner 1982).

The world's legal systems achieve the independence of judges in two different ways. In most civil-law countries, judges are civil servants who staff a judicial bureaucracy. New judges are appointed to the bottom of the hierarchy based mostly on academic performance, not ideology or party loyalty. Senior judges, however, determine promotions of junior judges by monitoring their decisions, possibly with some influence from politicians. The bureaucracy attempts to shield individual judges from direct political or economic influence.

The careers of federal judges in the United States follow a different path. The president appoints federal judges for life tenure with confirmation by the Senate. President and Senate carefully scrutinize the ideology and politics of the candidate. Thus politics, not academics, control appointment to the federal bench. Once appointed, however, ties are completely severed between the judge and politicians. Except in special circumstances, federal judges cannot even talk to politicians. Furthermore, the route to promotion among federal judges is utterly haphazard. Senior judges have little say about the promotion of junior judges. Instead of an independent bureaucracy, U.S. federal judges have little or no bureaucracy.[36]

In the civil-service system, senior judges scrutinize the performance and, possibly, the politics of junior judges seeking promotion. In the U.S. federal system, in contrast, politicians scrutinize the performance and politics of candidates to become judges. The difference between the two systems can be characterized as *ex ante political scrutiny versus ex post judicial scrutiny*. *Ex ante* political scrutiny implies examination of the politics of a judicial candidate before appointment as judge. *Ex post* political scrutiny implies examination of the politics of a judge after appointment and before promotion.

Independent judges play a crucial role in private and public bargains, which can be explained by an example. Suppose that private parties bargain together over a contract. Their bargaining is more likely to succeed if they know that the terms of any agreement between them will be enforced. In future disputes, a neutral adjudicator is most likely to enforce the contract according to its terms. Independent judges are neutral adjudicators, whereas dependent judges are biased adjudicators. So independent judges facilitate bargains, whether in private business or in politics. To illustrate by lawmaking, legislators can reach agreements over bills more easily if they have confidence that an independent adjudicator will interpret the legislation. Independent judges contribute to the success of political bargaining by providing neutral interpretation of legislation (Landes and Posner 1975).

---

[36] In contrast, some municipal judges in the United States must face regular elections, and some U.S. states require supreme court judges to be confirmed by a majority of voters.

Conversely, when judges are politically dependent rather than independent, political factions cannot rely on courts to enforce their agreements. In these circumstances, politicians must find alternatives to legislation and contracts to secure their bargains. (One possibility is to secure more agreements by embedding them in constitutional amendments.[37])

I explained that independent courts lubricate political deals. Did politicians give independence to courts, or do politicians sustain the independence of courts, in order to lubricate political deals? Independent courts help a government precommit to paying its debts. Some historical evidence suggests that English and Dutch monarchs increased their ability to borrow money by allowing more independence for courts.[38] In part, however, judicial independence results from party competition in government. Empirical evidence from several countries indicates that party competition sustains the independence of courts, whereas perennial rule by the same party undermines judicial independence.[39] A hegemonic party has no need to make deals with other parties, so a hegemonic party has no need for an independent court to lubricate such deals. Some empirical evidence from U.S. states suggests that when courts promote political deals by enforcing the bargain embodied in legislation, legislators reward courts by paying higher judicial salaries on average to the judges.[40]

The role of courts in enforcing agreements has implications for a theory of interpretation. In order to lubricate the economy, courts should enforce private agreements as embodied in contracts. According to the bargain theory of contracts, the bargain is the contract and the writing is its embodiment.[41] In any case, the fact is that the bargain guides the court in interpreting a written contract. Similarly, in order to lubricate politics, courts should enforce agreements among political factions as embodied in legislation. The political bargain should guide courts in interpreting the words in statutes.

When legislators negotiate with each other to obtain a majority, the courts have reason to interpret the resulting legislation in light of the underlying bargain. Sometimes, however, legislators vote on a bill without going through the bargaining process. To illustrate, a legislature that grows weary of negotiations may call for a vote without reaching an agreement. In the vote, the majority

[37] Crain and Tollison 1979. Using judicial tenure as a proxy for judicial independence, the authors found that it correlates negatively with constitutional amendment activity across U.S. states. The original result was confirmed using a different index of constitutional activity by Anderson et al. 1990. The authors understand their results as indicating that less judicial independence causes more attempts by politicians to embed bargains in the constitution in order to secure them against revision by judicial interpretation. This understanding is troubling since state courts in the United States interpret state constitutions. Courts have greater power to interpret the constitution as opposed to legislation. Instead of securing political bargains, embedding them in the constitution gives greater scope for court interpretation, including amending the political bargain as preferred by the court.

[38] North 1995, p. 22.

[39] See Ramseyer 1994.

[40] See Anderson, Shughart, and Tollison 1989. Notice, however, that rewarding judges by higher salaries makes courts more dependent on the legislature (Macey 1988).

[41] For the bargain theory of contracts, see Eisenberg 1982.

prevails without a bargain among its members. When a statute arises without a bargain, the court has little guide to interpretation except the ordinary meaning of the words in the statute. As discussed in chapter 2, "legislative intent" has no meaning without a political bargain.

Besides enforcing political bargains, courts have another important political role. Whereas legislators primarily bargain, the executive primarily gives orders. Courts increase the effectiveness of political control at the top by lowering the cost of monitoring officials at the bottom of state administration. Specifically, courts detect rule breaking by administrators. As explained in chapter 7, court detection of rule breaking alerts top political leaders to the diversion of purpose by lower-level civil servants.

I have explained that courts lubricate bargains for the legislature and effectuate orders by the executive. In addition, courts play other roles in the state. Next I discuss how courts make law more or less on their own by creating common law or interpreting general language in civil codes. (Part 4 examines the role of courts in protecting individual rights).

Questions

1. Economists often assume that civil servants try to maximize the size and income of their agency. Assume that civil service judges in Europe try to engross the court bureaucracy. How would this aim influence the way they decide cases?

2. In the United States, some municipal judges are elected, whereas political officials almost always appoint high-court judges. Contrast the difference in incentives between appointed and elected judges. Does this difference suggest that higher judges should be appointed rather than elected?

3. A famous legal philosopher, Ronald Dworkin, asserts that judges are better at deciding individual rights than they are at making social policies. Relate this account of the role of judges to their independence.

4. Some U.S. legal scholars have bitterly protested the application of political standards to the confirmation of judges. Discuss the incentive effects of applying political standards to the confirmation of U.S. federal judges.[42]

5. Discuss the jury as a device to protect against a judge with an interest in the case.

6. Important cases are usually decided by vote of a panel of judges. If votes were secret (courts announced outcomes but not the votes of individual judges), would judges become more independent?

---

[42] President Bush nominated Robert Bork for the U.S. Supreme Court. Bork was perceived as too conservative by the Senate, which refused to confirm his nomination. He subsequently wrote a stinging attack on the role of politics in the process of Senate confirmation of federal judges. See Bork 1990.

Efficient Common Law

Unlike the executive who creates an agenda, judges take cases as they arise. Unlike legislators who sit in an assembly where political factions bargain, judges mostly decide disputes. Unlike elected officials, judges cannot retain a staff to survey public opinion or seek a mandate from voters. The independence of judges circumscribes their competence in making public policy (Fuller 1978). For example, judges cannot manage macroeconomic policy, design an efficient poverty program, or administer a school district.

Unlike legislators or the executive, however, judges repeatedly see the consequences of applying a law to particular cases. This fact enables judges to make marginal adjustments to laws. For some kinds of rules, marginal adjustments over a period of time lead to the social optimum. Economists admire markets and courts for decentralizing decisions and responding to local information. Just as efficient economic decisions require local information that markets uncover, so the efficient application of rules requires local information that courts uncover.

The economic analysis of law has demonstrated more consistency between efficiency and some bodies of judge-made law, notably the common law of contracts and property, than anyone anticipated when the intellectual enterprise first began in the 1960s.[43] Judges, however, seldom mention efficiency explicitly in deciding cases. Apparently the mechanism driving some common law toward efficiency operates without judges explicitly pursing this aim. In this respect, the hand that directs the common law toward efficiency is invisible.

Adam Smith suggested, and general equilibrium theory proved (Arrow and Hahn 1971), that competitive markets allocate resources efficiently without anyone consciously striving for that goal. Reasoning by analogy, economists have searched for competitive mechanisms that cause the judge-made law to evolve toward efficiency without judges consciously striving for that goal.[44] Litigation, especially in U.S. courts, shares many features of a market. Like other investments, many people litigate for the sake of material gain. Like other services, litigation is costly and lawyers compete to provide it. Like auctions, litigation creates value and redistributes it. Is litigation pressure the invisible hand that directs the common law toward efficiency?

Theorists have considered three ways the litigation market could drive law toward efficiency. First, inefficient laws might cause more legal disputes than efficient laws. For example, a law that provides incentives for underprecaution causes more accidents than a law that provides incentives for efficient precaution. Second, legal disputes caused by inefficient laws might be more difficult to settle out of court than legal disputes caused by efficient laws. To illustrate, vague laws draw people into litigation by creating uncertainty over legal

---

[43] See the analysis of contract and property rules in the leading textbooks (Cooter and Ulen 1999; Posner 1992). Note that the common law of torts seems to lack the efficiency properties of contracts and property. Skepticism about the whole enterprise persists in some quarters (Kelman 1988).

[44] Cooter 1987b; Cooter and Kornhauser 1980; Goodman 1978; Hadfield 1992; Hirshleifer 1982; Hylton 1993; Ott and Schafer 1991; Priest 1977; Priest 1987; Rubin 1977; and Rubin 1994.

entitlements. Equivalently, vague laws increase the transaction cost of bargaining over entitlements, so parties will challenge such laws until the courts clarify the underlying entitlements.[45] Third, the winners win more than the losers lose from correcting a law's inefficiency, so expenditures on challenging an inefficient rule might exceed expenditures on defending it (Goodman 1978).

Unfortunately, these three arguments are more clever than convincing. A law is general in the scope of its application. Changing a law affects everyone who is, or will be, subject to it. The effects of a new precedent spill far beyond the litigants. Most plaintiffs appropriate no more than a small fraction of the value the new precedent creates and redistributes (Landes and Posner 1979; Rubin and Bailey 1993). With large spillovers, self-interest of the litigants cannot direct the litigation market toward efficiency.

The solution to the paradox of judge-made law's efficiency lies more in society and less in courts. The common law's efficiency comes in part from society generating efficient social norms and judges' working social norms into the fabric of the law. The traditional account of the "law merchant" provides an example. The merchants in the medieval trade fairs of England developed their own courts and practices to regulate trade. As the English legal system became stronger and more unified, English judges increasingly assumed jurisdiction over disputes among merchants. The English judges often did not know enough about these specialized businesses to evaluate alternative rules. Instead of making rules, the English judges allegedly tried to find out what rules already existed among the merchants and selectively enforce them. Thus the judges dictated conformity to merchant practices, not the practices to which merchants should conform. The law of notes and bills of exchange in the eighteenth century especially exemplifies this pattern.[46] In general, potential social norms compete for allegiance in solving coordination problems. In certain circumstances, the more efficient norms win the competition.[47] The common law evolved toward efficiency by enforcing norms that evolve toward efficiency.

---

[45] This is apparently Rubin's line of thought in his pioneering article (Rubin 1977). Priest tried to test whether uncertainty about law causes litigation that creates new precedent, or new precedent creates uncertainty that causes litigation. His data apparently show that doctrinal change and increased legal disputes occur in the same year, but not which occurs first, so the facts that he observed are consistent with either hypothesis (Cooter 1987b; Priest 1987).

[46] The extent to which the medieval law merchant was substantive, rather than procedural, is disputed, and its relationship with common law and admiralty law is difficult to reconstruct. The process of assimilating bills of exchange and negotiable instruments into the common law, which occurred in the eighteenth century, is well documented. The traditional theory is developed by Holden (1995). Holden is criticized by Baker (1979). A revised view, which stresses that Mansfield immersed himself in the minutiae of business practice in order to extract the best principles from it, is found in Rogers (forthcoming). I benefited from discussions on this point with Dan Coquillette, James Gordley, and Jim Rogers.

[47] Empirical evidence for the efficiency of social norms is found in Bernstein 1992; Cooter 1991b and Ellickson 1991. An explanation is found in Cooter 1997a. Research emphasizing inefficiency includes Kuran 1997 and Posner 1996.

TABLE 8.1
Judicial Preferences

	Case		
Judge	Civil Rights	Property Rights	State Power
liberal	P > > > D	D > P	D > P
libertarian	D > P	P > > > D	D > P
conservative	D > P	D > P	P > > > D

Questions

1. Explain why the pressure for judge-made law to evolve toward efficiency might be stronger in commercial law than in accident law.

2. Compare the inefficiency of litigation markets to the inefficiency of political lobbying.

Pareto-Inefficient Courts

I have explained why judge-made law might evolve toward efficiency by enforcing social norms. When judges disagree, however, the aggregation of their opinions causes an especially troublesome type of inefficiency. Appellate judges often decide cases in panels by majority vote. As explained in chapter 2, voting does not reflect intensity of sentiment. Without bargaining, voting can lead to a decision that all the judges like less than an alternative. To illustrate this problem for judicial panels, I will construct an example with three judges and three cases.

Assume that the appellate panel consists of three judges, each with a different conception of law and politics. One judge is left-liberal, another is libertarian, and the third judge is conservative. The three judges face three cases, each of which embodies a different issue. One case involves civil rights, the second case involves state power, and the third case involves property rights. The left-liberal judge intensively favors the plaintiff in the civil rights case and mildly favors the defendant in the other two cases. The libertarian judge intensively favors the plaintiff in the case on property rights and mildly favors the defendant in the other two cases. The conservative judge intensively favors the plaintiff in the dispute about state power and mildly favors the defendant in the other two cases. Table 8-1 summarizes these judicial preferences, where ">" denotes "prefers," and ">>>" denotes "strongly prefers."

Assume that judicial ethics forbid judges from bargaining or trading votes. If the panel proceeds by majority rule in each case, and if the judges conform to judicial ethics, the defendant will win by a vote of 2 to 1 in all three cases. Thus majority rule with no vote trading results in the outcomes (D,D,D).

If the outcomes are (D,D,D), each judge gets his way in the two cases that he cares mildly about and does not get his way in the one case that he cares intensely about. Assume that each of the judges would rather get his way on the one case than he cares intensely about than on the two cases that he cares mildly about. Under this assumption, all three judges prefer (P,P,P) rather than (D,D,D). Majority rule produces a result that all the judges consider worse than an available alternative. In other words, majority rule yields Pareto-inferior outcomes relative to judicial preferences.

Now assume that ethical norms change and allow judges to bargain. All three judges would presumably recognize that each of them prefers (P,P,P) to (D,D,D). Consequently, they might agree to vote unanimously for the plaintiff in each case, yielding (P,P,P). By trading votes, each judge wins the one case that he feels strongly about and loses the other two cases where his feelings are weak. This example illustrates that bargaining allows judges to achieve Pareto-efficient outcomes.

Keep in mind that independent judges base their decisions on their ethical and political philosophies, not their material self-interest. If the judges on the panel are perfectly independent, the fact that they "prefer" (P,P,P) to (D,D,D) means that they regard the former result as morally and politically superior to the latter. In other words, they regard (P,P,P) as more nearly right than (D,D,D).

Judges may form a political elite with unrepresentative preferences relative to the citizens. Alternatively, the preferences of judges may represent the preferences of citizens. For example, political parties select judges for the German constitutional court in proportion to the number of seats the parties hold in the legislature. Thus the distribution of political sentiment on the German constitutional court roughly resembles the distribution of political sentiment among German voters. Given representative preferences, Pareto-efficient decisions relative to the preferences of judges are also Pareto-efficient relative to the preferences of citizens.

In chapters 2 and 3, I explained that majority rule is the threat point from which legislators bargain. Legislators avoid Pareto-inferior legislation by trading votes. Judicial ethics in most countries, however, forbid vote trading among judges. To illustrate, a U.S. or German judge who traded her vote on one case to obtain the vote of another judge would be considered utterly unethical.

When formal rules obstruct Pareto efficiency, informal practices typically undermine the formal rules. The extent of implicit or covert bargaining among judges is difficult to ascertain.[48] In the United States, high-court judges form a small, exclusive, and intimate community. One judge often knows what another will say before she speaks. This atmosphere breeds a spirit of cooperation in which each judge takes account of strong convictions held by other judges. Given intimacy and a spirit of cooperation, judges facing cases like the ones in table 8-1 may defer to the strong convictions of other judges. For example,

---

[48] Contrary to general beliefs, an impressive statistical study of the so-called case files of U.S. Supreme Court justices suggests a substantial amount of implicit or explicit bargaining over cases. See Spriggs 1997 and Stearns 1999.

the conservative judge in table 8-1 may defer to the liberal judge's strong convictions about civil rights, and the liberal judge may defer to the conservative judge's strong convictions about state power. Cooperation and deference may produce the Pareto-efficient result without explicit bargaining.

Some courts avoid Pareto-inferior decisions by the mechanism for assigning cases to judges. For example, Mexico traditionally had a large supreme court that assigned cases to small panels of judges. Mexican judges could apparently bargain with each other over who got assigned to which case. This practice allowed each judge to decide the cases that he cared about the most. (This practice allegedly contributed to corruption of Mexican judges, who bargained to hear cases affecting their private interests.)

Why forbid bargaining among judges? Some people believe that morality eschews compromise. To illustrate by a famous example from Kant, suppose that someone bangs on your door and asks you to hide him from an assassin. After hiding him, the assassin bangs on your door and asks whether his victim is inside. According to Kant, you must reply truthfully (Kant 1970). Kant takes this view because he does not think that morality depends on an act's consequences. Applied to courts, Kant's nonconsequentialism forbids judges from causing a small injustice in one case to avoid a large injustice in another case.

Unlike Kant, people who take consequences seriously usually believe that morality allows compromise. To illustrate by the preceding example, murder is far worse than a lie, so most people would feel justified in lying to the assassin. Applied to courts, consequentialism permits a judge to cause a small injustice in one case to avoid a large injustice in another case.

A more practical objection to judges trading votes concerns the appearance given by bargaining. Bargaining among judges offends public decorum and undermines the legitimacy of courts. Perhaps the trading of votes would undermine the independence of judges and cause them to seek bribes. Another practical argument, which I develop later, asserts that courts will make fewer errors when judges vote on the merits of each case rather than trade votes across cases. In any event, the possibility remains that revising judicial ethics to allow vote trading under certain circumstances would produce results that almost everyone prefers.

Questions

1. Most readers of this book are not currently involved in litigation, but every one of you is a potential litigant. If you could choose the rules under which courts would decide any future dispute involving yourself, would you permit or forbid judges to bargain and trade votes? Defend your answer.

2. Bargaining often involves withholding information for strategic advantage. To what extent would trading votes corrupt the search for truth among judges by giving them an incentive to withhold information from each other?

3. Assume that ethical rules change to allow bargaining among judges. How would bargaining and vote trading complicate the writing of opinions by judges?

TABLE 8.2
Court's Intransitive Values

Judge	Political Values of Judges					
liberal	civil rights	>	state power	>	property right
libertarian	property rights	>	civil rights	>	state power
conservative	state power	>	property rights	>	civil rights

The Honorable Judges Chase Their Tails

Now I turn from decisions to the reasons given by judges. A French court frequently announces its decision without explaining it, and British courts usually write short opinions. In contrast, the U.S. Supreme Court writes very long opinions that explain the reasons for its decision in detail. Each justice can dissent or concur in writing. Perhaps these opinions are too long and windy for efficient communication. (Napoleon allegedly added the following postscript to a letter: "I did not have time to be brief.") In any case, by explaining its decision, the court helps citizens understand their legal obligations and predict how the court will decide future cases.

Unfortunately, the U.S. Supreme Court sometimes contradicts itself in its written opinions. The judges, however, may not be the cause of contradiction. Instead, the cause may be the system of majority rule by which the court reaches its decisions. Majority rule may preclude the court from giving a coherent explanation of its decisions because the underlying opinions of the judges are intransitive.

To illustrate, return to the same three-judge panel as in table 8-1, which faces three cases involving civil rights, property rights, and state power. Table 8-2 depicts how the three judges order these values by their importance. Thus, the liberal judge thinks civil rights are more important than state power, whereas the conservative thinks that state power is more important than civil rights.

Without bargaining, these preferences result in incoherent opinions by the court. To illustrate, assume that the judges decide the cases by majority vote and each one writes an opinion explaining his vote. The opinion of the court is the opinion of the majority. Two of the three judges agree that civil rights are more important than state power, state power is more important than property rights, and property rights are more important than civil rights. Each individual judge orders the three values consistently, but the majority of judges are intransitive. Thus the opinion of the court about the importance of these values runs in a circle.

In this example, the court does not transmit a coherent political philosophy, by which I mean an ordering of political states of the world from bad to good. Other examples are easily constructed concerning, say, abortion, affirmative action, drugs, or the military draft.[49] In general, hard cases for judicial panels make incoherent law (Easterbrook 1982).

In private exchange, bargaining moves goods from people who value them less to people who value them more. Similarly, in collective choice, bargaining moves control over each public good from people who value the good less to people who value the good more. Achieving Pareto efficiency and coherence are two arguments for allowing judges on panels to trade votes.

Questions

1. "Dig a hole" and "Do not dig a hole" are inconsistent commands. If someone gives you two inconsistent commands, obeying both of them is impossible. "Dig a hole and fill it up" is a pointless command. Obeying this command is possible, although obedience accomplishes nothing. Are intransitive commands inconsistent, pointless, or both?[50]

2. Recall that the person who controls the agenda has a lot of influence over the outcome of majority-rule voting. On the U.S. Supreme Court, the agreement of four justices is required for a case to be heard ("granting certiorari"). The chief justice determines the order in which to hear the cases that were granted certiorari. Discuss whether or not the chief justice has enough control over the Court's agenda to influence outcomes significantly.

3. The U.S. Supreme Court is supposed to obey the principle of "stare decisis," which means that precedent must be respected. Respecting precedent implies allowing time to pass before overturning a past decision. Does stare decisis solve the problem of intransitive cycles?

Winner's Curse: Aggregating Factual Judgments

Table 8-1 and table 8-2 depict situations where judges with different values could benefit from bargaining. In this section, I explain why judges with the same values and different information might want to vote instead of bargain. Early in this chapter I explained that aggregating individual judgments often cancels errors. This section applies that result to decisions by panels of judges.

I begin with a problem of group judgment among people with the same objective. Assume that the state proposes to auction the rights to oil under a

---

[49] Here is a formula for constructing such examples. Consider three possible legal positions on a politically controversial act such as abortion, affirmative action, using drugs, or drafting people for military service. First, assume that the absolutist believes in prohibiting the act absolutely, or, if that is impossible, prohibiting the act conditionally. Second, assume that the moderate believes in prohibiting the act conditionally, or if that is impossible, the moderate prefers complete freedom rather than an absolute ban. Third, assume that the rule-of-law proponent dislikes ambiguity in rules or discretion in officials, so the rule-of-law proponent believes in complete freedom, or if that is impossible, the rule-of-law proponent prefers an absolute ban rather than a conditional ban. For a three-judge court, a majority prefers an absolute ban over a conditional ban, a conditional ban over complete freedom, and complete freedom over an absolute ban.

[50] For more on this point, see Kornhauser 1986.

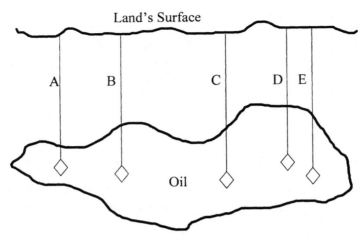

Fig. 8-5 Oil Field with Test Wells

parcel of its land. Five oil companies each drill a test well on the land, as labeled A, B, C, D, and E in figure 8-5. Company C's test well predicts more oil in the field than the other test wells, and Company A's test well predicts less oil than the others do.

Assume that antitrust law prevents the companies from pooling the results of their tests. Company C will probably bid the highest and win the lease. However, the test well yielding the most oil offers a biased estimate of the total oil in the field. Consequently, the winner may bid more than the rights are worth, in which case winning the auction is a curse—"the winner's curse."

In this example, antitrust law forbids the exchange of information, so each oil company based its bid on its own test well. Now modify the assumption about antitrust. Assume that the five companies are allowed to form a consortium, exchange information about the test wells, and make one bid. Everyone in the consortium has the same goal—to maximize the consortium's profits. To pursue this goal, the consortium needs an accurate estimate of the amount of oil in the field. To obtain the best estimate, the consortium should pool its data and compute the mean test result. Under certain assumptions, the mean of the five test wells provides the most accurate estimate of the amount of oil in the field.

Another decision process works almost as well as computing the mean test result. Instead of computing the mean, the group could decide by majority rule. In majority rule, the median voter will prevail. When errors are normally distributed, the median converges to the mean as the number of observations increases.

To generalize this result, assume that a group controls a continuous variable. The group sets the value of its control variable, and the value of the control variable determines the payoff to the group. Everyone has different information about how the control variable affects the payoff. If their information comes from independent observations with random errors (normal distribution of errors with zero mean), the best decision procedure is to pool their information and compute the mean. As the number of members of the group increases, allowing the median member to decide approaches the same result as computing the mean.

Applied to the courts, this reasoning provides a rationale for deciding cases by judicial panels with sincere voting. Assume that the issue in the legal dispute can be characterized as choosing a point on a dimension of choice. Also assume that the judges share the same underlying values, including the same conception of justice. The judges have common information supplied by the trial itself. In economic parlance, this information is "public." In addition, the judges bring to the case their knowledge based on past experiences and education, including knowledge about history, politics, and economics. In economic parlance, this information is "private," meaning it is not common to the judges. When the judges discuss the case with each other, they pool some of their private information and make it public. Judges arguing with each other about the effects of the case corresponds to the oil consortium's pooling information to compute the mean.

Even after lengthy deliberations, however, much information remains private. If private information contains random errors, a majority vote will provide a good estimate of the true value of the variable. In real cases, the judges do not know how to assign numerical values and compute the mean for the choices that they face. Given this fact, majority rule may be the best procedure for the judges to follow. When practical obstacles prevent the pooling of information, such as excessive transaction costs, then majority voting provides an inexpensive approximation to pooling the data. Majority rule is probably the best way for panels of judges to resolve factual disagreements.

When pooling information, the parties must be careful about how to frame the decision. In general, sequential decisions by majority rule do not yield the same results as do simultaneous decisions. This is important for choosing the procedures by which a panel of judges makes a decision in a case. For example, assume that a judicial panel must decide whether the plaintiff and defendant had a contract, and also whether the contract (assuming it exists) was breached. Sequential decisions may give a different result from simultaneous decision. In the sequential procedure, the court first decides by majority vote whether there was a contract. Assuming a positive decision on the first vote, the court next decides whether, assuming a contract, there was breach. By this procedure, the court might find for the plaintiff. If, however, the court adopted a simultaneous procedure, where the judges voted on the question of whether or not there was a contract and breach of a contract, a majority might decide for the defendant.

Here is an example from Geoff Brennan (Brennan 1998), drawing on the work of Bruce Chapman (Chapman 1998).

Judge X believes there was a contract and a breach.

Judge Y believes that there was no contract, but if there had been a contract there would have been a breach.

Judge Z believes that there was a contract but there was no breach.

Judges X and Z believe there was a contract, and judges X and Y believe that, assuming a contract, there was breach. So a sequential decision finds for the plaintiff by 2 to 1. However, judge Y believes there was no contract and judge Z believes that there was a contract and no breach, so a simultaneous decision finds for the defendant by 2 to 1. Which procedure is best? In general, rational court procedures must respond to the rules of probability theory, which I cannot explain here.[51] Instead, I return to the question of vote-trading by judges.

Differences in Beliefs and Values

The preceding argument for trading votes based on preference satisfaction assumes that judges have different values. In general, the greater the difference in values among judges, the larger the loss from forbidding bargaining. Conversely, the preceding argument for sincere voting based on factual accuracy assumes that judges have the same values. In general, the more similar the values of judges, the stronger the case for decisions based on sincere voting.

To illustrate the distinction between differences in values and information, recall the problem of rational abstention from a vote as discussed in chapter 2. In my example, a faculty member must decide whether to vote or abstain from voting on the proposed appointment of a new faculty member. The faculty member's decision only matters if her vote would be decisive. If her vote would be decisive, then abstaining would allow the chairman to decide the question instead of the faculty member. (The chairman breaks ties.) So the faculty member rationally abstains if she prefers for the chairman to decide rather than to decide for herself.

Whether the faculty member prefers to decide or allow the chairman to decide depends on differences in values and information. Values pertain to ends and information pertains to means. If the parties have the same ends, then each should defer to the one with the best information about means. Specifically, if the faculty member and the chairman have the same values and the chairman has more information, then the faculty member should abstain. If the faculty member and the chairman have very different values, then she should vote even though she has less information than the chairman does.

Now I summarize the application of this analysis to judicial panels. When judges share the same values, majority rule is a convenient way to aggregate private information. In voting, a judge with less information should defer to a

---

[51] To illustrate, assume that a judge must decide whether the defendant in a case is liable to the plaintiff for breach of contract. At the end of the trial, the judge decides that the probability of a contract equals .6, so the preponderance of the evidence favors the existence of a contract. On the basis of independent evidence, the judge also decides that assuming a contract, the probability of a breach equals .6. So, conditional on the assumption of a contract, the preponderance of the evidence favors breach. Given these facts, the judge, who is a good statistician, correctly concludes that the probability of a contract and breach equals $.6 \times .6 = .36$. The plaintiff has not proved his case by the preponderance of the evidence, so the judge finds for the defendant. Given that an individual judge correctly reasons in this way, the sequential procedure described in the preceding footnote is obviously inferior to the simultaneous procedure.

judge with more information and the same values. When values differ, however, judges do not want to defer to each other. Sincere voting case by case fails to aggregate the intensity with which different judges hold different values. To avoid needlessly sacrificing the realization of their values, judges with different values must find a means to decide cases (like bargaining) that responds to differences in the intensity of their sentiments.

Questions

1. Suppose you had to decide how many judges would be optimal for a nation's supreme court. Use figure 8-1 to discuss how to solve this problem.

2. Few American cases have aroused such passion in recent years as *Roe v Wade*, in which the Supreme Court decided, among other things, that states cannot forbid women to obtain an abortion during the first trimester of pregnancy. Instead of the first trimester, the Court could have chosen another point in the pregnancy, earlier or later. Apply the median rule to sincere voting by justices. How might the outcome change if the justices were allowed to bargain and trade votes?

CONCLUSION

Imagine a dispute among the branches of government over who should control an agency. Executive control would undermine liberty, declares the legislature. Legislative control would be grossly inefficient, declares the executive. Meanwhile, the high court contemplates setting aside both views and deciding the matter itself. Which branch of government will do best for which kind of decision? I have provided a framework for answering this question by sketching the special competency of each branch of government. Legislators especially bargain, the executive especially gives orders, and courts lubricate bargains for the legislature and effectuate orders by the executive. The next chapter examines differences in the behavior of the branches according to the extent of their separation.

Separation of Powers

I would rather be governed by 3 crazy people than by 1 crazy person.

—*Martin Shapiro*

OF ALL MONOPOLIES, the state's monopoly on force is the most profitable to control. Some politicians in a democracy would, if they could, perpetuate their power by undermining popular competition for office and moving toward dictatorship. Antitrust theory suggests how to constrain such politicians. According to antitrust theory, expanding the size of a cartel needed to monopolize an industry destabilizes it. The cartel destabilizes because each member has a stronger incentive to defect. Similarly, separating state powers destabilizes political cartels by requiring the cooperation of more officials to monopolize government. Elections provide voters with the primary means to control officials, but separating powers is also necessary (Persson, Roland, and Tabellini 1997).

Besides destabilizing cartels, separating powers influences the conduct of government. A superior gives orders to a subordinate, whereas equals proceed by bargains. Separating powers transforms subordinates into equals and replaces orders with bargains. The decision to separate powers in the constitution is a choice for bargains over orders as the way to conduct government. Bargains impose negotiation costs, whereas hierarchy imposes costs of supervision.

This chapter concerns the way separate powers relate to each other. The need for cooperation among the branches of government causes them to behave strategically toward each other, and the constitution partly determines their best strategies. Simple game theory can explain the logic of power in different constitutions. I will answer such questions as the following:

Example 1: The U.S. Supreme Court has much more discretion in interpreting law than does the House of Lords, which is Britain's highest court. Do courts usually enjoy more discretion in a presidential system than in a parliamentary system?

Example 2: Under an "open rule," a legislature can amend a bill before voting on it. Under a "closed rule," a legislature must vote on a bill without amending it. Most legislatures follow an open rule most of the time. However, the U.S. Congress sometimes follows a closed rule in voting on bills reported out of committees, and the Commission in the European Union

TABLE 9.1
Separation of Powers

type	powers	number	example
dictatorship	executive holds all power	1	former Soviet Union
rule of law + unicameral parliamentary	courts + one house of legislature with prime minister	2	Great Britain
rule of law + bicameral parliamentary system	courts + upper house + lower house with prime minister	3	Germany
rule of law + unicameral presidential	courts + one house of legislature + president	3	France
rule of law + bicameral presidential	courts + upper house + lower house + president	4	United States

makes proposals to the Council of Ministers under a closed rule. How does the change from open to closed rule change the ways bills get drafted?

Example 3: The European Union increasingly resembles a bicameral democracy. How will bicameralism change the power of the branches of European government, including the Commission and the Court of Justice?

FORMS OF SEPARATED POWERS

The executive, legislative, and judicial powers of government can be united or separated. A dictatorship such as the former Soviet Union unites all three powers in the executive, who governs by decree.[1] In contrast, any state with the rule of law, such as Great Britain, Germany, or the United States, separates the judiciary from the executive and legislature. A parliamentary system unites executive and legislative powers, as in Great Britain, where the Parliament's lower chamber elects the prime minister, or in Germany, where the lower chamber elects the chancellor.[2] In contrast, a presidential system separates executive and legislative powers as in France and the United States, where the citizens directly elect the president. A unicameral system unites legislative powers in a single house, as in Great Britain where the House of Commons governs and the House of Lords comments. In contrast, a bicameral system divides legislative powers between the lower and upper houses, as in Germany or the United States. Thus the number of divisions of power can range from 0 in a dictatorship to 4 in a presidential, bicameral democracy, as depicted in table 9.1.

---

[1] The Soviet Constitution provided for the separation of powers, but it had no effect on the real allocation of powers.

[2] The German president has ceremonial powers only.

Table 9.1 oversimplifies reality. To illustrate complexity, Japan and Korea have mixed systems with a president and a prime minister. The president has much executive power, but the prime minister heads the cabinet and the government day by day. Another complication occurs when the effective allocation of power in politics does not correspond to the legal allocation in the constitution. For example, a dominant political party can unite powers separated in the constitution, as illustrated by the Communist Party in the former Soviet Union. Conversely, fragmented parties can separate powers united in the constitution, as illustrated by the government in Israel. The effective separation of powers depends on law (the constitution) and politics (parties). This chapter focuses on the former, not the latter. To keep the analysis simple, I often assume that political parties reinforce the constitutional allocation of powers, rather than undermine it.

Students of industrial organization sometimes say that only four numbers should matter to antitrust policy: one, two, three, and four-or-more. These cryptic remarks mean that a market with four or more suppliers behaves much like a perfectly competitive market, whereas each reduction in suppliers below four increases the likelihood of monopolistic practices.[3] Generalizing, this rule of thumb implies that political conspiracy with four or more members is unmanageable. Assuming this generalization is true, dividing government into four branches provides the maximum protection against political conspiracies obtainable by constitutional separation of powers, and each decrease below four makes conspiracy more manageable.

Consequences of Separating Executive and Legislative Powers

In addition to destabilizing cartels, separating power causes government to proceed more by bargains and less by orders. Bargains impose negotiation costs, whereas hierarchy imposes supervision costs. According to table 9.1, different constitutions strike the balance differently. In a parliamentary system with tight party discipline, the prime minister gives orders to legislators of his own party. In a coalition government, the prime minister has some power to give orders to members of the government from different parties. In a presidential system, in contrast, the leading legislators do not sit in the cabinet and may not be members of the president's party, so the president typically needs to bargain with the leading legislators. To illustrate, the British prime minister issues orders to enact legislation in Parliament, whereas the U.S. president negotiates with Congress over legislation.

Several consequences follow from these facts. By increasing transaction costs, bargaining among the branches of government slows down the pace of legislation and reduces demand for it. Conversely, by reducing transaction costs, the unification of power speeds up legislation and increases demand for it.

[3] This belief is implicit in the common practice of measuring monopoly structure in an industry by its four-firm concentration ratio.

Figure 9-1 depicts these facts, where the horizontal axis indicates the quantity of legislation and the vertical axis depicts its price. The "demand" for legislation in figure 9-1 refers to the willingness of citizens to pay lobbyists for it. To keep the analysis simple, assume that lobbyists can exert their influence and obtain legislation for their clients. The "supply" of legislation refers to the cost to lobbyists of providing legislation. The separation of powers shifts the supply curve up, resulting in a rise in the price of legislation from p_0 to p_1, and a fall in the demand for legislation from x_0 to x_1.

Separating powers in figure 9-1 causes total expenditures by private citizens on legislation to change from $p_0 x_0$ to $x_1 p_1$. Total expenditures increase if demand is inelastic, and total expenditures decrease if demand is elastic. In consumer theory, demand for "necessities" is inelastic and demand for "luxuries" is elastic. Thus the separation of powers should increase total expenditures on legislation considered necessary by interest groups and decrease expenditures on legislation considered desirable but unnecessary. Whether aggregate expenditures increase or decrease depends on whether necessary or unnecessary expenditures predominate in the mix of legislation demanded by interest groups.

Besides changing total expenditures on lobbying, the separation of powers redirects it. When powers are separated, an interest group with influence over only one branch of government can block legislation. For example, an interest group with influence over the executive, and no influence over the legislature, might persuade the executive to veto a bill. Lowering the cost increases the demand by interest groups to block legislation. Conversely, when powers are separated, securing passage of new legislation requires influence with several branches of government. Raising the cost decreases the demand by interest groups to enact legislation. Thus the separation of powers privileges the status

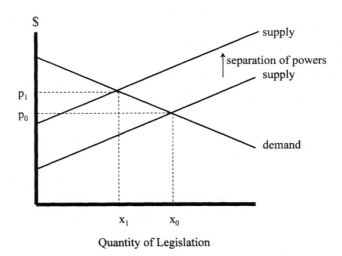

Fig. 9-1 Demand for Legislation

quo. (Recall the demonstration in chapter 3 that privileging the status quo can fill the empty core in a game of majority rule.)

Bargaining between Executive and Legislature

Now I will contrast a unicameral parliamentary system, which unites executive and legislative powers, and a unicameral presidential system, which separates executive and legislative powers. To keep the analysis simple, I assume that political parties reinforce the constitutional allocation of power, so that the constitutional allocation of powers corresponds to their effective allocation.

Bargain Set

Assume that the government considers a bill to spend funds on a new activity. In a unicameral parliamentary system, a majority in the legislature suffices to enact the bill. To illustrate, if the British prime minister enjoys a secure majority in Parliament and party discipline holds, she can decide her preferred expenditure level and enact it. She does not need to negotiate with another branch of government or another party. Any negotiations that occur will take place among the members of the ruling party, typically within the cabinet. In contrast, a unicameral presidential system requires cooperation of the executive and legislature to enact legislation. To illustrate, if the president belongs to one party and another party controls the legislature, enacting legislation requires bargaining between the president and the legislature.

I will explain the logic of bargaining between legislature and executive with the help of figure 9-2. Without the legislature's cooperation, the executive can block any bill, which results in expenditure level $0. The executive prefers for expenditures to increase from $0 up to $E, which is the executive's most preferred expenditure. Beyond $E, the executive prefers for expenditures to decrease. E_0 indicates the level of expenditure that makes the executive indifferent about whether the bill is enacted or not. In the notation of a utility function, indifference implies $u^E(0) = u^E(E_0)$.

No rational person makes an agreement unless he prefers the results of cooperating rather than not cooperating. Consequently, any proposal for cooperating

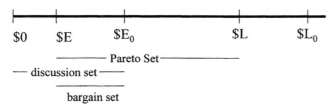

Fig. 9-2 Bargaining between Executive and Legislature

that is worth discussing must give each player at least his threat value. Rather than no expenditures, the executive prefers positive expenditures up to $\$E_0$. Thus the executive is prepared to discuss the set of points $[0, E_0]$ in figure 9-2.

Without the executive's cooperation, the legislature cannot enact a bill, thus obtaining expenditure level $0. The legislature prefers for expenditures to increase from $0 up to its most preferred expenditure $L, as depicted in figure 9-2. Beyond $L, the legislature prefers for expenditures to decrease. $\$L_0$ indicates the level of expenditure that makes the legislature indifferent about whether the bill is enacted or not: $u^L(0) = u^L(L_0)$. The legislature prefers no legislation rather than a bill larger than $\$L_0$. Any proposal for cooperation that is worth discussing must give the legislature at least its threat value, $u^L(0)$. So the legislature is prepared to discuss the set of points $[0, L_0]$.

As explained, the executive will discuss $[0, E_0]$, and the legislature will discuss $[0, L_0]$. The intersection of these two sets, which equals $[0, E_0]$ in figure 9-2, is the set of points that both parties are prepared to discuss. Thus $[0, E_0]$ is labeled *discussion set* in figure 9-2.

When the parties begin discussion, they will immediately identify some points preferred by both of them to other points. A change preferred by both parties moves from a point outside the Pareto set to a point inside the Pareto set given by [E, L]. The convergence of interests on points inside the Pareto set eliminates the need to bargain over points outside of it. To illustrate, starting from $0 in figure 9-2, both the executive and the legislature agree to move to the right. The situation changes, however, when movement to the right reaches the executive's most preferred point $E. The executive will resist demands by the legislature for further moves to the right. The legislature, however, may demand moving further to the right as the price of cooperation. Consequently, further moves to the right will become the subject of bargaining. In general, choosing among points within the Pareto set requires bargaining.

The *bargain set* refers to the range of possible values that rational parties will bargain over as the basis of cooperation. For a point to be in the bargain set, both parties must be prepared to discuss it, and they must disagree about whether any better point exists. In other words, the bargain set in figure 9-2 equals the intersection of the discussion set and the Pareto set: $[E, E_0]$.

Negotiations between the executive and legislature will focus on the bargain set. If the parties cooperate successfully, a bill will be passed by the legislature and signed into law by the executive that requires expenditure somewhere in the range $[E, E_0]$.

My analysis of bargaining in figure 9-2 assumes a unicameral presidential system in which different parties control the executive and legislature. Now I will describe bargaining under bicameralism. Depicting bargaining between the executive and the two houses of a legislature, as in a bicameral presidential system with weak party discipline, requires slight modification of figure 9-2. Instead of thinking of L in figure 9-2 as denoting the legislature, think of it as denoting the lower house. Let U denote the legislature's upper house. Adding U's preferred point $U to figure 9-2 and adding U's point of indifference with no

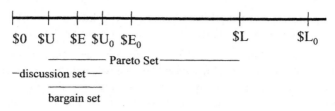

Fig. 9-3 Bargaining among Executive and Two Houses of Legislature

expenditure U_0 gives figure 9-3. By the same logic as before, $[0, U_0]$ indicates the discussion set in figure 9-2, $[U,L]$ indicates the Pareto set, and $[U, U_0]$ indicates the bargain set.[4]

By adding a third power and moving from figure 9-2 to figure 9-3, the bargain set decreases. In general, additional division of powers can "weakly decrease" or "weakly increase" the range of bargaining.[5]

The executive is usually a single person,[6] whereas the legislature is a collection of individuals and parties. The preceding discussion treats each chamber of the legislature as a single person for the purposes of bargaining. In reality, legislatures often organize themselves to overcome divisions and strengthen their bargaining position with the executive. For example, the U.S. Congress gives committee chairmen effective veto power over some legislation, thus counterbalancing the president's veto power (Diermeier and Myerson 1994). In addition, the legislature reduces the executive's power by creating unwieldy executive agencies that the executive imperfectly controls (Moe and Caldwell 1994).

Questions

1. If the preferences of the upper house move a little to the right in figure 9-3, does the Pareto set increase, decrease, or remain unchanged? What about a move to the left?

[4] Any one of the three powers can secure expenditures $0 without cooperating with the others. The upper house is indifferent between $0 and the expenditure level denoted U_0. Discussing levels of expenditure above U_0 with the upper house is pointless, so $[0, U_0]$ is the discussion set. The Pareto set is the range in between the most preferred points of the three actors, $[U, L]$. All three powers prefer a point inside the Pareto set to any point outside it. So bargaining converges to the intersection of the Pareto set and the discussion set, which can be written in notation as follows:

$$\underset{\text{discussion}}{[0, U_0]} \quad \cap \quad \underset{\text{Pareto}}{[U, L]} \quad = \quad \underset{\text{bargain}}{[U, U_0]}.$$

In general, the power that prefers the least expenditure determines the upper bound of the discussion set. The discussion changes when moving from figure 9-2 to figure 9-3 because I assume that U_0 is smaller than E_0. Similarly, the Pareto set expands when moving from figure 9-2 to figure 9-3 because U is smaller than E. In this example, the relative locations of U, E, and L are arbitrary assumptions made for purposes of illustration, rather than the actual preferences of real powers in a particular nation.

[5] "Weakly decreases" is a term of art that means "cannot increase and might decrease."

[6] In the Swiss federal system, however, the executive is a small committee of equals.

2. If the preferences of the lower house move a little to the right in figure 9-3, does the Pareto set increase, decrease, or remain unchanged?

3. Besides the legislature, executive, and the judiciary, Taiwan has two additional branches of government. A separate body of elected officials has the power to decide whether or not a person is qualified for office. The other elected body decides whether or not to impeach officials who violate the law or abuse their powers. Predict the effects of this further separation of power on the formation of political cartels and combating corruption of officials.

4. In discussing democracy's empty core in chapter 3, I mentioned that democracy in India allegedly endures because the country contains so many different kinds of people. Discuss how the fragmentation of social groups affects the *optimal* separation of powers in the constitution.

Timing and Commitment

Which point in the bargain set will be chosen? In unstructured bargaining, game theory cannot predict precisely where agreement will occur within the bargain set. (A reasonable solution, called the *Nash bargaining solution* in chapter 3, requires the parties to split the surplus from cooperation.[7]) Adding more structure to the bargaining process, however, can give the bargaining game an exact solution. I will discuss several processes yielding exact solutions and apply them to legislation.

TAKE-IT-OR-LEAVE-IT

Sometimes procedural rules give an official the power to make take-it-or-leave-it offers to the legislature. The recipient of a take-it-or-leave-it offer can accept or reject but cannot modify the proposal or offer an alternative. To illustrate using the European Union, the Commission makes proposals to the Council of Ministers that the Council can accept or reject but not amend. In the legislature, take-it-or-leave-it offers take the form of bills drafted in committee and proposed to the whole legislature under a procedural rule requiring legislators to vote for or against the bill without amending it. To illustrate, committees of the U.S. Congress sometimes report bills that the U.S. Congress decides under a "closed rule."

A *purely* take-it-or-leave-it offer is *final* in the sense that only one offer is made. In reality, the rejection of a take-it-or-leave-it offer often results in revising and resubmitting another offer. To illustrate, rejection of a proposal made by the Commission to the Council of Ministers or made by a committee to the

---

[7] To compute the Nash bargaining solution for the example in figure 9-2, let x denote the actual compromise reached. Cooperation yields the surplus $u^E(x) - u^E(0)$ to the executive, and $u^L(x) - u^L(0)$ to the legislature. Since x splits the surplus, it can be found by solving $u^E(x) - u^E(0) = u^L(x) - u^L(0)$. For the best justification of the Nash bargaining solution as a predictive theory, see Rubinstein 1982. Notice that the Nash solution involves combining the utilities of different people, without, however, the ethical significance that welfare theories give to interpersonally transferable utility.

U.S. Congress does not preclude an alternative proposal. Although these offers are not necessarily final, reformulating and resubmitting an offer uses valuable time and energy. Consequently, a rejected offer sometimes gets abandoned, in which case the logic of final offers applies.

In any case, the simple logic of final take-it-or-leave-it offers illuminates more complex cases. The power to make a final take-it-or-leave-it offer gives all the bargaining power to one actor. Consequently, an actor with this power will make an offer in the bargain set closest to his most preferred point. The other parties will accept this offer because they prefer it to the status quo.

To illustrate using figure 9-2, identify the executive with the Commission in the European Union. By assumption, the Commission most prefers point E. Identify the legislature in figure 9-2 with the Council of Ministers. By assumption, the Commission can make a final take-it-or-leave-it proposal to the Council of Ministers. The Council of Ministers prefers any point up to L_0 rather than 0. Bargaining will focus on the bargain set $[E, E_0]$. The Commission will propose its most preferred point E and the Council of Ministers will enact the proposal.

As another illustration, consider the presidential veto. The "presentment clauses" of the U.S. Constitution require bills to be presented for signature by the president before becoming law.[8] When the U.S. Congress enacts a bill, the president can sign or veto it, but he cannot modify it. I will model this process as a final take-it-or-leave-it offer by Congress to the president. To keep the example simple, assume that the Senate and the House have the same preferences, and they most prefer point L as depicted in figure 9-2. Identify the president's preferences with the executive in figure 9-2. By assumption, Congress can make a final take-it-or-leave-it proposal to the president. The president prefers any point up to E_0 rather than 0. Bargaining between the president and Congress will focus on the bargain set $[E, E_0]$. By assumption, Congress most prefers point L, which is above E_0. Therefore Congress will enact a bill slightly below E_0 and the president will sign it.

Questions

Assume that the executive nominates a candidate to serve as head of an administrative body and the legislature must confirm the nomination. Model the process as the executive's presenting the legislature with a final take-it-or-leave-it nomination. If the legislature refuses to confirm the nomination, the agency must function without a head.[9] Depict the logic of the situation in a figure.

STRENGTH THROUGH COMMITMENT

In any finite sequential bargaining game, the player who makes the final offer presents its recipient with a take-it-or-leave-it choice. After a final take-it-or-leave-it offer, the player who made the offer cannot compromise, so the responsibility to compromise devolves to the other player. Consequently, the player

---

[8] Article I, section 7, clauses 2 and 3.

[9] See McCubbins 1989; Ferejohn and Shipan 1990.

who makes the last offer has the power to extract the entire surplus of cooperation from the player who receives the final take-it-or-leave-it offer.

In general, a party who commits to a position reduces or loses the power to compromise. To illustrate, return to the preceding example of the presidential veto. As explained, if Congress most prefers point L in figure 9-2, then it will enact a bill slightly below E_0 and present the president with a final take-it-or-leave-it offer. Anticipating this fact, the president might try to commit to vetoing any bill above, say, E. If the president succeeds in making a credible commitment, then Congress will have to lower the bill to E in order to make it law. In general, the actor in a bargaining situation who succeeds in making a credible commitment gains an advantage by losing the power to compromise.

Businesses make their promises credible by signing enforceable contracts. Politicians, however, typically have to rely on the weaker power of reputation. Thus to lend credibility to a threatened veto, the president may have to put his reputation at stake by appropriate publicity, such as repeating publicly that he will veto any bill over E.

The preceding discussion of sequencing and commitment assumed final offers. Politics actually occurs through repeated interactions with tentative offers. The change from final take-it-or-leave-it offers to tentative take-it-or-leave-it offers complicates without threatening the economic logic of bargaining. In general, sequencing and commitment tip the balance of power in bargaining games in favor of the party who can eliminate his ability to compromise. In bargaining, there is strength in commitment. Structured bargaining has outcomes determined by sequencing and commitment, whereas unstructured bargaining has indeterminate outcomes.

LOGICAL OR PSYCHOLOGICAL?

Psychological experiments reveal some troublesome results for the economics of bargaining. Instead of demanding all of the surplus, the actor in experiments who makes the final offer often proposes to share the surplus as required by intuitive ideas of fairness. Furthermore, the party who receives an "unfair" final offer sometimes rejects it, even though he receives a higher objective payoff from accepting the unfair offer than from rejecting it.[10] In experiments with final-offer games, many people stop short of pure economic logic. Insofar as these experiments with college students apply to career politicians, the economic models require modification to allow some role for intuitive concepts of fairness.

Questions

1. In an experiment, you have the power to make one offer to divide $10 with another person. If your partner accepts the offer, you get the money as agreed. If your partner rejects the offer, the two of you get nothing. What would you

[10] Notice that the latter fact partly explains the former fact. Final-offer games are often called "ultimatum games" in experimental economics. Similar violations of economic rationality occur in "dictator games," where one party has all of the power and refuses to use it. See Hoffman and Spitzer 1985b and Hoffman et al. 1994.

offer? Does your offer depend on whether your partner knows who you are? Does your offer depend on whether you know who your partner is? Does your offer depend on whether you will play the game again with this partner?

2. The so-called gatekeepers in the U.S. Congress are powerful committees that can bottle up legislation and prevent it from reaching the floor for a vote. If the legislation reaches the floor for a vote under an open rule, however, the legislature can modify the committee's proposal. Modify figure 9-2 to depict bargaining between a "gatekeeper" committee and the whole legislature.

Executive's Line-Item Veto

The preceding section discussed how the U.S. president's veto power affects bargaining between the executive and legislature. Chapter 8 discussed how omnibus, multi-issue legislation with numerous riders can contribute to chronic government deficits in the United States and elsewhere. Responding to this problem, the U.S. Congress enacted legislation in 1996 giving the president the power to veto a single line or item in a multi-issue bill, without vetoing the entire bill, but this legislation was found unconstitutional in 1998.[11] Similar legislation in many American states gives the governor power to veto lines in the budget enacted by the state legislature (Krasnow 1991).

I will explain how changing the legal process from the conventional veto, which I call "total veto," to the line-item veto dramatically increases the president's power. Perhaps the greatest increase in the executive's power concerns his command over interest groups. Consider a line in the budget providing, say, a subsidy of $50 million to the developers of flat-screen computer technology. A clever president can threaten to veto the item while letting the industry know that a generous campaign contribution might change his mind. In principle the executive could extract a donation of up to $50 million in exchange for not exercising the veto. Thus the line-item veto gives vast powers to the executive to extract "rents" from the special interests that receive subsidies in the budget enacted by the legislature.

In addition to increasing the president's power over special interests, the line-item veto also increases the president's power over Congress. I will explain this fact using a graph. To be concrete, let x and y represent government expenditure on guns and butter, respectively. Given the government's budget constraint, the president most prefers point (x^*, y^*) in figure 9-4.

---

[11] *Clinton v City of New York*, 524 US 417 (1998). The legislation that was struck down by the court would have worked as follows: "The way it works is the president would sign a spending bill and then act within five days to reject an item. He could not rewrite spending figures—only reject them entirely—but he could cancel spending for new entitlement programs or eliminate tax breaks benefiting groups of fewer than one hundred. ... Congress then could pass a bill to reinstate the specific spending. And if the president vetoed that, a two-thirds vote in Congress would be required to override him and force the administration to spend the money. ... [T]he president's ability is limited compared to governors who can reduce the size of a budget line item" (Superville 1997, P. A3).

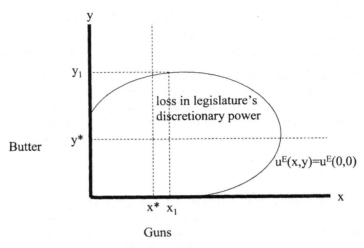

Fig. 9-4 President's Preferences and Line-Item Veto

Recall that in figure 9-2 the point E_0 indicates the level of expenditure that leaves the executive indifferent to the status quo: $u^E(0) = u^E(E_0)$. I generalize the point E_0 in figure 9-2 to two-dimensional choice in figure 9-4. The indifference curve $u^E(x, y) = u^E(0, 0)$ in figure 9-4 connects all levels of expenditure on guns and butter for which the executive remains indifferent relative to spending nothing. (Increasing expenditures on both items widens the deficit, so the indifference curves form ellipses rather than the usual shape in the theory of consumer demand.[12])

In order to contrast the legislature's discretionary power under the total veto and the line-item veto, I will model veto power as a final take-it-or-leave-it offer by the legislature to the executive. First consider the total veto. In the model of a final take-it-or-leave-it offer by the legislature, the executive will sign any bill enacted by the legislature with values (x, y) inside the indifference curve $u^E(0, 0)$. Thus the legislature can choose any point in the set inside the indifference curve $u^E(x, y) = u^E(0, 0)$ in figure 9-4. The set of points (x, y) satisfying $u^E(x, y) \geq u^E(0, 0)$ indicates the discretionary power of the legislature under the executive's total veto power.

Now consider what happens when the executive can veto lines of expenditure in a bill without vetoing the total bill. Line-item veto power has two general forms. In the simplest form to analyze, the executive can replace the legislature's proposed expenditure on an item with *any lower* level of expenditure. Some

[12] Let p_x and p_y denote the price of x and y, respectively, so total state expenditures are $E = p_x x + p_y y$. Let T denote tax revenues. Thus the deficit equals $T - E$. Write the executive's utility function as $w^E(x, y, T - E)$. The function w is concave in its three arguments, as with ordinary commodities in consumer demand theory. Substitute $p_x x + p_y y$ for E to obtain $w^E(x, y, T - p_x x - p_y y)$. Holding T constant, this expression defines u^E, where $u^E(x, y) = w^E(x, y, T - p_x x - p_y y)$. The indifference curves for u^E are elliptical in x and y.

U.S. governors have this power. In general, the executive will exercise this veto power whenever he prefers lower expenditures on an item rather than the expenditures in the legislature's bill. To illustrate, a bill calling for expenditure (x_1, y_1) in figure 9-4 would be line-item vetoed and replaced with expenditure (x^*, y^*). Consequently, replacing the total veto with the line-item veto sharply diminishes the discretionary power of the legislature. In figure 9-4 the change reduces the legislature's discretionary power by an area that includes (but is not limited to) the area to the northeast of (x^*, y^*) labeled "loss in legislature's discretionary power."[13]

The second type of line-item veto, which the U.S. president briefly enjoyed, allows the executive to accept or reject expenditures in a bill line by line, but does not allow the executive to reduce expenditures. Line by line, the executive's choice is binary, not continuous. To illustrate, if a bill calls for expenditures (x_1, y_1), the executive can sign the bill, veto the line of expenditure on guns thus yielding $(0, y_1)$, veto the line item on butter thus yielding $(x_1, 0)$, or veto both lines of expenditure thus yielding $(0, 0)$. Like the continuous line-item veto, the binary line-item veto shifts power from the legislature to the executive. The shift is smaller with the latter than with the former. (I omit a graphical demonstration because of its complexity.)

When the executive and legislature bargain successfully, the executive does not actually exercise its veto. Even if the executive seldom exercises the line-item veto, the threat tips the balance of power in favor of the executive relative to the legislature.

Bargaining between Houses of Legislature

Having discussed bargaining between the executive and legislature, now I discuss bargaining between the two houses of the legislature in a bicameral system. The logic of bargaining is easier to explain by focusing on constitutions giving equal power to the two chambers, as in the United States, rather than on constitutions giving less power to the upper chamber, as in Spain. My discussion only concerns a situation in which both houses must concur in order to enact the legislation at issue. When two chambers of the legislature disagree, they must bargain to a solution. To illustrate using the European Union, when the Council of Ministers and the Parliament disagree over proposed legislation, it sometimes goes to a "conciliation committee" drawn from both bodies. Similarly, when the U.S. Senate and House of Representatives enact somewhat different versions of the same bill, the differences must be resolved in a "conference committee." The conference committee members, who are drawn from both chambers, often have decisive power to shape the final legislation. They especially have this

---

[13] In figure 9-4, the line-item veto removes from the legislature's discretion any point such that there exists a point to the southwest that lies on a higher indifference curve for the executive. A complete map of this area, whose shape can be irregular, requires a complete map of the executive's indifference curves.

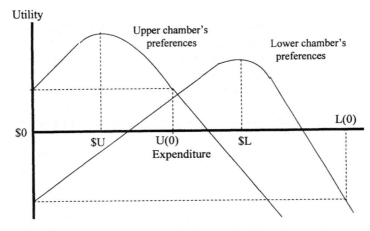

Fig. 9-5 Conference Committee's Discretion

power when rules of procedure enable them to make take-it-or-leave-it offers to the two chambers of the legislature.

To illustrate, recall that figure 9-3 depicts take-it-or-leave-it offers involving the executive and the legislature. To depict take-it-or-leave-it offers by the conference committee, figure 9-5 revises figure 9-3. The horizontal axis in figure 9-5 represents state expenditures on a certain project, and the vertical axis represents the utility of the upper and lower chambers of the legislature. The lower chamber would prefer spending $L, and the closer the actual allocation is to $L, the better the lower chamber likes it. Similarly, the upper chamber would prefer allocating $U, and the closer the actual allocation is to $U, the better the upper chamber likes it. (Thus I assume that each chamber has single-peaked preferences in the dimension of choice.)

Now suppose the lower chamber passes a bill whose implementation requires spending $L, and the upper chamber passes a bill whose implementation requires spending $U. A conference committee must reconcile the two bills. If the committee reaches an agreement, the reconciled bill will be reported back to the two chambers under a closed rule, which allows each chamber to vote "yes" or "no" but not to amend the bill. If both chambers enact the reconciled bill, it becomes law. If either chamber of Congress rejects the reconciled bill, it does not become law and the allocation equals $0.

The logic of choice is simplest when the conference committee can make final take-it-or-leave-it offers to the legislature. Under this assumption, each chamber will vote for the bill if they prefer the level of expenditure in the bill rather than $0. According to figure 9-5, the lower chamber will vote "yes" on any bill between 0 and $L(0)$, and the lower chamber will vote "no" on any bill outside the interval $[0, L(0)]$. Similarly, the upper chamber will vote "yes" on any bill between 0 and $U(0)$, and the upper chamber will vote "no" on any bill outside the interval $[0, U(0)]$. Therefore, the conference committee has power to choose any value in the intersection of $[0, L(0)]$ and $[0, U(0)]$.

Under a closed rule, the conference committee can make take-it-or-leave-it offers. These offers, however, are not necessarily final. Now I will modify the analysis to allow for the fact that if either chamber rejects a take-it-or-leave-it offer, both chambers can enact fresh bills. The legislature is most likely to reject the conference committee's offer and enact fresh bills under two conditions. First, the transaction costs of fresh legislation must be low relative to the value of a fresh bill. Second, both chambers prefer an alternative bill to the one the committee proposes. If both chambers prefer an alternative bill, they may bypass the committee and vote directly for the bill that they both prefer. By enacting identical bills in both chambers, no reconciliation in a conference committee is required.

To illustrate, if the conference committee chooses any bill above L in figure 9-5, both chambers would prefer a bill to the left with lower expenditure than L. Alternatively, if the conference committee chooses any bill above U and below L, no alternative exists that both chambers prefer. Therefore the conference committee can choose any point between U and L. The zone between L and U, written [U, L], is the Pareto-efficient set, defined with respect to the preferences of the lower and upper chambers.[14]

To summarize, the conference committee must also choose a point that both chambers prefer to no bill, as denoted by the intersection of [0, U(0)] and [0, L(0)]. Furthermore, assuming relatively low transaction costs of fresh legislation, the conference committee must choose a point in the Pareto set [U, L] to assure that its bill is not replaced by an alternative preferred by both chambers. Thus the conference committee's zone of discretion in figure 9-5 is given by the interval between U and U(0).

Questions

1. Redraw figure 9-5 so that the conference committee's most preferred point $K is outside the interval between $U and $L. Explain why the conference committee may not want to choose point $K.

2. Suppose the legislature were changed from bicameral (two chambers) to tricameral (three chambers). Would the Pareto sets in figure 9-5 increase, decrease, or remain unchanged?

SEPARATION OF POWERS AND JUDICIAL DISCRETION

Unlike the legislature or executive, courts are not supposed to bargain with politicians. Even without bargaining, however, the separation of powers in other branches affects the court's discretionary power to interpret the law. Specifically, multiple vetoes on fresh legislation increase the discretionary power of the court.

---

[14] Check for yourself that in the interval between L and U, no changes are possible that make one chamber better-off without making the other worse-off.

To see why, consider what happens when the government dislikes the court's interpretation of a statute. The government may try to enact a new law whose explicit language precludes the court's previous interpretation, in which case legislation *repeals* the court's interpretation. The discretionary power of a court stops short at the point where its interpretation of existing law provokes repeal by fresh legislation. (Notice that this analysis parallels the analysis of discretion by administrative agencies in chapter 7.)

To depict the court's discretionary power of interpretation caused by separating executive and legislative power, figure 9-6 modifies figure 9-2 by adding some points above the line, which I will explain. Assume that the legislature and executive bargain with each other and agree to enact bill B into law. (B is inside the bargaining set [E, E_0].) Changed circumstances subsequently reveal ambiguous drafting of the legislation, which creates room for dispute over its meaning. To illustrate, assume the government uses funds authorized for expenditure on "roads" to acquire land for bicycle paths, and the automobile manufacturers bring a suit contending that a bicycle path is not a "road" as meant by statute.

Competing theories proclaim how the court *ought* to interpret the statute's language. Perhaps the court ought to interpret the law according to the *legislative bargain* that enacted it, in which case the court would find that the law authorizes expenditure level B. This theory of interpretation requires examining legislative history to discover the intent of the law's makers.

Or perhaps the court should try to interpret the statute according to the *plain meaning* of the words in which it is written, even when the meaning is not plain. For example, the court might ask linguists whether or not most speakers would describe a bicycle path as a "road."

Or perhaps the court should interpret the law in the way that they think best serves the *public interest*. To illustrate in figure 9-6, let "J" indicate the point that, in the opinion of the judges, best serves the public interest. Under the public-interest theory, the court should interpret the statute to authorize expenditure level J.

Or, perhaps the judges should defer to the *preference of the government* by interpreting the law in the way most preferred by the executive, in which case the court would find that the law authorizes expenditure level equal to E.

Or, perhaps the judges should interpret the statute in light of changed preferences of the legislature and executive. To illustrate, assume that the executive's

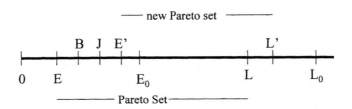

Fig. 9-6 Court Interprets Legislation

most preferred point shifts from E to E', and the legislature's most preferred point shifts from L to L', thus creating the new Pareto set [E', L'] for the executive and legislature. Notice that the original bargain B lies outside the new Pareto set [E', L']. Thus, the current legislature and executive prefer for the level of expenditure to increase above the value B favored by the enacting legislature. To implement these preferences, the government could enact fresh legislation. Alternatively, the court could save the government the transaction costs of fresh legislation by reinterpreting existing legislation to allow expenditures inside the new Pareto set [E', L'].

I have discussed some normative theories of interpretation. My present concern, however, is with the court's power, not its ethics. After a bill is enacted, the court must interpret legislation as cases arise. When cases expose ambiguities and unintended consequences of legislation, courts can change law by interpreting it. When the court makes law by interpretation, the government can respond by enacting fresh legislation that repeals the court's interpretation. Thus the court has discretionary power within the range of interpretations that will *not provoke* legislative repeal.

To repeal a court's interpretation of existing legislation, all the decision makers with the power to block legislation must prefer a fresh bill rather than the court's interpretation. In other words, the possibility of repeal requires the court's interpretation to be outside the Pareto set of the legislature and executive. Conversely, if the court's interpretation is Pareto efficient relative to the preferences of the decision makers who must cooperate to enact fresh legislation, no potential proposal exists that is preferred by all of them. So the *court's discretionary power of interpretation corresponds to the set of possible laws that are Pareto efficient relative to the preferences of the decision makers who must cooperate to enact fresh legislation.*[15]

To illustrate, consider the initial situation in figure 9-6 where the executive prefers E, the legislature prefers L, and, after bargaining, they enact bill B. The judges, however, believe that interpretation J best advances the public interest. If the judges interpret the bill to mean J, which is inside the Pareto set [E, L], then the executive and legislature cannot agree on an alternative. The executive prefers J to any alternative to the right, and the legislature prefers J to any alternative to the left. So the executive and legislature cannot agree to repeal the court's interpretation J by enacting fresh legislation. In general, the court has discretionary power to choose any interpretation in the Pareto set [E, L] without provoking repeal by fresh legislation.

Now consider what happens if the court's interpretation lies outside the Pareto set of the executive and legislature. Assume that the most preferred points of the executive and legislature shift to E' and L', so the new Pareto set is [E', L']. If the court interprets the legislation to mean J, which lies outside [E', L'], the executive and legislature prefer moving to the right. If transaction costs are not

---

[15] I implicitly assume zero transaction costs of fresh legislation. Positive transaction costs of fresh legislation increase judicial discretion and the discretion of government administrators, as explained in chapter 7.

too high, the executive and legislature will bargain and agree on fresh legislation to repeal the court's interpretation by moving to the right. To preclude this possibility, the court should interpret the legislation to mean a point inside the set [E', L']. Thus the Pareto set of the sitting legislature and executive defines the court's discretionary power of interpretation.

Now I relate the court's discretionary power to the alternative constitutional forms described in table 9.1. Under a dictatorship, the judges take orders from the executive, which the Russians call "telephone justice." The rule of law requires separating the courts from the executive.

Moving down the list in table 9.1, a unicameral parliamentary system separates the courts from the unified executive and the legislature, which figure 9-7 depicts by equating the most preferred point of the executive E_1 and the legislature L_1. In a unicameral parliamentary system, a disciplined governing party can repeal any judicial interpretation at will, so the court has little discretionary power of interpretation. In other words, the courts can only win when interpreting legislation differently from the government if the difference in opinion is so small that the government prefers to avoid the transaction costs and embarrassment of overriding the court. In important cases, the court might as well interpret statutes as preferred by the government in the sitting legislature, unless the court wants to put the government through the exercise of enacting fresh legislation.

Now consider the consequence of an additional separation of powers, producing a bicameral parliamentary system or a unicameral presidential system. Since fresh legislation requires cooperation of two powers, the court can interpret statutes anywhere between their most preferred points without provoking repeal by fresh legislation. For a bicameral parliamentary system, figure 9-7 depicts this fact by the distance between the most preferred point of the lower house L_1 and the upper house L_2. In a bicameral parliamentary system, the court's discretionary power corresponds to the Pareto set $[L_1, L_2]$. Similarly, for a unicameral presidential system, figure 9-7 depicts the court's discretionary

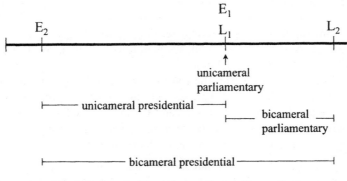

Fig. 9-7 Court's Discretionary Power (Pareto Set)

power by the distance between the most preferred point of the president E_2 and the legislature L_1, which equals the Pareto set $[E_2, L_1]$.

Finally, consider the consequence of an additional separation of powers, creating a bicameral presidential system. The court can interpret legislation anywhere between the most preferred points of the three powers. Figure 9-7 depicts this fact by the distance between E_2, L_1, and L_2, which equals the Pareto set $[E_2, L_2]$.

In general, the court's discretion in interpreting legislation equals the Pareto set for the officials who must cooperate to pass new legislation. Separating powers typically increases the court's discretionary power of interpretation, and unifying powers typically decreases it.

Besides the constitution, political organization influences the cost of legislation. Fragmentation of political parties increases the court's discretionary power, and concentration of parties decreases it. According to recent empirical research, these two variables—constitutional separation of powers and party fragmentation—explain much of the observed differences in the daring of courts in different countries (Cooter and Ginsburg 1996; Ramseyer and Rasmusen 1996). For example, the model correctly predicts judicial daring by U.S. courts, timidity by courts in Great Britain, and intermediate behavior by French and German courts.

These predictions about the discretionary power of courts assume that politics conforms to a democratic constitution with the separation of powers. Under these assumptions, obstacles that slow down legislation increase the discretionary power of the court. The effects may be different, however, in countries with a powerful executive and a weak tradition of democracy. In such countries, a slowdown in legislation may cause the executive to rule by degree. When paralysis afflicts the legislature, democracies look to the courts and autocracies look to the executive.

Questions

1. Why would you expect the discretionary power of the court to be roughly the same in a bicameral parliamentary system as in a unicameral presidential system? Why might they differ?

2. The United States has a bicameral presidential system, and Australia has a bicameral parliamentary system. A judge of Australia's High Court argued that his court is less willing to consider policy in deciding cases than is the U.S. Supreme Court. He explained this difference by the fact that the Australian constitution, unlike the U.S. Constitution, contains no bill of rights (Mason 1986–87). Explain this fact using the preceding analysis, without referring to a bill of rights.

Supreme Court on the Edge

An historical example illustrates the application of the so-called *spatial model* of court discretion. In 1964 the U.S. Congress passed the landmark Civil Rights

Fig. 9-8 Civil Rights Legislation and Bush Administration

Act, which ultimately caused much litigation and social change. Subsequently, Presidents Reagan and Bush appointed conservative Supreme Court justices who narrowed the interpretation of the Civil Rights Act and reduced its scope. I will use the spatial model to show how far the Supreme Court could go in this direction during the government of President Bush.

If the Supreme Court provoked fresh civil rights legislation, it could count on President Bush to veto it. Overriding the veto would require a two-thirds vote of *both* chambers of Congress. The Senate was more conservative than the House on civil rights issues. Thus the Senate constrained how conservative the Court's interpretation could be without provoking fresh legislation.

By this reasoning, the Supreme Court's zone of discretion in interpreting the Civil Rights Act was bounded on the right by the point at which two-thirds of the senators would vote for fresh legislation overturning the court's decision. This situation is depicted in figure 9-8. H, S, P, and C represent the most preferred points of the House, Senate, president, and Court, respectively. V indicates the point at which two-thirds of the Senate would override a veto.

In fact, the Supreme Court's decisions provoked a fresh civil rights bill in 1990, which passed both chambers of Congress and was vetoed by President Bush. The subsequent attempt to override the veto obtained the necessary two-thirds vote in the House, but fell two votes short of two-thirds in the Senate. Apparently the Supreme Court went to the edge without falling over. After examining the historical evidence, a prominent scholar concluded that the Supreme Court in fact acted as the model predicts.[16]

Questions

1. Suppose that preferences shift in just one branch of government, say the U.S. House, whereas preferences remain constant for the president and Senate. If existing legislation lies inside the Pareto set, no new legislation results. Use the spatial model to show that the change in the preferences of the House can change the court's zone of discretionary power.

2. If the transaction costs of legislation increase, does the discretionary power of courts increase or decrease? Explain your answer.

3. In the American system, a presidential veto can be overridden by a two-thirds vote in both chambers of Congress. Use the spatial model to depict how the possibility of an override bounds the Court's discretion.

[16] Subsequently political circumstances changed and President Bush signed a new Civil Rights Act (Eskridge 1991).

4. The U.S. House and Senate narrowly pass slightly different bills, which are reconciled in committee. Upon receiving the bill, the president, instead of signing or vetoing it, does nothing for eight days and Congress adjourns ("pocket veto"). At its next session, Congress enacts the bill again and sends it to the president. Again, the president does nothing. After ten days, the bill automatically becomes law.[17] Now administrators and courts must interpret law. Who made the law? What was their intent?

5. Justice Scalia of the U.S. Supreme Court especially favors "textualism," which means interpreting a statute by its text and ignoring legislative history. Explain how this approach simplifies the message sent to voters by a bill, but may increase the transaction costs of government.

Constitutional Interpretation

Unlike creating legislation, repealing interpretations of constitutions by courts requires constitutional amendments. For example, U.S. courts originally held that the U.S. Constitution prevents the federal government from taxing income, and the sixteenth Amendment repealed this interpretation by explicitly granting Congress the power to levy income taxes. Amending constitutions, however, is typically more difficult than enacting legislation, so constitutional interpretation typically conveys more discretionary power to courts than does statutory interpretation.

To depict the difference, consider a unicameral parliamentary system in which enacting a statute requires a vote by a majority of legislators, whereas amending the constitution requires a vote by two-thirds of legislators. To keep the example simple, assume that voting follows the median rule and the preferences of legislators roughly follow a normal distribution over a single dimension of choice as depicted in figure 9-9.

First consider ordinary legislation in figure 9-9. The median vote, labeled x^*, will command a majority in the legislature against any alternative. If the majority enacts legislation denoted by x^*, and if transactions costs are low, any attempt by the court to interpret the law as different from x^* will provoke repeal by fresh legislation. The court, consequently, has no discretionary power of statutory interpretation.

Constitutional interpretation is another matter. Beginning at the origin in figure 9-9, more than two-thirds of the legislators prefer moving to the right. A two-thirds vote will repeal the court's interpretation of the constitution, so a court interpretation of the constitution in this zone provokes repeal by constitutional amendment. As the court's constitutional interpretation moves farther to the right, however, it reaches point x_1, where at least one-third of the legislature opposes moving further to the right. The legislature cannot agree to repeal an interpretation of the constitution in this zone.

---

[17] Article I, section 7 of U.S. Constitution.

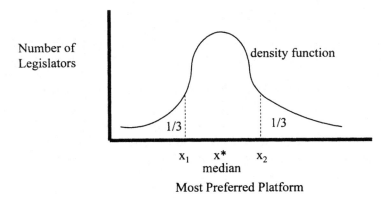

Fig. 9-9 Court's Discretion in Interpreting the Constitution

Equivalently, beginning at the far right of figure 9-9, more than two-thirds of the legislators prefer moving to the left. A court interpretation in this zone provokes repeal by constitutional amendment. As interpretation moves farther to the left, it reaches point x_2, where at least one-third of the legislators opposes moving further to the left. The legislature cannot agree to repeal an interpretation of the constitution in this zone.

As explained, when the court chooses any point between x_1 and x_2, at least one-third of the legislature will oppose any move to the left or the right. Thus the court's zone of discretion in interpreting the constitution equals the interval $[x_1, x_2]$.

In general, lowering the obstacles to changing the constitution, such as requiring a simple majority instead of a super-majority, decreases the discretionary power of the courts to interpret the constitution. To illustrate by referenda, fifteen U.S. state constitutions provide for constitutional amendment or legislation by majority vote of the citizens, and no state requires a super-majority vote by the citizens.[18] The courts in these states cannot easily shield unpopular decisions from the majority of citizens, and some highly publicized ballot initiatives have reduced minority rights.[19] Conversely, greater obstacles to changing the constitution increase the discretionary power of the courts to interpret the constitution. To illustrate, in the thirty-five U.S. states that do not provide for referenda, the courts can shield unpopular decisions from the majority of citizens.[20]

[18] Baker 1995, p. 146. When placing a proposal on the ballot, however, an initiative to amend the state constitution typically requires more signatures than an initiative to enact legislation.

[19] The most famous are Colorado's Amendment 2, which forbade the state or its localities to enact statutes protecting people from discrimination based on their sexual orientation or entitling them to affirmative action, and California's Proposition 209, which prohibits many forms of affirmative action or racial preferences by the state, including contracting and university admissions.

[20] In spite of these facts, Baker argues that peculiar features of U.S. federalism should cause the rights of minorities to increase from simple-majority rule by citizens seeking to amend U.S. state constitutions, as opposed to super-majority rule. As opposed to super-majority rule, simple-majority

Are court powers of constitutional interpretation excessive? Constitutions like that of the United States secure the independence of the court from politics, which gives the courts much discretionary power when interpreting the constitution. Constitutional review can set in motion a virtuous cycle that encourages compliance with the constitutional order and respect for basic civil and political liberties. Unlike the United States, some nations fear the insulation of constitutional interpretation from politics. Rather than allowing the court to impose its own views, some nations want courts to respond to the elected government when interpreting the constitution. To illustrate, the Supreme Court of Italy (Corte Suprema di Cassazione, which has nine divisions specialized in civil, criminal, and labor matters) does not decide constitutional questions. Instead, the Supreme Court refers constitutional questions that arise in its cases to the Constitutional Court. According to Article 135 of the Italian Constitution, the Constitutional Court consists of fifteen judges who serve for a nine-year term. Judges serving in other courts elect five constitutional judges, the president of Italy appoints five, and the united chambers of Parliament elect five. While the five judges chosen by the judiciary are relatively independent of politics, the other ten judges depend on politicians for securing high office upon completing their term on the Constitutional Court. Constitutional interpretation in Italy is thus a political activity by design.[21]

Other countries use various devices to circumscribe the court's power of constitutional interpretation. A procedure found in Mexico and Argentina, called "amparo," permits a court to decide that a government policy or law was unconstitutional as applied to a particular person in a given case. Such a finding, however, does not imply that the policy or law is generally unconstitutional, nor does such a finding provide a precedent for future disputes.[22]

In chapter 1 I explained that the constitution trumps statutes whenever they conflict. When a court case challenges the constitutionality of a statute, U.S. courts review the statute to determine whether or not it is constitutional. In contrast, constitutional courts in Europe are more reluctant to provoke a confrontation with the legislature by declaring legislation to be unconstitutional. Observers sometimes summarize the facts by saying that U.S. courts practice *constitutional review* of statutes and European courts do not. An intermediate procedure used in France permits a court to review the constitutionality of a

---

rule allows more constitutional amendments to pass. These amendments can expand or repeal individual rights in state constitutions. The U.S. Constitution typically blocks attempts by states to repeal individual rights, whereas attempts to expand individual rights in state constitutions are allowed under the U.S. Constitution. Thus, proponents of expanding individual rights should favor simple-majority rule, not super-majority rule, to amend state constitutions. See Baker 1995.

[21] Note, however, that the Constitutional Court does not decide the case that originally posed the constitutional issue. Having rendered its decision on the constitutional issue, the ordinary judge resumes his decision making on the original case. The fate of individual litigants is thus shielded from political influences. See Cappelletti, Merryman, and Perillo 1967, pp. 75–78, and Merryman 1985. Thanks to Francesco Paresi.

[22] Barker 1988; Provost 1992.

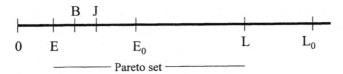

Fig. 9-10 Statutory Interpretation, Constitutional Interpretation, and Statutory Review

newly enacted statute. Once a new statute passes constitutional review, however, the statute's constitutionality cannot be challenged in subsequent cases. Thus the United States has ex post judicial review, France has ex ante judicial review, and most European countries have no judicial review.

Sometimes a court with wide powers, such as the U.S. Supreme Court, can choose whether to base its decision on statutory interpretation, constitutional interpretation, or judicial review. To appreciate the choices, consider figure 9-10's simplification of figure 9-6. The executive and legislature in figure 9-10 enact B as a bargain. The court believes that J is the best interpretation of the law for the public. The court considers whether to change the law by statutory interpretation, constitutional interpretation, or statutory review. Statutory interpretation allows the court to choose any point in the Pareto set [E, L] without fear of repeal by fresh legislation. Constitutional interpretation permits the court to choose any point in a much larger set than [E, L], which I do not depict in figure 9-10. Statutory review invalidates the statute, in which case the legislature and executive may enact a new bill. Assume the new bill will come as close to B as possible while respecting the court's decision. Thus the court's discretionary power in figure 9-10 is largest under constitutional interpretation, smallest under statutory review, and intermediate under statutory interpretation.

Questions

1. Suppose the majority needed to amend the constitution increases from two-thirds to three-quarters in figure 9-9. Depict the change in the court's discretionary power of constitutional interpretation. Would this change be larger or smaller if the distribution's variance increased?

2. In recent years the U.S. Supreme Court has interpreted the U.S. Constitution so as to resist congressional encroachment on the president's veto power. Under what conditions would you expect these interpretations to strengthen the Supreme Court's discretionary power?

EUROPEAN UNION: AN EXAMPLE

After the Second World War, Europe realized an ancient dream by creating its first unified government since the Roman Empire.[23] Beginning as a treaty of

[23] This section is based on Cooter and Drexl 1994 and Cooter and Ginsburg 1998. Also see Schmidtchen and Cooter 1997.

cooperation in coal and steel production, the European Union, or EU (to use its current name), deepened its cooperation to include new policy areas and broadened its membership to fifteen states, with many more in line to join. Free trade proved a stronger force in uniting Europe than did the armies of Napoleon and Hitler. Recently Europe's constitutional law has been the most innovative in the world, providing a model for prosperity and peace through regional government. I will use the methods developed in this chapter to analyze briefly the constitutional logic of the European Union.

Institutions of the European Union

Europe's "primary law" consists of the treaties establishing the EU, whose amendment requires ratification by all member-states.[24] Although Europe has no formal constitution, primary law is its de facto constitution. Primary law divides powers among Europe's four most important institutions of government: the Commission, the Council of Ministers, the Parliament, and the Court of Justice.[25]

The Commission is an administrative body currently consisting of nineteen commissioners and a president who is appointed by the Council. The Commission administers "common" policy areas, meaning the ever-expanding set of EU regulations. The governments of the member-states meet regularly, usually through the Council of Ministers, which is made up of cabinet-level officials from the member-states. The Council makes policy and enacts legislation. The European Parliament consists of 518 members, who were formerly appointed by the national governments, but now citizens directly elect a certain number of them in each country.[26] The European Court of Justice consists of one judge from each member-state plus one additional judge.[27] The Court interprets legislation and ensures that it is consistent with primary law. Cases may be brought before the Court by the main European organs of government, national

---

[24] Here are the main treaties constituting the primary law of the EU: European Coal and Steel Community Treaty, 1951; European Economic Community, 1957; European Atomic Energy Community, 1957; Merger Treaty, 1965; Single European Act of 1986 (providing for creating the Single European Market); and the Treaty of European Union, 1992.

[25] In addition to these basic institutions, there are other institutions in the EU that do not play a direct role in the formation and interpretation of European law. These include the Presidency of the Commission, a new Council of Regions, the Economic and Social Committee, and the Central Bank.

[26] European law allocates seats in the Parliament by country, not population. Thus Luxembourg has six seats, or approximately one for every 70,000 inhabitants, whereas Germans has 99 seats, or approximately one for every 800,000 inhabitants. Each country elects its representatives according to its own law, thus allowing district or at-large elections and allowing winner-take-all or proportional representation.

[27] In 1987, a Court of First Instance was introduced to try to reduce the backlog of cases before the court. The Court of First Instance has jurisdiction over those areas of policy that the EU directly administers.

governments, national courts of member-states,[28] and individuals who can show detriment from a Community Act.[29]

Europe's legislation comes in two basic types. *Directives* consist of instructions to the legislatures of all member-states requiring them to harmonize their legislation in order to unify European markets ("build the single market"). Directives must be implemented as national law by the legislature in each of the member-states, so different states may enact somewhat different laws to implement the same directive. *Regulations* are laws enacted by the EU that apply directly to the member-states. Unlike directives, regulations are uniform everywhere in Europe and they take effect without action by the member-states. Regulations are restricted to activities under the exclusive jurisdiction of the EU, such as the Common Tariff, the Common Agricultural Policy, and European competition policy.

Separation of European Powers

The interactions among European institutions in lawmaking are complex and varied. I will simplify greatly in order to explain how the division of powers in Europe's primary law shapes its legislation. The Commission has the exclusive power to propose legislation. The procedure required to enact legislation depends on the legislation's specific content. Different substantive laws must be enacted by different procedures. The procedures differ according to the level of agreement required in the Council. Some legislation requires a unanimous vote in the Council, whereas some legislation requires a "qualified majority." (A qualified majority is a weighted majority, with heavier weights going to ministers from larger countries.[30]) The procedures for enacting European legislation also differ according to the extent of participation required by Parliament. Depending on the issue, the Council can legislate unilaterally without any role for Parliament; the Council can legislate after consulting with the Parliament; the Council can legislate subject to a parliamentary veto; or legislation requires equal cooperation by the Council and Parliament.

To be precise, the following five procedures can be distinguished:

1. *Unilateral Unanimity (UU)*: The Council can adopt or amend the Commission's proposal by unanimous vote. If unanimity is not reached, the proposal is rejected.
2. *Unilateral Qualified Majority (UQM)*: The Council can adopt the Commission's proposal by qualified majority. Otherwise, the proposal is rejected.

[28] National courts in the member-states can ask the Court of First Instance for an advisory opinion when a suit before them raises an issue of European law.

[29] If the Court of First Instance finds detriment, relief is given to the plaintiff, but the Community Act in question remains valid.

[30] Under the current procedure of qualified majority, Italy, Germany, the United Kingdom, and France each have ten votes, Spain has eight, Belgium, Greece, the Netherlands, and Portugal each have five, Austria and Sweden four, Denmark, Finland, and Ireland three, and Luxembourg two. Adopting a proposal in most areas requires 62 out of 87 votes.

3. *Consultation (CS)*: Same as the two unilateral procedures, except Parliament has the right to be consulted.
4. *Cooperation (Coop)*: The Council can adopt the Commission's proposal by a qualified majority and amend by unanimity. If, however, Parliament rejects the proposal, the Council can only adopt by unanimity.
5. *Co-decision (CD)*: Adoption of a proposal by the Commission requires approval of the Council by a qualified majority and approval of Parliament by a majority.

The top of this list contains the original procedures for legislating, which gave almost all power to the Council and no power to Parliament. The Council represents governments and the Parliament represents people. Consequently, the original procedures were criticized for being undemocratic. Proceeding further down the list, changes describe the shift toward bicameralism and democracy.

Define the discretionary power of an institution as its ability to get the laws enacted that it prefers. Now consider how the trend toward bicameralism and democracy affects the discretionary power of European lawmakers, beginning with the Commission.

The Commission has the exclusive power to propose legislation. Some of its proposals will be enacted and others will be rejected or amended. The Commission has more discretionary power when it can choose among a larger range of alternatives from which to frame proposals that will be enacted into law. This range is set by the difficulty of enacting new legislation, which changes with the procedural rules. A change from unanimity rule in the Council to qualified majority rule increases the Commission's discretionary power by making its proposals easier to enact.[31] Conversely, a change in procedure that strengthens Parliament creates an obstacle to enacting legislation. Consequently, changes that strengthen Parliament decrease the Commission's discretionary power by making its legislative proposals harder to enact.

---

[31] To be precise, the unilateral procedure, or the procedure of consultation, permits the Council to enact proposals on its own, regardless of Parliament's opposition. Under the unilateral procedures, the Council enacts proposals under a unanimity rule or a qualified majority rule. The change in procedure from unilateral-unanimity to unilateral–qualified majority in the Council increases the power of the Commission because it only needs a qualified majority in the Council to enact its proposals. In general, a procedural change requiring a weaker majority to enact legislation increases the discretionary power of the executive to propose legislation.

In contrast, the change from unanimity to consultation, or from consultation to cooperation, or from cooperation to co-decision, decreases the power of the Commission because as the role of Parliament in making law increases, the Commission must anticipate objections by two bodies (Council and Parliament) when proposing legislation. The Commission has a smaller range of alternatives from which to frame proposals that will actually become law. In general, a procedural change requiring two houses of the legislature, rather than one, to approve a proposal before it becomes law decreases the discretionary power of the executive to propose legislation.

In reality, the Commission cooperates closely with the Council and Parliament in developing proposals. The power of the Commission over legislation, as explained above, presumably affects its strength in bargaining with the Council and Parliament, as well as in affecting the ideology defining appropriate behavior by the institutions of European government.

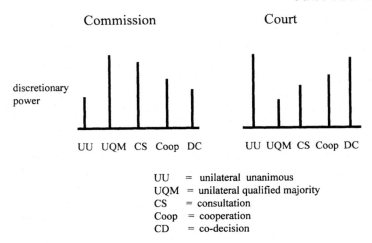

Fig. 9-11 Procedure Changes Power in European Union

Now I turn from the Commission to the Court. The latter is the mirror image of the former. As explained above, fresh legislation can be enacted to repeal judicial interpretation of existing law, so a court has discretionary power within the range of interpretations that will not provoke legislative repeal. A court's discretionary power of interpretation increases with the difficulty of enacting fresh legislation. A change from unanimity rule in the Council to qualified majority rule decreases the Court's discretionary power by making proposals easier to enact in the Council. Conversely, a change in procedure that strengthens Parliament increases the Court's discretionary power by making legislation harder to enact.

Figure 9-11 summarizes graphically how different procedures for legislation change the power of the Commission and Court. The judges on the Court have different philosophies about making law by interpreting law. These philosophies influence their willingness to exercise their power. I suspect that procedures giving the Court more real power will ultimately cause the judges to exercise more power.[32]

Questions

1. The co-decision process increases democracy by giving more weight to the European Parliament. Direct election of the head of the Commission is an alternative way to increase democracy. Predict the different consequences that these two ways to increase democracy have for the relative power of European institutions.

---

[32] For evidence that courts generally behave in this way, see Cooter and Ginsburg 1996. For evidence on the active political role of the European Court of Justice, see Garrett, Kelemen, and Schulz 1998.

2. Chapter 5 explains the difference between voting on proposals that combine different issues ("splicing") and voting on each issue separately ("factoring"). In the Council of Ministers, the national ministers for agriculture meet as the Council to decide European farm policy, the national ministers of transportation meet as the Council to decide European transportation policy, and so forth. Assuming that the Council factors issues and the Parliament splices issues, predict some differences in their behavior.

CONCLUSION

In a unified state, concentrating power tempts the executive to dispense with competition for office and end democracy. Conversely, separating powers effectively, which requires both law (constitution) and politics (parties), helps to stabilize competition for control of the state and preserve democracy. Separating powers, however, has consequences for the operation of government that are not easily discerned without analytical tools. Separated powers must bargain with each other to legislate. The need for agreement restricts possibilities to the set of Pareto-efficient outcomes relative to the preferences of the powers. Timing and sequencing of decisions affect the distribution of power among branches. An official who can make take-it-or-leave-it offers can obtain most of the surplus from cooperation by imposing the need to compromise on others. Even though courts do not explicitly bargain, the separation of powers in other branches determines the courts' discretionary powers of interpretation. Courts and administrators that interpret laws can exploit the scope of disagreement among the powers that must cooperate to change the law.

PART FOUR

Optimal Rights

REEF CORAL is the symbiosis of an animal (polyp) and a single-celled plant (zooxanthellae). The animal creates a shell around itself that protects the plants living within its flesh, and the plants produce most of the animal's food and energy. Similarly, the liberal state protects individuals and private organizations that produce the goods for society. Protection comes from the rule of law and individual rights.

Earlier I defined democracy as popular competition for government. Many people also consider democracy to encompass individual rights. Having analyzed the allocation of power to officials in part 3, part 4 turns to the allocation of rights to persons. Individual rights proceed from a philosophical tradition emphasizing personal autonomy and political liberty. Autonomy and liberty encourage self-expression and self-fulfillment. Community life, however, demands cohesion and restraint. When individuals conflict with communities, constitutional rights tilt the scale of justice in favor of individuals. In a democracy, individual rights impose limits on the scope of government by removing certain issues from ordinary politics.

To illustrate, if amending the constitution is difficult, and if the constitution effectively protects private property, then the legislature cannot expropriate one group's wealth for the benefit of another group. The constitution precludes such a battle for redistribution by removing expropriation from ordinary politics. Similarly, if the constitution effectively protects freedom of religion, then one religious community cannot use ordinary legislation to impose its practices on another religious community. In general, constitutional protection of individual rights dampens a group's impulse to use politics to subordinate others.

Normative philosophy, not positive science, tends to dominate discussions of constitutional rights. In response to this fact, chapter 10 explains how economics values rights, and chapter 11 relates these valuations to central philosophical traditions. The next three chapters—chapters 12, 13, and 14—return to positive analysis and consider the consequences of alternative understandings of three particular rights—property rights, free speech, and civil rights.

The people who enjoy rights usually value them, and a good constitution responds to peoples' valuation of rights. I will consider how to maximize the value of rights to the people who enjoy them. Chapter 12 explains how property rights, which belong to people as owners, give them liberty over material resources. Given liberty, the owners maximize the value of material resources. Chapter 13 explains how human rights, which belong to people as human beings, give liberty over nonmaterial aspects of life. Focusing on freedom of speech, chapter 13 explains how a constitutional prohibition on the regulation of speech can maximize its value. Chapter 14 explains how civil rights, which belong to people as citizens, give people an equal right to participate in public life and the private economy. Under perfect competition, the injurers pay the costs of discrimination. Correcting imperfections in competition, consequently, protects victims against the harm caused by discrimination.

The Value of Rights

> Like three distinct powers in mechanics, they [Parliament's two houses and the king] jointly impel the machine of government in a direction ... which constitutes the true line of the liberty and happiness of the community.
>
> —*Blackstone's* Commentaries[1]

> No man's life, liberty, or property is safe when the legislature is in session.
>
> —*Mark Twain*[2]

IN THE preceding quotation, Blackstone refers to the "liberty and happiness of the community." To achieve happiness, democratic constitutions create a framework of competition that fills offices with the candidates most preferred by the majority of voters. To preserve liberty, democratic constitutions divide the powers of government into several branches. Blackstone's homily suggests that a state with the proper division of powers serves the happiness of the community and the liberty of individuals.

The penetrating humor of Mark Twain suggests otherwise. Even a democratic legislature can threaten the individual.[3] To protect against the legislature, some constitutions entrench individual rights, so that a majority in the legislature cannot extinguish them. Entrenchment can protect the life, liberty, and property of citizens even while the legislature is in session.

I will restate this argument in economic terms. The preceding chapters view democracy as a mechanism to satisfy preferences through collective action. From this perspective, allocating constitutional powers creates incentives for officials to supply the public goods that citizens prefer, thus increasing the happiness of the community. Sometimes, however, some citizens prefer restricting the liberty of other citizens. In these circumstances, vulnerable individuals need protection against politics. Entrenching individual rights in the constitution provides some protection against politics.

---

[1] Blackstone 1979, book 1, chapter 2, p. 151. Thanks to David Lieberman for this quote.

[2] This quote is attributed to Twain by many people, but I can find no definite reference to when he said it. The same words were used by a judge in a mid-nineteenth-century case (1 Tucker 247, 249 [New York:Surr. 1866]).

[3] Joke: In the United States everything is permitted that is not forbidden. In Germany everything is forbidden that is not permitted. In Italy everything is permitted even if it is forbidden.

In a democracy, circumscribing the power of the majority of citizens or impeding their elected representatives requires justification. Rival philosophies disagree over the justification of individual rights. In this chapter and the next, I will use economic analysis to clarify these disputes without choosing among rival philosophies. In this chapter I explain different ways to measure the value of individual rights, which help answer such questions as the following:

Example 1: Laws create many different rights for many different people. How do constitutional rights differ from other legal rights?

Example 2: A consumer sues a credit-rating company to end its practice of disseminating personal information about loan applicants to lenders. The court must balance the value of credit and the individual's right to privacy. How do courts strike the balance? Do they implicitly use cost-benefit analysis?

Example 3: The state finances military defense, which is a public good, and the state subsidizes opera, which is a private good. In what ways do constitutional rights resemble military defense and opera?

INDIVIDUAL RIGHTS IN GENERAL

"Rights" are a multipurpose tool in the box of legal concepts. Some rights are entitlements created by a *duty*.[4] To illustrate, the promisor's duty to perform on a contract creates the promisee's right to performance. In this case, someone is entitled to a benefit because someone else has a duty to provide it. Instead of a contract, a statute can impose the duty creating the right. To illustrate, legislation that forbids employers from interfering with union organizing by worker gives workers the right to organize into unions.

These rights have legal effect insofar as the individual with the right can obtain a legal remedy for violation of the correlative duty.[5] To illustrate, the victim of breach of contract can sue for damages, and workers can seek an injunction against their employer's interfering with their efforts to organize a union. In general, law creates a right correlating with a duty whenever law gives a remedy for breach of duty to its victim.[6] Giving victims the legal power to remedy their wrongs relieves the state of responsibility for initiating every remedy, thus reducing the information that state officials need to do their jobs. Every developed legal system makes use of victim-initiated remedies, so every developed legal system creates some rights by imposing duties.

[4] Note that someone can have a duty to benefit another person and the beneficiary has no right to the benefit. For example, a policeman may have a duty to protect the citizens, but the citizens may not have a right to be protected by a policeman.

[5] But some entitlements have no remedy. A state official may be obligated to give me an explanation for rejecting my job application, but I may not have a legal remedy against an official who neglects his duty.

[6] There are many refinements of the fundamental legal concepts, which I leave to philosophy. Hohfeld 1964 (1919) provided an early system of such distinctions. Also see Radin 1938; Wright 1963; and Wellman 1985.

When contemporary people speak of "rights," however, they often adopt a lofty tone that implies something more than these work-a-day rights. Modern discussions of the individual and the state often concern special rights such as freedom of speech, press, assembly, and religion, contract, and the right to property and a fair trial. These individual rights are relatively modern inventions conventionally attributed to the eighteenth-century Enlightenment.

A difference in logic partly distinguishes work-a-day rights from individual rights. An *autonomous* person directs his own life. Many constitutional rights, such as those enumerated in the U.S. Bill of Rights, give the individual a zone of discretion to make life's fundamental choices without domination or manipulation by the state. Individual rights thus provide the legal foundation for a society of autonomous people. Admiration for an autonomous life and a society of individuals provides one motive for embedding individual rights in a constitution.

I refer to individual rights that provide autonomy as *liberties*. Two aspects of law secure liberty. First, the individual who possesses a liberty is neither obligated nor forbidden to do the act in question. Second, other people are forbidden to interfere with the liberty's exercise. To illustrate, a person who enjoys freedom of speech is not legally obligated to keep silent or to speak, and, if he chooses to speak, he is not legally obligated to say anything in particular. Furthermore, other people are prohibited from interfering with his speech, for example, by silencing him with threats.

By abstracting from these facts, I can formulate a handy definition of liberties. Let x denote an act such as "speak," "print," "assemble," or "worship." In general, a person has a liberty to x if he is not obligated or forbidden to x, and others are forbidden to interfere with his x'ing. A person who is not obligated or forbidden to x has *permission* to x.[7] Prohibiting others from interfering with x'ing protects it. Thus a liberty can be defined as a *protected permission*.

Now I can explain how individual rights differ from rights in general. Laws impose duties, create powers, distribute benefits, and supply remedies for a variety of purposes. For example, the duty to drive with reasonable care increases safety on the roads. Other purposes of legal duties include health, prosperity, coordination, predictability, compensation, deterrence, fairness, equality, competitiveness, communication, education, and cultural improvement. Different purposes require different logical structures for laws. Individual rights in constitutions have a distinct purpose that requires a distinct logical structure. The purpose of individual rights is to provide the legal basis of autonomy, and their logical structure is protected permissions.

Questions

1. Discuss how the following aphorisms relate to individual autonomy.

"Liberty is protected permissions."

"Anarchy is permission without protection."

"Dictatorship is protection without permission."

---

[7] This definition comes early in the axiomatic development of deontic logic by Wright 1963.

2. In what sense does a bill of rights "legalize freedom"?

3. Suppose the United States had no bill of rights. Would a bill of rights pass in today's Congress?

VALUING RIGHTS

An individual right is one thing and its value is something else. Philosophers worry about what things really are and economists worry about their value. My treatment of individual rights involves a little philosophy and a lot of economics. Having briefly described individual rights, I will devote the rest of this chapter to their value.

If a government violates your constitutional rights, what can you do about it? Sometimes you can sue for money damages,[8] in which case a court must place a price on, say, the right to speak, worship, vote, or a fair trial. Instead of damages, however, the usual court remedy is an injunction prohibiting the injurer from continuing to violate your rights. In these circumstances, increasing the scope of one right may require decreasing the scope of another right. The balancing of one right against another can be described as evaluating the opportunity cost of one right in terms of another right. A court that awards damages or balances competing rights places a value on them. Economics offers several different methods for valuing rights, which can clarify court practices. I will explain these methods in order of increasing complexity.

Commodities

Wealth can be ordered by its extent. For example, $200,000 is more than $150,000, and $150,000 is more than $75,000. Similarly, people typically speak as if liberties can be ordered by their extent. For example, contemporary Russia has more freedom of speech than czarist Russia, and czarist Russia had more freedom of speech than Stalin's Russia.

If a liberty can be ordered by its extent, then standard economic tools can represent its price. In microeconomics, the rate at which an individual will trade one good for another measures their relative value to him. The conventional graph in microeconomics depicts value by the slope of the consumer's

---

[8] To illustrate, a U.S. law permits suits for money damages, provided that the violation of constitutional rights occurred as a consequence of a policy pursued by the state or local government, not the federal government. See 42 U.S.C. 1983 (1988) for the following:

> Every person who, under color of any statute, ordinance, regulation, custom, or usage, of any State of Territory or the District of Columbia, subjects, or causes to be subjected, any citizen of the United States or other person within the jurisdiction thereof to the deprivation of any rights, privileges, or immunities secured by the Constitution and laws, shall be liable to the party injured in an action at law, suit in equity, or other proper proceeding for redress.

The "policy" requirement is formulated by the Supreme Court in *Pembaur v City of Cincinnati*, 475 U.S. 469, 483 (1986), which is discussed in Lewis and Blumoff 1992, p. 757.

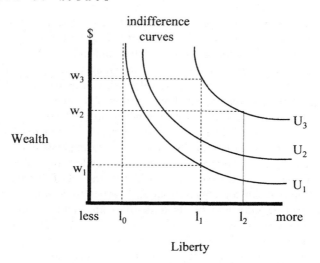

Fig. 10-1 Liberty as a Commodity

indifference curve. Thus the vertical axis in figure 10-1 indicates the level of wealth and the horizontal axis indicates the extent of a liberty, such as freedom of speech. Each utility curve represents the rate at which a person will trade wealth and liberty while remaining indifferent. For example, the point (l_1, w_3) lies on the same indifference curve as the point $(l_2, w_2,)$, so the person will trade $w_3 - w_2$ in wealth in exchange for an increase in liberty from l_1 to l_2. Thus $w_3 - w_2$ equals the *price* the person will pay to increase liberty from l_2 to l_1. Equivalently, as measured by the individual's preferences, an increase in wealth from w_2 to w_3 exactly compensates for a decrease in liberty from l_2 to l_1. Thus $w_3 - w_2$ equals perfectly compensatory damages for the person's loss in liberty from l_2 to l_1.

In general, a demand curve for an individual indicates the price he will pay for the good as its quantity varies. Each of the utility curves in figure 10-1 indicates the price the person will pay for liberty as its extent varies, holding other prices constant. Thus the utility curves are demand curves. (Strictly speaking, they are "utility-compensated demand curves."[9])

Presumably the person would be *willing* to pay more than indicated by curve U_1 for liberty if he were *able* to pay more, and he would be *able* to pay more if he had more *wealth*. More wealth could increase utility from U_1, say, to U_2 in figure 10-1. Compared to U_1, the demand curve U_2 indicates the price the person would pay for liberty after an increase in wealth and utility. In general, willingness to pay depends on ability to pay.

[9] The "compensated demand curve" indicates the quantity of the good that the person would buy as its price varies, holding constant other prices and *utility*. The conventional demand curve holds constant other prices and *income*. Compensated demand curves, which are important for welfare economics, are explained in any mathematical microeconomics textbook, such as Varian 1992.

Having discussed liberty's price, I consider its cost. The definition of a liberty as a protected permission suggests two kinds of costs. First, protecting liberty uses resources, such as expenditures on police and military. Second, increasing liberty can sacrifice other values, so liberty has an opportunity cost. For example, increasing the freedom of owners to develop their property may allow them to construct tall buildings that reduce light for their neighbors.

At first, increasing one liberty does not necessarily interfere with another liberty. Eventually, however, the set of liberties expands until increasing one liberty decreases another. To illustrate, if freedom of speech expands to encompass talking in church, then its exercise interferes with freedom of religion. When one liberty's expansion conflicts with another liberty, the set of liberties has reached the *liberty frontier*. On the liberty frontier, liberties trade off, and the value of one liberty can be measured by its trade-off with another liberty. In general, the opportunity cost of increasing one liberty equals the value of the resulting decrease in other liberties.[10]

I have explained that increasing a liberty can cause an increase in the cost of protecting it and a sacrifice of competing liberties. The supply curve S in figure 10-2 embodies these costs. As depicted in figure 10-2, the supply curve S slopes up, which implies that the cost of more liberty increases as its extent increases.[11]

Figure 10-2 also depicts the demand curve U_1 from figure 10-1, which I relabel D_1. As depicted, the demand curve slopes down, which implies that willingness to pay for additional liberty decreases as its extent increases.

Cost-benefit analysis measures value by price and cost. Applying standard cost-benefit analysis to figure 10-2, the optimum occurs where supply S equals demand D_1, which occurs when liberty's extent equals l_c^* and liberty's price equals p_c^*. If a court applied this method to decide the extent of a liberty given to citizens by law, the court would find the optimal extent of the liberty by comparing the demand for it by citizens and the cost of increasing its supply.

Question: Describe some examples where cost-benefit analysis seems appropriate for individual rights, and describe some examples where it seems inappropriate.

Public Good

The preceding section analyzed liberty as a private good. This description, however, is potentially misleading. Each person can have a different amount of the same private good. Democratic constitutions, however, typically guarantee

---

[10] The liberty frontier resembles the Pareto frontier, where increasing one person's satisfaction decreases that of another.

[11] Equivalently, a supply curve indicates the *quantity* of the good that private producers would supply at a given price, holding constant other prices. In terms of liberty, the supply curve indicates the quantity of liberty that the state can supply at a given cost.

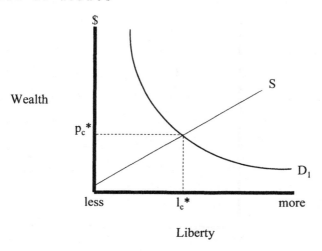

Fig. 10-2 Price and Cost of Liberty

the same liberties for everyone. Treating liberties as private goods conceals the equality constraint.

Given the equality constraint, one person's liberty cannot change without the same change in everyone's liberty. For example, my freedom of speech cannot increase without increasing your freedom of speech. I will adjust figure 10-2 to depict liberty as a good supplied equally to different people. The demand curve D_1 in figure 10-2 indicates the price that a particular person will pay for liberty. Presumably the person would be *willing* to pay more than D_1 for liberty if he were able to pay more, and he would be *able* to pay more if he had more *wealth*. More wealth could increase utility from U_1, say, to U_2 in figure 10-1. I reproduce the utility curve U_2 in figure 10-3 and relabel it D_2.

A modern democracy encompasses many citizens, whose aggregate demand determines the optimal supply of goods. To illustrate the method of aggregation as simply as possible, assume that the nation consists of two people, specifically a poor person with utility U_1 and a rich person with utility U_2. By assumption each one receives the same amount of liberty. Choose an amount of liberty, say l_p^* in figure 10-3. At l_p^*, liberty is worth p_1 to the poor person and p_2 to the rich person. Consequently, the aggregate value of liberty at l_p^* equals $p_1 + p_2$. Summing vertically in this same way for other quantities of liberty yields the aggregate demand curve $D_1 + D_2$. The value of liberty as measured by standard cost-benefit techniques equals the sum that the two people will pay for it: $D_1 + D_2$. The curve labeled $D_1 + D_2$ in figure 10-3 indicates the aggregate demand for liberty in a two-person state. Including more people in the state requires summing vertically more demand curves to obtain the aggregate demand.

At the cost-benefit optimum, the cost of increasing the extent of liberty by a small amount equals the aggregate amount that people are willing to pay for

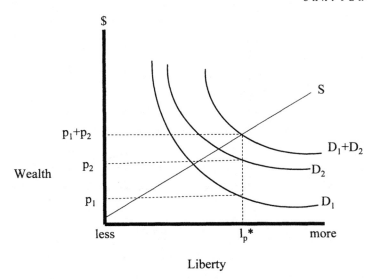

Fig. 10-3 Liberty as a Public Good

the increase. Consequently, optimal liberty in figure 10-3 corresponds to the point l_p^* where aggregate demand $D_1 + D_2$ intersects the cost curve S. If a court applied this method to decide the extent of a liberty given to citizens by law, the court would find the optimal extent of the liberty by comparing the demand for it by citizens and the cost of increasing its supply.

Notice that I computed aggregate demand for liberty by summing vertically. Summing vertically implies that everyone receives the same quantity of the good and different people value it differently. This is a characteristic of public goods such as military security and clean air. In contrast, demand for private goods such as apples or shoes aggregate by summing individual demand curves horizontally, because everyone in a free market pays the same price and different people buy different quantities. Treating liberties as public goods emphasizes the equality constraint according to which everyone enjoys the same quantity of each liberty supplied by the state, even though different people value liberties differently.

Questions: I discussed free speech and clean air as public goods. Discuss reasons for valuing free speech and clean air by the same method and by different methods.

Welfare

Jeremy Bentham, the English philosopher who invented utilitarianism, thought that liberty, apples, safe streets, and all other goods trade off at rates determined by the amount of pleasure they yield to a person. In contrast, many philosophers, lawyers, and judges treat individual rights as if their value must be measured differently from apples or safe streets. Bentham complained that the lofty language surrounding rights, especially among philosophers of natural rights, disguises the plain truth. For this reason he called natural rights "nonsense on stilts."[12] Many modern economists, who disagree with Bentham's use of pleasure as the universal measure, agree with Bentham in preferring pragmatism over philosophy of rights. Such economists would apply standard methods of cost-benefit analysis as described in the preceding sections to decide questions involving individual rights.

In spite of Bentham and pragmatic economists, philosophies that evaluate rights by methods other than cost-benefit analysis are very influential. I will, consequently, extend economic analysis to these philosophies. As depicted in figure 10-1, rich people will pay more for liberty than will poor people. In other words, the demand for liberty increases with wealth. Many lawyers and judges, however, assert that liberty is equally valuable to everyone. This assertion implies a distinction between market values and social values. I will use economics to distinguish between market and social values, and then I will apply the distinction to liberty.

A long tradition in economics, which is now out of favor, uses welfare, not wealth, to guide public policy.[13] According to the "material welfare school," a person's welfare depends on the satisfaction of needs (Cooter and Rappoport 1984). Needs form a hierarchy in order of urgency, with material needs at the base. Nonmaterial needs such as culture and entertainment are higher in the hierarchy. People usually satisfy urgent needs at the hierarchy's base before satisfying less urgent needs at the top of the hierarchy. For example, a person who is very hungry and very bored needs nourishment more than entertainment, so he usually prefers to eat rather than go to the opera. (A modern psychologist, A. Maslow, also arranged human needs in a hierarchy with a material base.[14])

According to the material welfare school, most people have the same hierarchy of needs, so comparing the level of satisfaction of the same needs by different people permits interpersonal comparisons of welfare. To illustrate, assume that person A has food and no entertainment, whereas person B has no food and no entertainment. The material welfare school says that person A has a higher level of welfare than person B. Furthermore, the material welfare school says that a malnourished person needs food more than a well-fed person needs entertainment. So giving food to person B increases total welfare in society by more than giving entertainment to person A does.

---

[12] This famous phase of Jeremy Bentham is the title of a recent book. See Waldron 1987. For Bentham's formulation of cost-benefit principles, see Bentham 1973, chapter 4, section 5, para. 6.

[13] For high points in the history of "welfare" as developed in Anglo-American economics, see Bentham 1973; Marshall 1925; Pigou 1950; Bergson 1938; Sen 1970a. For an overview, see Schumpeter 1986; Blaug 1978.

[14] From observing clients in clinical practice, Maslow distinguished five types of needs and arranged them in this order: physiological (survival, food, water, sleep), safety (security, protection), social needs (emotional attachments—friendship, love), ego (self-esteem, respect), and self-actualization (personal growth and development) (Maslow 1954).

Needs provide a basis for comparing levels of welfare for different people. Comparing welfare levels sometimes provides enough information to allocate resources. To illustrate, if providing nourishment to one person costs the same as providing entertainment to someone else, welfare increases more by spending the money on nourishment.

Often, however, comparing welfare levels does not provide enough information to allocate resources. To illustrate, assume that food for one malnourished person costs the same as a movie for fifty bored people. The fact that people need nourishment more than entertainment does not determine whether welfare increases more from feeding one person or entertaining fifty people. Allocating donations or subsidies between food and entertainment to maximize welfare requires measuring how much more food increases the welfare of a malnourished person than watching a movie increases the welfare of a bored person. In general, allocating resources to maximize welfare requires *measuring differences* in welfare between people, not just *comparing levels*.[15]

To solve such problems, scholars and international agencies like the World Bank have developed "welfare weights" to guide public policy (Feldstein 1974; Squire and Van der Tak 1975). For example, if $1.00 spent on nourishment increases welfare by the same amount as $2.00 spent on entertainment, then assign twice as much weight to expenditures on food as movies. Much like progressive taxation, welfare weights set public priorities about income redistribution.

Like other people, economists disagree about priorities for income redistribution. Consequently, no method of computing welfare weights commands a consensus among economists. Instead of explaining controversial ways to compute welfare weights, I will show how to apply any given set of welfare weights to liberty. To measure welfare, I will adjust the amount that people are willing to pay in light of their ability to pay.

To apply welfare weights to figure 10-3, assume a world consisting of one rich person and one poor person. The demand curve D_1 in figure 10-3 indicates the price the poor person will pay for liberty, and the demand curve D_2 indicates the price the rich person will pay. The philosophy under consideration asserts that liberty has the same social value for rich and poor people. To apply this philosophy to figure 10-3, convert prices to social values by using a welfare weight w that adjusts unequal prices. Specifically, using the rich person's price as a baseline, define w as equal to the difference between the rich person's price and the poor person's price.

To illustrate in figure 10-4, the welfare weight w equals the vertical distance between the demand curves D_2 and D_1, or, in notation, $w = D_2(1) - D_1(1)$. The rich person would pay p_2 for l_w^*, whereas the poor person would pay p_1. At l_w^*, the welfare weight w_1 equals $p_2 - p_1$. By assumption, the social value of providing l_w^* to the rich person equals p_2, and the social value of providing l_w^* to the poor person equals $p_1 + w_1$, where $p_2 = p_1 + w_1$.

---

[15] "Welfare differences" refer to the change in welfare caused by a change in consumption. Welfare differences must be measured to compare marginal values as required for maximizing welfare. In general, maximizing welfare requires different information than does comparing welfare levels.

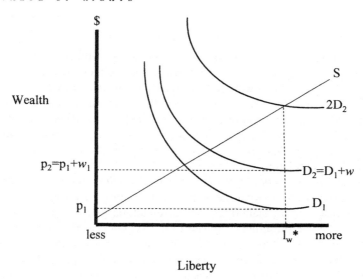

Fig. 10-4 Liberty as Welfare

To compute the optimum in figure 10-4, I proceed as in figure 10-3 except I use weighted prices instead of market prices. Applying welfare weights to the poor person's price, the state should supply the good until its cost equals the sum of its value to rich and poor: $S = D_2 + D_1 + w$, or, equivalently, $S = 2D_2$. In figure 10-4, the optimum occurs at l_w^*. Comparing figure 10-3 and figure 10-4, welfare weights increase the optimal supply of liberty relative to cost-benefit analysis from l_p^* to l_w^*. The increase is caused by assuming that the price poor people will pay for liberty underestimates its social value. (The opposite result follows from assuming that the price rich people will pay for liberty overestimates its social value.) If a court applied this method to decide the extent of a liberty given to citizens by law, the court would find the optimal extent of the liberty by comparing the weighted demand for it by citizens and the cost to the state of increasing its supply.

In this section I discussed how to determine the social value of each good by its contribution to welfare. This method of determining social value reduces all goods to a single good called welfare. In this respect, welfare analysis treats liberty the same as apples or safe streets. In the next section I consider another approach that attributes greater distinctiveness to different kinds of goods, including liberty.

Question: The rich presumably will pay more for liberty than will the poor. Assume that courts accept the principle that liberty is equally valuable to everyone. To implement this principle, the courts can use a weight either to increase the willingness-to-pay of the poor or to decrease the willingness-to-pay of the rich. Describe some differences that the choice will make to the court's decisions about the value of liberty.

Merit Goods

For conventional economics, the price that people are willing to pay for a good measures its value. For welfare economics, the welfare provided by a good measures its value, where welfare equals the price weighted by level of income. Outside economics, however, prices and welfare are not exclusive or ultimate standards of value. For example, when critics discuss a symphony's value, they do not mean how much people will pay to attend a performance. Similarly, when libertarian philosophers discuss the value of liberty, they do not mean how much it contributes to welfare.

Many discussions about liberty concern its *true* value. In terms of figure 10-1, the discussion concerns what the slopes of the indifference curves *ought* to be. Philanthropists and the state often subsidize cultural goods such as symphonies and opera. People presumably donate to the symphony or vote to subsidize it because they believe that symphonies have more value than their market price.

John Stuart Mill, a nineteenth-century British philosopher, developed this argument in a famous example. Pleasures, in Mill's opinion, differ in *quality*.[16] Thus poetry affords a higher quality of pleasure than "pushpin," which was a mindless barroom game of the nineteenth-century rather like pinball. Even if poetry yields the same *quantity* of pleasure to one person as pushpin yields to another, Mill asserted that the former should receive more weight in the social calculus than should the latter. For Mill, poetry is a good whose value exceeds some peoples' actual preferences for it.

In economics, the phrase *merit goods* refers to goods whose value to society exceeds their value to individuals.[17] Merit goods have irreducible social value, which tilts the optimal allocation of resources in their favor and may justify a subsidy from philanthropists or the state. The subsidy drives a wedge between the good's cost and the amount people are willing to pay for it.

Figure 10-5 applies merit to liberty. Recall that the aggregate demand curve $D_1 + D_2$ in figure 10-3 indicates the sum of the amount people would be willing to pay for a given extent of liberty. D in figure 10-5 represents such an aggregate demand curve, which I make a straight line for simplicity. The social value of the good exceeds what people will pay for it by the amount denoted M for merit. The social value of a good is the sum of its price and its merit. In figure 10-5, the good's social value is found by adding D and M, which is represented graphically by rotating the demand curve D upward by the amount of merit M to obtain the curve labeled D + M.

S in figure 10-5 indicates the cost of supplying liberty as its extent varies. The optimal amount of liberty differs depending on whether its cost is equated to its market value or its social value. Standard cost-benefit analysis measures value by willingness-to-pay, not by merit. Applying standard cost-benefit analysis to

---

[16] See "Utility" in Mill 1951.

[17] The concept of merit goods was pioneered in Head 1970 and Musgrave 1959. For more recent discussions, see the contributions in Brennan and Walsh 1990, including Cooter 1990.

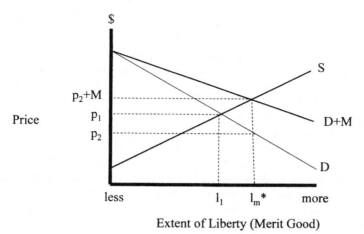

Fig. 10-5 Merit Good

figure 10-5, the optimal supply of the good equals l_1, where demand D intersects supply S. An analysis of merit reaches a different conclusion. Applying the merit approach, the optimal supply of the good equals l_m^*, where D + M intersects supply S.

If a private market supplies a merit good, achieving optimality requires state subsidies or private donations. If private sellers cannot collect a fee from users, as is the case for a purely public good, then the private market supplies none of the good. If private sellers can collect the price D from users of the good, a competitive market will equate cost S and demand D, resulting in the equilibrium quantity l_1 and price p_1. A subsidy M from the state or private philanthropists can increase the supply to its optimal level. With a subsidy equal to M, the market will equate cost S and the sum of demand and subsidy D+M, resulting in the equilibrium quantity l_m^*. At the equilibrium quantity l_m^*, the buyers pay price p_2, the state or philanthropists pay subsidy M, and the sellers receive $p_2 + M$. In figure 10-5, the subsidy is a wedge between private demand and supply.

If a court applied this method to decide the extent of a liberty given to citizens by law, the court would find the optimal extent of the liberty by comparing the cost to the state of increasing its supply and its social value, where social value equals the demand by citizens plus the good's merit.

Whose preferences determine the merit M of a good? The National Academy of the Arts? The Catholic bishops? The donor who created the Ford Foundation? This problem, which troubles economists, should trouble everyone who believes that the economy and the state should respond to the preferences of its citizens. In spite of troubling questions, however, the fact remains that the production of poetry in most countries enjoys substantial subsidies, especially through free education, whereas no state or private philanthropist subsidizes pinball.[18] As a

[18] At my university, some citizens got very upset when they realized that the student association runs an entertainment center that includes bowling, and state funds pay the costs of the building.

matter of fact, public policy and private philanthropy implement the merit goods concept.

Liberty resembles cultural goods in that some people attribute special merit to it. Judges and other officials seldom discuss individual rights as if they were commodities whose value can be established by voting or cost-benefit analysis. Instead, judges and other officials ascribe social value to liberty that is distinct from the value actually placed on it by individuals. The values in question are not regarded as matters of personal preference but of public responsibility. Public responsibilities concern what people ought to do, which can conflict with what they prefer to do. Thus some judges believe that people ought to value liberty more than they do. Instead of accepting passively the results of elections or cost-benefit analysis, defenders of liberty try to make people recognize its true value. If debate and discussion fail, then defenders of liberty try to prevail in the legislature and the courts.

The concept of merit spans the analytical gap between the values that people actually have and the values that people think others ought to have. To illustrate, D in figure 10-5 might denote the amount that voters will pay for liberty, as determined by political processes such as voting or technical evaluations like cost-benefit analysis. Judges, however, might believe that the constitution attributes merit M to liberty. Reasoning in this way, judges might conclude that the constitution requires liberty $l_m{}^*$, even though technical evaluations and elections indicate that people prefer liberty l_1.

A pluralistic society harbors alternative philosophies that diverge on some issues and converge on others. Convergence on the belief that the basic liberties should be entrenched in the constitution helps democracy flourish. Competing philosophies typically diverge over issues such as environmental protection, cultural subsidies, and redistribution for the sake of equality. When philosophies diverge over the values that people ought to have, cost-benefit analysis, while useful, cannot be decisive in convincing people to adopt one public policy rather than another. Instead the parties maneuver for political power or try to change preferences through debate. In general, people who feel responsibilities keenly are attracted to changing other peoples' preferences.

Questions

1. Does attributing "merit" to a good preclude cost-benefit analysis or merely modify the way it is conducted?

2. From a formal viewpoint, the merit M in figure 10-5 resembles the welfare weight w in figure 10-3. Explain how their interpretations differ.

3. Some judges take pride in "reasonableness" or "proportionality." Use some examples to discuss the connection among merit, reasonableness, and proportionality.

Perhaps the state and private philanthropists subsidize pinball, but they do not do so eagerly or even knowingly.

Trumps

The analytical device developed in figure 10-5 combines actual and ideal preferences. Sometimes, however, ideal preferences count for everything and actual preferences count for nothing, which brings me to my next topic. Some judges speak as if liberty's merit swamps its price. For example, a person cannot sell himself into slavery in most countries of the world, regardless of how much he values money and how little he values liberty. Sale is blocked even though buyer and seller agree on a price and both want to proceed with the exchange. Rights that the individual cannot transfer or extinguish are called "inalienable."[19] With inalienable rights, private value receives no public weight.

As in discussions of slavery, some people say that liberty is priceless, which implies that people ought not to sacrifice a small amount of liberty to obtain a large increase in wealth. Figure 10-1 above depicts this situation with a vertical indifference curve. As the quantity of liberty decreases toward l_0 in figure 10-1, the slope of the indifference curve U_1 becomes vertical, which indicates that no additional amount of wealth will compensate for a further loss of liberty. When the slope of an indifference curve becomes vertical, the two goods do not trade off.

Constitutions impose order on reasons, with some kinds of reasons defeating others. Many U.S. judges interpret the Constitution as giving so much weight to individual rights that very few reasons can justify their infringement. Trade-offs are common with consumer goods,[20] and, if you believe the language of judges, rare with individual rights. For example, some U.S. judges give little weight to the effects of individual rights on the nation's wealth or its people's welfare. Political philosophies with long pedigrees bolster courts in Western countries that refuse to trade off individual rights for other values such as wealth. For example, one of the most celebrated political treatises of our age, John Rawls's *A Theory of Justice* (1971), contends that a society with moderate scarcity should not trade off liberty for wealth. When faced with a public choice, officials in such a state should always choose more liberty, according to Rawls, even at the cost of a large loss of wealth. (See the next chapter for details.)

A card designated as "trump" in a game beats every other card. Similarly, constitutional rights trump other laws. In the United States, the rhetoric of judges suggests that individual rights trump legislation enacted by the representatives of a majority of citizens.[21] In practice, however, the extent to which constitutional rights trump legislation depends on the constitutional court's willingness to resist the legislature. To illustrate, the U.S. Supreme Court frequently rejects acts of Congress as violating individual rights found in the Constitution. In most other democratic countries, however, the constitutional court seldom oppose the legislature's interpretation of constitutional rights.

[19] Rose-Ackerman 1985.

[20] Here is an exception: A person who owns right and left shoes in equal numbers does not trade them off, because more right shoes are useless without more left shoes.

[21] An interesting discussion is in Epstein 1985a, pp. 9–16.

When interpreting individual rights, officials often deny that costs and benefits affect their decision. To illustrate, if the American Nazi Party would pay less to speak than others would pay to silence it, then cost-benefit analysis favors silencing the American Nazi Party. U.S. courts, however, would not use a cost-benefit test to decide whether the legislature can curtail the American Nazi Party's speech. Cost-benefit reasoning seldom figures in court interpretations of constitutional rights.[22] In addition to trumping legislation, constitutional rights often trump cost-benefit analysis.

If officials accept the principle that liberty trumps wealth, then they do not balance the former and the latter. Officials, however, may still trade off one liberty against another. For example, an increase in freedom of speech might justify a restriction on freedom of religion. To the extent that officials regard constitutional rights as trumps, constitutional argument trades off individual rights against each other, but does not sacrifice them for wealth or welfare.

Questions

1. Automobile insurance companies charge young men much higher rates than than they do young women. When sued for unconstitutional sexual discrimination, an insurance company makes two arguments. First, charging different rates by sex increases national wealth. Second, the constitutional right of contract protects the practice of charging different rates by sex. Relate the effectiveness of these two arguments to whether the judge regards constitutional rights as commodities, merit goods, or trumps.

2. Courts may enforce a contract to work for one year, two years, or even five years, but a lifetime contract is unenforceable against the worker as "slavery." Use the concepts of wealth, welfare, and trumps to discuss where to draw the line.

CONCLUSION

Preliminary to analyzing philosophies of rights, this chapter discusses methods for valuing rights in democratic countries. Cost-benefit analysis measures the value of private and public goods by peoples' willingness-to-pay. Evaluating rights by cost-benefit analysis implies treating them as a source of wealth and trading off with other sources of wealth. Regarded as sources of wealth, constitutional rights resemble commodities or public goods depending on whether they are distributed unequally or equally.

Instead of regarding rights as sources of wealth, regarding them as sources of welfare requires weighting willingness-to-pay by ability-to-pay. Regarded as sources of welfare, individual rights trade off with other sources of welfare, such as health care and housing.

---

[22] A review of economic influences on the U.S. Supreme Court is in Easterbrook 1994. Also see Dau-Schmidt 1990.

Courts, however, often speak as if markets and votes do not express the true value of individual rights. According to this view, individual rights have social value distinct from the value that individuals assign to them. To encompass this idea, I expanded economic value to include merit and trumps. Regarded as merit goods, intrinsic worth supplements price. Regarded as trumps, constitutional rights trade off with each other but not with other goods.

CHAPTER 11

Philosophies of Rights: Liberty and Redistribution

It works in practice, but will it work in theory?

To PROTECT MARKETS, a constitution can guarantee the rights of property and contract that keep markets free. Alternatively, to assure minimal welfare for everyone, a constitution can guarantee welfare rights such as medical care and housing. In practice, implementing welfare rights involves regulating markets and redistributing income, so liberty rights and welfare rights trade off with each other. The poles of the trade-off span the rival political philosophies of the right and left that figure prominently in modern political disputes.

Whether the aim is free markets or minimum welfare, a constitutional commitment can deflect redistributive contests away from the most wasteful and destructive ends and means that impoverish a nation. An effective constitution removes certain ends and means from ordinary politics. Instead of pursuing the special politics of constitutional interpretation and revision, politicians may change their ends or means. To illustrate, effective constitutional protection of private property blocks politicians from expropriating other peoples' wealth, thus diverting the politics of redistribution into less virulent forms than expropriation, such as state subsidies or regulations.

In many countries, constitutional rights work in practice to dampen redistributive contests, but people disagree sharply over how to explain and justify constitutional commitments. Do constitutional commitments arbitrarily empower one philosophy over its rivals? In this book I view the constitution as a mechanism to satisfy the preferences of citizens, and in this chapter I apply this perspective to the trade-off between free markets and redistribution. By doing so, I try to explain how some effective constitutional practices can work in theory. This chapter addresses such questions as the following:

Example 1: In addition to traditional liberties such as freedom of speech and freedom of religion, some people assert a right to education, health care, housing, and other benefits. What is the connection between these rights and the maximization of welfare?

Example 2: Some judges and philosophers refuse to sacrifice liberty for wealth. Do these beliefs contravene the preferences of ordinary people?

Example 3: Courts discuss ethical values whereas politicians pursue power. How do normative theories of constitutional rights based on justice relate to positive theories based on power?

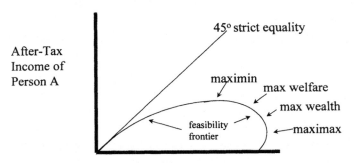

Fig. 11-1 Income Taxation and Redistribution

Distributive Ideals

The preceding chapter contrasted maximizing wealth and welfare. Figure 11-1 uses a diagram from public finance to depict the full range of appealing distributive ideals. To simplify, the figure assumes that society consists of two types of people. I will discuss representatives of each type, whom I call person A and person B. Person A, whose income is shown on the vertical axis in figure 11-1, has relatively low earning ability. In contrast, person B, whose income is shown on the horizontal axis, has relatively high earning ability. "Earning ability" means such things as quick intelligence and good judgment as required for business. If the state does not redistribute income, then A will have less income than B.

The state can use taxes and subsidies to redistribute wealth between the two people. The figure assumes that any tax subsidy must be based on income. For example, the state can tax high incomes and subsidize low incomes, which favors A and disfavors B. Alternatively the state can tax low incomes and subsidize high incomes, which favors B and disfavors A.

Assume that the state announces a schedule of taxes and subsidies based on income. A and B respond to the announcement by deciding how many hours to work. The state then applies the announced schedule to collect taxes from A and B, as well as to pay them subsidies. The result is after-tax-and-subsidy income levels of A and B. A feasible tax-subsidy system collects as much in taxes as it pays out in subsidies. In figure 11-1 the "feasibility frontier" depicts all the feasible after-tax-and-subsidy levels of income for A and B.[1]

If A and B have similar tastes for leisure, then B inevitably ends up with at least as much money after taxes as does A. Seeing why is not hard. Since the tax subsidy is based on income, the person with greater earning ability always has the option of earning exactly as much as the person with lower earning ability, thus paying the same tax and receiving the same subsidy. So B can

---

[1] Strictly speaking, the area inside the frontier is also feasible, but I ignore it because it is not Pareto efficient.

always enjoy at least as much after-tax-and-subsidy income as A. Furthermore, B normally chooses to work enough to earn more money than A does. B will choose to earn more than A so long as they have similar preferences regarding work and leisure.

A feature of figure 11-1 depicts this fact. The 45° line corresponds to all the points where A's after-tax income equals B's. The only feasible point of strictly equal income occurs at the origin of the graph, where taxes are so punitive that neither party earns any income. All the other feasible points lie below the 45° line, thus indicating that B enjoys more after-tax income than does A.

Start from the origin of figure 11-1 with strict equality and prohibitively high taxes. Allow taxes to fall and the parties begin working more and earning more, thus moving to the northeast in the figure. Continue moving northeast on the feasibility frontier to reach the highest point, which is labeled *maximin.* The maximin is the point where the relatively worse-off person (A) has as much income as feasible. In brief, the maximin is the point that maximizes the minimum income. Reaching the maximin typically requires taxing the relatively rich (B) at the rate yielding the largest subsidy for the relatively poor (A).

In *A Theory of Justice* (1971), Rawls argues that inequalities are only justified to the extent that they improve the well-being of the worst-off class of people.[2] This argument leads him to favor the maximin as the redistributive ideal of a just state.

Going beyond the maximin on the feasibility frontier in figure 11-1 requires lowering taxes and subsidies, which benefits B at the expense of A. Figure 11-1 depicts several salient points achievable by lowering taxes. As discussed in the preceding chapter, the material welfare school assumes that poor people get more welfare from additional income than do rich people. This normative ideal requires redistribution from rich to poor in order to maximize the sum of utilities. Maximizing the sum of utilities, however, does not require as much redistribution as maximizing the minimum income. Consequently, I locate the point labeled "max welfare" in figure 11-1 beyond the maximin.[3]

Next I consider maximizing wealth. An additional dollar earned by a rich person increases wealth by just as much as an additional dollar earned by a poor person. Consequently, the normative ideal of maximizing wealth gives equal weight to everyone's earnings, regardless of whether they are rich or poor. Reaching the point labeled "max wealth" in figure 11-1 requires lowering taxes on the rich and going beyond "max welfare." The point "max wealth" maximizes the sum of the incomes of A and B,[4] as required by cost-benefit analysis.

---

[2] The maximin is introduced in chapter 2 section 11 of Rawls 1971 and subsequently discussed in a variety of passages in the book.

[3] The precise location of the point of maximum welfare on this graph requires specifying how income translates into welfare. Depicting welfare in the graph requires social welfare curves analogous to individual utility curves.

[4] The point of wealth maximization occurs where a line with slope -45° is tangent to the feasibility frontier.

Going beyond wealth maximization in figure 11-1 eventually reaches the "maximax," which maximizes after-tax-and-subsidy income of the wealthiest person (B). The maximax is achieved by taxing the poor (A) and subsidizing the rich (B). Whereas the maximin implements egalitarianism, the maximax implements elitism.

In the twentieth century, public debate usually favors redistribution from rich to poor and overwhelmingly opposes redistribution from poor to rich. In practice, however, wealth goes with power. If the maximin is currently more favored in words than deeds, then the maximax is more favored in deeds than words. (How many heads of state have massive, secret accounts in foreign banks?)

In past centuries, however, the assumptions of public debate were different. For example, before the nineteenth century the English typically assumed that aristocracy was superior to democracy as a political ideal. According to the aristocratic ideal, some groups of people who embody superior values in their culture spend money better than others, and the people with superior tastes ought to enjoy more wealth than people with inferior tastes. Like merit goods, aristocracy assumes that some people have better preferences than others. This case for inequality rests on cultural values. The advance of democracy undermined the political power and the cultural values of the aristocracy.[5]

Along the feasibility frontier between the maximin and the maximax in figure 11-1, one person's income cannot increase without diminishing another person's income. Thus the points on the feasibility frontier between the maximin and the maximax are Pareto efficient. Pareto efficiency is consistent with redistributive ideals ranging from radical egalitarianism to radical elitism (as well as with skepticism that eschews ideals and proceeds from the actual). Choosing among Pareto-efficient points requires a normative standard to identify the preferred distribution of income.

Questions

1. Explain the difference between the feasibility frontier and the Pareto frontier in figure 11-1.

2. How would a constitution implement the maximax? the maximin?

ACTUAL VERSUS IDEAL

Aristotle argued that different types of societies would adopt different distributive principles.[6] He thought that democracies would adopt the principle that everyone gets an equal share, so democracies tend toward egalitarianism. In contrast, he thought that aristocracies would adopt the principle that the best get more, so aristocracies tend toward elitism. In practice, the state takes wealth from groups with less political power and gives wealth to groups with more

---

[5] For a devastating critique of aristocratic culture, see Veblen 1967. For the cultural case for inequality, see Cooter and Gordley 1994.

[6] Aristotle's theories of distribution are reviewed and applied to law in Gordley 1981.

political power. The alignment of power determines how the state redistributes wealth between rich and poor.

A constitution can stabilize economic competition and protect the resulting distribution of income, whatever it may be. Alternatively, a constitution can recognize welfare rights that embody a concept of economic justice. In either case, effective constitutions help secure a distribution of wealth and income. To illustrate the difference, Cass Sunstein argues that Roosevelt's New Deal in the 1930s changed the economic constitution of the United States Originally the common law gave the baseline for protecting the distribution of income under the U.S. Constitution. After the New Deal, the courts reinterpreted the U.S. Constitution as protecting a different baseline that allows redistribution in pursuit of ethical ideals (Sunstein 1987).

I will explain the connection between efficiency and distributive ideals in constitutions. To compare the efficiency of alternative laws, an economic model usually allows the laws under investigation to vary and holds other laws constant. No built-in limitations exist in such analyses concerning which rules vary and which rules remain constant.

The most popular style of analysis among economists, who are inclined to leave philosophy to others, evaluates changes in policy from the standpoint of the status quo. These models begin by characterizing equilibrium in an actual legal system and predicting the changes caused by modest legal reforms. To illustrate, an economic analysis might begin with existing guarantees of free speech and examine the consequences of redefining libel. The inherent conservatism of this approach lies in contemplating small changes in existing law.

Although economic analysis typically proceeds from the status quo, it need not. Alternatively, a model can begin with an idealized legal system that distributes rights according to a particular political or moral theory. To illustrate, an economic analysis might compare the consequences for defamation under alternative ideals of free speech, none of which characterizes actual legal systems. The inherent idealism of this approach lies in contemplating large changes in existing law.

Whether pragmatic or idealistic, an economic analysis usually asks whether changes increase or diminish the law's efficiency. "Efficiency" might refer to the Pareto standard—whether a change in law can make someone better-off without making anyone worse-off. Alternatively, "efficiency" might refer to the cost-benefit standard—whether the winners from a change in law gain more *wealth* than the losers lose. Or "efficiency" might refer to a welfare standard—whether the winners from a change in law gain more *welfare* than the losers lose.

Is Wealth the End of the State?

According to microeconomics, individuals maximize utility. The original inventors of utility theory, such as Bentham, considered utility to be a definite goal. Modern economics, however, has replaced substantive psychology with a logic of choice.[7] According to the modern view, "utility" describes the way a rational individual trades off a variety of goals. Utility in modern economics is an analytical construct for characterizing trade-offs among goals, not a single goal that dominates all other goals. In microeconomics, consumers purchase the combination of goods that maximizes utility subject to the constraint that expenditures do not exceed wealth. Wealth is a constraint not an end, as expressed in the saying, "I don't want money, I want the things money can buy."

Unlike individuals who trade off various goals, however, microeconomics typically assumes that firms maximize profit. Profit is a single, overarching goal for firms. Under this assumption, firms do not trade off profits for other goals.

Should the state maximize wealth like firms do or trade off various goals like individuals do? Some prominent law and economics scholars regard maximizing national wealth as the proper goal of the state (Posner 1981). When the state maximizes the nation's wealth, competitive politics provide citizens with public goods at low taxes. Plentiful public goods and low taxes increase the means for individuals to pursue their private ends. By providing individuals with means and not ends, the state remains neutral about the private goals that citizens ought to pursue. In general, the case for the state's maximizing wealth rests not on the proposition that wealth is intrinsically valuable but on the proposition that wealth provides citizens with the means for pursuing their private ends, without the state's favoring some private ends over others. Wealth is the *end* for the state and the *means* for individuals.

To illustrate, consider an imaginary state whose citizens work enough to satisfy their material needs and, after satisfying their material needs, they stop working in order to enjoy inexpensive activities such as playing the piano, cultivating orchids, reading books, walking in the park, watching television, and enjoying family life. Such people might want the state to maximize wealth so that citizens can maximize leisure. The citizens might object to public libraries or municipal orchestras that require the state to subsidize activities that some citizens value more than others.

Alternatively, consider another state where the citizens maximize consumption of market goods. In this state the citizens work long hours to earn money for large houses, luxurious cars, exotic trips, skiing, and fine dining. Such people might want the state to maximize wealth so that citizens can maximize consumption. As before, the citizens might object to the state's subsidizing particular activities such as skiing or housing.

A pure wealth maximizer has no values of its own apart from market values. In contrast, economic theory assumes that a consumer's tastes exist independently from market prices. An autonomous person creates or discovers his own values. For an autonomous person, markets provide constraints, not preferences. Lower prices imply less constraint. Instead of having values of its own, the wealth-maximizing state reduces the constraint on citizens.

---

[7] "[T]he utility theory of value has much better claim to being called a logic than a psychology of values" (Schumpeter 1986, p. 1058).

Autonomy is a virtue in people and a danger in states. Autonomous people subordinate the state, whereas an autonomous state subordinates its people. The "autonomy argument" provides the most compelling reason why states should act like firms, which maximize wealth, and not act like individuals, who maximize utility.

Wealth maximization by the state implies cost-benefit analysis of constitutional rights. To illustrate, cost-benefit analysis values liberty according to the actual price that people will pay for it. By applying cost-benefit analysis, the state respects individual values and refuses to guide decisions by its own values.

IS WELFARE THE END OF THE STATE?

Now I turn from wealth to welfare as a possible goal of the state. The preceding chapter described a long tradition in economics known as the "material welfare school" that uses welfare to guide public policy. According to this tradition, a person's welfare depends on the satisfaction of needs such as food, clothing, housing, and medical care. These needs form a hierarchy. Most people have the same hierarchy of needs, broadly defined, so comparing the level of satisfaction of the same needs by different people permits interpersonal comparisons of welfare.

After the second World War many governments created welfare states by extending the range of social benefits offered to citizens. The United Nation's Universal Declaration of Human Rights, adopted in 1948, raised these benefits to the level of rights:

> Everyone has the right to a standard of living adequate for the health and well-being of himself and his family, including food, clothing, housing, medical care and necessary social services, and the right to security in the event of unemployment, sickness, disability, widowhood, old age or other lack of livelihood beyond his control.[8]

Implementing welfare rights requires vast government expenditures to subsidize necessities and transfer wealth from rich to poor. In contrast, implementing liberty rights mostly requires government restraint. For this reason, a famous essay describes welfare rights as "positive" and liberty rights as "negative" (Berlin 1969). A rich country can implement both kinds of rights, whereas a poor country can implement liberty rights and not welfare rights. To illustrate, Denmark implements positive and negative liberties, whereas India implements negative liberties and not positive liberties.

According to the material welfare school, "needs" are well defined at low levels of income and undefined at high levels of income. At the lowest levels of income, people need material goods for survival, such as food, clothes, shelter, and medicine. Survival needs are relatively uncontroversial. At slightly higher levels of income, people need material goods for comfort, such as a house and

---

[8] Quoted and discussed in Waldron 1993, chapter 1, p. 14.

car. As wealth increases, however, all material needs get satisfied, so material needs recede as the basis for comparing the welfare of different people. Comparing the welfare of different people becomes increasingly difficult as their incomes rise.

To illustrate, a hungry person clearly needs food more than a bored person needs entertainment. It is unclear, however, whether one bored person needs to go to the opera more than another bored person needs to go bowling. With opera and bowling, the language of "needs" seems less appropriate than the language of "wants." Thus material welfare, which provides a clear basis for comparing welfare among very poor people, loses its relevance as wealth rises and poverty passes into affluence.

The case for redistribution among relatively affluent people rests not on material needs, but on equality. Utilitarians have argued that the marginal utility of income declines as people become richer, which implies that transferring a dollar from a person with relatively high income to a person with relatively low income increases society's total utility. In spite of several ingenious proposals, no method has gained general acceptance for measuring the rate at which the marginal utility of income declines.[9] General acceptance of a particular method would presumably imply a most unlikely event—the end to disagreements about political ideals of distribution.

As explained above, the public goal of maximizing wealth directs the state to help autonomous citizens pursue their private goals. In this respect, does the public goal of maximizing wealth differ from maximizing welfare? Does the state that adopts the public goal of maximizing welfare reduce the autonomy of citizens below the level achieved by maximizing wealth?

In principle, a state that redistributes income can remain neutral about how citizens spend their money. To illustrate using figure 11-1 the state can aim for any point on the feasibility frontier while allowing individuals to spend their money as they please. In particular, the state can use taxes for redistribution, and the state can refuse to use taxes to favor some consumer goods over others. For example, Rawls argues that a just state would pursue the maximin and remain neutral about how citizens use their wealth.[10]

In practice, however, states that pursue egalitarian ideals typically impose paternalistic restrictions on private contracts and regulate markets. To illustrate, original proponents of the material welfare school like Pigou argued in the 1920s for the state to invest in the health and education of workers, not merely give them money. Similarly, the material welfare approach easily leads to subsidies for necessities, such as food stamps and medicaid provided to very poor people by the U.S. government. Redistribution and regulation often go together as political goals. In practice, the state that adopts the public goal of maximizing welfare usually reduces the autonomy of citizens below the level achieved by maximizing wealth.

[9] The classic articles are Harsanyi 1953; Harsanyi 1955; Vickrey 1945; and Vickrey 1960.

[10] The view that the state should remain neutral toward different conceptions of goodness held by its citizens is especially developed in the sequel to *A Theory of Justice*. See Rawls 1993.

Questions

1. Give some examples of alleged rights that the constitution of your country does *not* recognize.

2. Discuss the advantages and disadvantages of including welfare rights in a constitution without implementing them by creating a welfare state.

3. Besides liberty rights and welfare rights, political discussion has turned to "third-generation rights," which encompass minority languages, national self-determination, the integrity of cultures, and environmental values. Discuss whether these rights resemble commodities, merit goods, or trumps.

Does Liberty Have Social Value?

In the preceding chapter I discussed valuing rights as commodities, welfare, and merit goods. Wealth maximization values rights as commodities, and welfare maximization values rights as a source of welfare. Insofar as the state recognizes merit, it abandons the passive role of aggregating values and assumes the active role of shaping values. The state shapes individual values by subsidizing merit and taxing demerit. Treating liberties as merit goods thus promotes liberty beyond the actual preferences of citizens.

Some defenders of liberty apparently believe that it should trump other values, not trade off with them. For example, libertarians and classical liberals, who achieved their greatest influence in Britain and the United States during the nineteenth century, believe that the state should protect liberty and not do much else. Specifically, the state should not maximize the nation's wealth or welfare. This philosophy minimizes the state. Another philosophy treats liberty as the first goal of the state and recognizes other secondary goals. In the formulation of Rawls, the state's first goal is maximum equal liberty. In other words, the state should provide people with the maximum liberty that can be made available to everyone. The liberty goal is "lexically prior" to other goals of the state, which means that liberty never trades off with welfare or wealth.

I have discussed wealth and welfare as possible goals of the state. In the next section I try to inject realism into these discussions and arrive at a more convincing account of the relationships among wealth, welfare, and liberty.

Wealth, Welfare, and Liberty Related to the Hierarchy of Needs

Citizens need liberty and wealth to pursue their private ends. Left-wing critics often argue that negative liberties such as those in the U.S. Bill of Rights have little value to people outside the circles of power. In general, a choice of whether or not to x requires the right to x and the means to x. The political left asserts that the right to x has no value without the means to x. For example, some Marxists assert that freedom of speech is valuable to the bourgeoisie who own

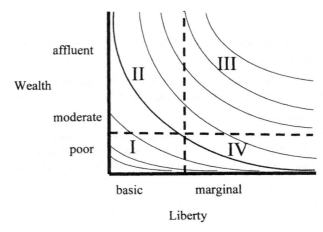

Fig. 11-2 Hierarchy of Desires

the printing presses but not to the working class who lack the means to circulate their views. Similarly, a feminist legal theorist asserted that freedom of speech is valuable to men who control the media but not to women (MacKinnon 1987).

I will graph the connection between wealth and the value of liberty. Figure 11-2 depicts wealth on the vertical axis. Beginning with affluence, a continuous decline in wealth passes through moderate prosperity and eventually reaches desperate poverty. Declining wealth eventually reaches the point where basic material needs go unsatisfied. For analytical simplicity, I assign a boundary on the dimension of wealth separating prosperity and poverty, as depicted on the vertical axis in figure 11-2. Above this boundary lies moderate prosperity, where basic material needs are satisfied. Below this boundary lies desperate poverty, where basic material needs are unsatisfied.

Similarly, I assume that people distinguish between basic and marginal liberties. Given a choice, people secure basic liberties before securing marginal liberties. The horizontal axis in figure 11-2 represents the extent of liberty. For analytical simplicity, I assign a boundary on the horizontal axis between basic liberties and marginal liberties.

The two boundaries divide figure 11-2 into zones labeled I, II, III, and IV. A person who suffers desperate poverty occupies zone I or IV, where the utility curves become almost horizontal. This fact indicates that the person strongly prefers more wealth rather than more liberty. For example, the person in zone I prefers to escape desperate poverty more than political tyranny.

A person who suffers political tyranny occupies zone I or II. In zone II, where the person escapes poverty, the utility curves become almost vertical. This fact indicates that the person strongly prefers more liberty rather than more wealth. As depicted in figure 11-2, moderate wealth makes a person prefer basic liberty rather than additional wealth.

In zone III, the person enjoys moderate wealth and more than basic liberty. The utility curves in zone III resemble utility curves for ordinary consumer

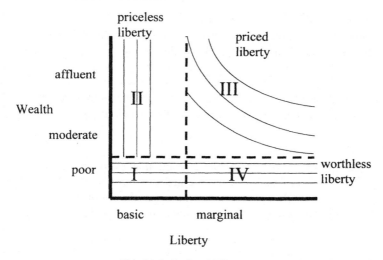

Fig. 11-3 Stylized Hierarchy

goods in microeconomics. As depicted in figure 11-2, moderate wealth and more than basic liberty makes a person trade off wealth and liberty like ordinary consumer goods.

Figure 11-3 stylizes the indifference curves in figure 11-2 by making *almost* horizontal indifference curves *perfectly* horizontal and making *almost* vertical indifference curves *perfectly* vertical. Consider a possible journey through the zones of figure 11-3. Beginning in zone I, desperate poverty gives wealth absolute priority over liberty. Stylizing the preferences of very poor people in zone I yields the socialist valuation of liberty. Now suppose wealth increases to a level of moderate prosperity, but a tyrant deprives the person of basic liberty. In zone II, the person prefers a small increase in liberty rather than a large increase in wealth, so liberty is priceless. Stylizing the preferences of people who enjoy moderate wealth and suffer political tyranny leads to the conclusion that liberty trumps wealth, as stressed by libertarians and some contractarians like Rawls. Finally, suppose the person secures more than basic liberty and enjoys moderate wealth. In zone III, marginal liberty and wealth trade off, so liberty has a price as stressed by economists.

Figure 11-2 presumably depicts the actual preferences of many people with respect to liberty and wealth, whereas figure 11-3 depicts the way some philosophers and judges talk about liberty and wealth. Many socialists talk as if policymakers should presume that society is in zone I, and many libertarians or Rawlsians talk as if society were in zone II, whereas economists talk as if society were in zone III. Each group has part of the truth insofar as liberty has little value to desperately poor people, paramount value to moderately affluent people living in tyranny, and ordinary value to people living in affluent democracies.

The preceding discussion concerns the subjective value of liberty. Another question concerns the causal connection between liberty and wealth. Does liberty increase wealth? Does wealth increase liberty? Empirical evidence from developing countries suggests that property rights and enforceable contracts promote development (North 1995; Olson 1992). Freedom of the press apparently articulates political needs with various beneficial effects such as averting famine (Dreze and Sen 1989; Sen 1994). Cross-country evidence, however, yields ambiguous results concerning the overall contribution of human rights and democracy to economic development (Trebilcock 1995).

Questions

1. In economics, a "necessity" is a good that everyone must have and a "superior" good is one for which demand increases more than proportionately with wealth. Discuss the extent to which the following resemble necessities or superior goods: (i) freedom of religion, (ii) freedom to travel, and (iii) privacy.

2. People value goods differently according to their wealth. Why should the state give equal rights to people who have unequal incomes?

DAMPENING CONTENTION OVER DISTRIBUTION

As noted, majority-rule games of distribution have no core, so a contest for distribution aggravates the problems of democracy. Embedding rights in the constitution distances them from democratic politics, especially when constitutional courts display independence from politics. A constitution committed to a particular distribution can dampen disputes over redistribution by removing them from ordinary politics.

To illustrate, redistribution from rich to poor requires heavy taxation. Many historical constitutions restricted voting to property owners, thus ensuring political domination by relatively wealthy people who prefer low taxes on high incomes. In the United States, courts blocked the implementation of income taxation on constitutional grounds until the Constitution was amended. In recent years, however, new constitutions in some new nations guarantee welfare rights, which apparently commit the state to redistributing in favor of the poor.

Effective constitutional rights, when difficult to change, can channel behavior away from conflict and into cooperation. Specifically, constitutional rights of property direct transactions away from politics and into voluntary exchange. The phrase "transaction structure" refers to the way that people interact with each other in allocating resources. By imposing a voluntary transaction structure on the allocation of resources, constitutions dampen conflict.

To illustrate, consider the difference between protecting land ownership by a constitutional right or protecting it by legislation. Sometimes the state needs private land for a public purpose, such as building a highway or creating a park. If a *statute* guarantees compensation of expropriated landowners at market prices, and if revising the statute only requires a majority of legislators, then the government may propose to revise the statute and expropriate private land without compensation. Given the instability of majorities, citizens may waste large resources contending over this legislation. Conversely, if the *constitution* guarantees compensation of expropriated landowners at market prices, and if revising the constitution requires a super majority of voters, a government program to take private land without compensation is probably infeasible politically. The constitutional provision against takings minimizes resources wasted on contending over public land acquisition.

Most constitutions distinguish the taking of private property from the regulation of it. Although the U.S. Constitution severely limits the power of government to take private property, twentieth-century courts allow extensive land-use regulations to effect property values. Political disputes are thus deflected from takings to regulations. To illustrate, environmentalists need not waste their efforts promoting the expropriation of ecologically sensitive lands, nor need developers defend against expropriation, but developers and environmentalists spend a lot of money lobbying at cross-purposes to influence regulations on land use. The next chapter discusses these facts in detail.

Constitution as Hypothetical Contract

After debate and bargains, the United States acquired its constitution by agreement among representatives of the states. Similarly, after debate and bargains, the European Union acquired its fundamental laws by treaties among the European nations. In these cases, the process of creating a constitution resembles the process of creating a contract. To justify state power, a great tradition in political philosophy conceives of *every* constitution as a hypothetical contract. Even without an actual bargain, the constitution resembles a contract insofar as its terms are the ones that rational people would have agreed to *if* they had bargained together.

By tracing the binding force of a constitution to an actual or hypothetical agreement among rational people, contractarianism rationalizes three of democracy's essential features. First, it captures the idea that state power derives from the consent of the governed. A "meeting of the minds" thus makes a state as well as a contract. Second, contractarianism views the state as serving people, not as people serving the state. Just as people freely enter contracts to improve their condition, not to worsen it, so the state should benefit everyone. Third, by acknowledging that people are free by nature, contractarianism provides a rationale for constitutional rights of individuals. Rational people will want to preserve their liberties when forming a state, so the constitution arising from contract will recognize individual rights.

The economic theory of bargaining can sharpen the logic of contractarianism. The contractarian approach begins with a description of what people would do in the absence of civil government, when military strength establishes ownership claims. This state of nature corresponds to the threats in a bargaining game,

TABLE 11.1
State of Nature

	Produced	Gained by theft	Lost by theft	Consumed
A	50	40	−10	80
B	150	10	−40	120
Totals	200	50	−50	200

which the parties exercise if they cannot agree. Next, contractarians describe the advantages of creating a government to recognize and enforce property rights. Civil society corresponds to the game's cooperative solution, which prevails if the parties can agree. The social surplus from creating the state corresponds to the cooperative surplus in the game. Finally, distribution of the surplus as prescribed in the constitution corresponds to the reasonable terms for cooperation in the game.

To illustrate numerically, imagine a world that consists of only two people, A and B.[11] In a state of nature, each one grows some corn, steals corn from the other party, and defends against theft. Each of the parties has different levels of skill at farming, stealing, and defending. Table 11.1 summarizes their payoffs in a state of nature. According to table 11.1, A grows 50 units of corn, A steals 40 units of corn from B, and A loses 10 units of corn to B through theft, so A consumes 80 units of corn. Similarly, B grows 150 units, steals 10, and loses 40 by theft, so B consumes 120 units of corn. In total the two of them produce 200 units of corn and redistribute 50 units through theft.

Instead of persisting in a state of nature, A and B can recognize each other's property rights and create an enforcement mechanism that puts an end to theft. Assume that cooperation will enable them to devote more resources to producing and fewer resources to redistributing, so total production will rise from 200 units to 300 units. In civil society there will be a mechanism for distributing the surplus, equal to 100 units, such as taxes and subsidies. The constitution stipulates general principles for distributing the surplus.

To induce cooperation, each party must benefit from it. To benefit, each party must receive at least his threat value, which equals the payoff that he can obtain on his own without the cooperation of others. Different contractarian theories characterize threat values differently. I will describe two different ways to characterize threat values in constitutional bargaining.

According to the first alternative associated with the philosopher Thomas Hobbes, no power exists to enforce morality in the state of nature that precedes law. Consequently, each person would exploit whatever strength he possesses in the state of nature to gain an advantage. In constitutional bargaining, according to this tradition, people would make all credible threats, including threats to

[11] This example first appeared in Cooter 1983 and was adapted in Cooter and Ulen 1988.

TABLE 11.2
Civil Society of Hobbes

	Threat Value	Share of Surplus	Consumption
A	80	50	130
B	120	50	170
Totals	200	100	300

harm others.[12] The "Consumed" column in table 11.1 describes the values of credible threats, which the "Threat Value" column in table 11.2 reproduces. A reasonable bargain gives each player his threat value and an equal share of the surplus from cooperation, as indicated by the "Share of Surplus" column in table 11.2. So, the social contract written in the spirit of Hobbes gives A 130 units of corn and B 170 units, as depicted in the "Consumption" column of table 11.3.

The theory of Hobbes assumes that no morality exists outside of civil society. According to the second alternative associated with the philosopher John Locke, however, moral obligations exist in nature. According to this view, people would recognize morality and restrain themselves by not threatening to harm each other when bargaining over the constitution. In nature, however, people will underenforce their rights and also interpret ambiguities in their favor. By creating a state, the parties can provide for adequate enforcement and authoritative interpretation of rights, thus creating a social surplus.

Table 11.3 depicts the social contract following Locke. In Locke's theory, unequal outcomes in the social contract come from unequal powers to produce, not from unequal powers to harm.[13] Instead of threatening harm, Locke restricts the parties to threatening noncooperation. With this restriction, the threat values of the parties equal the amount that they can produce on their own, as depicted in the "Threat Value" column of table 11.1 and reproduced in the "Threat Value" column of table 11.3. A reasonable bargain gives each player his threat value and an equal share of the surplus from cooperation, as indicated in the "Share of Surplus" column of table 11.3. So, the social contract written in the spirit of Locke allows A 100 units of corn and allows B 200 units, as depicted in the "Consumption" column of table 11.3.

[12] This is roughly the position of Thomas Hobbes and James Buchanan. See Buchanan 1975, and Hobbes 1651. Note, however, that Hobbes believed people would be unable to cooperate with each other unless intimidated by the state's coercive power. In Hobbes, the subjects give up almost all rights to the sovereign, except self-defense (Finkelstein 1998).

[13] This is roughly the theory of John Locke and Robert Nozick. See Locke 1961 (1690), and Nozick 1974. A third alternative excludes threats from constitutional bargaining. This is the position in Rawls 1971, where Rawls argues that moral equality prevents anyone from exploiting inequalities in talents and abilities when bargaining over the constitutional contract.

TABLE 11.3
Civil Society of Locke

	Threat Value	*Share of Surplus*	*Consumption*
A	50	50	100
B	150	50	200
Totals	200	100	300

Notice that the more efficient thief (A) benefits relatively more from the contract after Hobbes, which allows unequal thievery to cause unequal distribution. In contrast, the more efficient producer (B) benefits relatively more from the contract after Locke, which allows unequal production to cause unequal distribution.

Another alternative, not depicted in the figures, prevents *any* threats from influencing distribution in civil society, including the threat of noncooperation. According to Rawls, the social contract should be just, and justice denies the principle "to each according to his threat value." Rawls only allows *maximin inequality*, which gives more to the more able people only insofar as they produce more taxes to benefit the least able people.

A constitution built in the spirit of Hobbes allocates individual rights in response to natural powers of the social groups forming the state. A constitution built in the spirit of Locke allocates individual rights in response to the shared morality of the groups forming the state. Finally, a constitution built in the spirit of Rawls recognizes the welfare rights of the least able citizens. Each approach presumably leads to a different point on the welfare frontier in figure 11-1.

CONCLUSION

This chapter uses economic analysis to clarify constitutional philosophies of wealth, distribution, and liberty. By maximizing its value, a private firm maximizes the money available for stockholders to use as they please. Similarly, by maximizing wealth, a state maximizes the money available for citizens to use as they please. Maximizing wealth is the end of a state that seeks to minimize constraints on the available means for citizens.

A state can aim to redistribute wealth in pursuit of an ethical ideal as represented by point on the Pareto frontier. While disputes over ethical ideals permanently engage political debate, people who enjoy political power usually redistribute wealth to themselves. A constitution can dampen wasteful disputes by creating rights that limit the ends and means of redistribution.

Instead of pursuing wealth or its redistribution, a state can adopt a constitution that maximizes liberty. For affluent people, basic liberties apparently trump other values, whereas marginal liberties trade off with other values. Instead of maximizing liberty, citizens of an affluent country presumably prefer to secure basic liberty and trade off marginal liberties with other values. The people who enjoy constitutional rights value them, and a good constitution responds to peoples' valuation of their rights. In the next three chapters, I will consider how to maximize the value of property rights, free speech, and civil rights to the people who enjoy them.

Property Rights

[T]he right of property [is]... that sole and despotic dominion which one man claims and exercises over the external things of the world, in total exclusion of the right of any other individual in the universe.

—*Blackstone*, Commentaries on the Laws of England[1]

In the African tribe called the Barotse, "[P]roperty law defines not so much the rights of persons over things as the obligations owned between persons in respect of things."

— *Max Gluckman*, Ideas in Barotse Jurisprudence[2]

[T]he theory of the Communists may be summed up in the single sentence: Abolition of private property.

— *Karl Marx and Friedrich Engels*, The Communist Manifesto *(1848)*

THE LAW OF PROPERTY supplies the legal framework for allocating resources and distributing wealth.[3] As the preceding quotations indicate, people disagree sharply about these issues. Blackstone views property as providing its owner with freedom over resources, and he regards material freedom as the basis for other freedoms, "the guardian of every other right." In contrast, Gluckman found that property in the Barotse tribe in central Africa conveys responsibility, not freedom. Specifically, the Barotse hold a rich person responsible for contributing to the prosperity of his kin. Finally, Marx and Engels regard property as the institution by which the few enslave the many.

Instead of attempting to resolve such deep disputes over social organization, I proceed from a definition of private property sufficient to analyze capitalist democracies. Property can be viewed as a bundle of rights describing what a person may and may not do with the resources he owns. Property rights usually include the right to possess, occupy, use, consume, control, exclude,

---

[1] Blackstone 1765 (1992), book 2, Chapter 1, p. 2.

[2] Gluckman 1965, p. 171.

[3] The introduction to this chapter is based on the introduction to chapter 4 of Cooter and Ulen 1999.

expel, develop, transfer, assign, sell, mortgage, donate, or bequeath, and property rights often include the right to exploit, alter, transform, deplete, exhaust, waste, neglect, or destroy. The owner is free in the sense that no law forbids or requires him to exercise his property rights. Furthermore, the law forbids private persons and the state from interfering with the owner's exercise of his rights. Thus property creates a zone of privacy in which owners can exercise their will over things without answering to others in law.

Besides giving owners freedom over things, property conveys legal responsibilities. In common law owners must not harm the property or persons of others. Thus liability and regulations may require abating pollution, silencing noise, containing odors, and securing hazards.

The proponents of different visions of property try to imbed them in law and state institutions. This chapter will analyze the relationship between freedom and responsibility of owners as found in the constitutions of capitalist democracies. I will address such questions as the following:

Example 1: To construct a road, the state takes land from property owners and compensates them. Is compensation at market values too much, just right, or too little to create incentives for efficient behavior by property owners and the state?

Example 2: The owners of a small cottage on the beach apply for a permit to expand it into a house. The local zoning authorities refuse to issue the permit unless the owners "donate" a right-of-way across their property to enable the public to walk along the beach. When the owners sue the zoning authorities, the courts decide for the owners and prohibit such "donations." What are the economic consequences of this prohibition?

Example 3: The modern state often requires owners to apply for permits to develop property. Assume that a certain jurisdiction replaces the apply-and-appeal process with a system of transferable development rights (TDRs). How could TDRs increase efficiency and reduce corruption?

Example 1 concerns the taking of private property by the state. In most democracies, the government has broad powers of taxation and regulation, whereas the constitution restricts the taking of property. To illustrate takings, the courts may prevent government from taking the property of political opponents to raise revenues, and the courts may prevent the state from forcing private owners to allow public access to their land. Constitutional theory must distinguish takings, which most democratic constitutions restrict, from taxation and regulation, which most democratic constitutions do not restrict. This chapter uses economics to make the distinction and analyze its incentive effects.

Construction and new business activities often require permits, including variances from state regulations. As illustrated in example 2, owners must bargain with the state to obtain the permits, which involves risks. I will use economic theory to propose some constitutional guidelines for protecting individuals who must bargain with the state. Finally, I will explore the scope for replacing unwieldy regulations in property law with market-like instruments (example 3).

THUMBNAIL HISTORY: FROM MAXIMUM LIBERTY TO LOCHNER

I begin with a brief history of U.S. property law, which resembles developments in some other countries. Common law typically allows any use of land that does not interfere with other people or their property. Nuisance and tort law especially define "interference" in terms of physical harm and damage to health. Loss of amenity, such as the "quiet enjoyment" of one's land, receives only modest protection.[4] I use the phrase *maximum* liberty to refer to a legal system that allows an owner to do anything with her property that does not interfere with others. Common law imposed relatively few restrictions on the owners of property, so common law approximates a legal system of maximum liberty. Before the regulatory state emerged in the twentieth century, the common law of property was probably more important than regulations, so nineteenth-century America approximated a regime of maximum liberty for property owners.

In the twentieth century, however, governments in the United States imposed regulations restricting owners far more than common law did. As population grows and urbanization proceeds, one person's use of land becomes more entangled in another's. When uses entangle, distinguishing injurers from victims requires a difficult judgment about freedom and responsibility. The science of ecology identified forms of interdependence in the natural world that common law ignores, and the study of cities has done the same for urban property.[5] So twentieth century land-use regulations can be defended in principle as protecting the ecology of country and town. In practice, however, many regulations restrict competition and create monopoly profits for the friends of politicians.[6]

The U.S. Constitution guarantees both human rights and property rights. In the years since the Second World War, the Supreme Court has moved aggressively to protect human rights, especially in such areas as racial discrimination, freedom of speech, and freedom of religion. The Supreme Court has also moved aggressively to protect process rights, especially "due process" (the right not to be harmed by government actions in which the procedures are illegal). In this same period, however, the court has permitted wide interference by government with property rights in the form of zoning laws, regulation of industry, and redistributive taxation. In recent years, the U.S. Supreme Court has vigorously protected human rights, but not property rights.[7]

The opposite was true of the Supreme Court in the early years of this century, when property rights were vigorously protected, but human rights, as currently conceived, were relatively neglected. The symbol of the earlier view on property is the 1905 case of *Lochner v New York* (198 US 45, 1905), where the Supreme

---

[4] A good discussion is Passmore's exploration of the normative resources in common law and Judeo-Christian religion for addressing ecological problems. See Passmore 1974. For the argument that industrialization eroded the protections formerly afforded by the common law of nuisance, see Horwitz 1977.

[5] For a classic that remains fresh, see Jacobs 1993.

[6] For application to zoning, see Ellickson 1977 and Fischel 1985 as discussed in chapter 6 of this book.

[7] See Sunstein 1987.

Court struck down a New York statute prohibiting employers from requiring or permitting bakers to work for more than sixty hours a week. In a similar decision in 1923, the Supreme Court invalidated a minimum-wage statute for women and children.[8]

The *Lochner* case arose when a legislature tried to outlaw contracts that were enforceable under common law. By declaring the legislation unconstitutional, the court effectively entrenched common-law rights of contract and property in the constitution. Thus the *Lochner* case can be viewed as adopting common-law rights as the baseline for the constitutional protection of property. Under this doctrine, the taking of private property occurs when a law departs from the common-law baseline. The constitution, according to this view, requires neutral regulations with respect to the existing distribution of wealth as determined by common-law entitlements.[9]

In 1937 the U.S. Supreme Court began a new era by upholding a minimum-wage law for women, which marked the beginning of the repudiation of *Lochner*.[10] The *Lochner* principle was fully repudiated when Roosevelt's New Deal imposed many new regulations that vigorously intruded upon property rights. In early twentieth-century America, constitutional obstacles were also removed to increase the scope and rate of taxation.[11] According to one theory, these taxes and intrusions on property established the constitutionality of redistribution. The U.S. government now collects progressive taxes from income and pays benefits to unmarried mothers, retirees, the disabled, elderly people who are sick, corporate tobacco farmers, coal-shale extractors, manufacturers of flat computer screens, and many others.

Having eroded common-law restrictions on redistributing income, the New Deal did not establish a clear ideal for income distribution. Much of the political philosophy of justice concerns the ideal income distribution.[12] Instead of an alternative ideal for property rights and income distribution, the new understanding of the U.S. Constitution allows different ideals to contend for political power.

When governments redistribute income, the beneficiaries come to rely on these payments like stockholders rely on their quarterly dividends. Stockholders own their stocks, so they enjoy constitutional protection against the taking of their property. States must follow restrictive procedures when taking private property. In contrast, the beneficiaries of state programs do not own their benefits. When terminating someone's benefits, a welfare office must satisfy conditions of legality such as following its own rules.

---

[8] *Adkins v Children's Hospital*, 261 US 525 (1923).

[9] A discussion of this conception of property and its repudiation by Roosevelt's New Deal is in Ackerman 1984.

[10] *West Coast Hotel v Parrish*, 300 US 379 (1937).

[11] Notably, the sixteenth Amendment to the U.S. Constitution overcame obstacles the courts found in the Constitution to the taxation of income.

[12] There are many theories of just distribution. See, for example, Rawls 1971.

Some reformers want to change this situation and put needy beneficiaries of state programs (but not corporate beneficiaries) on legal foundations similar to those of stockholders.[13] According to this approach, hierarchy and patterns of coercion are more relevant to people than the formal lines separating private property and the state. Consequently, courts should regard certain kinds of state benefits as property of the beneficiary. If this approach became law, then terminating someone's state benefits might become as difficult as expropriating their property. This idea of the "new property" takes the repudiation of *Lochner* to its logical conclusion.

The *Lochner* controversy persists in alternative political visions connecting property rights, human rights, and democracy. Conservatives emphasize that private property protects liberty by making people economically independent of the state, whereas socialism weakens resistance to political authority by turning all workers into government employees. In this view, centralization of the economy causes centralization in politics. Conservatives note that communists abolished human rights and markets wherever they gained political control. The conservative vision emphasizes that clear property rights protect liberty and promote efficiency. Clear property rights are found in common law or civil codes supported by constitutional protections.

In contrast, political theorists since Aristotle have argued that free markets result in vast accumulations of private wealth, whose owners can purchase political power. In this view, the unequal distribution of property undermines democracy and promotes plutocracy.[14] The left-liberal vision focuses on the need for the state to protect workers and correct inequalities created by free markets. This vision admires social welfare legislation and the protection of human rights by courts.

Questions

1. Describe your ideal income distribution. If you could draft a constitution, how would you imbed your ideal income distribution in it?

2. Conventional microeconomics predicts that minimum-wage laws redistribute income and cause unemployment. According to conventional theory, who pays the cost of redistribution and who suffers unemployment?

3. If government benefits were treated as property by the courts, would you expect expenditures on lobbying for such benefits to increase or diminish?

---

[13] Reich 1964.

[14] The historical relationship among economic inequality, socialism, and democracy is confusing. India's democracy persists in spite of vast disparities in wealth, a relatively small middle class, and a recent history of socialism. In Poland, the move to restore democracy was led by a labor union (Solidarity). Chile elected a socialist government in 1970, which was overthrown by the military in 1973. General Pinochet imposed an authoritarian regime with a strictly capitalist economy that flourished, and the military eventually yielded power to democratically elected officials. These facts imply that the correct model relating democracy to the economy must involve multiple variables.

BRIEF ECONOMIC THEORY OF PROPERTY

Before analyzing constitutions, I will sketch an economic theory of property. The wealth of a nation depends on the efficient use of resources. Market exchange, which is voluntary, tends to move resources from people who value them less to people who value them more, as required for efficiency. To illustrate from chapter 3, Blair's purchase of Adam's 1957 Chevrolet creates a surplus because Blair values it more than Adam does. In a sale, "voluntary" means that the owner freely agrees to the price. The fact that both parties must consent to the sale usually guarantees mutual gain. Private owners also internalize the benefits and costs of alternative uses of their property, which prompts them to use their resources efficiently. So a regime of private property tends to maximize a nation's wealth.

In contrast, a taking does not require the consent of the property owner. Whereas voluntary exchange causes mutual gain, a taking causes unilateral gain. A property owner may value his property more than whoever takes it. A taking, which is involuntary, can move resources from people who value them more to people who value them less, thus causing inefficiency.

Protection of property rights by criminal sanctions and injunctions channels transactions into voluntary exchange. Conversely, when the rights of an owner are unprotected, others can acquire the property in an involuntary transaction. To illustrate, in condemnations the owner need not agree to the price, in warfare the conquered need not agree to the conquest, and in an emergency the common law authorizes a person lost in the woods to break into a cabin to find shelter and food.

The prohibition against interference and the legal power to exclude others protects the owner's right to use property. Besides the right to use property, the owner has an interest in its value. The requirement that other people who damage or take property must compensate at the market rate protects the owner's interest in the value of the property, but not the owner's right to use it. To illustrate, condemnation and the emergency doctrine allow one person to acquire or use another's property with compensation at the market price and without the owner's consent. In condemnation or an emergency, the owner's interest in the property's value enjoys protection, but the owner's right to exclusive use of the property goes unprotected.[15]

When the owner values the property at the market price, the difference between protecting interests and rights is small. Conversely, when the owner values the property at more than the market price, the difference between protecting interests and rights is large. To illustrate, assume that the market value of the estate Blackacre is $1 million. The fact that the owner retains Blackacre rather than sell it indicates that he values the property at more than the market price. Now assume that the state takes Blackacre and pays $1 million in compensation. If the difference between subjective and market values is small, say $1.1 million

---

[15] The difference between property and liability rights is explained in Calabresi and Melamed 1972 and elaborated in Klevorick 1985. Also see Posner 1985 and Shavell 1985.

versus $1 million, then protecting the owner's interest closely resembles protecting his right. Conversely, if the difference between subjective and market value is large, say $5 million versus $1 million, then protecting the owner's interest falls far short of protecting his right. Rapid turnover in ownership indicates little difference between subjective and market values, whereas enduring ownership often indicates subjective values exceeding market values.

Now reverse the example and assume that the state values the property much more than its private owner. Specifically assume that the owner of Blackacre values it at the market price of $1 million, whereas the state values the land at $21 million. This situation might occur because the public badly needs a road through Blackacre. If the state must buy Blackacre in a voluntary transaction, then the owner will typically extract part of the state's surplus value in the bargain. To illustrate, the surplus in this transaction equals $20 million, so dividing the surplus from exchange equally requires setting the price at $11 million.[16] Alternatively, if the state can condemn the property and pay compensation at the market price, then the state will receive all of the surplus value of $20 million. So protecting the owner's property right enables him to obtain a share of the surplus in transactions with the state, whereas protecting his interest allows the state to obtain all of the surplus.

The difference between the right and interest of the owner is often described as the difference between a "property right" and a "liability right."[17] In general, owners obtain an advantage by receiving a property right rather than a liability right.[18]

As explained, voluntary transactions move resources from lower- to higher-valued uses, as required for efficiency, whereas involuntary transactions can move resources in the opposite direction. Maximizing a nation's wealth, consequently, requires voluntary transactions as the rule and involuntary transactions as the exception. Channeling transactions into voluntary exchange requires protecting the owner's rights, not merely protecting the owner's interests. For example, most transactions must occur through markets, not takings.

To provide public goods and redistribute income, the state requires large revenues. In most democracies, the legislature can impose taxes by majority vote. Unlike takings, taxes are general levies that fall on a broad sector of the public. Economists have shown that broad taxes distort the economy less than narrow taxes.[19] To illustrate, a tax on food distorts less than a tax on vegetables, and a tax on vegetables distorts less than a tax on carrots. This principle follows from the fact that avoiding broad taxes is harder than avoiding narrow taxes.

[16] $20 million equals the difference between the state's willingness-to-pay for the land and the private owner's willingness-to-sell. Dividing the surplus equally requires the private owner to gain $10 million net of his loss of $1 million from giving up the property.

[17] Calabresi and Melamed 1972.

[18] This proposition is explained and proved in chapter 4 of Cooter and Ulen 1999.

[19] In general, the distortion caused by a tax on a good increases with elasticity of demand, and broad categories of goods are demanded less elastically than narrow categories. This proposition was first proved by Ramsey 1928. For an exposition, see Musgrave and Musgrave 1976 or Cooter 1978.

Thus avoiding a tax on food requires eating less, whereas avoiding a tax on carrots requires eating another vegetable such as cucumbers. In addition, broad taxes establish a baseline in tax law that is easier than narrow taxes to monitor and defend against political chicanery and special interests. So public finance economists favor taxes that fall on a broad base such as income, sales, profits, or real property.

As the base of a tax narrows, it distorts the economy more and provokes more political activity than obtaining equivalent revenue by a broad tax does. Narrowing a tax to its logical extreme ends with the taking of a particular good from a particular person. From this perspective, takings are simply the most distorting kind of taxes. Thus the economist's case against narrow-based taxes is the same as the case against raising revenues by taking private property.

Now I turn from takings to regulations. When uses entangle, the law must make judgments about freedom and responsibility among owners. These judgments often find their origins in pronouncements about who *caused* the harm.[20] Judgments about causation typically assign responsibility for the harm according to social norms. In small groups, social norms that regulate the practical affairs of daily life tend toward efficiency (Ellickson 1991). To illustrate, when a certain use of property impinges upon contiguous landowners, efficient social norms typically emerge to control the external harm. So commonsense judgments about the causes of harm often embody important facts about efficiency. (Like Epstein and unlike Coase, I believe that causation must play a central role in assigning legal liability in property cases.[21])

Legal prohibitions against interfering with others find justification in the economic concept of external cost. Whereas market transactions are voluntary, external costs are imposed without agreement of the harmed party. Externalities are outside the market system of exchange—hence their name.

As explained, when an externality affects small numbers of contiguous landowners, social norms usually emerge to control the behavior. In the absence of social norms, a small number of contiguous landowners can often bargain together and reach voluntary agreement over control of an externality. To illustrate, contiguous landowners may bargain with each other over control of smoke from a lime kiln. Clear rights, such as the right of polluters to emit smoke, or the right of pollutees to be free from smoke, facilitate bargaining and compromise. Bargains result in private agreements without the use of courts. When externalities affect a small number of contiguous landowners, social norms and bargains cure the problem with little need for law. Thus the courts stand ready to enjoin *private bads* in the confident expectation that they will seldom need to do so.

When an externality affects large numbers of owners, however, an efficient social norm may not emerge and transaction costs may obstruct bargaining. To illustrate, social norms and private bargains have failed to control air pollution

---

[20] I argue this point in Cooter 1987a. Also see the classic Hart and Honore 1985.

[21] Epstein 1973 and Coase 1960. Coase argues that the victim causes the harm just as much as the injurer in nuisance law, so cause provides no guide to liability.

from automobiles in the world's urban areas. Air pollution often resembles a public good (no rivalry and no exclusion within a natural air-quality zone), except pollution is bad and not good. *Public bads* affect too many parties for private bargains to resolve the problem. The law matters more to the efficiency of public bads than to private bads.[22]

The rule of law, however, can affect the number of people who need to participate in a bargain. Keeping numbers small improves the chance of success by lowering transaction costs of private bargains. This fact explains why efficiency requires injurers who cause harm to compensate victims, instead of making victims bribe injurers to cease causing harm. If the victims must pay injurers *not* to cause harm, then a large number of potential injurers may demand payment from their victims. To illustrate, if I must pay *potential* polluters not to pollute, then many people may proclaim themselves to be potential polluters. Conversely, if injurers who cause harm must pay the victims, then bargaining only needs to encompass the *actual* injurers and victims. To illustrate, if polluters must pay for the actual harm they cause, then potential polluters will take care not to harm too many people. In general, requiring injurers to compensate victims, instead of requiring victims to bribe injurers, increases the probability of private cooperation by lowering its transaction costs. By being willing to exercise its "police powers" to protect citizens from harming each other, the state gives citizens the power to suppress externalities.

Beside private law, public regulations constrain the use of property. Several differences distinguish public regulations from private law. First, public regulations typically involve state officials' monitoring for compliance before harm results, whereas liability law applies after the harm is done. Ex ante regulation differs in timing from ex post liability. Second, private owners seldom have the power to vary public regulations by mutual agreement. Replacing liability rights with state enforcement centralizes control of externalities. Conversely, decentralized control of externalities in a dynamic economy requires the continual creation of new forms of property, such as transferable pollution rights, the right to broadcast on a certain band of the electromagnetic spectrum, or the right to exclude others from using a computer program.

In chapter 3 I discussed the fact that majority-rule games of redistribution have no equilibrium ("democracy's empty core"). Applied to property, this fact implies that the citizens of a democracy can waste resources and effort contending over the distribution of property. For example, contests over distribution contribute to instability in some countries like Russia that are now emerging from communism. Social norms and constitutional law can help stabilize the income distribution in several ways (Cooter 1997b). First, the alignment of law with social norms creates a common understanding of the rights of owners. A common understanding about property rights provides the basis for bargaining

---

[22] For a brief discussion of the Coase Theorem, see chapter 3 of this book. For a detailed discussion, including the difference between damages and injunctions as remedies, see the discussion of the Coase Theorem in chapter 4 of Cooter and Ulen 1999 and the discussion of *Boomer v Atlantic Cement* in chapter 5 of the same book.

and cooperation, as required for efficiency and productivity. Second, alignment of law with social norms causes informal and formal sanctions to complement each other. When social norms and formal law complement each other, citizens and officials cooperate together in ways that make enforcement effective. Third, constitutional guarantees of property dampen contests of redistribution by removing some distributive issues from ordinary politics.

Question: Sketch how the economic theory of property gives freedom and responsibility to owners.

TAKINGS

Having sketched an economic theory of property, I apply it to some constitutional issues involving property.[23] In many countries, the constitution circumscribes the state's power to take private property. For example, the "Takings Clause" of the Fifth Amendment to the U.S. Constitution reads, "[N]or shall private property be taken for public use, without just compensation." Thus the Fifth Amendment prohibits the state from taking private property unless the private property is taken for a public use and the owner is compensated. "Public use" means a public purpose such as building a road, not a private purpose such as giving the property to the friend of politician. "Just compensation" means that fair market value must be paid to the owner of any property taken by the government.[24]

I will explain the economic rationale for the "public use" and "just compensation" requirements, which are common in democratic constitutions. Tyrannical or corrupt states sometimes finance government and enrich officials by taking property from powerless citizens. If the private property owner receives compensation equal to the market value for his property, the state cannot profit from taking it. To raise revenue by taking private property, the state must undercompensate the private owner whose property gets expropriated. So the "just compensation" requirement prevents the state from raising revenues by taking private property.

Viewed from this perspective, the requirement of compensation channels government finance away from takings and into taxes. I explained above that broad taxes do not distort the economy and provoke as much political activity as narrower taxes, and I also explained that narrowing a tax reaches its logical extreme by taking a particular good from a particular person. So the constitutional requirement of compensation at fair market value directs state finance in ways that reduce economic distortion and dampen redistributive contests.

The constitutional requirement of fair compensation, however, does not preclude another political abuse. Involuntary transactions can move resources from people who value them more to people who value them less. To illustrate,

---

[23] Also see Epstein 1985b; Fischel and Shapiro 1989; and Miceli and Segerson 1994.

[24] Fischel and Shapiro 1989 argue that this constitutional rule is in the interests of everyone facing an uncertain future, including the framers of the Constitution.

assume that Blackacre's owner values the estate at $5 million, the friend of a politician values it at $1.2 million, and the market price equals $1 million. The politician directs state officials to take Blackacre, pay $1 million in compensation to the owner, resell the estate to the politician's friend for $1 million, and the friend then donates $.1 million to the politician's reelection campaign. By these transactions, the politician gains $.1 million, the politician's friend gains $.1 million, and the state loses nothing. Thus the winners gain $.2 million. The original owner of Blackacre, who is the only loser, loses $4 million. The loss of $4 million far exceeds the winners' gain of $.2 million.

In this example, the politician's friend wants Blackacre for private use. Consequently, the taking violates the "public use" requirement that forbids the state from using its powers of condemnation to transfer private property involuntarily from one private person to another. To conform to the "public use" requirement, the state must take the property for a park, school, highway, or some other use by the general public.

The preceding example shows that the "public use" requirement reduces the scope for takings that destroy value. The "public use" requirement, however, does not completely solve the problem of inefficient takings. To illustrate, assume that motorists would be willing to pay $1.2 million for a highway through Blackacre. The state can take Blackacre and pay compensation at the market price of $1 million. So motorists will gain more than the state must pay to acquire the property. However, the owner values Blackacre at $5 million. Taking the property for use as a public highway thus destroys $3.8 million in value.

This example illustrates why the state should not *take* property with compensation *merely* to produce public goods. In most cases, the state should *buy* property to produce public goods. A voluntary transaction guarantees that the state must pay at least as much as the value of the private property to its owner. Consistent with his principle, the state buys most of the resources that it uses in production such cement, pencils, trucks, light bulbs, and labor.

Special circumstances are needed to justify *taking* private property to produce a public good. Developing public projects such as military bases, airports, highways, and wilderness areas often requires combining different parcels of land. When a developer owns almost all of the parcels, the last parcels become especially valuable. The need for contiguous parcels of land creates opportunities for owners to hold out for higher prices. Even when owners do not hold out, the hope of being the last seller gives each owner an incentive to delay the sale, thus increasing the project's transaction costs. (Holdouts are also discussed in chapter 5.)

To illustrate, assume that the state proposes to construct a road across three parcels of land owned by three different people. The state determines that motorists would pay $200,000 more than the construction costs for such a road. Consequently, efficiency requires undertaking the project provided that the land's value to the private owners is less than $200,000. Assume that the state acquires an option to buy one of the parcels for $30,000. The state could pay up to $170,000 for the other two parcels and still break even. Knowing this, each owner demands, say, $100,000 for her parcel of land. By acceding to these demands, the state would pay $230,000 for three parcels that the public values at $200,000, so the state should not accede to these demands. If the sellers do not lower their demands, the project must fail. In a real-life example, the developers of a new baseball stadium in Denver purchased all the land except for one small "holdout," whom the newspaper called "the guy who owns first base."

The state's power to condemn land eliminates the problem of holdouts. Except for the holdout problem, few reasons exist for the state to take property rather than buy it. In general, takings should be guided by the principle that *the government should only take private property to provide a public good when transaction costs preclude buying it.*

Questions

1. Assume that a private person owns the only suitable site for the state to build a satellite-tracking station. Explain the case for and against allowing the government to take the property and pay its fair market value as compensation.

2. The state of Michigan condemned many properties in a residential neighborhood on the border of Detroit known as "Poletown," assembled a large parcel of land, and sold it to General Motors to construct an automobile factory. The courts upheld the taking of private property for this project as a "public purpose." In terms of the economic distinction between private and public goods, does this project have a public purpose?

3. Compare the efficiency of the following two methods of amending the just-compensation constraint:

   a. Define just compensation to be fair market value plus, say, 20 percent.
   b. Allow each private property owner to make her own assessment of the value of her property. The property owner agrees to pay property taxes on that self-assessed value. If the government ever takes her property, it agrees to pay her self-assessed property value as just compensation.

Risk of Takings

Some assets such as land, a house, or a shop constitute a significant proportion of the owner's wealth. Most people are highly averse to the risk of losing a significant proportion of their wealth. To reduce this risk, most owners purchase insurance against the destruction of such assets by fire, flood, or other foreseeable disasters. Condemnation by the state also destroys the asset or takes its value from the owner. The "just compensation" clause in effect requires the state to insure the owner against takings. If law did not require the state to compensate owners, private insurance companies might sell protection against government takings, just like they sell protection against fires.

Why not extend the trend toward deregulation by repealing the Fifth Amendment and letting people insure privately against the loss of their property by takings? This question challenges us to compare the efficiency of private and public insurance and show the superiority of public insurance against takings.[25]

Competition causes a higher level of administrative efficiency in private insurance than in state insurance. Some state insurance, such as depository insurance provided to banks in the United States, have cost taxpayers vast sums of money due to mismanagement and fraud.[26] Thus, administrative efficiency argues against government insurance and for private insurance.

Two other reasons, however, argue for government insurance and against private insurance.[27] People buy insurance to get rid of risk. The insurer spreads the risk among all the policyholders. Spreading risk more broadly reduces the amount that anyone must bear. The state can spread the risk of takings among all taxpayers, which is broader than the base of all policyholders in any insurance company. In general, public insurance has the advantage over private insurance of a broader base for spreading risk.

This advantage of public insurance, however, is not so decisive as the second advantage. Government controls the frequency and extent of takings. The constitutional requirement that government compensate owners for taking their property provides government with a strong incentive not to take property unnecessarily. By not taking property unnecessarily, the total amount of compensation, which ultimately must be paid out of taxes, is less than it might otherwise be. If the state did not have to pay compensation, it might take property to finance itself, or to redistribute among the friends of politicians, or to purchase too many public goods.[28]

This argument for public insurance also explains the advantage of imbedding the compensation requirement in the constitution, as with the Fifth Amendment, rather than merely writing it into a statute. Writing protection into a statute has the disadvantage that the legislature that votes to take property could also vote to reduce the compensation paid to its owners.

I have explained that the incentive effects on government provide the decisive reason for making the state liable for takings, rather than leaving compensation to private insurers. Many writers outside the economic tradition, who remain confused about this point, mistakenly suppose that public compensation improves private incentives. These writers mistakenly believe that public insurance prevents "demoralization" of private investors.[29] In the next section I

---

[25] Blume and Rubinfeld 1984.

[26] The failure of the Federal Savings and Loan Insurance Corporation, which insured a special class of U.S. banks known as "savings and loan associations," cost American taxpayers between $100 and $500 billion. See, for example, Romer and Weingast 1991.

[27] See Fischel and Shapiro 1989; see also Kaplow 1986.

[28] For more on takings as insurance, see Blume and Rubinfeld 1984, and Kaplow 1981a.

[29] The misunderstanding of the "demoralization effects" of takings mars an otherwise superb paper on property by Michelman 1967. Also see Rose-Ackerman 1988.

explain that the opposite is true—insurance erodes private incentives for efficient behavior.

Questions

1. Conservatives who favor deregulation of, say, airlines and banking, often want to strengthen the protection of private owners against takings. Given that private insurance could protect against takings, are these people consistent?

2. Susan Rose-Ackerman has proposed the following guideline for courts to use in applying insurance theory to takings: "[C]ompensate [for a taking by the government] when the asset represents a major proportion of the owner's wealth so that a hypothesis of risk aversion is plausible. Employ a presumption in favor of risk aversion for individuals and risk neutrality for publicly held corporations. In addition, compensate even risk-neutral individuals whose loss represents a large proportion of their wealth if these individuals are politically ineffective."[30] Her guideline would make government's obligation to compensate depend in part on the wealth level of the owner whose property was taken. Describe some strengths and weaknesses of this proposal.

3. Another prominent scholar, Richard Epstein, argues that American courts should consider many forms of land regulation as takings under the U.S. Constitution.[31] How would you predict whether adopting his proposal would cause the total rental value of land to go up or down?

Takings v Regulations

Earlier I explained that when uses entangle, the law must make judgments about freedom and responsibility among owners. In cases involving a few contiguous properties, social norms and bargaining in the law's shadow usually solve the problem. In cases affecting a large number of people, however, private law does not work so well to correct the externalities caused by interdependent utility or production functions. In these circumstances, the state may enact regulations that restrict the activities of particular owners for the benefit of a wider public. Such restrictions raise difficult questions about compensation.

Regulations typically cause a fall in the value of some property whose owners may sue for compensation. To illustrate, an industrialist who acquires land to build a factory may be blocked when local government "down-zones" and forbids industrial uses. The industrialist may sue, alleging that the state took the value of his property without taking the title. A taking requires compensation and a regulation requires no compensation. When courts find for the plaintiff in such cases, they say there was a "taking." When courts find for the defendant in such cases, they say there was a "regulation."

[30] Rose-Ackerman 1988, p. 1707.

[31] R. Richard Epstein has argued that the current boundaries of the taking-regulation distinction permit government to avoid compensation in far too many cases. See Epstein 1985b. Also see Schambia 1982.

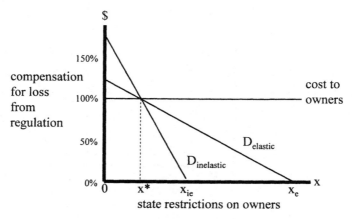

Fig. 12-1 Demand for State Restrictions by State Officials

In practice, obtaining building permits can be political or even corrupt. Instead of political reality, I focus on economic efficiency. The ideal boundary between regulating and taking requires an economic theory to distinguish between compensable and noncompensable acts by the state. In order to explain how to draw the boundary for the sake of economic efficiency, I will analyze incentive effects of compensation.

If the state need not compensate the private victims of public acts, the government has an incentive to take too much from private persons. Specifically, if the state need not compensate the losers from regulation, the government has an incentive to overregulate. Figure 12-1 depicts these facts. Demand curves in figure 12-1 indicate two possible schedules for the willingness of officials to pay compensation to owners for state restrictions on property. Perfect compensation of private owners equals 100 percent of the costs of state restrictions that they bear. If compensation equals 100 percent in figure 12-1, the state imposes restrictions on private owners equal to x^*, where the cost curve intersects the demand curves.

Alternatively, if compensation falls below 100 percent, the state imposes more restrictions than x^*. How much more depends on the amount that state officials are willing to pay as compensation to private owners for restrictions administered by the officials. If courts hold that a state restriction is a mere regulation, then compensation equals 0 percent. The inelastic demand curve $D_{inelastic}$ and 0 percent compensation yield state restriction x_{ie}. Alternatively, 0 percent compensation and the relatively elastic demand curve $D_{elastic}$ yield state restriction x_e. *In general, the more elastic the price elasticity of demand by state officials for state restrictions, the more state restrictions increase in response to a fall in required compensation to the private owners.*

Now I turn from state officials who impose regulations to private citizens who must comply with them. If the state must compensate the private victims of public acts, the private owners have an incentive to overinvest. Specifically, if the

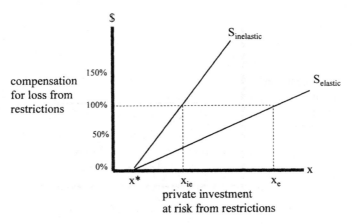

Fig. 12-2 Supply of Private Investments

state must fully compensate the losers from takings, the property owners have an incentive to make improvements on property whose value will be destroyed by a taking. In the case where the state must compensate fully for the harm caused by regulations, property owners will invest in improving their property as if there were no risk that regulations will destroy the value of their investment.

To illustrate, assume that an entrepreneur owns property suitable for development as retail stores or manufacturing. The property is currently zoned for either use, but the state may soon down-zone and forbid manufacturing. Down-zoning will destroy the value of investments in manufacturing facilities. If the state must compensate for property harmed by down-zoning, then the entrepreneur has an incentive to invest in manufacturing as if there were no risk.[32]

Figure 12-2 depicts these facts. If a state restriction is a regulation, then compensation equals 0 percent. The two supply curves indicated by an S in figure 12-2 represent two possible investment schedules for private owners. With 0 percent compensation, private owners invest x^* that is at risk. Alternatively, if the restriction is a taking and compensation equals 100 percent, private owners invest more than x^*. How much more depends on the slope of the supply curve for private investments at risk. In figure 12-2, 100 percent compensation and the inelastic supply curve $S_{inelastic}$ yield investments x_{ie}. Alternatively, 100 percent compensation and the relatively elastic supply curve $S_{elastic}$ yield investments x_e. *In general, the more elastic the supply curve for private investments at risk from state restrictions, the more investments increase in response to a rise in compensation above 0 percent.*

Second-Best Theory of Regulatory Takings: The Elasticity Principle

In the preceding section I explained that the elasticity of the state's demand for regulations and the elasticity of the supply of investments by private owners

---

[32] See chapter 5 of Cooter and Ulen 1999.

determine the response to different levels of compensation for taking property. Now I relate these facts to the efficient level of compensation. The internalization of benefits and costs creates incentives for rational actors to behave efficiently. Internalization, however, involves a paradox, as I will explain.

First consider internalization by the state. In figure 12-1 the state internalizes the cost of restrictions when it must compensate private owners for 100 percent of their losses. Insofar as the state behaves like a rational actor, x* in figure 12-1 indicates the efficient level of state restrictions. Under this assumption, any level of compensation below 100 percent results in too many state restrictions. Furthermore, the excess in restrictions becomes larger as the demand for restrictions by state officials becomes more elastic.

Now I turn from incentives for state officials to incentives for private owners. As with state officials, the internalization of benefits and costs creates incentives for rational owners to behave efficiently. In figure 12-2 the private owners internalize the risk that state restrictions will destroy the value of their investment when the state must compensate 0 percent of their losses. Thus x* in figure 12-2 indicates the efficient level of private investments at risk from state restrictions. Under this assumption, any level of compensation above 0 percent results in too much private investment at risk. Furthermore, the excess in investment becomes larger as the supply of investment becomes more elastic.

According to the preceding argument, the state internalizes the private costs of restrictions when it must compensate 100 percent of the losses, whereas private owners internalize the risk that restrictions will destroy the value of their investments when they receive compensation of 0 percent for their losses. Given these facts, liability law can provide efficient incentives to state officials or private owners, but not to both of them. Instead of a perfect solution, the courts often have to choose between finding that a state restriction is a regulation (100 percent compensation) or a taking (0 percent compensation).

An economic theory for making this distinction, which I call the *second-best theory of takings*, presumes that one party will have efficient incentives and the other party will have distorted incentives. For purposes of efficiency, the choice of whose incentives to distort depends on the elasticity of the response. As explained in figures 12-1 and 12-2, high elasticity raises the cost of a distortion in incentives. Conversely, low elasticity lowers the cost of a distortion in incentives. For the sake of second-best efficiency, the law should set liability so that the relatively elastic party internalizes costs and the relatively inelastic party externalizes costs. In general, *when the state responds elastically to the level of compensation for a restriction and private investment responds inelastically, courts should find that a state restriction is a taking.*

To illustrate, assume that requiring the government to compensate the victims of state restrictions will cause it to impose far fewer of them. Also assume that compensating private citizens for the loss in value from state restrictions has little effect on their investment decisions. The court should find that a restriction is a taking. To illustrate concretely, assume that the environmental agency's willingness to preserve wetlands responds highly to the amount of compensation it must pay to private owners. Also assume that investments by developers respond little to the probability of compensation for environmental restrictions. The court should find that an environmental restriction on wetlands is a taking.

Conversely when the state responds inelastically to the level of compensation for a restriction and private owners respond elastically, courts should find that a state restriction is a regulation. To illustrate, assume that requiring the government to compensate the victims of state restrictions has little effect on the extent of the restrictions that it imposes. Also assume that compensating private citizens for the loss in value from state restrictions causes a sharp increase in investments at risk. The court should find that a restriction is a taking. To illustrate concretely, assume that the environmental agency is highly committed to preserving wetlands regardless of its costs. Also assume that investments by developers respond greatly to the probability of compensation for environmental restrictions. The court should find that an environmental restriction on wetlands is a regulation.

To develop the second-best theory of regulatory takings, I need to predict the relative elasticity of the government and private owners. In general, people respond elastically to the price of a good that has close substitutes. Applying this principle, chapter 7 explained that a state organization responds elastically to prices when close substitutes exist for the act in question. For politicians at the top of a ministry, a close substitute is one that sustains the minister's political power, which might depend on popularity with voters and financial contributors. For civil servants, a close substitute is one that sustains the organization's revenues and employment, which might depend on the availability of alternative projects.

Notice that the contrast between no compensation and compensation for regulations is another form of the contrast between no liability and strict liability for accidents. A rule of no liability provides an incentive for injurers to take too many risks. Conversely, a rule of strict liability with perfect compensation provides an incentive for victims to take too many risks.[33]

Questions

1. Assume that a retail shop wants a brightly illuminated sign, regardless of its cost. Use the second-best theory of regulatory takings to explain why this fact is a reason for the court to find that a state restriction prohibiting brightly illuminated signs is a taking. (Hint: When the private investor responds little to incentives, the law can focus on getting the right incentives for state officials.)

2. Assume that a retail shop will not pay much more for a brightly illuminated sign than for an unlighted sign. Use the second-best theory of regulatory takings to explain why this fact is a reason for the court to find that a state restriction prohibiting bright signs is a regulation. (Hint: When the private

---

[33] This problem is explained in torts, contracts, and property in Cooter 1985. For a formulation of a first-best rule for takings, see Miceli and Segerson 1994.

investor responds greatly to incentives, the law should focus on getting the right incentives for private investors.)

3. "The theory of constitutionalism, as I understand it, tries to find a way to minimize the sum of the abuses that stem from legislative greed on the one hand, and judicial incompetence on the other."[34] In order to extend the second-best theory of takings to a situation where judges often make mistakes, use the elasticities in figures 12-1 and 12-2 to compare the consequences of different judicial errors.

4. According to the second-best theory of regulatory takings, if state officials prefer to withdraw a restriction rather than compensate its victim (elastic), this fact is a reason why courts should find the restriction to be a taking (100 percent compensation). Explain why this fact will bring courts into conflict with state planning officials.

BARGAINING WITH THE STATE

Viewed from an ecological perspective, adjacent parcels of land are so interdependent that anything one owner does affects the others. When the science of ecology encounters the "transformative economy" (Sax 1993), almost any restriction can be justified as controlling an externality. In such cases, property owners often bargain with the state over permits. Sometimes the state grants a permit provided that the owner *mitigates* the harm to the public. Sometimes the state grants a permit provided that the owner *offsets* the harm to the public by donating something valuable to the state. Mitigation and offset differ in their economic consequences for bargaining with the state. I will explain how an imperfect understanding of the difference resulted in an inferior court decision in a landmark case decided in the U.S. Supreme Court in 1987, *Nollan v California Coastal Commission*.[35]

Nollan

North of Los Angeles, the magnificent coastline of California remains largely unspoiled by development and the California Coastal Commission is responsible for keeping it that way. This case arose when a property owner sought a permit from the commission to enlarge a small coastal dwelling into a house. The property was located between the beach and a public road, as depicted in figure 12-3. The house would have diminished and degraded the view of the coast from the road.

The commission wanted to protect the view from the road, but that was not its only purpose. In addition, the commission wanted to obtain a walking path along the beach so the public could stroll there at high tide. Instead of

[34] Epstein 1985a, pp. 9–16.
[35] 107 SCt 3141 (1987). For a discussion of it, see Michelman 1988.

Aerial View

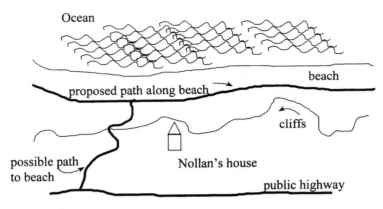

Fig. 12.3 Nollan

refusing permission to build the house, which the Supreme Court suggests that the commission could have done legally, the commission required the owner to donate a public path along the beach in exchange for permission to build the house. The owner sued and the case was eventually appealed all the way to the U.S. Supreme Court.

The state can regulate property to protect the public against harm, but the supply of public goods must be financed from general taxes, not by expropriating selected property owners. Was the Coastal Commission protecting the public or forcing a private person to pay for a public easement? The U.S. Supreme Court reached the latter conclusion in a complex opinion written by Justice Scalia. The Court remarked that the commission could require the property owner to draw up new plans for the house in order to reduce its intrusiveness. Redrawing the plans would mitigate the harm. Another form of mitigation, which is problematic but probably constitutional, would require the property owner to donate a path from the road to the beach, so the public could walk around the object obstructing its view.

Instead of requiring the owner to redesign the house or donate a path from the road to the beach, however, the commission required the owner to donate a path along the beach. A path along the beach would not mitigate the harm suffered by users of the road. The court looked for a "nexus" between the harm caused by the owner (obstructing the public view from the road) and the remedy demanded by the commission (donating a public path along the beach). The Court could not find a nexus. The Court reasoned that without such a nexus, the regulation was an illegal taking.

A legal principle can be abstracted from this conclusion. In order for a restriction to count as a regulation, not as a taking, the restriction must mitigate the harm that justifies it. Mitigation reduces harm, whereas offsets compensate for harm. *Nollan* can be interpreted as standing for the principle that government cannot present property owners who want to use their property in a particular way with the choice of offsetting the harm caused by the use or not using it.

An offset is compensation in-kind, whereas damages are compensation in money. *Nollan* prevents government from requiring in-kind compensation for harm to the public caused by private uses of property.

Mitigate or Offset?

I will explain the economic difference between mitigation and offset abstractly and by example. Perfect mitigation completely eliminates the harm in question, thus leaving victims indifferent between no harm and harm-and-mitigation. In reality, mitigation is usually imperfect. When mitigation of the public harm from a private act is imperfect, the public would prefer to forbid the act rather than allow it, conditional on mitigation. So when the state faces only two alternatives, it will often choose no-permit rather than permit-plus-imperfect-mitigation. This outcome blocks development.

Blocking development, however, can be wasteful. If the act's private value exceeds the public harm, then the owner could pay more than perfect compensation to the public. In other words, the owner could pay for an offset that makes the public and the owner better-off than if the act were forbidden. In so far as *Nollan* is interpreted to prohibit offsets, the Court's decision creates inefficiencies.

The Court's impulse to prevent offsets, however, has a sound motive. The Constitution gives government many more powers of regulation than it chooses to exercise against property owners. If building permits could be conditioned on offsets, government might choose to cash in on its potential power. To cash in, government would regulate, or threaten to regulate, solely in order to obtain valuable offsets. Allowing regulation to become a source of government revenue creates an incentive for overregulation and gives officials an opportunity to victimize politically disfavored property owners. For example, a mayor elected by tenants might avoid raising taxes by demanding offsets whenever property owners apply for building permits.

Allowing governments too much scope for bargaining with private owners invites another abuse as well. To speak of mitigating more than 100 percent makes no sense, so the upper limit on mitigation is the full extent of the harm. In contrast, the upper limit on an offset is the value of the building permit to the owner, which often exceeds the cost of the harm. Thus allowing government to require offsets empowers the state to extract most of the surplus value of private acts.

I have explained that forbidding offsets creates incentives for state officials to block too many developments, whereas allowing offsets creates incentives for state officials to extract the value from private developments. Before solving this dilemma, I illustrate it numerically.

TABLE 12.1
Value of Alternative Acts in Nollan

	Act (build house)	Don't act (don't build house)
Property owner	+1, 000	0
Public commission	− 300	0

TABLE 12.2
Cost of Mitigation and Offset in Nollan

	Private Property Owner	
	Redesign house (mitigate)	Path along beach (offset)
Property owner	−300	−250
Public commission	+250	+400

Hypothetical Example: Stylizing Nollan

To illustrate with numbers, assume that an owner will either act (build house) or not act (not build house). The consequences of this decision for the owner and the public are given in table 12.1. The numbers in the figure indicate that the permit to build the house is worth 1,000 to the property owner, whereas the cost to the public from loss of view is 300 as estimated by the commission.

In addition, the commission may require the owner who acts to mitigate (redesign the house) or offset (build a path along the beach). According to table 12.2, redesigning the house would cost the property owner 300, and redesigning the house would convey benefits of 250 on the public. Alternatively, donating a path along the beach will cost the owner 250 and convey benefits of 400 upon the public.

Combining tables 12.1 and 12.2 gives the net values of the alternatives as summarized in table 12.3. Redesigning the house and building it results in a net benefit of 700 for the property owner ($1000 - 300 = 700$) and a net loss of 50 to the public ($-300 + 250 = -50$). Alternatively, donating a path along the beach and building the house results in a net benefit of 750 for the property owner ($1, 000 - 250 = 750$), and a net gain of 100 for the public ($-300 + 400 = 100$). By definition, the most efficient course of action maximizes the sum of the net benefits to the property owner and the public. Thus, the efficient cell in table 12.3 requires building the house and donating a public easement along the beach (act and offset), which results is in net benefits of 850 to the owner and the public. Both parties most prefer "act and offset," so it is the "Pareto-superior" alternative.[36]

[36] One alternative is "Pareto superior" to another if one or more of the affected people prefers the first alternative over the second alternative, and no one prefers the second alternative over the

TABLE 12.3
Net Values in *Nollan*

	Don't act	Act and mitigate	Act and offset
Property owner	0	700	750
Public commission	0	−50	100
Total	0	650	850

According to one reading of the case, *Nollan* forbids the state from requiring an offset. Given this legal constraint, the commission must either refuse to issue a building permit or issue a permit conditioned on mitigation. If the commission refuses to issue a building permit, the public will suffer no harm. In contrast, if the commission issues a building permit and requires mitigation, the public will lose 50. So a public-minded commission will refuse to issue a building permit. This is true even though the private owner and the public would prefer the issuing of a permit conditional upon an offset.

By prohibiting offsets, the courts strengthen the bargaining position of private owners. To speak of mitigating more than 100 percent makes no sense, so the upper limit on mitigation is the full extent of the harm. In contrast, the upper limit on an offset is the value of the building permit to the owner, which often exceeds the cost of the harm. To illustrate by the preceding example, the largest amount of money that the commission could extract from the owner in exchange for the building permit would be the value of the latter to him. If money offsets are allowed, the commission could extract up to 1,000 for the building permit, even though the building only causes harm of 300 to the public. Thus, allowing officials to require offsets as a condition for obtaining permits empowers the state to extract a private development's value.

A Better Understanding of Nollan

I have explained that allowing offsets creates incentives for state officials to extract the value from private developments. In one interpretation, *Nollan* strengthens the bargaining position of owners against the state by forbidding offsets. Forbidding offsets, however, creates incentives for state officials to block too many developments. Fortunately, game theory suggests how to avoid this dilemma by a better interpretation of *Nollan*.

As illustrated above, the problem in game theory posed by *Nollan* is to allow offsets without weakening the position of the property owner, who must bargain

---

first. In other words, a change to a Pareto-superior alternative makes someone better-off without making anyone worse-off. (You might wonder, "Why would the property owner litigate the public commission's demand to act and offset, given that acting and offsetting is Pareto superior to act and mitigate?" The answer is that the property owner hoped the court would grant the right to act without mitigating or offsetting.)

with the state. To do so, the law might allow state officials to offer private owners the choice of mitigating or offsetting. The law, however, would not allow the state to require the private owner to offset without the alternative of mitigating. The proposed law would prohibit offsets unless the property owner also has the opportunity to mitigate. Game theory commends interpreting *Nollan* as standing for the principle that *government cannot require an offset as a condition for granting a building permit unless government also gives the applicant the alternative of mitigating.*

Applying this rule to the numerical example, the owner has the option to act and mitigate, yielding a payoff of 700 to the owner. Given this option, the owner will not accept an alternative yielding less than 700. The owner is, consequently, in a strong bargaining position. The owner need not accept the alternative of offsetting unless his net payoff exceeds 700. Giving the property owner the additional alternative of offsetting cannot make him worse-off than simply requiring mitigation. And the additional option of offsetting may make both parties better-off. Given that the owner has the right to develop and mitigate, there may be scope for a mutually beneficial bargain. If the private owner and the public both prefer offset to mitigation, the law should not prevent them from striking this bargain. In this example, "act and offset" yields 750 to the owner. Consequently, the owner will accept offsetting as an alternative to mitigating. Thus the law achieves Pareto efficiency by the rule "offsets permitted only when mitigation is allowed."

This analysis of *Nollan* illustrates a general feature of game theory: restricting the freedom of one party can strengthen its bargaining position. In this case, the bargaining position of owners strengthens by prohibiting them from agreeing to offset except when they have the opportunity to mitigate.

The U.S. doctrine of "unconstitutional conditions" restricts freedom for similar reasons. To illustrate, state governments in the United States can decide whether or not to provide benefits to unemployed workers, but if a state adopts an unemployment program, it cannot exclude striking workers from receiving the benefits. This constitutional requirement strengthens the bargaining position of unions. Similarly, the states can decide whether or not to permit foreign banks to operate in the states, but the states cannot require a foreign bank to waive its legal rights as a condition for doing business in the state. This constitutional requirement strengthens the bargaining position of foreign banks against the states. According to one commentator, the doctrine of unconstitutional conditions generally asserts that a state with absolute discretion to grant or deny a privilege cannot grant the privilege subject to conditions that pressure the waiver of constitutional rights.[37]

Questions

1. What would be the result in table 12.3 if the commission gave the property owner the choice of mitigating or offsetting?

[37] See Epstein 1988, p. 6.

2. Do offsets undermine the very idea of private property by giving government the power to extract a price for the exercise of any property right?

3. Assume the government wants to protect the environment by preventing construction of homes on a specific sand dune near the ocean. Government provides disaster insurance that enables landowners to build homes in places subject to flooding, such as sand dunes. If the government takes private property on the sand dune, either by condemning it or by imposing regulations that forbid any construction, should compensation include or exclude the increase in the value of the land caused by government disaster insurance?

4. In *Lucas v. South Carolina Coastal Commission*, the U.S. Supreme Court took a step toward requiring the state to pay compensation for restrictions on land use that diminish traditional property rights in common law. Use the second-best theory of legislative takings to characterize situations where this decision will increase or decrease economic efficiency.

Transferable Development Rights (TDRs)

Regulatory reform in recent years often replaces "command and control" with "market-like instruments" (Schultze 1977). For example, transferable emission permits are extensively traded in the United States, resulting in pollution abatement at less cost (Dwyer 1993). For land-use planning, however, market-like instruments have hardly developed. I will explain how a system of transferable development rights (TDRs) could achieve economic efficiency while solving difficult constitutional questions about takings.

Efficiency of TDRs

Assume that state officials construct a standardized measure of the development of land. Having constructed such a measure, the state determines through politics or administration that a certain region should undergo no more than, say, 100 units of development. I will show graphically how transferable rights over 100 units of development could cause an efficient pattern of development.

To keep the analysis simple, assume that the region has only two property owners, so 100 units of development rights must be allocated between owner A and owner B. The horizontal axis in figure 12-4 depicts development rights used by A and B. Measuring left to right indicates the development rights used by A, and measuring right to left indicates the development rights used by B. Notice that exactly 100 units of development rights are used by A and B at every point on the horizontal axis. For example, the point on the horizontal axis where A uses 25 corresponds to use of 75 by B.

Different owners value development rights differently. The demand curve labeled D_A indicates the amount that A is willing to pay for development rights, and the demand curve labeled D_B indicates the amount that B is willing to pay

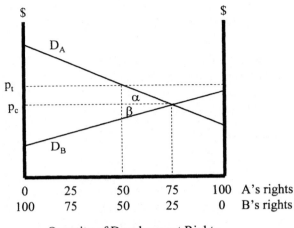

Quantity of Development Rights

Fig. 12.4 Transferable Development Rights

for development rights. The intersection of the demand curves, which occurs where A has 75 development rights and B has 25 development rights, indicates the efficient allocation of development rights between A and B. The allocation of development rights (75,25) is efficient because A and B are willing to pay exactly the same amount for an additional development right.

In contrast, consider the allocation of development rights (50,50), which is inefficient. At the point (50,50), D_A is higher than D_B, which indicates that A is willing to pay more for development rights than is B. To increase efficiency, A should receive more development rights and B should receive fewer development rights. This process of giving to A and taking from B should proceed until to the point (75,25), where A and B place the same value on additional rights.

The vertical distance between D_A and D_B measures the amount by which A values each right relative to B. Consequently, the vertical distance between D_A and D_B measures the social gain from giving an additional right to A and taking an additional right away from B. Thus the triangle $\alpha + \beta$ in figure 12-4 indicates the social gain created by moving from (50,50) to (75,25).

Some people may feel that fairness requires giving equal development rights to every owner. This policy, however, does not respond to the difference in the value of development rights by different owners. If owners receive equal development rights, and if they cannot trade them, then the resulting pattern of development results in waste measured by the triangle $\alpha + \beta$ in figure 12-4.

A market in transferable development rights (TDRs) would allocate them efficiently. To illustrate, assume that the state originally gives 50 development rights to each owner. At the initial allocation (50,50), A is willing to pay more than B is for additional development rights. Consequently, both owners can benefit from B's selling some development rights to A. Sales should continue so long as one party values additional rights more than the other. Sales cease when the market reaches the efficient allocation (75,25). If competition controls prices, then A receives α in surplus from the purchase of 25 units of TDRs, and B receives β in surplus from the sale of 25 units of TDRs.

TDRs have three advantages over the usual administrative process for development. First, TDRs economize on information. In order to allocate development efficiently without TDRs, planners must determine how much different owners value development rights. In terms of figure 12-4, the planner must know the demand curves of A and B. Without a market, administrators must determine the private value of development by conducting costly and inaccurate studies. The needed information is virtually impossible to obtain because A and B will respond strategically to questions about value. Instead of administrators deciding whether A or B values a development right more, the market can do so automatically. Thus at the point (50,50), the market reveals that the private value of a development right equals p_t, and this value falls to p_c at the point (75,25). A market for TDRs automatically allocates development efficiently by assuring that in equilibrium, all developers place the same value on additional developmental rights.

Second, besides allocating a fixed number of development rights among developers, the state must determine the total extent of development by all developers. Rational decisions require balancing the private value of development and the public value of conservation. With a market, the sale price of TDRs reveals the private value of development at the margin. The market in TDRs thus helps administrators and citizens balance the value of development and conservation more accurately.

Third, when land-use decisions by administrators make a vast difference to the value of a parcel of land, owners will spend large amounts to obtain political influence. In practice, developers often bribe planning officials in many jurisdictions around the world. Even without bribes, planning decisions concerning development prompt wasteful lobbying. TDRs, however, reduce political investment and bribery. Developers will focus more on buying TDRs and less on buying officials. Each particular owner is less likely to lobby or bribe officials under a system of TDRs than under the usual system of application-and-appeal.

TDRs have an attractive characteristic from the viewpoint of constitutional law. I explained that general taxes falling on a broad base cause small distortions relative to taking specific property from a specific person without compensation. TDRs resemble taxes in that they can spread the cost of restraining development among all owners of property rather than focus the costs on the specific property of specific people. The state can restrict development by reducing the numbers of TDRs, which harms many owners a little. In contrast, the usual building restrictions harm a few people a lot, thus raising constitutional questions about takings.

(I note in passing that taxation of development could result in a system almost identical to a market in transferable development rights. TDRs, however are more viable politically than the tax solution.[38])

---

[38] To illustrate, assume that the state wishes to limit development to 100 units. Initially the state imposes a tax of p_t in figure 12-4, and allows anyone paying the tax to proceed with development.

Example

To illustrate TDRs, imagine that a beach with sand dunes, an agriculture valley, or the airspace above some low-rise buildings comes under development pressure. The planning authorities want to restrict the total amount of development. The authorities first distribute TDRs to all property owners in proportion to the size of their holdings. Each TDR authorizes its owner to build one unit. The authorities next set the value of each unit in terms of cubic meters of development.

I will explain how TDRs work from the viewpoint of an individual owner and the planning authority. Assume that each TDR allows its owner to build 9 cubic meters. An owner of one parcel with 10 TDRs has the right to construct 90 cubic meters. Assume the owner wants to construct a building with 180 cubic meters of space. Instead of applying for a variance in the rules, the owner will have to buy 10 TDRs from someone else. Thus, TDRs channel the energies of developers into markets rather than politics.

While the number TDRs remains fixed forever, the authorities will need to vary their worth in cubic meters as policies and needs change. For example, the authorities might initially create 1,000 TDRs valued at 9 cubic meters each, thus allowing total development of 9,000 cubic meters. In time, however, authorities may revise their plans and decide to allow 10,000 cubic meters in total development. To accomplish the change, the authorities would set each TDR equal to 10 cubic meters. Alternatively, the authorities might review their plans and decide to allow 8,000 cubic meters in development and thus set each TDR equal to 8 cubic meters. Notice that revaluation spreads the effects of changing development plans across all owners of TDRs, thus distorting their behavior much less than do specific restrictions on specific properties.

TDRs have enjoyed limited use in the United States. For example, New York City sometimes grants a developer of a high-rise building the right to develop a fixed number of square feet above the parcel of land. The developer is free to decide how to configure the development above the parcel of land, such as choosing between a rectangular building or a more complex form. Sometimes the developer can even sell the development rights to the owner of an adjoining

---

At this price, A develops 50 units and B develops 0 units. Observing these facts, the state responds by lowering the tax rate. The state continues lowering the tax rate until it hits its target of 100 units. When the tax falls to p_c, A develops 75 units and B develops 25 units, so the goal of 100 units is achieved.

Development taxes have the same information characteristics as TDRs. Specially, the tax reveals the private value of development and assures that every developer values development equally. The major difference between TDRs and taxes is that the former gives the revenues from the sale of TDRs to private owners, whereas the latter gives the revenues to the state. Self-interested developers and property owners, consequently, prefer the current apply-and-appeal system to development taxes. Self-interested developers and property owners, however, might come to prefer TDRs in time, assuming TDRs could be made to work. For this reason, TDRs are more feasible politically than development taxes in many jurisdictions.

parcel.[39] If TDRs were further developed as a planning instrument, some authorities might abandon all restrictions other than TDRs, whereas other authorities would supplement TDRs with conventional restrictions such as zoning rules and site-specific permits. In general, the aim of TDRs is to eliminate or reduce reliance on specific restrictions on specific properties.

The history of transferable emission rights may provide a lesson for transferable development rights. After overcoming initial political objections and implementation problems, transferable pollution rights in southern California and elsewhere now yield large benefits relative to pollution regulation. Perhaps a concerted effort to develop TDRs would repeat this hopeful history. Certainly the inefficiency and corruption characterizing land-use planning in much of the world demands an innovative remedy.

Questions

1. Compared to TDRs, why do conventional land-use regulations require more constitutional protection of private property?

2. Use bargaining theory to explain how TDRs would reduce the value of the bribes that unscrupulous planning officials could extract from developers.

3. Describe some situations in which TDRs could easily replace land-use regulations, and describe some situations in which TDRs could not easily replace land-use regulations.

CONCLUSION

By giving people freedom over things, property promotes exchange and internalizes the benefits of efficient use. Democracy, however, allows wasteful contests of redistribution among competing majorities. A constitution can dampen these contests by removing some disputes about property from ordinary politics. A good constitution channels the politics of redistribution away from takings and into disputes about general taxes.

Entangling uses make owners responsible to each other. Private law can internalize most externalities that involve small numbers of people. Public law must respond to externalities that involve large numbers of people. Restricting property owners for the benefit of a diffuse public raises difficult questions about the boundary between regulations and takings. The ideal solution requires the state to compensate only the victims of excessive restrictions, or else limits the victims to compensation for investments justified in light of the risk that the state would impose the restrictions. In practice courts can seldom make these judgments about the efficiency of state restrictions and private investment.

Instead of ideal solutions, the real world usually offers the second-best solution. When the courts must choose between no compensation or full compensation, the elasticity of the response by state and private owners should control

---

[39] *Penn. Cent. Transp. Co. v New York City*, 438 US 104, 98 SCt 2646, 57 LEd2d 63 (1973).

the decision. If the state is highly elastic to the price of the restriction, then the restriction should be judged a taking so that the state internalizes the restriction's costs. Alternatively, if private investment is highly elastic to the price of the restriction, then the restriction should be judged a regulation so that owners internalize the risk of their investments.

Developers often have to bargain with the state over permits. If the state can demand that the developer offset the public cost of development, then the developer's bargaining position is weak. The state may be able extract the full surplus from the project in exchange for the permit. To solve this problem, the courts can prohibit offsets. A prohibition against offsets obstructs mutually beneficial bargains between the developer and the state. To obtain the best of both, the state should give the developer the right to mitigate, thus strengthening his bargaining position, and allow offset by mutual consent, thus facilitating mutually beneficial bargains.

The command-and-control approach, which has been discredited for most forms of regulation, remains the only possibility in the minds of most land-use planners. Transferable development rights could supplement or substitute for conventional permits and variances. TDRs reduce the information required for rational planning and channel the efforts of owners into market activities rather than political activities. TDRs also reduce constitutional problems by spreading the cost of restrictions among all owners, rather than focusing those costs on a few developers.

CHAPTER 13

Free Speech

> Language forms a kind of wealth, which all can make use of at once without
> causing any diminution of the store, and which thus admits a complete
> community of enjoyment; for all, freely participating in the general treasure,
> unconsciously aid in its preservation.
>
> —*Auguste Comte*[1]

HAVING ANALYZED property rights, I turn to human rights. Whereas property rights belong to people as owners, human rights belong to people as human beings. Since human rights belong to people as such, everyone has the same amount and no one can get rid of them. Thus human rights are equal and inalienable, whereas property is unequal and alienable.

A conventional list of human rights includes free speech and other forms of self-expression, printing and broadcasting, worship, group meetings ("assembly"), and contracting. The items in this conventional list are "liberties," which I defined in chapter 10 as "protected permissions." In recent years, political theorists and politicians have sought to expand the list of human rights beyond liberties. The expanded list includes civil rights, by which I mean the prohibition of discrimination on grounds of race, ethnicity, gender, or religion. Proposals for further expansion include welfare rights (living wage, health care, housing, food, paid vacations, etc.) and cultural rights (minority languages, cultural distinctiveness, national self-determination, etc.).

Each human right has its own history and character as developed in law and philosophy. Rather than survey all human rights briefly, I will analyze two of them in detail, specifically free speech in this chapter and civil rights in the next chapter. As Comte suggests in the preceding quotation, speech in many of its forms is a public good, from which economists conclude that speech tends to be undersupplied. I will use public-goods theory to explain when speech needs protection to increase its supply. The public-goods theory of speech developed in this chapter addresses such questions as the following:

Example 1: A professional association punishes a member for "intemperate political advocacy" and "unprofessional commercial advertising." After a lawsuit, the court orders the association to stop interfering with its members' political speech, and the court allows the association to continue punishing members for advertising. Can economic theory justify this difference?

---

[1] Quoted in Lessig and Resnick 1998.

Example 2: Statutes effectively limit expenditures on political campaigns in Britain, whereas court interpretations of the Constitution obstruct effective limits in the United States. How do effective limits on campaign expenditures affect competition in politics?

Example 3: A public writer falsely alleges that his neighbor had an illicit sexual affair with a famous politician. The neighbor and the politician sue the writer for libel. The court allows the neighbor's suit and disallows the politician's suit. Should the boundary between free speech and libel differ depending on whether the victim is a famous politician or an ordinary person?

The first example concerns the difference between political speech and commercial speech. Economic theory can justify more rigorous protection of political speech than commercial speech because the danger of monopoly in politics far exceeds the danger of monopoly in a particular market.

The second example concerns limits on political campaign expenditures. Media advertising requires money, whereas community barnstorming requires organization. Effective limits on campaign expenditures channel political competition away from fund-raising and into organization. Earlier this book contrasted the median rule and political bargaining. Media advertising moves politics toward the median rule, whereas political organizing moves politics toward bargaining.

The third example concerns the boundary between libel and free speech. A good location of the boundary minimizes the sum of the errors from false speech and too little speech. A good location of the boundary differs for different classes of victims, including ordinary neighbors and famous politicians.

Free Speech and Valuable Talk

People praise God, find a spouse, coordinate work, undermine rivals, campaign for office, and perform dramas through talk. Talk is the medium of social life much as money is the medium of business life. If speech is so valuable, why should it be free? The answer turns on a distinction between two meanings of "free." Consider the First Amendment to the U.S. Constitution: "Congress shall make no law ... abridging the freedom of speech." Freedom of speech is abridged by restrictive legislation. By prohibiting government regulation of speech, the First Amendment uses "free" in "free speech" to mean much the same as "free" in "free markets." Speech and markets are "free" when government does not interfere with them.

Applied to goods rather than markets, "free" has another meaning. As the price falls toward zero, a good gets cheaper and eventually becomes "free" like sunshine or country air. In this sense of "free," talk becomes cheap when people communicate nothing of value. "Free speech" in the U.S. Constitution does not mean cheap talk. On the contrary, free speech promotes valuable talk. Indeed, economic analysis justifies elevating free speech to a constitutional right by proving that doing so maximizes the value of talk, much like free markets maximize the value of commodities.

I will sketch the proof that a constitutional guarantee of free speech maximizes its value. Defined broadly, "speech" means any act of communication. Communicative acts transmit information that people value, including new ideas. As discussed elsewhere in this book, ideas are a special good from an economic viewpoint. If one person takes a bite from an apple, less remains for someone else to eat. Because one person's consumption diminishes another's, ordinary commodities like apples are "rivalrous." However, if one person uses an idea, it remains undiminished for other users, so ideas are "nonrivalrous." A person who possesses a nonrivalrous good can share it with others at no cost. Since including more people costs nothing, efficiency requires the broad dissemination of ideas, much like efficiency requires everyone to share in the enjoyment of military security, safe streets, and clean air.[2]

In economic theory, an "externality" refers to a transfer of value without payment. With harmful externalities, such as smoke or noise, the supplier does not pay for the harm imposed on others. A familiar proposition in economics, which I analyzed in chapter 5, asserts that a free market supplies too many goods that create harmful externalities. When production is naturally excessive, restrictive regulations can improve the situation. Conversely, with beneficial externalities, such as flower gardens or lighthouses, the supplier is not paid for the benefit created for others. The free market supplies too few goods that create beneficial externalities.

Many kinds of speech have beneficial externalities, especially transmitting ideas. Consequently, free markets provide insufficient quantities of beneficial speech. Regulations restricting speech aggravate the problem. The constitutional principle that speech should be free guards against legislation that aggravates the undersupply of ideas. This justification of free speech parallels standard economic arguments for efficient allocation of resources.

In addition to the argument from efficient allocation, economists defend free markets by an argument from innovation and growth. An innovator who discovers a valuable new technique or product gains a temporary advantage over competitors. The temporary advantage creates extraordinary profits, which dissipate with time as competitors emulate the innovator. Thus a free market promotes vigorous competition that stimulates and disseminates inventions.

Similarly, a speaker who discovers a new concept or expresses a new insight distinguishes himself from others, which can yield esteem and material advantage. The esteem and material advantage dissipate with time as the improved idea disseminates. Thus free speech promotes vigorous competition that stimulates innovation and disseminates ideas. These facts lead some observers to describe free speech as a "marketplace of ideas."[3]

[2] For more details, see the discussion of information economics in chapter 5 of Cooter and Ulen 1999.

[3] For a critical history of this concept, see Ingber 1984. He traces the idea to Milton and John Stuart Mill, and he traces the name to Holmes.

Markets for commodities presuppose property rights, but property rights in information are difficult to enforce. Transmission of information is so cheap that people who make valuable discoveries often cannot keep them secret. The information leaks out, whether it concerns a computer chip, a corporate merger, or a politician's illicit love affair. When information leaks, the discoverer cannot appropriate its full value. Foreseeing this fact discourages people from investing in finding information. Law can sometimes solve the problem of the nonappropriability of information by giving property rights to the creator. Thus copyright and patent law grant creators the right of exclusive use of their creation for a fixed period of time. Much like temporary monopoly, exclusive use-rights can create extraordinary profits.

I have explained that intellectual property rights circumscribe the use of ideas in order to reward their creation. In the special case of intellectual property, restrictions on ideas actually increase their supply. In general, the law should allow restrictions on ideas that increase their supply. Most restrictions, however, decrease the supply of ideas. Like most monopolies, most restrictions on speech create special advantages to benefit the few by harming the public.

By institutionalizing political competition, democracy makes political officials insecure. Political officials inevitably seek security by controlling political information. A constitutional guarantee of freedom of speech ideally prevents public officials from reducing political competition by restricting speech. By transferring the locus of control over speech from politicians to judges, the constitution ideally removes restrictions on speech from ordinary politics. In general, the constitutional right of free speech increases the effectiveness of competition among political candidates.

As explained, economic theory favors protecting speech for the sake of beneficial externalities and political competition. Implementing a constitutional right typically requires courts to balance various competing values. The greater the protection of free speech, the more other rights must be sacrificed. Economic theory implies a simple rule to determine the level of constitutional protection for different kinds of speech. *For any particular type of speech, constitutional protection should increase with increases in two variables: (i) its beneficial externalities, and (ii) the monopoly power created by its regulation.* Constitutional adjudication often follows this prescription, as I will show by comparing political speech, commercial speech, and pornography.

Political Speech

Maintaining democratic competition, rather than lapsing into dictatorship or oligarchy, requires many institutional props, including free political debate and wide dissemination of information among voters. Any abridgment of political speech undermines democracy by diminishing political competition. Democracy requires continual protection of speech against zealots proclaiming special privileges for their understanding of truth ("I have the right to persecute you because

I am right and you are wrong."—Bossuet[4]). Political speech should enjoy the highest constitutional protection in a democracy because of its centrality to political competition.[5]

Free speech increases the responsiveness of government in surprising ways. To illustrate, Jean Dreze and Amartya Sen demonstrate that a free press often prevents famine in developing countries by publicizing policy disasters that public officials, especially dictators, prefer to hide (Dreze and Sen 1989).[6] Although many citizens underestimate the worth of free political speech, liberal political theorists treat it as very valuable. From this perspective, free speech is a "merit good." (For merit goods, see chapter 10.) The next section connects this fact to regulations limiting expenditures in political campaigns.

REGULATING POLITICAL EXPENDITURES

In a public corporation, stockholders vote in proportion to their investment. Government by the rich works well in private corporations and badly in states. Few citizens would trade democracy for plutocracy. The difficulty is finding a way to limit the political influence of money. Techniques include capping the amount that any one person or organization can donate to a particular candidate, or capping the total amount that any one candidate can spend on a single campaign, or limiting the amount that any candidate can spend from his personal wealth on his own political campaign.

Different countries have different laws concerning donations to political candidates. To illustrate, Britain severely limits campaign expenditures by any candidate for Parliament in an election. The limit equals a fixed sum of money plus modest additional expenditures based on the number of electors in the constituency.[7] British elections are, consequently, short and cheap. In contrast, the United States has no effective ceiling on campaign expenditures or donations, so U.S. elections are long and expensive. This fact inspires the quip, "The golden rule of American politics is, 'He who has the gold rules.'"

The theory of rent-seeking provides a rationale for limiting political contributions. Recall that a rational corporation will invest in lobbying out to the point where the rate of return from political influence equals the return on manufacturing, research, marketing, etc. However, much lobbying wastes money on nonproductive activities. Corporations, unions, artists, charities, medical doctors,

---

[4] Quoted in Rawls 1993, p. 61 n. 16.

[5] Political speech has been called a "double public good" because it conveys ideas and constitutes participation in the public life. See Farber 1991.

[6] Note, however, that free markets in food and credit probably have at least as large a role as freedom of speech in suppressing famine.

[7] Representation of the People Act of 1983, sections 75–76. To be specific, the law imposes a limit of 14,592 pounds as of 1989, together with an additional amount for every entry in the register of elections to be used at the election. The additional amount is 16.4 pence in county constituencies and 12.4 pence in borough constituencies. This limit applies to the candidate's campaign expenditures. No person other than the candidate or his election agent may incur expenses with a view to promoting or procuring the election of a candidate. I am grateful to Anthony Ogus for this information.

the elderly, and military veterans in the United States, to name a few, spend large sums of money on lobbying. An effective cap on political contributions may reduce the waste of money on nonproductive activities.

There is, however, another side to the story. Many campaign contributions are spent on political advertising. Political advertising conveys information to voters concerning the platforms of the candidates. As discussed above, political information is a public good. Consequently, restrictions on campaign contributions may aggravate shortages in political information. Finding the optimal cap on political contributions for purposes of the law involves balancing the gain from less investment on redistributive contests against the loss from less dissemination of political information.

Advertisers count the number of "exposures" of a person to a commercial message. In television and radio advertising, the cost per exposure falls with the scope of the broadcast. Television and radio advertising, consequently, have large economies of scale. Like commercial advertising, political advertising targets television and radio in order to achieve economies of scale. Since television and radio advertising is expensive, effective limits on campaign expenditures reduce the amount of television and radio advertising.

When U.S. regulators stifled competition for airfares in the 1960s, some airlines put piano bars on their large planes to attract customers. Stifling one form of competition generally channels it into other forms. When politicians cannot compete through the media, they need to compete through party organizations. A typical party organization forms a pyramid with elected officials at the top and volunteers at the bottom. Local political organizations pay workers little or nothing for canvassing neighborhoods and getting out the vote. In general, effective limits on campaign expenditures channel political competition from media to labor. Conversely, ineffective limits on campaign expenditures channel political competition from labor to media.

Labor campaigns and media campaigns have different attributes. Labor campaigns require an organized party to direct the efforts of volunteers. Some volunteers expect political payoffs in exchange for their work. Organization facilitates bargaining over issues among the leaders of different factions and interests. In contrast, media campaigns increase the information to voters about the positions of politicians on issues. In media campaigns, politicians must increase their popularity, not build organization.

Previous chapters in this book elaborated the difference between the median rule and political bargaining. Media politics provide little scope for bargaining, thus increasing the force of the median rule. In contrast, political parties increase the scope of bargaining by organizing it. So an analysis of the effects of limiting campaign expenditures must consider a possible diminution in bargaining and an increase in the influence of the median voter.

PACs

Recent U.S. history of "political action committees" illustrates the practical difficulty of limiting campaign expenditures. From time to time Americans wonder whether the large sums required to win office are wasteful and corrupting. In the wake of scandals that forced President Nixon's resignation from office, Congress passed a law imposing a $1,000 limit per person on contributions to the campaign of any one candidate.[8] In *Buckley v Valeo*,[9] however, the Supreme Court distinguished between expenditures to help elect a candidate and contributions to the candidate's campaign. The Court allowed government to limit the amount of private contributions that a candidate could accept from each donor.[10] However, the Court held that government cannot limit expenditures by individuals on behalf of candidates. Such a restriction is an unconstitutional interference with free speech. One justice said that a $1,000 limit on expenditures by individuals to promote a candidate was "much like allowing a speaker in a public hall to express his views while denying him the use of an amplifying system."[11] By holding that anyone could spend any amount to elect someone to office, provided that the money was not given to the candidate's campaign fund, the Supreme Court destroyed the effectiveness of the law restricting political contributions.

In response to these legal developments, corporations funneled campaign contributions through organizations called "political action committees" (PACs). The history of PACs, which were unimportant until after the Federal Election Campaign Act of 1971, has a bizarre twist. Labor unions, whose total political contributions far exceeded those of corporations in the 1960s, feared that federal restrictions on political donations would curtail their practice of funding candidates. In response to this perceived danger, the unions obtained revisions in the bill that became the 1971 act and subsequently pursued other legislation and court rulings to allow generous political contributions by organizations.

Corporations, however, took far greater advantage of these opportunities than unions did. According to Federal Election Commission statistics, PAC contributions increased from $35 million in 1977–78 to $159 million in 1987–88. Furthermore, there were 1616 corporate PACs in 1987–88, which contributed $56 million to political candidates, whereas there were 256 labor PACs, which contributed $35 million.[12]

The dramatic change in the balance between union and corporate political contributions has affected American politics. Unions tend to contribute to liberal Democrats. In contrast, corporate PACs seek influence with whoever holds office, so corporate PACs tend to give to incumbents, regardless of party. When the incumbent steps down and a seat in Congress becomes vacant, however, corporate PACs tend to favor conservative Republicans. On balance, the surge in corporate giving made American politics more conservative.

[8] The Federal Election Campaign Act passed in 1971 and was amended in 1974 and 1976.

[9] 424 US 1,96 SCt 612,46 LEd 2d 659 (1976).

[10] Major party candidates receive some federal funding of their campaigns, and Congress can limit the acceptance of private donations as a condition for receiving federal funds.

[11] *Federal Election Commission v National Conservative Political Action Committee*, 470 US 480, 493, 105 SCt 1459, 1467 (1985).

[12] Epstein 1979 tells the history and provides early data. An unpublished lecture by Epstein updated the data as cited.

Instead of limiting campaign expenditures directly, an indirect approach might prove more successful. Until the end of the last century, citizens voted publicly in Britain and America, so any observer could see how a person voted. With public voting, a person who "buys" a vote can observe whether the seller kept the bargain. With the introduction of voting booths, buyers could no longer monitor the sellers, so the sale of votes by citizens diminished or disappeared.

Like nineteenth-century citizens, legislators typically vote in public, so donors can monitor the behavior of legislators who receive political gifts. Trade in donations and votes flourishes between lobbyists and legislators. A novel proposal to disrupt this market would impose anonymity upon donors. According to this proposal, political donations would be funneled through a "donation booth" consisting in a blind trust. The donation booth would prevent the legislator from knowing who made the donation. Consequently, the legislator would be unable to deliver precisely targeted political payoffs in exchange for donations (Ayres and Bulow 1998). This proposal, however, may restrict self-expression in ways that U.S. courts would find to violate the constitutional right of free speech.

Questions

1. The following constitutional amendment has been proposed: "The Congress may enact laws regulating the amounts of contributions and expenditures intended to affect elections to federal offices." Would this amendment increase or diminish the value of political speech? Would this amendment increase or diminish political competition?

2. Explain why media campaigns increase the median voter's influence, whereas campaigns based more on volunteer labor increase the role of political bargaining.

3. A corporation is a "legal person" and not a "natural person." The U.S. constitutional right of free speech protects natural persons but not corporations. Should corporations enjoy freedom of speech?[13]

Commercial Speech

Now I turn from political to commercial speech, whose main form is advertising. Advertising increases demand for selected goods by supplying information and altering tastes. The supply of information through advertising promotes competition, whereas the regulation of commercial speech can suppress competition. For example, an empirical study found a significantly lower price for eyeglasses in those U.S. states with fewer restrictions on advertising by optometrists.[14] Business groups sometimes seek "rents" by inducing officials to impose limits on advertising and other forms of commercial speech.

According to U.S. courts, the suppression of commercial speech sometimes violates the U.S. Constitution. For example, the state bar associations formerly

---

[13] Dan-Cohen 1991.
[14] Benham 1972.

prohibited lawyers from advertising. The bar's ban on advertising went so far as to forbid a lawyer from writing his specialty on his professional card,[15] thus enabling lawyers to collect fees for referrals. U.S. courts found that some of the bar associations' restrictions on advertising violated the right of commercial free speech.[16] After these restrictions were overturned, lawyers began to advertise, which intensified competition and increased accessibility of legal services to citizens.

The example of lawyers illustrates that U.S. courts protect commercial speech, but commercial speech enjoys much less protection than does political speech. The economic theory of free speech provides a rationale for protecting political speech more than commercial speech. While free speech promotes competition in politics and business, the two types of protection differ in importance. Given the state's monopoly on force, sustaining competition for office is more important than sustaining competition in a particular product market. The risk to democracy from the loss of political competition poses greater danger to the public than the risk of monopoly in some markets.[17] So the centrality of political competition provides the first reason to protect political speech more than commercial speech.

The second reason concerns the difference between private and public goods. Private goods mostly effect those who consume and produce them. Most benefits of advertising, consequently, accrue to the target consumers and the advertiser-seller, not to third parties. In this respect, advertising resembles a private good with few external benefits, not a public good with many external benefits. In contrast, laws have general effects. Larger externalities in political markets than in commodity markets justify greater legal protection of political speech than commercial speech.

Questions

1. Free speech maximizes the value of talk and free markets maximize the value of commodities. Assuming the goal of maximizing value, explain why courts protect speech more rigorously than they protect markets.

2. Some law and economics scholars advocate similar constitutional protection of property as speech.[18] To implement these views, the U.S. Constitution could be changed. Instead of merely protecting private property from being taken, the Constitution might prohibit government from "abridging property rights." Predict some consequences of such a change in the Constitution.

Pornography

Now consider an extreme example of privately valued "speech," specifically pornography. The consumers of pornography value the pleasure that it gives

---

[15] See an old copy of the ABA Code of Ethics, such as in Black et al. 1991.

[16] *Virginia State Board of Pharmacy v Virginia Citizens Consumers Council*, 425 US 748 (1976).

[17] Note, however, that Ronald Coase apparently disagrees. See Coase 1974.

[18] The closest to such a view is Epstein 1985b.

them, as evidenced by the large amount they pay for it. Many people, however, think that pornography creates harmful, not beneficial, externalities. For example, some feminists and conservative Christians allege that pornography prompts violence against women. If these assertions are true, then the case for constitutional protection is weak for pornography as compared to commercial speech or political speech. U.S. courts have in fact given only limited constitutional protection to pornography.[19] Instead of a high and uniform level of constitutional protection, U.S. communities have some scope to apply their own standards to regulate pornography.

PORNOGRAPHY TAX?

People differ in their definition of and response to pornography. Many people believe that advertising involuntarily exposes them to objectionable images, while other people find nothing objectionable in the same images. When people suffer involuntary exposure to pornography, the injurer does not have to pay for the harm experienced by some people. Like air pollution, involuntary exposure to images that the viewer finds objectionable is an externality. Willingness-to-pay is the standard measure of external costs. Since economics respects the preferences of individuals, their feelings determine the social costs of viewing pornography involuntarily. In principle, the amount that people who object to pornography would be willing to pay not to look at it measures the external cost of public pornography.

Economists often recommend controlling externalities by market-like instruments, not command-and-control regulations. For example, instead of quantitative restrictions, economists typically favor controlling some kinds of pollution by taxes or transferable emission rights.[20] Reasoning by analogy from pollution to pornography, the state could replace conventional restrictions with a pornography tax. In principle, standard economic techniques can measure the amount that people who object to pornography would be willing to pay not to look at it. Following the usual economic logic, a pornography tax should equal its external harm. The tax would apply to whoever exposed the public to the pornographic image of the type defined in the tax schedule. Exposing a few people to mild pornography would trigger a small tax, and exposing a lot of people to strong pornography would trigger a large tax. (The most objectionable kinds of pornography, such as child pornography, would remain crimes.)

Like a pollution tax, a pornography tax has advantages over conventional regulation. Faced with a tax, advertisers who can easily substitute nonpornographic advertisements for pornographic advertisements will do so, whereas advertisers who benefit most from using pornographic pictures will continue to do so. Thus the cost of reducing public pornography will fall on suppliers who can "abate" at least cost. By adjusting the tax schedule, the tax authorities can decrease the supply of different types of pornographic images to meet any goal.

[19] See Post 1990 discussion of *Hustler Magazine v Falwell*, 108 SCt 876 (1988).

[20] Chapter 12 discusses transferable development rights to protect the environment. For a discussion of pollution taxes and pollution rights, see Baumol and Oates 1979.

A pornography tax also has constitutional advantages. Prohibitions are more coercive than taxes, so judges should guard constitutional liberties more carefully against regulations than taxes. Vigilant judges who wish to protect expression by pornographers will find taxes less dangerous than prohibitions. In addition, a pornography tax might provide officials with more flexibility in dealing with an unmanageable problem. Instead of separating all speech into "permitted" or "forbidden," this proposal allows for a third alternative, "taxed speech."[21]

In addition to the enumerated advantages, a pornography tax has disadvantages, notably the cost of administration. A pornography tax would apply to more images than criminal prohibitions. Frequent imposition of a tax costs more than occasional imposition of a fine. Perhaps administration costs would not prove a decisive objection so long as tax revenues exceed administrative costs. From the viewpoint of moralists, another disadvantage of a pornography tax is that it does not clearly condemn pornography. In spite of this shortcoming, moralists would presumably welcome a significant reduction in involuntary exposure to pornography. Given the demonstrable disadvantages of pornography regulation, pornography taxes seem worth exploring.

PORNOGRAPHY IN PRIVATE

I have been discussing the external costs of involuntary exposure to pornography. What about voluntary exposure in private? Does private viewing of pornography hurt other people? Psychologists disagree. An old psychological tradition associated with Freud asserts that pornography channels sexual energy into imaginary acts that dissipate sexual impulses without harming anyone. According to this tradition, pornography viewed in private might actually benefit other people by reducing more objectionable behavior such as sexual harassment at work. If confirmed in fact, this view implies the social desirability of private viewing of pornography.

More recently, however, some legal scholars have vehemently asserted that private viewing of pornography causes some men to harm women.[22] According to this view, pornography prompts violence by dehumanizing the object of desire. If confirmed in fact, this view implies that private viewing of pornography harms other people. A third view holds that private viewing of pornography has little or no effect on the way men treat women.

At present, no reliable body of scientific knowledge exists to determine whether private viewing of pornography causes or averts harm to women. A new line of

---

[21] In an innovative paper on Internet pornography, Lessig writes: "Speech, it is said, divides into three sorts—(1) speech that everyone has a right to (political speech, speech about public affairs); (2) speech that no one has a right to (obscene speech, child porn); and (3) speech that some have a right to but others do not (in the Universities, *Ginsberg* speech, or speech that is 'harmful to minors,' to which adults have a right but kids do not). Speech protective regimes, on this view, are those where category (1) speech is dominant; speech repressive regimes are those where categories (2) and (3) dominate." (Lessig and Resnick 1998, p. 1).

[22] For strong allegations without any evidence beyond anecdotes, see MacKinnon 1987.

inquiry might provide such evidence in the future.[23] In the absence of evidence, political debates must continue to rely on moral intuitions, religious conventions, and philosophical theories, including discussions of liberty and efficiency by philosophically minded economists.[24]

Most citizens want to ban child pornography and limit children's access to pornography. The explosive growth of the Internet poses difficulties for such controls. Internet transmissions originate with the sender, pass through intermediaries, and eventually arrive at the recipient. Different jurisdictions have different laws for different types of recipients (e.g., minor or adult). The sender, however, often does not know the jurisdiction and type of the recipient, or even the route traveled by the transmission. To obtain this information, senders need to create various controls on recipients, such as limiting access by passwords. By applying a tax or sanction to the sender, policymakers can give the sender an incentive to find the lowest cost technique for conforming to the law. Techniques include self-rating by senders and limiting access to precleared recipients.[25] Taxes and sanctions on senders of pornography relieve law makers of the burden of attempting to regulate a very complex communication system.

ENFORCE CIVILITY?

An overlapping consensus about some political values can cause most citizens voluntarily to obey the law.[26] Without voluntary obedience to law by many citizens, the rule of law presumably collapses.[27] How should the state sustain the overlapping consensus required by the rule of law?

An economic analogy helps answer this question. Most modern economists believe that the economy flourishes best without extensive state interference. In eighteenth-century Europe, however, the dominant philosophy of mercantilism held that the state should extensively regulate the economy in order to increase national wealth. The attack on this view by Adam Smith marks the conventional beginning of modern economic theory.

These economic developments mirror moral developments. In the eighteenth century, England had a state religion and censored the press, as well as punished adultery and homosexuality. Blackstone, the great historian and philosopher of the common law, defended press censorship and state religion as necessary to the moral consensus that sustains the state.[28] In the twentieth century, however, only the vestiges of these past laws remain in England and other liberal democracies.

---

[23] As an example of the possible results from experimental psychology, Borgida 1994 conducted an experiment showing that exposure to sexually explicit advertising (1) alters performance in perceptual tasks and recall in direction of sexuality, and (2) leads to stereotyping and dominance behavior in job interviews of women by men.

[24] An article by Sen contrasting the "lewd" and the "prude" (1970b) provoked many published responses.

[25] For a thoughtful, pioneering paper on regulating Internet speech, see Lessig and Resnick 1998.

[26] For a profound meditation on overlapping consensus and political theory, see Rawls 1993.

[27] For models on this point, see Cooter 1997c.

[28] Thus Blackstone writes, "[T]o censure the licentiousness, is to maintain liberty, of the press" (1765 (1992), p. 153). In general, see his chapters defending established religion.

Apparently political philosophers and many citizens think that the state should do much less to cultivate moral consensus than it did in the past. Perhaps the state should provide a framework to prevent one person from harming another, then let the economy and morality look after themselves. In much of the world, the mercantilist spirit has declined in economics and morality.

Questions

1. Use monopoly theory to explain why private schools might be allowed to restrict the speech of their students more than public schools can.

2. The First Amendment of the U.S. Constitution explicitly protects speech and printing, but its protection has extended to most acts of communication and many forms of self-expression. How does public-goods theory determine whether or not to protect an act?

3. U.S. law permits employers to forbid sexually offensive talk in the workplace, while allowing the same speech in a public forum. Offer an economic justification of these facts.

MY SPEECH, YOUR NETWORK:
ORGANIZATIONS RESTRICTING MEMBERS' SPEECH

As developed above, the public-goods theory of free speech makes two fundamental claims. First, speech transmits ideas with beneficial externalities that the market undersupplies, and the constitutional protection of speech guarantees that government does not aggravate the shortage. Second, abridging speech rights reduces competition, which results in harm that increases with the forum's importance.

I cannot fully elaborate this theory, but I will discuss several details, beginning with an example of how organizations restrict the speech of their members. The Prodigy Services Company, a joint venture of a retailer (Sears) and a computer company (IBM), connects personal-computer users to a network providing various services and the exchange of information.[29] When Prodigy recently sought to increase the fees charged to subscribers, some subscribers used the network to mount a campaign of protest, including complaining to the advertisers of products sold through it. Prodigy apparently responded to this campaign by terminating some subscribers. Some terminated subscribers alleged interference with their constitutional right to free speech. Prodigy replied that although messages sent from one consumer to another are private and protected, messages sent by consumers to advertisers over the network can be restricted by it.[30]

Many other organizations restrict the speech of their members in various ways. To illustrate, legislators must follow the agenda, students may not speak

---

[29] The Internet is evolving so fast that my remarks about this company may be history by the time this book appears.

[30] See "Home-Computer Network Criticized for Limiting Users," *New York Times*, 27 November, 1990, C1.

in class unless called upon, Catholic priests may not advocate abortion, workers may not make racial slurs while on the job in some companies, and most state employees may not promote political causes while at work. Without restrictions on speech, the effectiveness of organizations would be impaired. For example, debate in Congress would be chaotic without an agenda, and racial slurs in a factory might create a ruckus. On the other hand, an organization's restrictions on speech can oppress its members. For example, procedural rules can suppress debate in the legislature, and a company can pressure employees to follow its owner's political dictates.

A vigorous competition among organizations for members provides protection against such oppression. When organizations compete with each other, a disgruntled member can resign from one organization and join another. An economist calls such protection "exit."[31] Whereas competition keeps the exits open, monopoly closes the exits. When an organization has monopoly power over its members, they cannot switch to a close substitute. For example, physicians who do not belong to the American Medical Association (AMA) cannot practice in most U.S. hospitals, so doctors who disagree with the AMA pay a high price for leaving it. Similarly, the state monopolizes political power within a nation. Most people who disagree with their government cannot emigrate. When exit is impractical, people need rights to preserve their freedom. Human rights must be imbedded in the constitution to protect citizens against the state's monopoly power.

This line of thought suggests how courts should set the legal limits on the power of organizations to restrict the speech of members. An organization typically justifies restricting the speech of members as a way to increase its effectiveness. More effective organizations provide greater rewards to their members, including higher salaries. The intrusiveness of restrictions must be balanced against the higher rewards from belonging to more effective organizations. Competition for members will drive organizations to find the balance between liberty and effectiveness that most people prefer. Organizations that strike the preferred balance will flourish in an open competition for members. If courts intervene to alter the restrictions on speech that competitive organizations impose on members, dissatisfaction among members will increase.

When an organization has monopoly power over its members, however, individuals may need the court's protection against the organization's restrictions on their liberty. The greater the monopoly power an organization possesses over its members, the greater the loss in liberty from restrictions that it can impose on them. For example, the cheapest configuration of an electronic network directs transmissions through a central switch, which creates an element of natural monopoly. To the extent that a private network like Prodigy actually has monopoly power, its subscribers may need some court protection of their free-speech rights. Conversely, to the extent that Prodigy has competitors, it lacks monopoly power and its subscribers do not need court protection of their speech rights.

[31] Hirschman 1970.

In general, *courts should scrutinize an organization's restrictions on individual liberty in proportion to the organization's monopoly power.* If the court finds no monopoly power, the law should take no interest in an organization's restrictions on speech. If the court finds monopoly power, it should ask whether the restrictions on speech strike a reasonable balance between intrusiveness and effectiveness. A reasonable balance yields a high level of satisfaction for the organization's members.

Economic principles can justify a difference in standards applied to private and public organizations. A person who dislikes a private organization's restriction on speech can usually escape by leaving and going to another private organization. Exit costs are relatively modest. In contrast, a person who dislikes a government restriction on speech cannot emigrate easily to another country. The high cost of exit from a country reflects the greater monopoly power of the state as opposed to that of a private organization. The difference in costs of exit justifies higher protection of free speech in public organizations as opposed to private organizations.

"Hate speech," such as diatribes insulting racial groups, disrupts social relations and interferes with an institution's legitimate purpose. For example, hate speech in a factory can disrupt production, and hate speech in a university can disrupt education. The cost of exit should condition the attitude of judges toward restrictions on hate speech. Changing factory jobs is easier than changing government jurisdictions. A characteristic of actions by the state is that citizens have difficulty avoiding their consequences. As interpreted by courts, the U.S. Constitution possibly allows a private organization to regulate hate speech that would disrupt its legitimate purpose, whereas the U.S. Constitution might disallow a similar restriction in a public organization such as a state university.[32]

Instead of contrasting private and public organizations, I contrast different levels of government in a federal system. Changing neighborhoods is often easier than changing cities, changing cities is often easier than changing states, and changing states is often easier than changing nations. In general, escaping jurisdiction by a less comprehensive government is easier than escaping jurisdiction by a more comprehensive government. Differences in the cost of exit from different levels of government justify different degrees of vigilance by courts in protecting individual liberties. As discussed in chapter 6, restrictions on individual liberty at the level of neighborhood government can increase the range of individual choices, whereas such restriction at the national level intrudes intolerably on individual liberty. The "exit principle" implies the "federalism of individual rights," by which I mean that courts should tolerate more interference with individual liberty when the effects are localized.

[32] *Doe v University of Michigan*, No. 89-71683, United States District Court for the Eastern District of Michigan, Southern Division, 721 F. Supp. 852 disallowed restrictions on hate speech at a public university. It is unclear as yet how far these speech rights extend in a private university. See preliminary injunction by Santa Clara Superior Court Judge Peter Stone in *Corry v Stanford University*, Case No. 740309 (Santa Clara County, Feb. 27, 1995).

FREEDOM AND LIABILITY

Some ideas, like democracy and vaccinating children, benefit people. Other ideas, like bolshevism and phrenology, harm people. In a liberal state, however, the people who promote bad ideas are not legally liable for the resulting harm. To illustrate, the economist who commended government by a randomly chosen dictator (its Pareto efficient) is not liable for the harm suffered by an organization that follows this recommendation. The liberal vision of society ascribes rationality to people, including the capacity to evaluate ideas. People with such capacities should decide for themselves whether ideas are good or bad, rather than have law preempt the decision.

Ideas can be beneficial or harmful, but not true or false. Truth and falsity belong not to ideas but to propositions and assertions, such as "All swans are white" or "It is snowing in Jamaica." True assertions often provide valuable information, whereas false assertions spread confusion and doubt. Unlike bad ideas, however, false assertions can give rise to liability for the harm caused by them. As developed above, the economic theory of free speech focuses on the external benefits of ideas. Now I turn from freedom to liability, and I also turn from ideas to factual propositions.

To illustrate liability, consider that people, organizations, and products have valuable reputations. Speech that harms someone's reputation can provoke a suit in which the victim seeks damages or injunctive relief. To be concrete, a newspaper reporter may allege that a politician dined with a notorious criminal. Alternatively, Able Plumbing Supply Company may allege that Best Plumbing Supply Company does not use real copper in its hot water pipes. In both cases, the speaker possibly commits the tort of libel or slander.

Strict Liability v Negligence in Libel Law

A successful libel suit has several elements. First, the plaintiff must allege that the defendant made a *false* assertion. Truth is a complete defense against the tort of libel in common law.[33] (Unlike common law, statutes sometimes hold a person liable for the harm done by a true assertion.[34]) Second, the plaintiff must allege that he suffered harm as a consequence of the assertion. Harmless lies provide no basis for a legal action.

If the plaintiff wins by proving that the defendant's assertion was false and harmful and not proving anything more, then the libel rule can be called *strict*

---

[33] Truth, however, was not a complete defense in prosecuting the common law *crime* of libel, such as the crime of libeling the king (Post 1990).

[34] To illustrate, dissidents may be forbidden to incite troops to mutiny in times of war, and agitators may be forbidden to incite a crowd to violence in times of racial tension. In the United States the question of the extent to which Congress can outlaw incitement without contradicting the constitutional right of free speech was answered by Justice Holmes in a famous formulation of the "clear and present danger" standard. See *Schenck v United States*, 249 US 47, 39 SCt 247, 63 LEd 470 (1919) and *Whitney v California*, 274 US 357, 47 SCt 641, 71 LEd 1095 (1927).

liability. In many situations, however, the plaintiff must allege something more to succeed in a libel suit. The third element, if required, often concerns the evidence justifying the defendant's assertion. Evidence differs by degrees. A modest legal standard requires the speaker to have "reasonable evidence" for an assertion, thus turning libel law into a form of the negligence rule. A speaker is negligent who fails to satisfy a community standard of care in obtaining evidence to justify an assertion. For example, a credit company may be negligent in collecting information used to determine someone's credit rating.

Beyond negligence, a higher standard requires the plaintiff to prove that the defendant was grossly negligent. For example, in U.S. law libel of a "public personality," like a politician or actor, requires the defendant to show a "reckless disregard for the truth."[35] Still worse is a deliberate lie. A speaker lies by making an assertion that he knows to be false with the intention to deceive. Under this standard of libel, liability requires the defendant to know that his assertion was false when he made it.

I cannot develop the distinctions between no liability, strict liability, negligence, gross negligence, and intentional libel here, but I will sketch the contours of the underlying economic problem.

Given incomplete evidence, a speaker is seldom entirely certain of a proposition's truth. A rule of strict liability allocates all the risk to the speaker. If the speaker internalizes most of the benefits of a true assertion, then a rule of strict liability for false assertions provides efficient incentives. If, however, the speaker internalizes little of the benefits of a true assertion, then a rule of strict liability for false assertions deters too much speech. When speech has external benefits, a libel rule of strict liability chills too much speech.

A negligence rule can ameliorate the problem. Given a negligence rule with clear standards, a speaker can immunize himself against liability by gathering a reasonable amount of evidence before making an assertion. Immunity from liability makes the speaker more willing to convey social benefits on others by speaking.

In some circumstances, however, far larger benefits from speech accrue to the public than to the speaker. In these circumstances, even a negligence rule chills too much speech. In these circumstances, the standard of libel may require deliberate lies or gross negligence in obtaining evidence.

The Politician and the Mob

To clarify the economic logic, I will discuss some examples of libel. Assume that a newspaper reporter asserts that a politician dined in a restaurant with a notorious criminal. The report, which turns out to be false, harms the politician's reputation. A suit for libel might begin by asking whether or not, given the evidence, the reporter should have made the assertion. Consider a cost-benefit test for answering this question. By this test, the reporter should have made the assertion if the expected benefits exceeded the expected costs to society. The

[35] *New York Times Co. v Sullivan*, 376 US 254 (1964).

expected benefits equal the probability that the assertion is true multiplied by the social benefit of making a true assertion. The benefits include the gain from discrediting a corrupt politician. Conversely, the expected costs from the assertion equal the probability that the assertion is false multiplied by the social cost of making a false assertion. The social cost includes the loss from discrediting an honest politician.

As the speaker's confirming evidence increases, the probability increases that making the assertion passes the cost-benefit test. Similarly, as the benefit to society increases from discrediting a corrupt politician, the probability increases that making the assertion passes the cost-benefit test. Thus, the likelihood of the court's finding libel decreases when the reporter possesses more confirming evidence and when benefits to society increase from discrediting a corrupt politician.

So far I have discussed whether or not the reporter, given the evidence he possessed, was negligent in making the assertion. Now consider whether the reporter was negligent in gathering the evidence for the assertion. Confirming evidence comes from diners who reported observing the criminal at the politician's table. Disconfirming evidence comes from diners who failed to observe the criminal at the politician's table. The number of diners who were interviewed by the reporter might indicate the quantity of evidence.

Next I apply expected net-benefits test to gathering evidence for the assertion. By the cost-benefit test, the reporter is negligent for failing to gather more evidence if the cost of gathering the evidence is less than the expected net benefit to society. In this example, the cost of gathering the evidence equals the cost of interviewing another diner. Thus the likelihood of the court's finding negligence decreases as the cost of interviewing another diner increases. The expected net benefit equals the probability that the new evidence will cause the reporter not to make the assertion, multiplied by the expected savings in harm from not making the assertion. Thus the likelihood of the court's finding negligence increases as the probability increases that another interview will tip the balance against making the assertion.

Libel law can make speakers internalize the cost of false assertions. In many cases, however, the speaker does not internalize the benefits from making a true assertion. For example, investigative reporting creates public benefits beyond the resulting increase in profits from selling more newspapers. In this example, the public benefits from learning about corruption among elected officials. If investigative reporters do not capture all the benefits from true assertions, and if liability law makes investigative reporters bear all the costs of false assertions, then incentives are deficient for investigative reporting. In general, the nonappropriability of external benefits results in deficient supply of speech, which liability aggravates. In the language of the courts, liability "chills" public discussion.

Discussions of public figures such as politicians have external benefits that are lacking in discussions of private persons. This fact explains why politicians and other public figures should face greater difficulty than should ordinary people in recovering damages for libel.[36] Thus in *New York Times Co. v Sullivan*,[37] the U.S. Supreme Court recognized that a finding of liability would cause commercial newspapers to strike the wrong balance between costs of inaccurate information and the benefits of more information.

Able v Best

As another example of the cost-benefit standard of negligence, assume that Able Plumbing Supply Company suspects that its competitor, Best Plumbing Supply Company, does not use real copper when installing hot water pipes. If this proposition is true, asserting it will create a net social benefit by improving consumer information. If this proposition is false, asserting it will create a net social cost by confusing consumers.

The need for libel law arises because speakers do not pay the social cost of making a false assertion. For example, if Able falsely asserts that Best does not use real copper in hot water pipes, consumers will mistakenly avoid Best, whose profits will fall, and some of these consumers will be diverted to Able, whose profits will rise. Absent liability, the harm caused by the false assertion falls upon Best and its customers, whereas Able benefits. Libel law can make Able compensate Best, thus shifting Best's loss to Able. In general, libel law can make speakers internalize the social cost of the confusion created by their false assertions.

Before making the assertion, Able should collect evidence by such means as inspecting pipes installed by Best. The investigation should proceed until the cost of additional evidence equals the probability of gathering disconfirming evidence multiplied by the harm averted by not making the assertion. By following this rule, Able will collect the reasonable amount of evidence.

Having collected reasonable evidence, Able should weigh benefits, costs, and probabilities. Able should make the assertion if the expected benefits exceed the expected costs to society. The expected benefits equal the probability that the assertion is true multiplied by the social benefit of making a true assertion. The benefits include the gain to consumers from discrediting a shoddy plumbing company. Conversely, the expected costs from the assertion equal the probability that the assertion is false multiplied by the social cost of making a false assertion. The social cost includes the loss of competition to consumers from discrediting a conscientious plumbing company.

Rain Developing toward Evening

Now I develop a precise test for libel based on expected net benefits to society. The problem of when to stop gathering more evidence is conceptually difficult.

---

[36] In *Hustler Magazine v Falwell*, 108 SCt 876 (1988), the U.S. Supreme Court held that a "public figure ... could not recover damages without demonstrating the existence of a false statement of fact which was made with actual malice." For private persons, recovery is possible without proving malice.

[37] 376 US 254 (1964).

For purposes of exposition, I reduce this general problem to the specific problem of whether to bother obtaining a weather report before going to the beach.

Assume that you need to decide whether to go to the beach or stay at home. Going to the beach yields benefits B when the sun shines and costs C when it rains. To make this decision, you need some information about the weather. You look up at the sky and estimate the probability p of sunshine. Rationality requires that you go to the beach if pB exceeds $(1 - p)C$ and stay at home otherwise:

$$[pB - (1 - p)C \geq 0] \Rightarrow \text{go to beach.} \quad (13.1)$$

$$[pB - (1 - p)C < 0] \Rightarrow \text{stay at home.} \quad (13.2)$$

Assume that inequality (1) is satisfied, so you make a tentative decision to go to the beach. Before making a final decision, you ask yourself whether you should phone the weather service and get some more information. The weather service is predicting either sunshine or rain. If you phone the weather service and learn that it is predicting sunshine, your tentative decision will be confirmed and you will go to the beach. In this case, you gain nothing from calling the weather service except more confidence.

To indicate this fact formally, let p_s denote your subjective probability that the weather will be sunny when you know that the weather service predicts sunshine. Your subjective probability that the weather will be sunny is higher when you know that the weather service predicts sunshine than when you do not know the weather forecast: $p_s > p$. If inequality (1) holds before calling the weather service, then inequality (1) holds after calling the weather service and obtaining the prediction of sunshine:

$$[pB - (1 - p)C \geq 0] \Rightarrow [p_s B - (1 - p_s)C \geq 0]$$
$$\Rightarrow \text{go to beach.}$$

Now consider the possibility that you call the weather service and learn that it predicts rain. Since the weather service predicts rain, you will revise downward your subjective probability that the weather will be sunny. To indicate these facts formally, let p_r denote your subjective probability that the weather will be sunny when you know that the weather service predicts rain, where $p > p_r$.

The fact that the weather service predicts rain causes your subjective probability of sunshine to fall. If your subjective probability of sunshine falls far enough, you will change your mind and decide to stay at home. I assume that p is revised downward far enough so that inequality (2) is true:

$$[p_r B - (1 - p_r)C < 0] \Rightarrow \text{stay at home.}$$

In this case, your phone call saves the expected net cost of going to the beach on a day when rain is likely. Specifically, by changing your decision and staying at home, you save expected net costs equal to $[p_r B - (1 - p_r)C]$.[38]

---

[38] Let q denote the probability that the weather service is predicting sunshine. Note that the following relationship holds among p, q, p_s, and p_r:

$$p = qp_s + (1 - q)p_r.$$

Now I can formulate how to decide whether or not to call the weather service. Assume that phoning the weather service is a toll call that costs w. Let q indicate your subjective probability that a phone call will reveal that the weather service is predicting sunshine. If the weather service is predicting sunshine, you will gain nothing from making the toll call except greater confidence in your tentative decision to go to the beach. Thus making the toll call to the weather service, which costs w, yields no gain with probability q.

Let $(1 - q)$ indicate your subjective probability that the weather service is predicting rain. If the weather service is predicting rain, the decision to stay home will save you the net cost of going to the beach on a day when rain is likely, which equals $[p_r B - (1 - p_r)C]$. This savings occurs with probability $1 - q$. Thus making the toll call to the weather service, which costs w, saves expected net costs equal to $(1 - q)[p_r B - (1 - p_r)C]$.

Now I can formulate precisely the expected costs and benefits of calling the weather service. At a certain cost of w, the benefit equals 0 with probability q, and the benefit equals $[p_r B - (1 - p_r)C]$ with probability $(1 - q)$. So you should call the weather service if expected benefit exceeds the cost, or, in notation,

$$[-(1 - q)[p_r B - (1 - p_r)C] > w \Rightarrow \text{call weather service.}] \qquad (13.3)$$

According to formula 3, you should call the weather service if the expected savings from disconfirming your belief in sunshine exceeds the cost of the call.

Reasonable Evidence

By reinterpreting formulas 1, 2, and 3 in the weather model, I can develop a cost-benefit test for libel. Assume that someone must decide whether or not to make an assertion. If the speaker makes no assertion, the payoff to society is 0. If the speaker asserts the proposition and it is true, the social benefits equal B. If the speaker asserts the proposition and it is false, the social costs equal C. Let p denote the probability that a particular proposition is true, and let $1 - p$ denote the probability that it is false. Efficiency requires the speaker to make the assertion if, and only if, the expected benefit exceeds the expected cost:

$$pB - (1 - p)C \geq 0 \Rightarrow \text{assert the proposition.} \qquad (1')$$

$$pB - (1 - p)C < 0 \Rightarrow \text{remain silent.} \qquad (2')$$

The probability p in inequality $(1')$ depends on the available evidence concerning the assertion's truth. How much evidence would a rational person gather before making the assertion? In general, the answer depends on the cost of gathering information and the harm it averts.

Assume that the speaker will make the assertion unless he obtains new evidence that the proposition is false. In other words, assume that inequality $(1')$ is satisfied under existing evidence. Should the speaker gather more evidence before making the assertion? If new evidence confirms the prior belief, then p is revised upward to p_s. The new evidence gives the speaker more confidence in making the assertion that he tentatively planned to make. Confirming evidence, however, does not change the speaker's plan to make the assertion. So confirming evidence has no value beyond greater confidence.

Let q denote the probability that gathering more evidence will *not* cause the speaker to change plans. In other words, let q denote the probability that (1′) continues to be satisfied after gathering some more evidence. By causing no change in plans, the additional evidence has no expected benefits or costs. Consequently, the speaker expects to gain q[0] from gathering more evidence.

Conversely, the new evidence might disconfirm the prior belief. If new evidence disconfirms the prior belief, then p is revised downward to p_r. The downward revision in p might tip the balance and cause inequality (2′) to be satisfied. If the balance is tipped, the speaker should remain silent. Disconfirming evidence that is strong enough to change the speaker's plan has an objective effect. By causing the speaker to change his plan and remain silent, the speaker expects to save $[p_r B - (1 - p_r)C]$.

Let $1 - q$ denote the probability that gathering more evidence will cause the speaker to change plans. In other words, let $1 - q$ denote the probability that gathering some more evidence will cause probability p to fall far enough to satisfy inequality (2′).[39] By causing the speaker to change his plan and remain silent, the speaker expects to save $[p_r B - (1 - p_r)C]$. Consequently, the speaker expects to save $(1 - q)[p_r B - (1 - p_r)C]$ from gathering more evidence.

Now I can formulate the decision rule for gathering more evidence. Let w denote the cost of gathering more evidence. In general, the speaker should gather more evidence if it costs less than the expected harm averted by remaining silent:

$$-(1 - q)[p_r B - (1 - p_r)C] \quad > \quad w \quad \Rightarrow \quad \text{gather more evidence.} \quad (3')$$

$$\underbrace{\hphantom{-(1 - q)[p_r B - (1 - p_r)C]}}_{\substack{\text{expected harm averted} \\ \text{by remaining silent}}} \qquad \underbrace{\hphantom{w}}_{\substack{\text{cost of} \\ \text{more evidence}}}$$

The analysis has identified the formal elements of a negligence theory of libel. Inequality (2′) suggests that a speaker makes an assertion negligently if the expected social cost of making a false assertion exceeds the expected social benefit of making a true assertion. Inequality (3′) suggests that not gathering more evidence to support an assertion was negligent if the expected harm averted by remaining silent exceeds the cost of the evidence. Now I can state precisely the negligence theory of libel. Given available evidence, a speaker's assertion is negligent if inequality (2) is satisfied. Given the opportunity to gather more evidence, a speaker's assertion is negligent if inequality (3) is satisfied.

---

[39] In order to tip the balance, the probability p must fall at least to the level given by solving inequality (2): $p < C/(B + C)$.

Questions

1. Suppose a legislator proposed to make economists liable for the consequences of any bad ideas that they develop. Make an economic argument against the proposal.

2. In order to apply formulas (1') and (2') to a case, the variables must be interpreted. Explain how each of the variables might be interpreted in the hypothetical case of *Best Plumbing Company v Able Plumbing Company*.

3. The crime of libel concerns harm to the public. Rewrite the cost term in formula (1') as two terms, one of which denotes the harm to an individual and other harm to a community. Discuss the application of this revised formula in criminal law. To deter the crime of libel, when must damages exceed what is necessary to compensate the victim?

4. Formula (2') concerns whether to gather more evidence in support of a proposition that you plan to make. Instead, suppose you plan *not* to make the assertion based on existing evidence. Can you derive the formula for determining whether you ought to gather one more unit of evidence? (The answer is in a footnote.[40])

CONCLUSION

The university cherishes freedom of speech, yet students are graded and professors promoted on what they say. This fact illustrates the complexity and subtlety of free speech. Many scholars resist simple models of complex behavior. In my view, simple models are necessary to understand the main causes of complex behavior. A good constitution maximizes the value of human rights to the people who enjoy them. This chapter explains how freedom can maximize the value of speech.

Speech transmits ideas and information with beneficial externalities that markets undersupply. Regulating speech aggravates the shortage of ideas and information by promoting monopoly. Restricting commercial speech harms particular markets, and restricting political speech threatens democracy. Conversely, effective constitutional protection of speech prevents the state from aggravating the natural shortage of ideas and information. Unlike ideas and information, some speech harms other people, such as involuntary exposure of people to pornography. In principle, a pornography tax could internalize this externality.

[40] Assume that (1) is not satisfied with existing evidence. Gathering one more unit of evidence is confirming with probability q, which causes p to rise to p', and disconfirming with probability $(1 - q)$, which causes p to fall. If the evidence is disconfirming, the speaker will not make the assertion, which is what he would have done without any additional evidence by hypothesis. If the evidence is confirming, we assume the speaker then ought to make the assertion: $p'B - (1 - p')C \geq 0$. Thus the expected payoff increases from 0 to $p'B - (1 - p')C$ with probability q at the cost w of an additional observation. The observation should be made if the expected net benefit is positive

$$q[p'B - (1 - p')C] \geq w \Rightarrow \text{make the observation.}$$

Many organizations try to increase their effectiveness by restricting the speech of members. Open competition among organizations for members, such as competition of corporations for employees, allows individuals to balance restrictions on speech and larger rewards from membership. As competition lowers the cost of exiting from an organization, courts have less reason to scrutinize restrictions on speech of members.

Free speech stimulates beneficial ideas and undermines harmful ideas. Consequently, no liability should attach to the invention and promulgation of bad ideas. Unlike bad ideas, false assertions can create liability. The threat of liability discourages people from making false assertions based on inadequate evidence. A cost-benefit test can clarify the efficient amount of evidence required for making an assertion. The efficiency standard provides a basis for contrasting alternative rules for libel law, such as no liability, negligence, gross negligence, and strict liability.

CHAPTER 14

Civil Rights

> It is of great importance in a republic not only to guard the society against
> the oppression of its rulers, but to guard one part of the society
> against the injustice of the other part.
>
> —*James Madison*[1]

> If you think you know the solution to affirmative action,
> you don't understand the problem.
>
> — *Michael Heyman, Chancellor, University of California at Berkeley*

HUMAN RIGHTS belong to people as such, so everyone has the same amount and no one can get rid of them. Political philosophers, however, disagree about the list of human rights. A standard list includes liberties, such as freedom of speech, worship, and assembly. In addition to liberty rights, the list of human rights advocated by many political philosophers includes freedom from discrimination on grounds of race, ethnicity, sex, and religion. The struggle for freedom from discrimination in the United States focused originally on the rights of citizens, such as voting in elections and equality in court, and now extends to nondiscrimination in many private transactions, including freedom from discrimination in purchasing services and finding employment in private organizations.

"Civil rights" now refers to freedom from all forms of discrimination. The absence of discrimination gives different kinds of people an equal opportunity to compete for offices, jobs, wealth, privileges, and honors. Civil rights are especially those equality rights concerned with opportunities.

Sex, ethnicity, religion, etc., form part of each person's identity, which lies at the core of personality. Discrimination based on these traits involves an indignity that provokes powerful emotions, which motivate strong moral judgments. The moral judgments of different people, however, contradict each other. As expressed in the quote from Chancellor Heyman, conflicts in deeply held moral judgments preclude consensus solutions.

Powerful feelings cloud judgment, which makes analysis urgent and controversial. This chapter uses economic theory to analyze the consequences of different forms of discrimination and alternative legal remedies. Although a careful analysis cannot solve the problem of discrimination, it can improve the quality

---

[1] Hamilton, Madison, and Jay 1961, p. 323, cited by Amar 1991, pp. 1132–33.

of debate and provide reasons for each person to modify his views. Here are some examples of questions analyzed in this chapter.

Example 1: The owner of a profession basketball team that refused to hire African-American players would suffer a competitive disadvantage and lose a lot of money. When does market competition tend to eliminate discrimination by making discriminators pay its costs? Conversely, when does market competition aggravate discrimination by making victims pay its costs?

Example 2: Assume that one ethnic group prevents employers from hiring people from another ethnic group to work in skilled jobs. How will a law ending discrimination affect the wages of skilled and unskilled workers in each group?

Example 3: A public housing project with equal numbers of European-American and African-American residents finds that applications from blacks to fill vacancies exceed applications from whites. Management decides to fill vacancies with whites and blacks in equal numbers. Is this decision unconstitutional discrimination against blacks or a legal method of preserving residential integration?

Example 4: An automobile insurance company's statistics reveal that Latinos and young males create more risk of accidents than do other people, so the company charges them higher rates. What is the best means for law to prevent the insurance company from using ethnic traits or gender to set rates?

U.S. CIVIL RIGHTS: BRIEF LEGAL HISTORY

The struggle against bigotry and discrimination toward African Americans preoccupies much of American history.[2] I will apply economic analysis to some of the doctrines of constitutional law that figure prominently in this history. First, however, I sketch briefly the history leading to recent developments in U.S. civil rights laws.

When African captives were first imported into British colonies in the beginning of the seventeenth century, slavery was common in many countries, but not in western Europe. British law did not recognize the status of "perpetual, hereditary slave." The closest status in British colonies was that of "indentured servant," which was not hereditary or perpetual.[3] In response to the slave trade, colonies of Britain and other European countries created the legal institution of slavery. Humanitarians were appalled by the cruelty of slavery, but slave owners wanted to keep their wealth. The slave trade in the British colonies created a powerful movement to abolish slavery and a vested interest in perpetuating slavery.

---

[2] My thanks to Robert Post for help with this section.

[3] "Servitude" was common in Britain, whereas "indentured servitude" was restricted to colonies as a device to assure repayment of travel costs. The U.S. colonies apparently got much of its slave law from British Caribbean colonies, which in turn got it from the Portuguese in Brazil and Dutch in the Guyanas. (Wiecek 1977).

In the United States, the abolitionists prevailed in the North, which gradually eliminated slavery in the eighteenth and early nineteenth centuries, whereas slave owners prevailed in the South, which gradually eliminated the status of "free Negro" (Wiecek 1977). In the new territories of the West, the two legal orders confronted each other and struggled for superiority. The attempted secession of the Southern states prompted the bloody Civil War that ended with the South's military defeat in 1865 and implementation of the U.S. Constitution's Thirteenth Amendment, which outlaws slavery and any form of "involuntary servitude."

Northern victory left the Southern states under the control of the occupying army and the abolitionists, who tried to impose a legal framework that would bring African Americans into full participation in political life. Thus the Fourteenth Amendment to the U.S. Constitution excluded secessionists from holding many federal offices, and the Fifteenth Amendment forbade states from denying the right to vote on grounds of "race, color, or previous condition of servitude." The Civil Rights Act of 1866 made it a crime to deprive anyone of a broad list of rights.

For black Southerners, the years immediately following the Civil War were a time of political and social liberation, tempered by economic hardship and unreliable law enforcement. In contrast, many white Southerners experienced these years as a period of vindictive foreign domination and anarchy. Control of the South by Northerners did not last long. The former soldiers of the Southern armies formed vigilante organizations that imposed their version of rough justice and often terrorized African Americans. Once the occupying armies withdrew, white Southerners regained control of governments and excluded blacks from political power by law and practice.

Southern legislatures eventually enacted the so-called Jim Crow laws that facilitated or required segregation in public services such as transportation, restaurants, and schools. To illustrate, these laws relegated African Americans to sitting in the back of buses and streetcars, thus ending the practice of people sitting wherever they wanted. Economic historian Jennifer Roback has argued that many forms of segregation, such as separate seating in public transportation, were unsustainable without the force of law. She concludes that law, not the market economy, segregated the South (Roback 1989). (Endemic discrimination in the North is another story.)

Just as slavery induced a political movement for abolition, segregation induced a political movement for integration. The civil rights movement challenged segregation on constitutional grounds. "Judicial review" refers to the power of U.S. courts to scrutinize legislation for consistency with the constitution. Laws mandating segregation were potentially in violation of the Fourteenth Amendment, which guarantees "equal protection of the laws" to everyone, regardless of race, and which forbids states from depriving "any person of life, liberty, or property, without due process of law.[4] After a series of cases, the Supreme Court ruled

---

[4] A technical point of law worth noting is that the Fourteenth Amendment's strictures against discrimination apply to actions by state governments. To reach the federal government, the courts have found similar strictures in the Fifth Amendment.

in *Plessy v Ferguson* (1896) that state and local governments can permit or require separate facilities for blacks and whites, provided that the facilities are equally good. "Separate but equal" provided the legal foundation for segregation through the first half of the twentieth century.

Although separate facilities were in fact unequal, the civil rights movement had little success in attacking discriminatory laws during the first half of the twentieth century. Civil rights litigants, however, patiently pursued a sequence of minor victories that built up to the breakthrough in 1954 when the Supreme Court gave the Fourteenth Amendment a new interpretation. In *Brown v Board of Education*, Chief Justice Earl Warren wrote:

> Does segregation of children in public schools solely on the basis of race, even though the physical facilities and other "tangible" factors may be equal, deprive the children of the minority group of equal educational opportunities? We believe that it does ... in the field of public education the doctrine of "separate but equal" has no place. Separate educational facilities are inherently unequal. Therefore, we hold that the plaintiffs and others similarly situated ... are, by reason of the segregation complained of, deprived of [equal protection of the laws under the Fourteenth Amendment].

Brown eventually came to stand for rejecting the old principle of "separate but equal" in favor of the new principle of integration.[5]

The integration of public transportation and restaurants took a different course. After the Civil War, protestors sometimes disrupted integrated businesses in order to promote segregation. In the 1960s, this practice was reversed, with protesters disrupting segregated businesses in order to promote integration. The most famous example was the boycott of segregated public transportation in Selma, Alabama, which was organized by a young black minister named Martin Luther King. His philosophy of active, nonviolent disruption of segregated businesses proved effective in integrating transportation, restaurants, and other services across the South. The triumph of civil rights in the streets was not without its blood and tears, or its heroes and villains. Instead of retelling these dramatic tales about a time when "giants walked the earth," I will return to developments in law.

Federal judges became intensely active in pursuit of civil rights during the 1960s and 1970s. Courts issued orders, called "structural injunctions," requiring schools and other institutions to change fundamental practices and policies that sustained segregation. Later, judicial activism on civil rights dampened under the influence of conservative judges appointed by Presidents Nixon and Reagan.

Congress did not enact civil rights laws until a decade after the Supreme Court decided *Brown*. The assassination of President Kennedy in 1963, the forcefulness of his successor President Johnson, and a massive march on

[5] After *Brown*, the fourth circuit interpreted *Brown* to mean "No segregation," whereas the fifth circuit interpreted *Brown* to mean "Integration." Over a period of years, the fifth circuit's interpretation won.

Washington organized by Martin Luther King eventually persuaded Congress to overcome the opposition of Southern senators and enact civil rights legislation. The Civil Rights Act of 1964 and its subsequent amendments attack discrimination in politics, courts, business, and work. Congress subsequently enacted legislation to withhold federal financial aid from school districts that remained segregated.[6]

I will discuss briefly some doctrines that courts developed to promote integration. As noted in *Brown*, U.S. courts frequently review statutes affecting civil rights to see whether they conform to the "equal protection" and "due process" clauses of the Fourteenth Amendment. U.S. courts have struggled to give more precise and definite meaning to this amendment. Courts have found that laws violate the Fourteenth Amendment if, among other things, they discriminate against some groups of people ("unequal protection") or restrict their rights without following correct procedures ("illegal process"). Explaining the reach of these expansive doctrines would require many pages.[7] Instead, I will suggest the flavor of the arguments by discussing some key terms.

Some racial and ethnic groups have been deprived of the laws' protection more than others. If a statute draws a distinction based on the race or ethnicity of people who have historically suffered discrimination ("suspect class"), then the courts subject the statute to "strict scrutiny" of its constitutionality. To survive strict scrutiny, the state must need the racial distinction in the statute to achieve a "compelling purpose." Not many statutes that explicitly refer to race or ethnicity can survive strict scrutiny. Strict scrutiny removed many racial and ethnic categories from state laws.

Many statutes differentially affect races or ethnic groups without the law's explicitly referring to race or ethnicity. Such a statute is racially neutral on its face. Instead of strict scrutiny, facially neutral statutes are examined for the lawmaker's intent to discriminate.[8] Laws with discriminatory intent violate the U.S. Constitution. A statute that is neutral on its face may have a "disparate

---

[6]The traditional view that court activity following *Brown* had large effects on prompting integration has been challenged in Rosenberg 1993. According to Rosenberg, schools in the South remained segregated for ten years after *Brown*, whereas congressional legislation tying school funding to integration in the 1960s induced school integration in the South.

[7] U.S. Supreme Court Justice William Brennan wrote: "The Declaration of Independence, the Constitution and the Bill of Rights solemnly committed the United States to be a country where the dignity and rights of all persons are equal before all authority. In all candor we must concede that part of this egalitarianism in America has been more pretension than realized fact. But we are an aspiring people, a people with faith in progress. Our amended Constitution is the lodestar for our aspirations." If the Supreme Court views the Constitution as the lodestar of national aspirations for equality, then the Constitution will require much amendment by interpretation.

[8] The demonstrations in earlier chapters that many people with dissimilar intentions act collectively to make a law should make the reader uneasy about finding a unified "intent"—whether discriminatory or nondiscriminatory—in the making of a statute. Perhaps the relevant court cases can be understood without relying on the concept of intent articulated in them. One scholar has suggested that the key to these cases is the significance of the racial minority's interest. According to this view, the court will strike the practice down if it adversely affects the vital interests of the minority, even without a showing of discriminatory intent. See Ortiz 1989.

impact" on a minority group that historically suffered discrimination. Disparate impact alerts courts to the possibility of discriminatory intent by lawmakers. For example, school boundaries with a disparate impact were often found by the courts to have been drawn by the school district with the intention to discriminate.

Even without discriminatory intent, laws with disparate impact may violate U.S. civil rights statutes.[9] For example, Title VII of the U.S. Civil Rights Act prohibits employment discrimination based on race, sex, or age. State officials who have no intention to discriminate may adopt a practice that violates federal law by depriving a racial group of equal opportunity in employment.

To illustrate these complicated doctrines, consider a case of alleged employment discrimination among police. The city of Washington, D.C., required applicants for its police force to take a test of basic verbal skills (reading, vocabulary, and so forth). The rules for applying the test did not refer to race or ethnicity, so the practice was "facially neutral" and thus escaped "strict scrutiny" by the Supreme Court. More African Americans, however, failed the test than did individuals from other groups, so the test had a "disparate impact." To decide whether the examination violated the Constitution, the Supreme Court had to ask whether or not the test was designed with the intent to discriminate. The Supreme Court did not find an intent to discriminate when applying this test to job applicants.

Having disposed of constitutional issues, the question remained as to whether the test violated Title VII of the Civil Rights Act, which guarantees "equal opportunity" in employment without regard to race. To comply with this statute, the Supreme Court required the city to demonstrate the *validity* of the test, which means that the test measures characteristics relevant to job performance. Thus Washington had to try to demonstrate that greater literacy makes better policemen.[10]

Employees have used title VII in many suits alleging discrimination. Statistical analysis of Title VII lawsuits discloses a paradox and also resolves it. Most people believe that employment discrimination against women and minorities declined in the United States between 1970 and 1989. During these years, however, employment discrimination suits increased over twenty times. How are these facts reconciled?

Many of the original suits were brought against hiring practices that discriminated against classes of people. The success of these suits and the abatement of discrimination for other reasons caused more minorities and women to move into better jobs and more integrated work environments. These changes greatly increased the possibility for a new wrong: discriminatory firings. As time passed, the character of Title VII complaints changed from discriminatory hiring of classes to discriminatory firing of individuals.

---

[9] *Arlington Heights v Metropolitan Housing Dev. Corp.*, 429 US 252, 97SCt 555, 50 LEd2d 450 (1977) and *Personnel Adm'r of Massachusetts v Feeney*, 442 US 256, 99 SCt 2282, 60 LEd2d 870 (1979).

[10] *Washington v Davis*, 426 US 229, 96 SCt 2040, 48 LEd 2d 597 (1976).

Generalizing, if more persons enjoying legal protection against discrimination are employed and the economy slumps, then more protected employees get discharged. Discharging more employees in protected classes causes more lawsuits. The frequency with which a company experiences suits alleging discriminatory discharge depends on the number of its protected employees and the state of the economy.[11]

Many people feel that the historic victims of discrimination deserve something more than an equal chance to compete. Instead of passive equality, many Americans take affirmative action to reverse the consequences of past discrimination. To illustrate, many law schools search for able students from minority groups, urge them to apply, and admit them with lower grades and test scores than those of other applicants. To pass review under the Fourteenth Amendment, affirmative action programs in state schools must have a compelling purpose for making racial and ethnic distinctions, such as reversing the consequences of a specific discriminatory practice in the past.

In groping for the boundary between "affirmative action" and "reverse discrimination" in the *Bakke* case, the U.S. Supreme Court distinguished "targets" from "quotas."[12] Thus a medical school may aim to have, say, 20 percent African-American students if this is a "target" chosen for the sake of "diversity," but the goal is illegal if it is a "quota" chosen to remedy "social wrongs." Although U.S. law permits racial targets under *Bakke*, a referendum in the state of California banned such practices by the state. In addition, federal court decisions are placing more restrictions on the advantages that can be given legally to the historic victims of discrimination. Lower courts have recently forbidden some forms of affirmative action, and many commentators believe that the Supreme Court is poised and waiting for the right case to limit affirmative action as now widely practiced in the United States.

Questions

1. U.S. states organize and administer elections. Some states and localities formerly prevented African Americans from voting. Most of these laws and practices were eradicated in the 1960s and Southern blacks now vote in large numbers. Use the "median rule" to predict the consequences of enfranchising African Americans in the South. Use a model of legislative bargaining to make the same prediction. How do the predictions differ?

2. California ended many affirmative action programs by the state as a consequence of a ballot initiative called Proposition 209. Use the median rule to explain why direct democracy might treat minorities less favorably than representative democracy would.

3. "Judges should be one step ahead of society, but not two steps." Do you agree with this saying as applied to civil rights?

---

[11] See John J. Donohue III, "Further Thoughts on Unemployment Discrimination Legislation: A Reply to Judge Posner," *University of Pennsylvania Law Review* 136 (1987): 523.

[12] *University of California Regents v Bakke*, 438 US 265 (1977).

EQUAL OPPORTUNITY

In the United States and other countries, the law restricts the criteria that can be used when employers fill jobs, universities award scholarships, or retailers sell commodities. To discriminate against people by race, sex, religion, ethnicity, age, or disability may violate morality and law. Fairness in competition generally requires that the criteria for sorting winners from losers measure performance on dimensions appropriate to the activity in question, such as speed, accuracy, comprehension, endurance, originality, or productivity.[13] Traits of persons such as race, sex, ethnicity, or age do not measure performance. Antidiscrimination laws prohibit sorting winners and losers by personal traits rather than performance. The absence of discrimination gives people with different personal traits an equal opportunity to compete for offices, jobs, wealth, privileges, and honors.

Given an equal opportunity to compete, skill and luck determine outcomes. Because people differ in skill, an equal opportunity to compete does not give everyone an equal probability of winning. Because people differ in luck, an equal opportunity to compete does not assure victory for the most deserving people. Some philosophies, such as the theory of justice developed by John Rawls and discussed in chapter 11, advocate an ideal distribution that reduces the influence of skill and luck. These ideals imply redistributive policies that go beyond equal opportunity.

Equal opportunity to compete in economic transactions can conflict with freedom of contract. Complete freedom of contract implies the right to deal or not deal with anyone for whatever reason, including personal traits. In contrast, antidiscrimination laws prohibit parties from allowing some traits to affect their transactions. In general, equality rights conflict with liberty rights, because the former regulates transactions to achieve equality, whereas the latter creates a sphere of autonomy.[14] To illustrate, a law forbidding economic discrimination would prohibit a black Muslim bakery from hiring only black Muslim employees. In this example, the right of job applicants to nondiscriminatory evaluation conflicts with the baker's preference for employees with specified traits. Similarly, a law forbidding economic discrimination would prohibit a white supremacist who owns a restaurant from dealing exclusively with white customers. In this example, the customer's right to nondiscriminatory service conflicts with the restaurant owner's freedom of contract.

DISCRIMINATION UNDER PERFECT COMPETITION

In most countries, economic activity follows historical patterns that involve discrimination against some groups. Designing laws to undo discriminatory

---

[13] See, for example, the discussion of "pure procedural justice" in Rawls 1971, chapter 14, esp. p. 86.

[14] There is a large philosophical literature on "negative liberty" and "positive liberty," beginning with Berlin 1969.

practices presupposes an understanding of them. Some laws succeed in reducing discrimination, while other laws merely increase the transaction costs of continuing the same discriminatory practices. To develop the required understanding, I begin by analyzing the effects of competition on discrimination.

Competition among organizations generally undermines discrimination by them.[15] In labor markets, discriminatory employers constrain themselves by refusing to hire or promote people with disfavored traits. The constraint imposes higher costs to obtain the same quality of labor. In perfect competition, lower-cost producers eliminate higher-cost producers. Thus perfect competition eliminates discrimination by employers.

To illustrate, a professional football team in the United States recruited the best available white players in the 1950s and refused to recruit African Americans. The discriminatory team competed against other teams that recruited the best available players, regardless of race. Over time, the discriminatory team's popularity and profits plummeted as it lost more of its games, so it eventually abandoned discriminatory recruitment.

Having discussed how competition affects discriminatory employers, now consider how competition affects discriminatory employees. Imagine a world whose people are blue or green, in which some blues refuse to work with greens, but otherwise people are nondiscriminatory. Workers of different color substitute perfectly for each other on the job, except that organizations employing discriminatory blues must pay the extra cost of segregating them from greens. Thus the value of a discriminatory worker to an employer equals the value of any nondiscriminatory worker minus the incremental cost of segregation. Competition in the labor market aligns each worker's wages with his value to employers. The perfectly competitive wage of discriminatory workers thus equals the wage of equivalent nondiscriminatory workers minus the incremental cost of segregation. Perfect labor-market competition imposes the cost of segregation on workers who demand it.

These facts are depicted in figure 14-1. The horizontal axis indicates the quantity of labor and the vertical axis indicates the wage rate. Workers are distinguished into those who discriminate, indicated by a subscript "d," and those who do not discriminate, indicated by a subscript "n." The curves S_d and S_n indicate the quantity of labor each group will supply as a function of the wage. The demand curves D_d and D_n indicate the value of the two kinds of labors to employers.

Initially, assume that the cost of segregation is nil in figure 14-1, so both kinds of labor are equally valuable to employers and they receive the same wage, $w_d = w_n$. Now assume that segregating the workplace becomes costly. As the cost of segregation increases, the demand curve for discriminatory labor shifts down from D_d to D_d' as shown, and the discriminatory wage falls from w_d to w_d'. The reduction in use of discriminatory labor causes an increase in demand for nondiscriminatory labor, as indicated by the upward shift in demand from D_n to D_n'. Consequently, a gap opens in the wage of the two groups, with

[15] See Becker 1973.

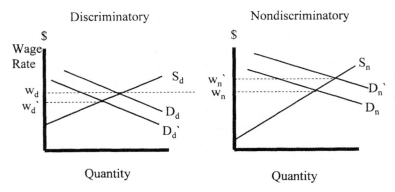

Fig. 14-1 Discriminatory Employees

discriminatory labor receiving the lower wage w'_d and nondiscriminatory labor receiving the higher wage w'_n.

I have explained why perfect competition causes discriminatory workers to pay for segregation. In general, perfect labor markets impose an increase in the cost of production on anyone who demands special working conditions. If segregation increases the costs of production, workers who demand segregation will pay its costs.

Now I turn from labor markets to markets for goods and services. Discriminators sometimes refuse to buy or sell goods or services to some groups of people. A similar argument can be made about "refusal to deal" as was made about employment discrimination. As before, first consider discriminatory sellers and nondiscriminatory buyers. If sellers refuse to deal with some buyers, the discriminatory sellers may bear additional costs. In perfect competition, all goods sell at cost, so discriminatory sellers will charge more than nondiscriminatory sellers for the same good. By assumption, buyers are nondiscriminatory, so they will purchase from the sellers with the lowest prices. Thus perfect competition eliminates discriminatory sellers, just as it eliminates discriminatory employers.

For example, a restaurateur who insisted on segregated dining facilities might have higher costs, which nondiscriminatory patrons would refuse to pay. If all restaurant patrons are nondiscriminatory, then the higher prices charged in the segregated restaurant will cause it to fail.

Now consider the case of discriminatory buyers. Once again, product markets strictly parallel labor markets. Specifically, consumers who prefer discriminatory sellers will pay a surcharge for the products they buy relative to nondiscriminatory consumers. The surcharge will equal the additional cost of segregating buyers. For example, diners who discriminate will pay the extra cost of segregating dining facilities.[16]

---

[16] A related question is whether the satisfaction of discriminatory preferences should ever count as a social benefit. Some economists, who are true to the tradition of Bentham, count all preference

Insofar as the model of perfect competition is accurate, discriminators pay its costs. Some people with strong preferences for segregation may be willing to pay the cost of discrimination. Should the law allow people to "buy" as much segregation as they are willing to pay for, or should the law prohibit segregation? Fortunately, debates about segregation and the law seldom have to address this question, because the most troubling cases of segregation do not involve the discriminators paying the cost of segregation. Rather, the most troubling cases of segregation occur when the victims of segregation pay its costs. In other words, the most troubling forms of discrimination occur in social interactions different from perfect competition. As explained in the next section, these interactions occur outside of markets or in imperfectly competitive markets.

Questions

1. In *Diaz v Pan American World Airways, Inc.*,[17] males alleged discrimination in airline hiring, such as exclusive employment of pretty, young female stewardesses. The court found that discriminatory preferences of customers cannot justify discrimination in hiring airline staff. Economic theory counts satisfying discriminatory preferences as a social benefit. In a case like *Diaz*, do you agree with standard economic methodology?

2. Assume that some workers demand more integration than maximizes the firm's productivity. In perfectly competitive labor markets, who would bear the cost of the additional integration?

3. Assume that some men refuse to be led by women, but most women are willing to be led by men. The state seeks to implement a law prohibiting sex discrimination in hiring and promotions. What obstacles will the labor market present to implementing this law?

DISCRIMINATORY POWER

As explained, the model of perfect competition predicts that discriminators will pay for discrimination. Testing this prediction requires estimating the effects of discrimination on earnings, which is notoriously difficult. The best empirical estimates, however, do not confirm the prediction that discriminators pay for it. Rather, empirical studies suggest that the targets of discrimination in the United States historically received lower wages than others with equivalent skills, and that civil rights laws helped raise the income of African Americans.[18] Given the

---

satisfaction as equally valuable, regardless of whether the preferences are immoral, but others disagree. For discussion and citations, see Lewin and Trumbull 1990.

[17] 311 Supp 559 (1970).

[18] The empirical evidence is reviewed in Epstein 1992, chapter 12, "The Effects of Title VII." For especially careful econometric work, see Heckman 1991.

evidence, the model of perfect competition apparently cannot explain discriminatory practices in the United States. Although the perfectly competitive model describes powerful forces at work in the economy, something goes wrong in its simple application to discrimination.

In subsequent sections of this chapter, I will consider several market failures that might explain how discriminators shift the burden of segregation to its victims. To begin, I develop a model of discrimination based on power, not competition. Just as producers collude to fix prices and obtain monopoly profits, so social groups sometimes collude to obtain the advantages of monopoly control over markets. To enjoy the advantages of monopoly, a social group must reduce competition from others by excluding them from markets. In this way, the more powerful social group can shift the cost of segregation to its victims, so that the victims of discrimination are worse-off and the discriminators are better-off.

To illustrate, recall the hypothetical example in which some blues discriminate against greens, and perfect competition causes the discriminatory blue workers to bear the cost of segregation. Now suppose that discriminatory blue workers organize themselves and acquire enough power to disrupt the workplace. The blues could use this power to threaten employers who failed to discriminate against greens. Faced with the power of the blues, employers might find that they could maximize their profits by avoiding disruption, even at the cost of segregating workers and confining greens to lower-level jobs. This example describes circumstances in which segregation reduces productivity and its victims bear the cost.

The consequences of discriminatory power in the market for skilled and unskilled labor are depicted in figure 14-2. The demand for skilled labor is indicated by the curve labeled D_s, and the supply of skilled labor by greens, blues, and the sum of greens and blues, is indicated by the curves S_g, S_b, and $S_g + S_b$, respectively. In the absence of discrimination, the wage for all skilled workers is w_s. The demand for unskilled labor is indicated by the curve labeled D_u, and the supply of unskilled labor (blue and green) is indicated by the curve S_u. In the absence of discrimination, the wage for unskilled workers is w_u.

Now consider how discrimination changes wages in figure 14-2. If blues exclude greens from the market for skilled labor, the supply falls from $S_g + S_b$ to S_b, and the skilled wage rises to w_s'. Discrimination forces greens to work as unskilled labor. The additional greens entering the unskilled labor market swells the supply from S_u to S_u', which causes wages to fall from w_u to w_u'. Thus discrimination increases wages for skilled blue workers and lowers wages for unskilled blues and all greens.

Discrimination as depicted in figure 14-2 divides blues against each other by increasing the wage of skilled blues and decreasing the wage of unskilled blues. However, the unskilled blues could also use discrimination to their advantage if they obtained power in the market for unskilled labor. For example, unskilled blues might distinguish the tasks of unskilled labor into two types, "blue work" and "green work." If more greens seek unskilled work than do blues, and if

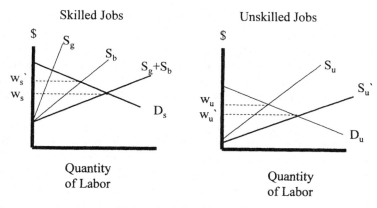

Fig. 14-2 Discriminatory Power

demand is higher for "blue work" than for "green work," then segregating tasks will cause the wage of unskilled blue workers to rise above the wage of unskilled green workers.

This market analysis can be applied to Title VII of the U.S. Civil Rights Act of 1964. The law prohibits employment discrimination based on race, sex, or age. In practice, most workers fall within its protection except for young white males. Complaints of discrimination must be filed with a commission (Equal Employment Opportunity Commission) that vets them. The commission can issue a finding but cannot issue an injunction. Unresolved complaints can be taken to court, which can order the defendant to cease the discriminatory practice. The court can also order the injurer to pay foregone wages to victims.

To illustrate, a court might order a company that wrongfully denied a job to someone two years ago to hire the person and pay compensation equal to the difference between his current wage and the higher wage in the better job for two years. In terms of figure 14-2, a skilled green worker who was forced to accept unskilled employment could sue for the difference between w_s and w_u. The fact that the law limited damages to back-pay discouraged lawyers from taking small cases on a contingency fee. Revisions in Title VII in 1992 brought employment discrimination closer to tort law by broadening damages, which makes employment discrimination cases more attractive to lawyers.

ANTIDISCRIMINATION AS ANTITRUST

In general, the members of a group benefit from reducing competition with outsiders for business. This is true regardless of whether the group is a cartel of industrialists or a group based on race, ethnicity, religion, age, or sex. Discriminatory social groups resemble business cartels, and a discriminatory norm resembles a price-fixing agreement. Thus I will borrow from monopoly theory and antitrust law to analyze discriminatory market power.

Cartels are unstable because each member can increase its profits by defecting from the group. For example, the Organization of Petroleum Exporting Nations (OPEC) tried to fix prices in the early 1970s, but countries like Algeria secretly discounted oil in order to sell more of it. As a cartel becomes large, detecting and preventing such "cheating" by members becomes harder. Without legal backing and formal enforcement of their agreements, large cartels like OPEC usually collapse.[19]

Similarly, social groups can exert power to increase their wages by restricting competition in the labor market, but individuals can profit from violating the restrictions. To illustrate, recall figure 14-2 in which blue workers exclude green workers from skilled jobs. An employer can reduce wages from $w_{s'}$ to w_s by ending segregation and integrating the workplace. To prevent employers from ending segregation, blue workers must bear the inconvenience, expense, or danger of threatening employers and participating in industrial disruptions. Skilled blue workers who cease to participate in these activities, however, continue to enjoy the discriminatory wage $w_{s'}$. In economic jargon, individual blues have an incentive to "free-ride" with respect to discriminatory norms by withholding enforcement effort. So the self-interest of employers and blues as individuals does not prompt them to sustain discriminatory norms.

In general, sustaining discriminatory norms requires the collusion of many people, which presupposes sanctions to discipline them. Informal sanctions such as gossip, ostracism, and boycotts can operate spontaneously, especially when a culture stresses group solidarity.[20] In the past, many Americans used informal sanctions to punish individuals who failed to keep the races separate or women "in their place." However, informal sanctions were probably not enough to sustain many forms of segregation in the United States without buttressing by formal laws.[21] To illustrate, Southern states formerly outlawed the integration of schools, and the board of realtors in many localities prohibited its members from selling houses to black families in white neighborhoods.

Antidiscrimination laws, which ideally increase competition, can sometimes diminish it. To illustrate, suppose the greens in figure 14-2, who were the historic victims of discrimination, acquire legislative power and enact laws mandating preferential hiring of greens. For example, the law might mandate filling job openings for skilled workers with greens until 60 percent of the workers are green. (Perhaps 60 percent of the population is green.) Thus blues cannot compete with greens for jobs until the green quota is filled, which causes the green wage to rise above the blue wage for skilled workers.

Figure 14-3 depicts these arguments, which underlie the claim that affirmative action is reverse discrimination. Figure 14-3 reproduces the supply curve for skilled green workers S_g as already depicted in figure 14-2. As already explained in figure 14-2, the wage in a free market without discrimination or reverse

---

[19] The instability of cartels is a standard topic in the economic theory of monopoly. For example, see Telser 1978.

[20] See Akerlof 1985.

[21] Roback 1989.

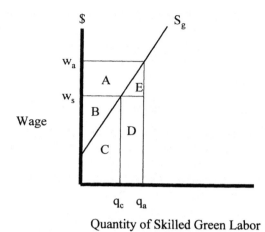

Fig. 14-3 Quotas and Wages

discrimination equals w_s. As depicted in figure 14-3, the wage w_s results in the supply of q_c of skilled green labor. The quota, however, requires the employment of q_a skilled green labor. To satisfy the quota, the wage for skilled green labor must rise to w_a. In order to satisfy the quota, skilled green labor must be paid more than skilled blue labor. The quota causes the "surplus" enjoyed by skilled green workers to increase from B to A + B.[22]

The phrase "rent-seeking" refers to the efforts of people to secure laws that convey monopoly power and profits upon themselves. Writing a law into the constitution can reduce rent-seeking by removing the law from ordinary politics. For example, constitutional protection of private property inhibits state officials from expropriating private property for themselves. Similarly, constitutional guarantees against discrimination can reduce rent-seeking by social groups. Constitutional protection against discrimination, like constitutional guarantees of property, can facilitate competition and preclude wasteful efforts to redistribute income among social groups by political means.

On the other hand, the creation of vague and uncertain constitutional rights by courts can unleash extensive rent-seeking through litigation. Social groups, including racial and ethnic groups, are paradigmatic interest groups in many respects. Like other interest groups, they seek to collude and redistribute wealth to themselves by inefficient restrictions on competition.

Self-interest and morality, however, often prompt individuals to evade these restrictions. Thus, discriminatory social groups suffer the same problems of instability as do other cartels. To sustain discriminatory norms, evaders must be

---

[22] By definition, the surplus equals the difference between wages and the value of labor to the people supplying it. Without the quota, the skilled green workers receive B + C in wages, and they value their labor at C, so their surplus equals B. With the quota, the skilled green workers receive A + B + C + D + E, and they value their labor at C + D + E, so their surplus equals A + B.

punished by a combination of informal sanctions and formal laws. By under-mining these sanctions, law can cause the discriminatory norms to disintegrate. As with business cartels, the best public policy against a racial or ethnic cartel undermines it by aggravating its natural instability.

Questions

1. Compare a discriminatory social norm to a price-fixing agreement.

2. In some circumstances, a country gains an advantage by imposing a tariff on the products of another country, especially if the other country cannot retaliate by imposing its own tariffs. Similarly, one ethnic group could gain an advantage by imposing a tariff on hiring people from the other ethnic group. What would it mean for one ethnic group to "impose a tariff" on another?[23]

3. Most discussions of discrimination in the United states presume that majorities subordinate minorities, which is not always the case. Majorities often charge minorities with discrimination. For example, in the United States males are less than 45 percent of the population, the economically dominant Chinese are a small fraction of Indonesia's population, and east Indian merchants are a small fraction of the population in Africa. Use collective-choice theory to predict different outcomes depending on whether the victims of discrimination are the majority or the minority.

4. Racism divides workers and retards unions. Under what conditions might employers promote racism among workers in order to hold down wages?

DISCRIMINATORY SIGNALS AND ASYMMETRICAL INFORMATION

I first considered discrimination in the context of perfect competition, and then I considered monopoly power. Now I consider a different kind of market imperfection, specifically imperfect information on the part of buyers and sellers.[24] To understand the problem of imperfect information, I begin with a familiar example concerning insurance against automobile accidents. Insurance companies classify drivers into broad groups and set premiums according to the probability that the average driver will have an accident. For example, young drivers cause more accidents on average than middle-age drivers, and young males cause more accidents on average than young females. The sex and age of policyholders, which are cheap for insurance companies to discover, predict the risk of accidents with sufficient accuracy to be useful for setting insurance rates. Thus, insurance companies charge higher premiums for being young and male.

Now I turn from insurance to employment. Just as insurance companies know little about individual policyholders, so employers know little about job

[23] See Krueger 1963.
[24] See Arrow 1973.

applicants. In choosing among them, employers rely on signals to predict performance. For example, a job applicant with a college degree can easily provide the employer with a copy of his transcript. The college degree may signal traits that the employer values, like intelligence. Education effectively signals intelligence because more intelligent people can acquire education more easily and cheaply than can less intelligent people.[25]

"Good signal" is the name economists give to a characteristic that predicts accurately on average and is cheap to observe. In transactions with imperfect information, the parties search for good signals to reduce their uncertainty. Examples of good signals include the smell of a peach, the height of a basketball player, the speed in megahertz of a computer chip, the class rank of a law student, the rating of a bond, and the brand name of an automobile. Similarly, sex and age of drivers signal future claims against insurance companies.

In discriminatory signaling, a fixed trait like sex or race signals an unobserved variable. To illustrate, sex is an easily observed trait, whereas strength is a variable that is relatively difficult to observe. Men are physically stronger than women on average, so some employers reject all female applicants for jobs requiring strength. By adopting such policies, an employer will often make mistakes like rejecting a strong woman and accepting a weak man, just as an automobile insurance company sometimes overcharges safe males and undercharges dangerous females. *In general, if mistakes of overgeneralization cost less than gathering more individualized information, the use of the signal maximizes profits and competition will reinforce the discriminatory practice. This is a case of rational discrimination.* Conversely, *if the cost of overgeneralization exceeds the cost of gathering more individualized information, then the use of the signal is inefficient and competition will eliminate its use.* This is a case of *irrational prejudice.*

Suppose that the government prohibits employers from using discriminatory signals. For example, a statute might give strong women the right to sue employers who hire men exclusively for jobs that require strength. If the prohibited signals are inefficient, the law bans what competition will eliminate. If the prohibited signals are efficient, the law augments the cost of production, which someone must bear. Competition drives the market price of a good down to the cost of producing it. Thus a reduction in an industry's efficiency typically causes the consumers of its products to pay higher prices.

To illustrate, assume that sex efficiently signals the physical strength of job applicants. If the law bans the use of this signal and the prohibition is effective, rational employers will adopt the best substitute for the banned signal. The best substitute may be a direct measure of physical strength, or the best substitute may be another signal, such as the applicant's height, weight, or age. In any case, competition translates any increase in the cost of sorting job applicants into higher product prices.[26]

[25] Spence 1974.

[26] Behind these remarks lies a complicated incidence theory developed in public finance. For a survey, see Musgrave and Musgrave 1976.

In the absence of regulations, the victims of discriminatory signals may have private remedies. To illustrate by the preceding example, if sex signals strength and employers have no irrational prejudice against hiring women, then strong women would probably find it in their interest to undergo tests and provide employers with the results. The selective use of direct testing would occur without government intervention in the labor market.

An objection to private remedies in this example is that by assumption, female applicants would have to bear the cost of a test that men need not take. Regulations would be required to overcome this objection. The employer might be required to test directly the strength of any applicant requesting it. Or the state might provide direct tests of strength without charge.

These remedies have a distinct advantage over requiring the employer to base hiring decisions on a test of strength administered to job applicants. Such a requirement forces employers to test *every* job applicant. In contrast, the alternative remedies result in testing the strength of a small fraction of applicants.

In general, *the economic strategy for correcting discriminatory signals is to increase the flow of information to the market so that relying on them is unnecessary.* This approach usually suggests a cheaper solution than banning the use of the discriminatory signal. The savings arise from limiting the gathering of information to potential victims of discrimination, rather than forcing the gathering of more information about everyone.

Many social critics believe that decision makers frequently rely on false signals that reflect social stereotypes, not accurate averages. Competition can teach a sharp lesson to businesses that rely on false signals. Decision makers whose prosperity depends on the accuracy of their perceptions are better situated than social critics or legislators to penetrate myths. However, competitive pressures are blunted in many organizations, especially in the public sector or the nonprofit sector. Blunting competition allows decision makers to persistently rely on bad signals.

A telling example comes from the criminal courts in New Haven, Connecticut. When the state charges a person with a crime, the judge sets bail. The law requires judges to set bail at the minimum amount that creates a reasonable certainty that the accused will appear for trial. If the accused posts bail, then he can go free pending trial. The state returns the bail to the accused if he appears for trial, whereas the state seizes the bail if the accused fails to appear for trial.

In reality, most people accused of a crime in the United States post bail by borrowing the money from a specialized lender called a bail bondsman. In exchange for a fee, the bail bondsman assumes the risk that the defendant will not appear for trial. A study that compared 1,118 black and white defendants in New Haven found that bail amounts averaged 35 percent higher for blacks charged with the same crime as whites. This fact suggests that judges believed that compared to white defendants, black defendants in this sample had a higher propensity to flee. If this belief were accurate, it might justify higher average bail for blacks than whites.

This justification for judicial behavior, however, is inconsistent with the observed behavior of the bail bondsmen. Bondsmen charged black defendants rates that were 19 percent lower than the rates charged to white defendants. In a competitive market the bond rate should approximate the probability of flight (given the judicially set bail). The lower rate indicates that bail bondsmen think blacks are less likely than whites to flee when facing the same bail as set by the courts.

The evidence indicates that the bondsmen and the judges attach opposite signs to the racial signal. The authors of this study believe that competition among bondsmen causes them to estimate probabilities accurately, whereas the absence of competition among judges permits their prejudices to go uncorrected. The market for bail bonds apparently eliminates half of the effect of discrimination in bail setting.[27]

Questions

1. Discuss whether the following characteristics are likely to be cheap and accurate predictors of automobile accidents in the United States:

prior traffic accidents

age

sex

Hispanic surname

race

2. What effects would follow from a legal prohibition against using the signals in the preceding question to set insurance rates?

3. The gap in reading and writing skills between white students and black or Hispanic students has narrowed slowly over the last fifteen years.[28] What effect should the narrowing of this gap have on labor-market signaling?

4. A secretary with a master's degree in English and ten years of experience may earn less per hour than a plumber with a high school degree, four years of apprenticeship, and ten years of experience. Secretaries are disproportionately women and plumbers are disproportionately men. The proponents of "comparable worth" want the state to require employers to pay secretaries at least as much as they pay plumbers. Predict the different effects of such a law based on the following three alternative assumptions about the labor market: (i) perfect competition, (ii) discriminatory power of males, (iii) sex signaling.

---

[27] Ayres and Waldfogel 1994.

[28] "Tests Show Reading and Writing Lag Continues," *New York Times*, 10 January 1990, B7. In the period 1971–1988, the tested reading skills of black students improved modestly along some dimensions while those of white students were unchanged, so the gap narrowed somewhat. No narrowing of the gap was found for other dimensions of reading or writing skills.

EXTERNALITIES AND TIPPING POINTS: TRAGIC SEGREGATION

When each person's action depends on what others do, the interdependency of behavior can create instabilities. To illustrate, if each buffalo follows the one in front, the whole herd may run over a cliff. Similarly, "white flight" has allegedly destabilized integrated schools and neighborhoods in the United States White flight in the United States resembles ethnic polarization that occurs in other countries. Most recently, ethnification in Rwanda and Yugoslavia produced the slaughter of civilian populations. In this section I analyze the instabilities created by interdependent preferences toward mixed social groups.

I begin with a simple model of white flight.[29] Assume that an all-white neighborhood consists of one hundred families who can be ranked according to their attitudes toward residential integration. At one end of the ranking, the one-hundredth white family would move out of the neighborhood if one black family moved in. Similarly, the ninety-ninth family would move out if two black families moved in. Proceeding down the ranking, the first family would move out when ninety-nine black families had moved in.

I also assume that blacks have a continuous distribution of attitudes toward living in neighborhoods with whites. Some black families would be willing to move into an all-white neighborhood, many black families would be willing to live in an integrated neighborhood, and some black families would be unwilling to live in a neighborhood with any whites.

Now assume that large numbers of blacks migrate to the city containing this neighborhood. The demand and supply in the housing market is such that whenever a house becomes vacant in a particular white neighborhood, more black families than white families want to buy it. It is not hard to see that if one black family moves into the white neighborhood, a process will be set in motion that may not end until all whites have moved out. Specifically, if one black family moves in, the one-hundredth white family will move out. Now the house of the one-hundredth white family must be sold. The buyer of the vacant house is more likely to be black than white, so it is likely that two black families will now reside in the neighborhood. As a result, the ninety-ninth white family will move out. Now it is likely that there will be three black families in the neighborhood and the ninety-eighth white family will move out. The process continues until the neighborhood is all black.

The tragedy of this situation is that many whites and blacks in the neighborhood may positively value residential integration. In spite of sentiment favoring integration, unrestricted sale of houses in a free market cannot achieve integration. Instead, the integrated neighborhood inexorably unwinds and becomes segregated. The beneficiaries are blacks and whites who want to live in segregated neighborhoods.

Notice that this model's dynamics make no special assumptions about the cause of attitudes toward integration. For example, the attitudes of whites or

---

[29] This model is based on Schelling 1978b.

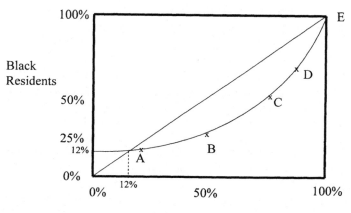

Whites Planning to Move Out

Fig. 14-4 White Flight

blacks in the model may reflect skin prejudice, cultural pride, class-consciousness, fear of violence, or beliefs about housing prices. In every case, the basic dynamics of the model are the same.

The most familiar economic models compare equilibria ("comparative statics"), whereas this model describes a dynamic path. Indeed, this model probably describes the actual dynamic in U.S. cities after the Second World War when many neighborhoods went from all white to all black. It also probably describes forces at work in many public schools today. Since the model is unfamiliar and important, I will develop it better with a graph.

Figure 14-4 graphs the attitudes toward integration of residents in a neighborhood that is all white. The horizontal axis shows the proportion of white residents in a neighborhood who plan to move out. The vertical axis shows the proportion of black residents. Thus the graph shows the proportion of white residents who would plan to move out as a function of the proportion of black residents who move in.

To illustrate the interpretation of figure 14-4, suppose that the graph consisted of a single point at the northwest corner, corresponding to the value (0%, 100%). This would indicate that no white family in the neighborhood would plan to move out even if all the other residents were black. Conversely, suppose that the graph consisted of a single point at the southeast corner of the graph, corresponding to the point (100%, 1%). This would indicate that all whites in the neighborhood would plan to move out if only 1 percent of the neighborhood became black. The curved line in figure 14-4 represents a more realistic case in which there is a continuous distribution of sentiment toward integration.

I will analyze the dynamics of white flight created by the distribution of preferences represented by the curved line in figure 14-4. As the curve is constructed, 100 percent of the white residents would be willing to remain if less than 12 percent of the residents were black. Thus, up to 12 percent of the white families can move out and be replaced by blacks without provoking white flight. However, once the proportion of black residents reaches 12 percent, white flight begins, as can be seen by considering point A on the graph. Since Point A lies below the 45-degree line, point A indicates that more than 12 percent of the white residents would plan to move out if the neighborhood were 12 percent black. This is an unstable situation in which integration starts to unwind, as is illustrated by considering several other points on the graph. At point B, approximately 60 percent of the white residents would be planning to move out if approximately 25 percent of the residents were black. At point C, approximately 75 percent of the whites would be planning to move out if 50 percent of the residents were black. And so the flight goes on until no whites remain in the neighborhood.

To complete the model, another graph should be drawn showing the distribution of black preferences toward integration. In this graph, the vertical axis would show the proportion of whites in the neighborhood, and the horizontal axis would show the proportion of blacks who would be willing to move into the neighborhood. The blacks who are most tolerant of white neighbors would move into it first, and the blacks who are least tolerant of white neighbors would move into it last. I omit this graph for the sake of simplicity.

In a neighborhood characterized by figure 14-4, 12 percent blacks or fewer is an unstable equilibrium, and 100 percent blacks is the only stable equilibrium. The stability conditions can be stated precisely in terms of the diagonal line in figure 14-4. The model assumes that whenever a house becomes vacant, it is more likely to be purchased by a black family than by a white family. So long as the neighborhood is at a point where the curved line representing white attitudes toward integration lies below the diagonal line, more whites plan to move out in response to the existing proportion of black residents. This is a disequilibrium. There is an equilibrium at any point where the curved line representing white attitudes toward integration touches the diagonal line. To have a stable equilibrium, the curved line must intersect the diagonal line from below as it does at point E. Stable segregation occurs when the intersection is near the diagonal line's end, as at point E in figure 14-4. For stable integration, the curved line must be redrawn so that it intersects the diagonal line from below at a point near the middle of the diagonal line.

An application of this theory comes from Starrett City,[30] which is a private housing project in Brooklyn whose construction was partly financed by the federal government. In 1977 Starrett City had approximately 20,000 tenants, with whites occupying nearly 65 percent of the 5,881 apartments and the other 35 percent being occupied by blacks and Hispanics. The managers set a racial quota of 65 percent white and 35 percent nonwhite, which they defended on the grounds that it was necessary to maintain a stable, integrated community. There were, however, fewer white applicants for vacant units than there were black or Hispanic applicants.

[30] "New York Housing Complex Ordered to End Race Quotas," *New York Times*, 6 May 1987, Y1.

The National Association for the Advancement of Colored People (NAACP) challenged these quotas in a suit brought in 1979, which was settled in 1984 with the provision that allocation by race should continue, but 174 additional units should be made available to nonwhite applicants. Apparently the owners of Starrett City and the NAACP agreed that color-blind apartment allocation would lead to segregation (as in figure 14-4). Their settlement, however, was challenged by the Civil Rights Division of the Justice Department, who contended that any such system of racial quotas, even one whose purpose is integration, violates the Federal Fair Housing Act. The view of the Justice Department prevailed in federal court, which ordered an end to the racial quotas. A follow-up story reported that Starrett City was evading the court order in a way that advantaged blacks.[31]

Spontaneously segregated neighborhoods resemble a tragic drama in which social laws lead inexorably to an end that many people do not want. The people who want to live in homogeneous neighborhoods can satisfy their preferences, but the people who want to live in diverse neighborhoods cannot satisfy their preferences. The outcome frustrates the desire of many people of both races to live in an integrated community or to attend integrated schools.

Racially restrictive covenants ("ceiling quotas") can avoid tragic segregation and stabilize integration. To illustrate, if 50 percent of the houses in the hypothetical neighborhood described in figure 14-4 had enforceable deeds restricting ownership to whites, the neighborhood would have stabilized with 50 percent white families and 50 percent black families. Furthermore, the 50 percent white families and the 50 percent black families in the neighborhood would tend to be those with the most positive attitudes toward integration. The federal courts have struck down racially restrictive covenants, which were used historically to keep neighborhoods all white.[32]

Can economists devise a way to end tragic segregation other than by relying on ceiling quotas? From the viewpoint of economic theory, continuous preferences of individuals over the racial mix in social groups causes tragic segregation. Preferences over the racial mix in social groups are economic externalities. Economists typically propose to remedy externalities with a tax, subsidy or transferable rights, rather than quotas. In principle, these remedies could be applied to racial mixing. Thus a tax might be assessed on housing sales that worsen a neighborhood's racial mix, or a subsidy might be paid on housing sales that improve the neighborhood's racial mix. Alternatively, a solution using transferable property rights might be developed.[33] Similar devices could be used

---

[31] Starrett City avoided the court order by not filling any vacant apartments from its waiting list of applicants who fit the poverty criteria, black or white, but instead keeping them vacant until someone applied who was above the legal definition of poverty. The middle-class applicants who were above the poverty line were disproportionately black. See *New York Times*, 14 July 1990.

[32] In *Shelly v Kraemer*, 334 US 1, 14023 (1948), the Supreme Court found unconstitutional a covenant in a deed prohibiting the sale of the property to Negroes.

[33] It might work like this: Racially restrictive rights of residence would be issued to property owners in participating neighborhoods by the government. The distribution of rights would correspond

in schools, such as school vouchers that increase in value when the enrollment of a pupil in a particular school improves its racial balance.

Questions

1. The intersection of a demand curve and a supply curve represents a static equilibrium. Figure 14-4 graphs a dynamic process. To make sure that you understand this technique, redraw the curve in figure 14-4 so that it has a new shape. Put arrows along the curve to indicate areas of instability and the resulting direction of change. (For example, you need to put arrows at points A, B, C, and D pointing up the curve toward E.)

2. Your vacation takes you to a foreign city inhabited by Muslims and Christians. You observe that all the neighborhoods are strictly segregated by religion. You also observe that a substantial number of people of both religions would prefer to live in a neighborhood inhabited by people of both religions. Adapt the model of white flight to explain these observations.

3. The model of white flight assumes that "tastes" remain unchanged as events unfold. How do you think that attitudes toward integration will change as segregation proceeds in figure 14-4?

4. Economists typically oppose quotas as inefficient. For example, quotas for reducing pollution tend to be inefficient because they do not reflect differences in abatement costs by different firms. Suppose the government imposes racial or sex quotas on a firm (e.g., 50 percent of the plumbers must be female). Explain how the resulting inefficiency resembles the inefficiency from pollution quotas. Explain how the inefficiency can be overcome in principle by pursuing the same goal through the use of taxes or transferable rights, rather than quotas.

CONCLUSION

Perfect competition eliminates discrimination or makes the discriminators bear the cost. Removing the obstacles to competition, consequently, attacks discrimination. By releasing market forces, constitutional guarantees of equal opportunity can undo discrimination. Statistical studies, however, often conclude that discrimination persists in the United States and the victims pay for it. Understanding the persistence of discrimination requires a theory of market failure. Monopoly power, asymmetric information, and externalities are three fundamental types of market failures that explain the persistence of discrimination.

---

to the government's ideal racial mix for the neighborhood. To sell a property in the neighborhood to a prospective buyer, the owner would have to possess a right of residence corresponding to the prospective buyer's race. For example, if the best prospective buyer of a property were black, but the owner of it possessed a "white occupancy right," the sale could not be consummated without buying a "black occupancy right" from someone else.

Like any business cartel, a social group can gain an advantage for itself by blocking entry into labor markets by other people. A social cartel, furthermore, suffers from the same instability as a business cartel. Sustaining a social cartel requires the group to overcome free-riding by its members. Some groups overcome free-riding by private enforcement of social norms. Other groups cannot overcome free-riding except by enacting state laws to enforce discrimination. To destabilize social cartels, the state can use the same techniques as antitrust law uses against business cartels. For example, courts can strike down discriminatory laws and refuse to enforce discriminatory private contracts.

Even without market power, asymmetrical information can cause discrimination to persist in markets. Irrational prejudice consists in making decisions about individuals by using statistical averages based on false inferences from personal traits. Market competition sharply penalizes irrational prejudice. Rational use of prejudicial signals consists of making decisions about individuals by using statistical averages based on *true* (but objectionable) inferences from personal traits. Market competition rewards rational prejudice. To combat rational prejudice, the state must improve the information available to decision makers, so they no longer need to rely on objectionable statistical inferences from personal traits.

In addition to social cartels and discriminatory signals, the attitudes of people toward each other can create externalities that free markets cannot internalize. In the case of tragic segregation, a continuous distribution in attitudes toward mixing with other races can destabilize any integrated environment. Externalities can be corrected in principle by ceiling quotas, although U.S. courts seldom allow the use of this device. A more promising remedy comes from tax subsidies or transferable rights, such as school vouchers whose value increases when used to improve the racial balance of a school.

Summary and Conclusion

THE PHILOSOPHY of mercantilism, which prevailed in Europe until the late eighteenth century, praised monopoly as a device to enrich the state. By convention, modern economics originates with Adam Smith's attack on mercantilism in his book *The Wealth of Nations* (1776), which praises competition as a device to enrich the nation. In social science's most famous metaphor, Smith proposed that competition directs the butcher and baker, who look only to their own advantage, to maximize the nation's wealth, as if directed by an "invisible hand." A century passed before the marginalist revolution of the late nineteenth century mathematically formulated this metaphor (Blaug 1978; Schumpeter 1986). Mathematical improvements culminated in general equilibrium theory in the 1950s and 1960s, which provides a rigorous defense of competitive markets and a framework for analyzing market failures (Arrow and Hahn 1971). Subsequent developments in game theory detailed more precisely how competition usually works and sometimes fails (Fudenberg and Tirole 1991).

In 1776, the same year that Adam Smith published his most famous book, the United States issued its Declaration of Independence. Many Americans hoped to create the world's first mass democracy. After a false start, the present U.S. Constitution was adopted, which some of its framers described as a machine for good government by self-interested people.[1] Judging from *The Wealth of Nations* and the U.S. Constitution, the ideal of competition began its ascent in economics and politics at roughly the same time. Two hundred years later, with the collapse of communism after 1988, the principle of competition dominates the world's economic and political institutions, as well as economic and political theory. At least for a while, capitalism and democracy lack serious rivals.

Competitive markets cause private businesses to supply abundant private goods at low prices. Similarly, competitive elections ideally cause public institutions to supply abundant public goods with low taxes. Market competition satisfies the preferences of consumers for commodities better than an economic cartel does, and political competition satisfies the preferences of citizens for laws and public goods better than a political cartel does. Specifically, elections (democracy) satisfy citizens more than a self-perpetuating bureaucracy (civil-service state), a dominant social class (aristocracy), a ruling family (monarchy), an all-powerful individual (dictatorship), a priestly caste (theocracy), or a vanguard party (communism) does.

Whereas Adam Smith intuited the efficiency of market competition, general equilibrium theory proved it. Ideally, the economic analysis of politics would do

---

[1] See, for example, Madison 1981b, p. 160. Or see the letter from John Adams to Richard Henry Lee, 15 November 1775, reprinted in Adams 1851, quoted in Krasnow 1991.

for democracy what general equilibrium theory did for capitalism—prove that competition best satisfies the preferences of citizens. But is the efficiency of political competition provable? From the beginning, attempted proofs encountered difficulties. Instead of positive proof, mathematical theories discovered impossibility theorems demonstrating the limits of democracy. Decisions over public goods require collective choices, and Kenneth Arrow proved that a no democratic constitution can guarantee stable, Pareto-efficient, collective choices (Arrow 1963). Competition does not produce good results as predictably in politics as it does in economics. Unlike the economy, irreducible power and unending redistribution destabilize cooperation in politics. When cooperation collapses, selfishness destroys instead of energizing.

Even so, political competition aligns the ambition of politicians and the public good better than any noncompetitive system of political organization. This book predicts the extent to which alternative forms of democracy satisfy the preferences of citizens. I have used the positive methodology of individual rationality and the normative standard of preference satisfaction to justify democracy and critique its various forms.

In 1825 a revolt in Russia aimed to replace Tsar Nicholas with his brother, Constantine, and to promulgate a constitution. At the climax, revolting soldiers and aristocrats in St. Petersburg chanted "Constantine and constitution! Constantine and constitution!" Many of the common people apparently thought that "constitution" was Constantine's wife.[2] In any case, the Decembrist Revolt failed in part because too many Russians did not understand what a constitution is. A social scientist reading contemporary constitutional scholarship might wonder whether its authors know what a constitution is. Constitutional scholarship focuses too much on the constitution as an historical agreement and a repository of values, and not enough on the constitution as an incentive structure that affects behavior. Predicting the effects of a constitution on behavior requires social science, especially a policy science that predicts effects on policy variables like liberty, efficiency, and distribution. In this concluding chapter, I recapitulate the justification and critique of democracy by summarizing my major predictions. After the summary, I discuss the success of the strategic theory of democracy and its limits.

SUMMARY

Being a policy science, economics makes predictions about policy values. Statements about the consequences of alternative policies on values can be formulated as predictions or prescriptions. The prediction "x causes y" becomes the prescription "To achieve y, do x." I will summarize my predictions and prescriptions in the same order that they appear in this book.

---

[2] Nicholas Riasanovsky, professor of Russian history at Berkeley, told me in private communication that insufficient documentation supports the claim of historical accuracy for this event, but the vignette accurately represents the mentality of common people in Russia. My thanks go to Nicholas Riasanovsky, Greg Grossman, and Blair Dean for discussing this point.

TABLE 15.1
Factoring, Splicing, and the Character of Politics

	Constitutional Forms	Character of Politics
Factor	special governments, ballot initiatives	median democracy
Splice	comprehensive legislature	bargained democracy

Median Democracy v. Bargained Democracy—
Optimal Number of Governments

According to part 2 of this book, a constitution and other fundamental laws can factor or splice the functions of government. To factor, the constitution creates many narrow governments, each with a limited purpose, such as the special governments common in the United States. The constitution can also factor by allowing ballot initiatives and referenda, each on a single issue. Alternatively, the constitution can splice the functions of government. To splice, the constitution creates one broad government to make all laws and supply all public goods.

Single-purpose governments and single-issue referenda increase the transaction costs of bargaining across issues. Taken to its logical limit, factoring eliminates political bargaining, which tends to eliminate vote trading and strategic behavior. Nonstrategic voting on a single dimension of choice often yields a stable equilibrium at the most preferred point of the median voter. I call such a political system, which the first row of table 15.1 summarizes, *median democracy*.

Alternatively, a constitution can splice functions by creating a few broad governments, each with many purposes. In such a system, the central legislature and executive hold most power, as they do in France or Japan. Comprehensive government by a central legislature decreases the transaction costs of bargaining across issues. Taken to its logical conclusion, splicing results in government by an encompassing bargain. Reaching a bargain requires vote trading and strategic behavior. I call such a political system, which the second row in table 15.1 summarizes, *bargained democracy*.

Median democracy and bargained democracy have different strengths and weaknesses, as summarized in table 15.2. The median rule is stable, so referenda and single-purpose governments tend toward stability. In addition, everyone who votes contributes to determining the median, so referenda respond to voters. Besides these two strengths, median democracy has the weakness of obstructing trade across issues. Without trade, politics is inefficient relative to the preferences of citizens. In addition, referenda and single-purpose governments increase the number of elections, which can strain civic virtue. Oscar Wilde reputedly said, "The trouble with socialism is that it takes up too many evenings."[3] Similarly, referenda and single-purpose governments absorb the resources and time of many talented people.

---

[3] This quote is often attributed to him, but my trusted reference librarian, Debby Kearney, could not find the sentence in his writing.

TABLE 15.2
Median Democracy versus Bargained Democracy

	Strengths	*Weaknesses*
Median democracy	responsive, stable	no trades, possibly exhausted citizens
Bargained democracy	possibly efficient	possibly unresponsive, possibly unstable

Conversely, by splicing functions and reducing the number of governments, bargained democracy demands less participation by citizens in elections, which conserves civic virtue. In addition, a multipurpose legislature facilitates bargaining. By trading across issues, politics can achieve efficiency relative to the preferences of citizens. In practice, however, political bargaining may not realize the best possibility. Indirect democracy requires citizens to monitor representatives, but each citizen has an incentive to free-ride on monitoring efforts by others. Imperfect monitoring by citizens enables their representatives to pursue objectives contrary to the interests of most voters.

Besides this agency problem, indirect democracy can provoke contests of distribution over the surplus from cooperation. A contest for redistribution wastes resources and can paralyze government. In markets, perfect competition forces everyone to trade at market prices, which solves the distribution problem. No one, however, has contrived a perfectly competitive mechanism to control the state's natural monopoly powers. As long as a democratic constitution stops short of perfect political competition, a problem of distribution will persist. Self-interested rationality does not dictate how to divide the surplus from cooperation. The resulting destabilization of political coalitions constitutes the problem of democracy's empty core.

I have explained that bargained democracy has the potential to outperform median democracy, and bargained democracy also risks performing worse than median democracy. For this reason, the optimal number of governments differs by place and time. Table 15.2 suggests how to adjust democracy in a particular country in light of actual performance. When elections pick faithful representatives who bargain successfully with each other, legislatures produce the laws and public goods that citizens want. Under these conditions, the constitution should consolidate power held by the national legislature. Conversely, when legislators do not serve the interests of citizens, legislatures produce unwanted laws and undesired public goods. Or when legislators cannot cooperate with each other, the legislature produces little law and few public goods. A state plagued by unresponsive officials or legislative paralysis should tilt toward median democracy. To tilt toward median democracy, the state should favor single-purpose governments, ballot initiatives, and referenda. The tilt toward median democracy must stop short of exhausting the citizens with too many elections.

Table 15.2 has a special application to unresponsive administrators. When freed from control by voters, administrators engorge the bureaucracy or enrich themselves by corruption. The mechanical application of rules can reduce corruption and promote political control over administration, at the cost of inflexibility. By increasing the number of elections, the state can narrow and shorten the administrative hierarchy, thus reducing administration and increasing government. Assuming honest elections, increasing the number of elections can reduce corruption, while retaining flexibility.

Treaty, Association, Federation—Optimal
Relations between Governments

The problem of the optimal number of governments focuses on the quantity of elections. A related problem, also analyzed in part 2, concerns the terms on which different governments relate to each other. Treaty, association, and confederation represent increasing levels of centralization. Optimal centralization partly depends on the character of the goods that the states must supply. For local public goods, a legal framework of free mobility allows citizens to sort themselves by preferences for local public goods. Given free mobility, states must satisfy the preferences of citizens in order to attract residents. Even without mobility, the right of communities to contract freely with governments for the supply of local public goods can make governments compete with each other. Free mobility and free contract ideally create competition among governments that increases efficiency in the supply of local public goods.

In addition to supplying local public goods, states also supply private law. The right of citizens to stipulate the state with jurisdiction over contracts can force governments to compete in supplying private law. Competition to supply private law promotes efficient government. Conversely, forced harmonization of law precludes competition among jurisdictions.

I have explained how competition among states improves the supply of local public goods and private law. Instead of competition, however, some problems of government require coordination or cooperation among states. Pure coordination problems merely require a framework for exchanging information. A treaty among states can establish the organization needed to exchange information. Beyond coordination, some public problems require cooperation. Sovereign states cooperate under unanimity rule, under which the most independent regions and localities can demand the best terms. As summarized in table 15.3, unanimity rule strengthens the bargaining power of the party who least needs collective action. Alternatively, federal states cooperate under some form of majority rule. Majority rule strengthens the bargaining power of the parties inside the national coalition that governs the country.

I explained how unanimity rule and majority rule differ with respect to distribution. In an ideal world of zero transaction costs, the form of cooperation affects distribution and not efficiency. In reality, however, the form of cooperation affects its likelihood. Given increasing returns to the scale of cooperation

TABLE 15.3
Sovereign v. Federal

	Constitutional Form	Empowered Group	Efficiency Problem
Unanimity rule	sovereign states	least need for collective action	paralyzed by holdouts
Majority rule	federal system	national coalition	contest of distribution

TABLE 15.4
Relations among States

Public Need	Incentive Mechanism for States	Legal Form
Private law of contracts	Competition for jurisdiction	Right to stipulate jurisdiction in contracts
Local public goods	Competition for residents and public goods contracts	Individual's right of mobility and locality's freedom of contract
Coordinate among states	Information exchange	Treaty
Cooperation by few states	Unanimity rule	Association
Cooperation by many states	Majority rule	Federation

among regional or local governments, unanimity rule creates a problem of holdouts. Small groups usually solve the problem of holdouts, whereas a solution usually eludes large groups. To solve the problem of holdouts, a large group must switch to majority rule, which usually creates another problem. Under majority rule, the parties inside the national coalition can shift the costs of government to the parties outside of it. So majority rule creates opportunities for politicians to waste resources in a contest of distribution. The last column in table 15.3 summarizes these conclusions about efficiency.

Combining the results in table 15.2 and 15.3, table 15.4 suggests how to adjust intergovernmental relations in light of actual performance by states. To improve private law arising from contracts, lower the obstacles to stipulating jurisdiction in contracts. To improve the supply of local public goods, lower the cost of mobility to citizens and remove obstacles to communities contracting with governments. To improve coordination among states, create a treaty organization for the exchange of information. To improve cooperation among a few states, form an association governed by unanimity rule. To improve cooperation among many states, create a federation with majority rule. When holdouts obstruct

TABLE 15.5
Bargains v. Orders

	Constitutional Forms	*Character of Politics*
Fragment	Proportional representation, bicameralism, presidential system	Bargained democracy
Unify	Single-district winner-take-all, Unicameralism, prime minister	Command democracy

needed collective action, reduce the scope of unanimity rule and increase the scope of majority rule. Conversely, when states compete to redistribute wealth through control of the central government, increase the scope of unanimity rule and reduce the scope of majority rule.

*How Many Branches?—Optimal Division of
Powers within a Government*

The analysis of the optimal number of governments and the optimal relations between governments in part 2 of this book views each state externally. Part 3, however, turns to the internal structure of government and considers the division of powers among its branches. To summarize the results, first contrast unification and fragmentation of political power. Proportional representation fragments the legislature's power by encouraging many political parties, whereas single-district winner-take-all elections unify power by consolidating parties. Bicameralism also fragments legislative power, whereas unicameralism unifies legislative power. Indirect election of the prime minister unifies legislative and executive power, whereas direct election of the president fragments legislative and executive power.

Fragmenting power requires government to proceed by bargains, which I have already called "bargained democracy." By contrast, unifying power can enable the executive to proceed by commands, which I call "command democracy." In the purest form of bargained democracy, the legislature dominates, whereas the executive dominates in command democracy. Table 15.5 summarizes this contrast.

Table 15.6 summarizes the strengths and weaknesses of bargained democracy and command democracy. As explained, bargaining can aggregate political preferences efficiently, or, alternatively, failed bargains can destabilize politics. In contrast, the executive in a command democracy can formulate a consistent plan of action and proceed decisively. Like the central planner under communism, however, the executive in a political system lacks the information required to match public goods and the preferences of citizens. Under the best conditions, insufficient information makes a strong executive unresponsive, and under the

TABLE 15.6
Strengths and Weaknesses of Bargained and Command Democracy

	Strengths	*Weaknesses*
Bargained democracy	possibly efficient	possibly unstable
Command democracy	decisive	unresponsive, possibly dictatorial

worst conditions a strong executive ends democracy by eliminating political competition.

Tables 15.5 and 15.6 suggest how to adjust the allocation of internal power in light of actual performance by a state. When failed bargains cause instability, unify power by such measures as single-district winner-take-all elections or by strengthening the dominant house of the legislature. Alternatively, when the executive threatens the rule of law, fragment power in order to move from command democracy toward bargained democracy. Implement the change to bargained democracy by adopting proportional representation, dividing power between two equal houses of the legislature, or, possibly, shifting power from prime minister to president. (The change from indirect to direct election of the executive has uncertain effects on the executive's power.[4])

Now I turn from politics to administration. Proceeding down through the state hierarchy, politics intersects administration where political appointment ends and civil-service jobs begin. At the top of the hierarchy, political control makes administration respond to the electorate. Below the top, however, independence of the civil service keeps administration honest.

Chapters 4 and 7 develop theories of administration that imply some prescriptions to increase responsiveness and reduce corruption in administration. To increase responsiveness, decrease the breadth and depth of bureaucracy by increasing the number of elections; impose uniform procedures on administrators, thus lowering the transaction costs of review by official bodies; and change the way courts, legislative committees, and other official bodies review the performance of administrators. A shift from cooperative oversight to unilateral oversight by several official bodies can force civil servants to respond more to elected officials and judges.

To reduce corruption in administration, decrease political appointments and increase civil-service jobs; reduce the discretion of officials by making them follow rules; adopt uniform procedures that make administration more transparent to citizens; and reduce the depth and breadth of administration by increasing the number of elections.

---

[4] Being outside the legislature, a president typically suffers a disadvantage relative to a prime minister in controlling the legislature. A directly elected president, however, enjoys a popular mandate that the prime minister lacks. The question is whether a popular mandate strengthens the executive's control over the legislature more or less than absence from the legislature weakens the executive's control.

TABLE 15.7
Problems and Solutions for Administration and Courts

Public Problem	Legal Solution
Unresponsive administration	More elections; uniform procedures; unilateral oversight
Corrupt administration	Fewer patronage jobs; more rules; uniform procedures; more elections
Insufficient rule of law	Judicial civil service or once-for-all political appointments of judges
Weak courts	Constitutional review by courts of general jurisdiction; divide legislative power; judicial review of administrative procedures

Now I turn from administrators to courts. Independent courts secure the rule of law, which enables politicians to make credible commitments. To secure independence, either create a judicial civil service as in most civil-law countries, or else allow once-for-all political appointments as in the U.S. federal courts. By one means or the other, prevent politicians from influencing the salaries or promotions of individual judges.

Given independent courts, the extent of their power responds to several variables. To increase (decrease) the discretionary power of the court to interpret law, give (take away) the power of constitutional review to courts of general jurisdiction and divide power among more (fewer) branches of government that must cooperate to enact new statutes. To increase (decrease) the power of courts over civil servants, allow (prohibit) courts to impose procedures on administrators. Administrators will respond by reducing the burdened activity, and the extent of the decrease usually depends on the administrators' ability to substitute another public good in place of the one burdened by more costly procedures. When substitution is easy politically and technically, imposing a more costly procedure causes a large decrease in the supply of the good in question. Table 15.7 summarizes these prescriptions for administration and courts.

Protecting Individuals—Optimal Rights

Having analyzed the allocation of powers to officials in parts 2 and 3, part 4 turns to the constitutional rights of individuals. The people who enjoy rights usually value them, and a good constitution responds to these valuations. For affluent people, basic liberties often trump other values, whereas marginal liberties trade off with other values, including wealth. These facts suggest that the constitution for an affluent country should secure basic liberty and maximize the value of marginal liberties. Table 15.8 summarizes how to maximize the value

TABLE 15.8
Problems and Solutions Involving Constitutional Rights

	Public Problem	*Legal Solution*
Property rights	Redistributive contests	Restrict takings and allow general taxes
	Private activity harms the public	Elesticity principle; TDRs
	Bargaining with state	Duty to mitigate; offset by mutual agreement
Speech rights	Undersupply of ideas and information	Free speech and intellectual property protection
	Organizations restrict speech	Mobility principle for speech restrictions
	False information causes harm	Balancing test for libel
Civil rights	Discrimination by a social cartel	Prohibit discriminatory laws; nonenforcement of discriminatory contracts
	Rationally prejudicial signals	Increase market information
	Unstable integration; racial flight	Ceiling quotas; tax subsidies; transferable rights

of constitutional rights to the people who enjoy them, focusing on property rights, free speech, and civil rights.

By giving people freedom over things, property law promotes exchange and internalizes the benefits of efficient resource use. Many politicians, however, want to expropriate their enemies' wealth and restrain their friends' competitors. A constitution can dampen contests of redistribution by removing some disputes from ordinary politics. A good constitution channels the politics of redistribution away from takings and into broad taxes. For example, a constitution can guarantee the rights of property and contract that keep markets free, while allowing politics to determine the level of taxation.

Entangling uses by property owners cause externalities. When externalities involve small numbers of contiguous owners, they can usually solve the problem themselves through bargaining and social norms. When externalities involve large numbers of owners, however, transaction costs obstruct bargaining and the evolution of social norms. In these circumstances, the state often takes measures to control externalities. The courts must decide whether these measures regulate property, which requires no compensation of owners by the state, or takes property, which requires compensation of owners by the state. According to the elasticity principle for regulatory takings, the answer ideally depends on the relative magnitude of the response by the state and owners to compensation.

An elastic response by the state and an inelastic response by owners commend a high level of compensation, whereas an inelastic response by the state and an elastic response by owners commend a low level of compensation.

In the minds of most administrators, the command-and-control approach, which has been discredited for most forms of regulation, remains the only possibility for land-use planning. With more imagination, transferable development rights could supplement or replace conventional land-use restrictions, including zoning. TDRs reduce the information required for rational planning and channel the efforts of owners into market activities rather than political activities.

Developers often have to bargain with the state over permits. If the state can require the developer to offset the public harm from development, then the developer's bargaining position is weak. The state may exploit this weakness by extracting the full surplus from the project in exchange for the required building permit. To strengthen the owner's bargaining power, give owners the right to develop provided that they mitigate the public harm from development. Given this right, however, allow owners and the state to bargain to an agreement substituting an offset for mitigation.

Turning from property to speech, note that speech transmits beneficial ideas and useful information that markets undersupply. Regulating speech promotes monopoly, which aggravates the shortage of ideas and information. Specifically, restricting political speech threatens democracy and restricting commercial speech harms product markets. Conversely, effective constitutional protection of speech prevents the state from aggravating the natural shortage of ideas and information in markets and politics. Unlike speech that provides beneficial ideas and information, some speech harms other people, such as involuntary exposure of people to pornography. In principle, a pornography tax could internalize this externality.

Many organizations try to increase their effectiveness by restricting the speech of members. Each organization strikes a different balance between restrictions on speech and larger rewards from belonging to a more effective organization. Competition for members allows individuals to strike their preferred balance by choosing among organizations. As competition lowers the cost of exiting from an organization, members can escape unwanted restrictions more easily, so courts have less reason to scrutinize restrictions on speech of members and more reason to defer to the balance struck by individuals. Conversely, as monopoly power raises the cost of exiting from an organization, courts have more reason to scrutinize restrictions on speech of members. The mobility principle asserts that courts should scrutinize organizational restrictions on members' speech in proportion to the cost of leaving the organization.

A free market for ideas stimulates beneficial ideas and undermines harmful ideas. Consequently, no liability should attach to the invention and promulgation of bad ideas. In this respect, false assertions differ from bad ideas. A person who wishes to make an assertion should balance the expected gain from its truth against the expected loss from its falsity. A libel standard based on a balancing test can motivate people to obtain adequate evidence before making an assertion.

Now I turn from free speech to civil rights. Perfect competition usually eliminates discrimination or makes the discriminators bear its cost. Statistical studies often conclude, however, that victims pay for persistent economic discrimination in the United States. If these statistics tell the truth, then civil rights laws should correct market failures that cause harmful discrimination.

Monopoly power, asymmetric information, and externalities are three fundamental types of market failures that can cause harmful discrimination. Like any business cartel, a social group gains an advantage by blocking competition from other people, as when an ethnic group reserves the best jobs for its own members. Like a business cartel, however, a social cartel suffers from instability. Cartel members who "cheat" by surreptitiously breaking its rules harm their group while benefiting themselves and outsiders. To survive, a social cartel must use social norms or public laws to suppress cheating by members. Destabilizing social cartels requires the same techniques that antitrust law uses against business cartels. Specifically, courts should strike down discriminatory laws and refuse to enforce discriminatory contracts.

Another type of problem concerns information-based discrimination. Businesses base many decisions on statistical inferences. Irrational prejudice, which competition punishes, consists of making decisions about individuals based on false correlation between personal traits and average economic behavior. Rational prejudice, which competition rewards, consists of making decisions about individuals based on true correlation between personal traits and average economic behavior. To combat rational prejudice, the state should increase information so decision makers no longer rely on objectionable inferences from statistical averages.

Besides social cartels and discriminatory signals, the attitudes of people toward each other can create externalities that disrupt markets. For example, a continuous distribution of attitudes toward mixing with other races can destabilize an integrated environment, causing racial flight. In principle, externalities can be corrected by ceiling quotas, tax subsidies, or transferable rights such as school vouchers.

Motives and the Institutions of Democracy

To make the preceding predictions and prescriptions, I attempt to understand politics as a strategic interaction among self-interested people. This approach has a long history, going back at least to Machiavelli and Hobbes. Alternatively, political theory can proceed by assuming that officials directly pursue moral values such as justice, fairness, or the public interest. The normative approach goes back at least to Plato's *Republic* and it continues today as exemplified by the writings of Rawls, Habermas, and Thompson.[5]

While the normative approach focuses on how officials *ought* to act, its usefulness depends on how officials actually act. If norms affect officials, then ana-

[5] For example, see Rawls 1993; Habermas 1996; and Thompson and Guttman 1996.

lyzing norms is useful for predicting and influencing the behavior of officials. Conversely, if norms do not affect officials, then analyzing norms is useless for predicting or influencing the behavior of officials. To explain why strategic theory is more useful than normative theory for understanding democracy, I will compare motives and democratic institutions.

Interests

Democracy is a system of popular competition for office. Successful politicians aim to win elections. Some founders of the United States hoped that democratic competition would select a "natural aristocracy" to lead.[6] Most successful politicians, however, resemble power brokers more than aristocrats. Industrialists want subsidies, artists want grants, students want fellowships, parents want tax deductions, the elderly want pensions, and so forth. To obtain political influence, these individuals must organize. Organized interests look to their own advantages, not to the public good.

To create a winning coalition of voters, politicians must bargain and make deals that give organized interests the laws and public goods that they most desire. From this perspective, the real work of the legislature involves bargaining, whereas debates among politicians about the public interest are mostly rhetoric. Perhaps the democratic process occasionally shakes loose from the constraints of self-interest, but these moments occur seldom, if ever.[7] Most state officials try to do well and a few try to do right.

Reason

I have argued that electoral competition selects politicians who pursue power most skillfully. In addition to competitive government, democracy encompasses the rule of law, which requires insulating judges from political pressure. Instead of satisfying interests, courts evaluate arguments. Courts are ideally moved by reasons, especially reasons about fairness, morality, and the public interest. Insofar as these reasons move courts, normative theories are useful to predict, and influence, the behavior of courts.

As summarized in the first and second rows of table 15.9, legislators especially bargain over interests, and courts especially debate over reasons. Shifting lawmaking power from legislators to judges, consequently, tilts government toward reason and away from interests.

[6] Jefferson wrote to Adams, "I agree with you that there is a natural aristocracy among men. The grounds of this are virtue and talents. . . . May we not even say that that form of government is the best which provides for a pure selection of these natural aristoi into the offices of government?" Letter of 28 October 1813, in Jefferson 1984, pp. 1305–06.

[7] Ackerman has proposed that special moments occur in the political history of a country when people can rise above the normal politics of self-interest and create constitutional provisions from better motives (Ackerman 1984; Ackerman 1989). As examples from U.S. history, he offers the original Constitutional Convention, Reconstruction after the Civil War, and Roosevelt's New Deal.

TABLE 15.9
Motives and Politics

Motive	Process	Institution
interest	bargain	legislature
reason	debate	court
passion	oratory	campaign
will	commands	executive

A good constitution tilts without tumbling over. To appreciate the risk of tumbling over, consider Plato's great meditation on justice, *The Republic*, which stands near the beginning of Western political philosophy. To make government respond to reason, Plato's constitution gives the most power to the best philosopher. The philosopher-king in Plato's republic has no use for competitive elections. In reality, however, power without competition corrupts ambition. If a state organized by Plato's prescription, the philosopher-king would quickly cease being a philosopher and begin acting like a king.

Besides restraining power, elections provide officials with information about the political preferences of citizens. The absence of elections in Plato's republic deprives officials of information about the laws and public goods that citizens want. Instead of responding to citizens, Plato's philosopher-king regulates the details of their lives, even controlling marriages through the rationalizing power of a great lie.[8] In Plato's view, the philosopher-king perceives the forms of reason and thereby understands the requirements of justice. This conception of lawmaking, which represents the political conceit of intellectuals, disastrously overestimates the power of reason and underestimates the power of empirical knowledge.

Plato's *Republic* exhibits the best and worst that philosophy offers constitutional law.[9] As primary lawmakers, judges suffer from the same weaknesses as Plato's philosopher-king. Distancing judges from the pressures of competitive elections removes the motivation and information needed to satisfy the preferences of citizens.

Passion

Having considered the motives of politicians and judges, I turn to citizens. A single vote seldom influences the outcome of a large election. Large elections

---

[8] Reproduction was to be regulated through the "myth of the metals," according to which different people are made from different metals that differ in their value. In his history of philosophy, Bertrand Russell says that "compulsory acceptance of such myths is incompatible with philosophy, and involves a kind of education which stunts intelligence." See Russell 1945, chapter 14, "Plato's Utopia," p. 113.

[9] Bertrand Russell wrote in his history of philosophy that he would treat Plato "with as little reverence as if he were a contemporary English or American advocate of totalitarianism." See Russell 1945, chapter 13, "The Sources of Plato's Opinions," p. 105.

and the secret ballot eliminate material sacrifice by a citizen who votes his conscience rather than his interests. Given low costs, citizens enjoy expressing political values, rather like people enjoy telling others how to live. As voters, citizens have mixed motives that combine self-interest and a conception of the public interest. Sometimes a person's conception of the public interest merely rationalizes his self-interest. Sometimes, however, self-interest and a person's conception of the public interest drift apart. To the extent that citizens vote against their interests, normative theories presumably have a role in explaining voting.

Like most judges, citizens are free from electoral competition. Unlike most judges, however, few citizens carefully listen to lengthy arguments and deliberate before casting a vote. Furthermore, ordinary citizens do not have training in law and government comparable to that of judges. Inchoate feeling presumably influences citizens more than judges, whereas explicit reasons presumably influence judges more than citizens. Understanding these facts, politicians use oratory and symbols to arouse feelings and influence voters in electoral campaigns, as indicated in the third row of table 15.9.

Will

Since passions are unstable, a mature adult needs the strength of will to override momentary impulses. Strength of will enables a person to pursue enduring goals consistently. Like a person, a state needs to pursue enduring goals consistently. This ability especially comes from the political leadership provided by the executive. The executive leads by his ability to command civil servants and the members of his own party. As indicated by the last row in table 15.9, the executive especially supplies will to the state.

By shifting lawmaking power from legislators to the executive, a constitution can tilt toward will and away from interests. In times of war or great crisis, citizens narrow their goals for the nation. In an emergency, a democracy that eschews dictatorship sometimes invests the executive with emergency powers.

DEMOCRACY'S SUPERIORITY

Table 15.9 contrasts the role of interest, reason, passion, and will in democratic politics.[10] To the extent that bargains matter in politics, interests must be important, so the legislature needs power. To the extent that debate matters in politics, reasons must be important, so the courts need power. To the extent that oratory matters in politics, passions must be important, so campaigns influence politics. To the extent that commands matter in politics, will must be important, so the executive needs power.

The superiority of democracy, I believe, rests on an institutional framework that makes law respond especially to interests and gives lawmaking power to the legislature. The interests of people in order, liberty, and prosperity provide the

---

[10] Hirschman 1977 contrasts interests and passions in politics and political theory. Similar distinctions are used by Elster 1995 to contrast the drafting of the U.S. and French constitutions.

most reliable motivation for political cooperation. Democracy responds to these interests by providing citizens with the laws and public goods that they prefer.

Conversely, too much influence on lawmaking by reason, passion, or will can frustrate citizens. Since reason is abstract, judges are too remote from citizens to be the principle lawmakers. Since passion is unstable, the law must constrain demagogues by channeling political campaigns. Since will is instrumental, the citizens must give ends to the executive rather than have the executive impose ends on citizens.

Conclusion

I used strategic theory to make prescriptions for democracy. Now I conclude by discussing the limits of strategic theory and how to transcend them.

Better Data and More Applications

Strategic theory explains the logic of interaction among rational people. Replacing intuition with logic often reveals causal connections that no one previously articulated. Logic, however, guarantees consistency, not predictive accuracy. Predictive accuracy comes from empirical validity. How valid is constitutional law and economics?

"Not very valid" is the answer suggested by two quips. "In legal scholarship, one anecdote is empirical evidence and two anecdotes are data." "Proving the efficiency of a legal institution by an economic model resembles shooting an arrow into a tree and then drawing a bull's eye around it." While these quips have enough truth to sting, they underestimate the empirical validity of the models in this book. This book builds models from stylized legal facts, makes predictions from the models, compares the predictions to facts, and then revises the models. Thus facts feed back into models.

As scientific method, empirical feedback falls short of testing hypotheses. Testing hypotheses involves making predictions from models, then confirming or disconfirming the predictions by statistics. The economic analysis of constitutional law currently lacks the data needed to test its hypotheses. The desire to test hypotheses is not merely physics envy, but the aspiration for a science of government. Testing hypotheses gives confidence in results that cannot be obtained in another way. Finding the data to test legal hypotheses, however, requires too much donkey work for most legal scholars. In addition, relatively few constitutional scholars have the necessary statistical training. Hypothesis testing in constitutional law awaits improved government statistics and a new generation of constitutional scholars with mastery over empirical methods. At this stage in its development, the field of constitutional law and economics must draw on stylized facts and informal observations to ground its theories. (J. S. Mill believed that economics necessarily has this character.[11])

---

[11] Mill believed that data would always be inadequate to choose among several possible economic theories, so the final choice would rest on intuition and common sense (Mill 1844). In this respect,

In addition to having insufficient data, constitutional law and economics suffers from a deficiency in the *level* of research. Influencing disputes in constitutional law requires research at the same level of generality as the issues posed in court cases. In fact, most research in constitutional law and economics proceeds at a higher level of abstraction than arguments in legal disputes. Scholarly research is thin at the level where judges and other officials make decisions. I hope that this book stimulates concrete, applied research aimed at influencing constitutional law.

By advocating empirical research and applications, I have offered a conventional prescription to improve law and economics. Next I turn to prescriptions that economists find controversial or unpalatable. Specifically, I will discuss modeling more diverse motives than interests.

The Internal Point of View

Why obey the law? Oliver Wendell Holmes urged scholars to consider the law from the viewpoint of a "bad man," who obeys the law because the price of disobeying is too high.[12] The threat of sanctions deters bad people from disobeying the law. Conventional economics follows the advice of Holmes and views laws externally like prices.

Even though people often experience law as coercive,[13] when asked why they obey law, most Americans give moral reasons. The form of these reasons often predicts the person's attitudes toward law (Tyler 1990). If this psychological research is accurate, most Americans obey the law out of respect. Understanding their behavior requires considering the law from the viewpoint of a "good man," who internalizes the law and obeys it out of respect.

Perhaps the "good man" theory explains why most people obey the law most of the time, whereas the "bad man" theory explains the behavior of actors who balance on the edge between obeying and disobeying the law. In other words, the "good man" theory explains the average person's behavior and the "bad man" theory explains the marginal person's behavior.

If people were angels who internalized law perfectly, state coercion would be unnecessary. Although people are hardly angels, even imperfect internalization reduces the need for state coercion. Given the inverse relationship between internalization and coercion, the long tradition in economics that admires limited government should also admire internalization. Beyond government, respect for the law enhances the efficiency of markets that link strangers in a decentralized economy.[14]

his views differ sharply from those of Milton Friedman, who argued that the realism of assumptions is irrelevant to building economic models (Friedman 1953).

[12] Holmes 1897. "If you want to know the law and nothing else, you must look at it as a bad man, who cares only for the material consequences which such knowledge enables him to predict, not as a good one, who finds his reasons for conduct, whether inside the law or outside of it, in the vaguer sanctions of conscience."

[13] MacCormick 1998 stresses the "heteronomy of the will" in politics.

[14] Before his recent death, Mancur Olson became deeply interested in the way law and morality augment markets. A conference inspired by his ideas, "Market Augmenting Government," was held

The contrast between the external and internal viewpoint toward law relates to the contrast between prices and preferences in economics. An economist analyzes an external obligation as a price and an internal obligation as a preference. In economics, a person "prefers" whatever he is willing to pay for, including obeying the law. The price can be denominated in money, effort, time, or any other scarce resource. The amount the person is willing to pay measures the intensity of the preference.

From a psychological viewpoint, however, respect for the law does not *feel* like a preference for asparagus or waterskiing. Internalized obligations differ markedly from conventional economic preferences. The difference is so great that noneconomists balk at calling so many different things "preferences."

The important point, however, does not concern feelings or semantics. Rather, the important point concerns a difficulty in applying the economic theory of preferences to respect for the law. Most people value wealth and power, and they face obstacles to fulfilling their desires. In contrast, few people value poverty and vulnerability, and these desires are easily fulfilled. Competition ensures that successful politicians have a sharp, unsatisfied desire for power and wealth. Consequently, the assumption that each politician wants more power and wealth is a good starting point for political theory.

Respect for the law, however, differs from one country to another. Aristotle thought that good government makes good citizens.[15] Political institutions presumably explain part of the variation. To illustrate, democracy requires citizens to participate in government, which may increase their respect for law. A political theory should explain why some political institutions create respect for law and other political institutions create cynicism.

Insofar as political institutions affect the respect of citizens for law, political theory should explain respect for law. An explanation requires a theory of how people acquire and lose respect for law. Developing such a theory is especially urgent for advocates of limited government and a decentralized economy. Unfortunately, conventional economics takes tastes as given. No accepted theory of endogenous preferences exists in economics. Consequently, this book offers no explanation of how a constitution can create respect for the law. For example, I offer a mixed theory of voting by citizens that combines self-interest and a conception of the public interest. I do not, however, offer an explanation of why some citizens internalize a particular conception of the public interest.

A good political theory explains, not assumes, respect for law. Being based on game theory, this book suffers from the absence of an explanation of respect for law. Unlike conventional economists, however, I do not think that modeling respect for law as a "preference" excuses me from explaining it. I will conclude

in Washington in March 1999 by Institutional Reform and the Informal Sector. The conference papers will be published.

[15] Aristotle wrote, "... Legislators make the citizens good by forming habits in them, and this is the wish for every legislator, and those who do not effect it miss their mark, and it is in this that a good constitution differs from a bad one" (*Nicomachean Ethics*, 1103^{b}5). I witnessed a dramatic example of this fact in 1994, when I played soccer in Chicago with Serbs and Croats. The same people were perfectly civil in the United States and monstrous to each other in Bosnia.

with a few remarks sketching how I eventually hope to overcome this weakness in theory.

Toward a Theory of Internalization

Constitutional scholars, lawmakers, and judges vigorously debate about the values that people *should* have. Public debate does not take preferences as given. Instead of implementing values, public debate often tries to change them. In these debates, scholars offer reasons that justify one set of political principles rather than another. This is a central task of political and moral philosophy. To illustrate, Bruce Ackerman argues that under liberal restrictions on discourse, claims supported by neutral reasons yield a unique set of distributive principles.[16]

By offering reasons for values, philosophy offers a rational basis for internalization. Unlike philosophy, psychological theories such as behaviorism and Freudianism explain internalization by irrational processes. Social conditioning, habit formation, and transference are often inaccessible to thought or choice. "Depth psychology" searches for the unconscious and involuntary foundation of articulated values. Some modern linguists take a similar approach through the study of metaphors (Lakoff and Johnson 1980).

Economics is more rational than psychology and more predictive than philosophy. Economics should contribute to understanding respect for law by developing a theory that is rational and predictive. I have some idea of how to retain the core assumptions of economics and extend them to encompass the internal viewpoint toward law. In games, the players sometimes deliberately worsen the payoff that they will receive in the future from choosing a particular strategy. Deliberately worsening your own payoff from a particular strategy commits the player to choosing another strategy. To illustrate, an advancing army commits to the offense by burning the bridges behind it. Burning the bridges increases the absolute cost of retreating, thus increasing the relative gain from advancing.

Similarly, internalizing a social norm attaches a personal penalty to the forbidden act. The personal penalty increases the absolute cost from doing wrong, thus increasing the relative gain from doing right. In most cooperative activities, people prefer partners with moral commitments. Consequently, a rational person can gain from making moral commitments in cooperative games. A rationally self-interested person with the power to make moral commitments would internalize a norm when the commitment conveys an advantage. (I call such commitments *Pareto self-improvements*.[17])

Many people view respect for law and allegiance to the state as requirements for being a good citizen. Being perceived as a good citizen conveys advan-

---

[16] Ackerman 1980. For a profound meditation on the rules of political debate in a democracy, see Rawls 1993.

[17] Cooter 1998a and Cooter 1998c.

tages on a person, in particular the advantages of participating in cooperative ventures organized according to democratic social norms. Perhaps a democratic constitution and a democratic culture convey advantages on people who internalize democratic ideals. In this way, democracy makes good citizens. (In my language, internalizing respect for law is a *Pareto self-improvement*.[18])

Internalization implies the possibility of alternative selves. Much of personality development concerns choosing whom to become. A complete theory along these lines would explain how democracy forms the self in which an actor has an interest.[19]

A related point concerns self-expression. I explained that signaling moral commitment conveys an advantage by increasing trust as needed for cooperation. Moral commitment, however, can be fake or genuine. For most people, a cool lie comes easier than a fake emotion. So emotional expression plays a role in certifying genuine moral commitment (Frank 1988). In politics, the symbols whose manipulation arouses passion often concern loyalties to ethnic groups, social classes, or localities.[20] An economic theory of expressive law, however, is in its infancy.[21]

The role of emotion in expressing internalized values makes law and politics relatively hot. The strategic theory of democracy, however, is relatively cool. Extending strategic theory to the internal viewpoint might warm people to constitutional law and economics.

Earlier I stated that democracy's superiority over other forms of government rests partly upon legal institutions that respond to the interests of citizens. In addition, part of democracy's superiority rests upon self-reinforcement. Specifically, democracy enlists the support of citizens for government, and participation of citizens in government improves civic morality.[22] When good citizens make good government and good government makes good citizens, democracy reinforces itself.

Some social theorists like Locke aim for balance, whereas other theorists like Hobbes aim for purity. The strategic theory of democracy developed in this book relies on the positive methodology of individual rationality and the normative standard of preference satisfaction. I have attempted to work these ideas pure as applied to constitutional democracy. I have argued that strategic

---

[18] Ibid.

[19] Emphasizing the development of one aspect of a person rather than another requires self-control. In contrast, the standard economic model of decision making does not encompass the problem of self-control, so the faculty of the will is not modeled. The economic analysis of law has made little use of the economics of self-control and self-monitoring. I have written two papers on this subject. See Cooter 1991c and Cooter 1998c.

[20] The political process of inventing tests of loyalty to social groups has been called "ethnification" (Kuran 1998).

[21] See Cooter 1998a.

[22] Rawls argues that a more just state has an advantage in competition with less just states. Rawls emphasizes that people who experience the state as just will increase their allegiance to it. See Rawls 1971, esp. chapter 8, "The Sense of Justice."

theory encompasses the larger part of democratic politics and philosophical theories encompass a smaller part of it. By working strategic theory pure, I have omitted part of constitutional theory, but I hope to correct this omission in the future by helping economics to assimilate the internal point of view toward law.

BIBLIOGRAPHY

Ackerman, Bruce A. 1997. "The Rise of World Constitutionalism." *Virginia Law Review* 83: 771–97.

———. 1989. "Constitutional Politics/Constitutional Law." *Yale Law Journal* 99: 453–547.

———. 1984. "The Storrs Lectures: Discovering the Constitution." *Yale Law Journal* 93: 1013–72.

———. 1980. *Social Justice in the Liberal State.*

———. 1972. "The Uncertain Search for Environmental Policy: Scientific Factfinding and Rational Decisionmaking along the Delaware River." *University of Pennsylvania Law Review* 120: 419.

Adams, John. 1851. "Letter from John Adams to Richard Henry Lee (Nov. 15, 1775)." In *The Works of John Adams*, edited by C. F. Adams, Vol. 4, pp. 185–86. Boston: Little Brown.

Adams, J., and C. F. Adams. 1850. *The works of John Adams, second president of the United States: with a life of the author, notes and illustrations.* Boston: Little Brown.

Adams, W. J., and Janet L. Yellen. 1976. "Commodity Bundling and the Burden of Monopoly." *Quarterly Journal of Economics* 90: 475–98.

Akerlof, George A. 1985. "Discriminatory, Status-based Wages among Tradition-oriented, Stochastically Trading Coconut Producers." *Journal of Political Economy* 93: 265–76.

Alesina, Alberto, and Enrico Spolaore. 1997. "On the Number and Size of Nations." *Quarterly Journal of Economics* 112: 1027–56.

Alexander, H. E. 1979. *Political Finance.* Beverly Hills, CA: Sage Publications.

Allison, Graham T. 1971. *Essence of Decision: Explaining the Cuban Missile Crisis.* Boston: Little Brown.

Amar, Akhil Reed. 1991. "The Bill of Rights as a Constitution." *Yale Law Journal* 100: 1131–1210.

Anderson, G., D. Martin, W. Shughart II, and R. Tollison. 1990. "Behind the Veil: The Political Economy of Constitutional Change." In *Predicting Politics—Essays in Empirical Public Choice*, edited by W. Crain and R. Tollison, 89–100. Ann Arbor: University of Michigan Press.

Anderson, G., W. Shughart II, and R. Tollison. 1989. "On the Incentives of Judges to Enforce Legislative Wealth Transfers." *Journal of Law and Economics* 32: 215–28.

Aristotle. 1962. "Actual Constitutions and Their Variety." In *The Politics of Aristotle*, edited by Ernest Barker. New York: Oxford University Press.

Arrow, Kenneth J. 1973. "The Theory of Discrimination." In *Discrimination in Labor Markets*, edited by Orley Ashenfelter and Albert Rees. Princeton: Princeton University Press.

———. 1963. *Social Choice and Individual Values.* 1951. Reprint, New York: Wiley.

Arrow, Kenneth J., and F. Hahn. 1971. *General Competitive Analysis.* San Francisco and Edinburgh: Holden-Day, Inc., and Oliver and Boyd.

Ayres, Ian, and Jeremy Bulow. 1998. "The Donation Booth: Mandating Donor Anonymity to Disrupt the Market for Political Influence." *Stanford Law Review* 50: 837–91.

Ayres, Ian, and Joel Waldfogel. 1994. "A Market Test for Race Discrimination in Bail Setting." *Stanford Law Review* 46: 987–1047.

Baird, Douglas, Robert Gertner, and Randall Picker. 1994. *Game Theory and the Law.* Cambridge, MA: Harvard University Press.

Baker, John. 1979. "The Law Merchant and the Common Law before 1700." *Cambridge Law Journal* 38: 295.

Baker, Lynn A. 1995. "Constitutional Change and Direct Democracy." *University of Colorado Law Review* 66: 143–58.

Bardhan, Pranab. 1996. "Disparity in Wages But Not in Returns to Capital between Rich and Poor Countries." *Journal of Development Economics* 49: 257–70.

Barker, Robert S. 1988 "Constitutionalism in the Americas: A Bicentennial Perspective." *University of Pittsburgh Law Review* 49: 891.

Baumol, William, Wallace Oates, and Sue Blackman. 1979. *Economics, Environmental Policy, and the Quality of Life.* Englewood Cliffs, NJ: Prentice-Hall.

Bebchuk, Lucian Arye. 1992. "Federalism and the Corporation: The Desirable Limits on State Competition in Corporate Law." *Harvard Law Review* 105: 1437.

Becker, Gary. 1973. *The Economics of Discrimination.* Rev. ed. Chicago: University of Chicago Press.

Benham, Lee. "The Effects of Advertising on the Price of Eyeglasses." *Journal of Law and Economics* 15 (1972): 337–52.

Bentham, Jeremy. 1973. *The Utilitarians: An Introduction to the Principles of Morals and Legislation.* Garden City, NY: Doubleday.

Bergh, Roger vanden. 1997. "The Subsidiary Principle and the EC Competition Rules: The Costs and Benefits of Decentralization, " 142–83. In *Constitutional Law and Economics in the European Union,* edited by D. Schmidtchen and R. Cooter. Cheltenham and Lyme, Eng., Edward Elgar Publishing.

Bergson, A. 1938. "A Reformulation of Certain Aspects of Welfare Economics." 310–34.

Berlin, Isaiah. 1969. "Two Concepts of Liberty." In *Four Essays on Liberty,* 118–72. New York: Oxford University Press.

Bernstein, Lisa. 1992. "Opting Out of the Legal System: Extralegal Contractual Relations in the Diamond Industry." *Journal of Legal Studies* 21: 115–57.

Black, Duncan. 1958. *The Theory of Committees and Elections.* Cambridge: Cambridge University Press.

Black, Henry Campbell, Joseph R. Nolan, Jacqueline M. Nolan-Haley, and West Publishing Company. 1991. *Black's Law Dictionary: Definitions of the Terms and Phrases of American and English Jurisprudence, Ancient and Modern.* Abr. 6th ed. St. Paul: West Publishing.

Blackstone, William. 1979. *Commentaries on the Laws of England.* Facsimile of the 1765–1769 ed. Chicago: University of Chicago Press.

———. 1765 (1992). *Commentaries on the Laws of England.* Buffalo: William S. Hein and Co.

Blaug, Mark. 1978. *Economic Theory in Retrospect.* 3rd ed. New York: Cambridge University Press.

Blume, Lawrence, and Daniel Rubinfeld. 1984. "Compensaton for Takings: An Economic Analysis." *California Law Review* 72: 569–628.

Bohnet, Iris. 1998. "Fairness, Inequality and the 'Identifiable Victim Effect': A Behavioral Institutional Analysis." Paper presented at the Seminar on Law, Economics, and Organizations, University of California at Berkeley.

Bolton, Patrick, and Gérard Roland. 1997. "The Breakup of Nations: A Political Economy Analysis." *Quarterly Journal of Economics* 112: 1057–90.

Borgida, Eugene. 1994. "Gender Stereotyping and Sexual Harassment: Social Psychology in and on Trial." Paper presented at the Law and Society Seminar Series, University of California at Berkeley.

Bork, Robert H. 1990. *The Tempting of America: The Political Seduction of the Law.* New York: Free Press.

Boudreaux, Donald J., and A. C. Prichard. 1993. "Rewriting the Constitution: An Economic Analysis of the Constitutional Amendment Process." *Fordham Law Review* 62: 111–62.

Brennan, Geoffrey. 1998. "Collective Irrationality and Belief." Working paper, Rearch School of Social Science, Australian National University.

Brennan, Geoffrey, and Loren Lomasky. 1993. *The Pure Theory of Electoral Preference.* Cambridge: Cambridge University Press.

Brennan, Geoffrey, and Cliff Walsh, eds. 1990. *Rationality, Individualism, and Public Policy.* Canberra: Centre for Research in Federal Financial Relations.

Brenner, Saul. 1982. "Ideological Voting on the U.S. Supreme Court: A Comparison of the Original Vote on the Merits with the Final Vote." *Jurimetrics Journal* 22: 287–93.

Breton, Albert. 1996. *Competitive Governments: An Economic Theory of Politics and Public Finance.* Cambridge: Cambridge University Press.

Breyer, Stephen. 1982. *Regulation and Its Reform.* Cambridge, MA: Harvard University Press.

Brinig, Margaret F., and F. H. Buckley. 1997. "Welfare Magnets: The Race for the Top." *Supreme Court Economic Law Review* 5: 141–77.

Brueckner, J. 1983. "Property Value Maximization and Public Sector Efficiency." *Journal of Urban Economics* 14: 1–15.

Bruno, Michael, and Boris Pleskovic. 1997. *Annual World Bank Conference on Development Economics, 1996.* Washington, DC: The World Bank.

Buchanan, Allen E. 1991. *Secession: The Morality of Political Divorce from Fort Sumter to Lithuania and Quebec.* Boulder: Westview Press.

Buchanan, James. 1991. *Constitutional Economics.* Oxford: Blackwell.

———. 1990. "The Domain of Constitutional Economics." *Constitutional Political Economy* 1: 1–18.

———. 1975. *The Limits of Liberty: Between Anarchy and Leviathan.* Chicago: University of Chicago Press.

Buchanan, James M., and Gordon Tullock. 1962. *The Calculus of Consent: Logical Foundations of Constitutional Democracy.* Ann Arbor: University of Michigan Press.

Buckley, F. H. "The Market for Migrants." 1997. In *Economic Dimensions in International Law*, edited by J. Bhandari and A. Sykes, 405. Cambridge: Cambridge University Press.

Buscaglia, Edgardo, William Ratliff, and Robert Cooter, eds. 1997. *The Law and Economics of Development.* Greenwich, CT: JAI Press.

Buxbaum, Richard M. 1991. *European Business Law: Legal and Economic Analyses on Integration and Harmonization.* New York: W. de Gruyter.

Cain, Bruce E., and David Butler. 1991. "Redistricting Myths Are at Odds with Evidence." *Public Affairs Report, Institute of Governmental Studies, University of California at Berkeley* 32, no. 5.

Calabresi, Guido. 1970. *The Costs of Accidents: A Legal and Economic Analysis.* New Haven: Yale University Press.

Calabresi, Guido, and Douglas Melamed. 1972. "Property Rules, Liability Rules and Inalienability: One View of the Cathedral." *Harvard Law Review* 85: 1089–1128.

Campbell, Angus, Philip E. Converse, Warren E. Miller, and Donald E. Stokes. 1960. *The American Voter*. New York: Wiley.

Cappelletti, Mauro, John Henry Merryman, and Joseph M. Perillo. 1967. *The Italian Legal System*. Palo Alto: Stanford University Press.

Casson, Mark. 1991. *The Economics of Business Culture: Game Theory, Transaction Costs, and Economic Performance*. Oxford: Clarendon Press.

Cavalli-Sforza, Luigi Luca. 1995. "Human Migration." Paper presented at the Migration Work Group, Gruter Institute, Stanford University.

Cavalli-Sforza, Luigi Luca, and Francesco Cavalli-Sforza. 1995. *The Great Human Diasporas*. Translated by Sarah Thorne. New York: Addison-Wesley.

Chang, Howard F. 1996. "Liberalized Immigration as Free Trade: Economic Welfare and the Optimal Immigration Policy." *University of Pennsylvania Law Review* 145: 1147–1244.

Chapman, Bruce. 1998. "Law, Incommensurability, and Conceptually Sequenced Argument." *University of Pennsylvania Law Review* 146: 1487.

Choi, Stephen. "Market Lessons for Gatekeepers." 1998. Paper presented at the American Law and Economics Association, University of California at Berkeley.

Choper, Jesse H. 1980. *Judicial Review and the National Political Process: A Functional Reconsideration of the Role of the Supreme Court*. Chicago: University of Chicago Press.

Christensen, Raymond V. 1994. "Electoral Reform in Japan." *Asian Survey* 34: 589–605.

Coase, Ronald. 1974. "The Market for Goods and the Market for Ideas." *American Economic Review* 64: 384.

———. 1960. "The Problem of Social Cost." *Journal of Law and Economics* 3: 1–44.

———. 1937. "The Nature of the Firm." *Economica* 4: 386.

Coleman, Jules. 1980. "Efficiency, Utility, and Wealth Maximization." *Hofstra Law Review* 8: 509.

Condorcet, Marquis de. 1976. "Essay on the Application of Mathematics to the Theory of Decision Making." In *Condorcet: Selected Writings*, edited by K. Baker. Indianapolis: Bobbs-Merrill.

Cooter, Robert. 1998a. "Expressive Law and Economics." *Journal of Legal Studies* 27: 585–607.

———. 1998b. "Liability Rights as Contingent Claims." In *The New Palgrave: A Dictionary of Economics*, edited by John Eatwell, Murray Milgate, and Peter Newmann. New York: Stockton Press.

———. 1998c. "Self-control and Self-improvement for the 'Bad Man' of Holmes (The 1997 Oliver Wendell Holmes Conference)." *Boston University Law Review* 78: 903–30.

———. 1997a "Normative Failure Theory of Law." *Cornell Law Review* 82: 947–79.

———. 1997b. "The Rule of State Law versus the Rule-of-Law State: Economic Analysis of the Legal Foundations of Development." In *Annual World Bank Conference on Development Economics, 1996*, edited by Michael Bruno and Boris Pleskovic, 191–218. Washington, DC: The World Bank.

———. 1997c. "The Rule of State Law versus the Rule-of-Law State: Economic Analysis of the Legal Foundations of Development." In *The Law and Economics of Development*, edited by Edgardo Buscaglia, William Ratliff, and Robert Cooter, 101–48. Greenwich, CT: JAI Press Inc.

———. 1992. "The Minimax Constitution as Democracy." *International Review of Law and Economics* 12: 292.

————. 1991a. "The Coase Theorem." In *The New Palgrave: The World of Economics* edited by John Eatwell, Murray Milgate, and Peter Newman, 457–60. New York: Stockton Press.

————. 1991b. "Inventing Market Property: The Land Courts of Papua New Guinea." *Law and Society Review* 25: 759–801.

————. 1991c. "Lapses, Conflict, and Akrasia in Torts and Crimes: Towards an Economic Theory of the Will." *International Review of Law and Economics* 11: 149–64.

————. 1990. "Merit Goods: Some Thoughts on the Unthinkable." *In Rationality, Individualism, and Public Policy*, edited by Geoffrey Brennan and Cliff Walsh, 186–92. Canberra: Centre for Research in Federal Financial Relations.

————. 1989. "Towards a Market in Unmatured Tort Claims." *University of Virginia Law Review* 75: 383–411.

————. 1987a. "Torts as the Union of Liberty and Efficiency: An Essay on Causation (in 'Symposium on Causation in Tort Law')." *Chicago Kent Law Review* 63: 523.

————. 1987b. "Why Litigants Disagree: A Comment on George Priest's Measuring Legal Change." *Journal of Law, Economics, and Organization* 3: 85, 227–34.

————. 1985. "Unity in Torts, Contracts and Property." *California Law Review* 73: 1.

————. 1983. "Justice and Mathematics: Two Simple Ideas." In *New Directions in Economic Justice*, edited by Roger Skurski, 198–231. Notre Dame: University of Notre Dame Press.

————. 1982. "The Cost of Coase." *Journal of Legal Studies* 11: 1.

————. 1978. "Optimal Tax Schedules and Rates." *American Economic Review* 68: 756–68.

Cooter, Robert, and Josef Drexl. 1994. "The Logic of Power in the Emerging European Constitution: Game Theory and the Division of Powers." *International Review of Law and Economics* 14: 307–26.

Cooter, Robert, and Tom Ginsburg. 1998. "Division of Powers in the European Constitution." In *The New Palgrave: A Dictionary of Economics*, edited by John Eatwell, Murray Milgate, and Peter Newman, New York: Stockton Press.

————. 1996. "Comparative Judicial Discretion: An Empirical Test of Economic Models." *International Review of Law and Economics* 16: 295–314.

Cooter, Robert, and James Gordley. 1994. "The Cultural Justification of Unearned Income: An Economic Model of Merit Goods Based on Aristotelian Ideas of Akrasia and Distributive Justice." In *Profits and Morality*, edited by Robin Cowan and Mario J. Rizzo, 150–75. Chicago: University of Chicago Press.

Cooter, Robert, and Lewis Kornhauser. 1980. "Can Litigation Improve the Law without the Help of Judges." *Journal of Legal Studies* 9: 139.

Cooter, Robert, and Peter Rappoport. 1984. "Were the Ordinalists Wrong about Welfare Economics?" *Journal of Economic Literature* 22: 507.

Cooter, Robert D., and Thomas Ulen. 1999. *Law and Economics*. 3rd ed. New York: Addison Wesley.

————. 1996. *Law and Economics*. 2nd ed. New York: Addison Wesley.

————. 1988. *Law and Economics*. Glenview: Scott, Foresman.

Cox, Gary W. 1994. "Strategic Voting Equilibria under the Single Nontransferable Vote." *American Political Science Review* 88: 608–21.

Crain, W. M., and R. Tollison. 1979. "Constitutional Change in an Interest-Group Perspective." *Journal of Legal Studies* 8: 165–75.

Dahl, Robert. 1982. *Dilemmas of Pluralist Democracy: Autonomy vs. Control*. New Haven: Yale University Press.

Dan-Cohen, Meir. 1991. "Freedoms of Collective Speech: A Theory of Protected Communications by Organizations, Communities, and the State." *California Law Review* 79: 1229–70.

Dau-Schmidt, Kenneth G. 1990. "An Econmic Analysis of Criminal Law as a Preference-Shaping Policy." *Duke Law Journal* 1: 1–38.

Demsetz, Harold. 1968. "Why Regulate Utilities." *Journal of Law and Economics* 11: 55–66.

Dharmapala, Dhammika. 1998. "Campaign Contributions, Expenditures, and Rational Voting Behavior." Paper presented at the Public Sector Seminar, Economics Department, University of California at Berkeley.

———. 1996. "Comparing Tax Expenditures and Direct Subsidies: The Role of Legislative Institutions." Paper presented at the Public Sector Seminar, Department of Economics, University of California at Berkeley.

Diermeier, Daniel, and Roger Myerson. "Bargaining, Veto Power, and Legislative Committees." Working Paper, Northwestern University.

Donohue, John J. III. 1987. "Further Thoughts on Unemployment Discrimination Legislation: A Reply to Judge Posner." *University of Pennsylvania Law Review* 136: 523.

Downs, Anthony. 1957. *An Economic Theory of Democracy.* New York: Harper.

Dreze, Jean, and Amartya Sen. 1989. *Hunger and Public Action.* Oxford: Clarendon Press.

Dworkin, Ronald. 1986. *Law's Empire.* Cambridge, MA: Belknap Press.

———. 1977. *Taking Rights Seriously.* London: Duckworth.

Dwyer, John. 1993. "The Use of Market Incentives in Controlling Air Pollution: California's Marketable Permit Program." *Ecology Law Quarterly* 20: 103.

Dyzenhaus, David. 1998. "Why Carl Schmitt?" In *Law and Politics: Carl Schmitt's Critique of Liberalism,* edited by David Dyzenhaus, 1–22. Durham: Duke University Press.

Easterbrook, Frank H. 1994. "The Supreme Court, 1983 Term—Forward: The Court and the Economic System." *Harvard Law Review* 98.

———. 1982. "Ways of Criticizing the Court." *Harvard Law Review* 95: 802.

Eisenberg, Melvin Aron. 1982. "The Bargain Principle and Its Limits." *Harvard Law Review* 95: 741.

Elhauge, Einer. 1997. "Are Term Limits Undemocratic?" *University of Chicago Law Review* 64: 83–201.

———. 1991. "Does Interest Group Theory Justify More Intrusive Judical Review?" *Yale Law Journal* 101: 31.

———. 1995. "Term Limits: Voters Aren't Schizophrenic." *Wall Street Journal,* 14 March.

Ellickson, Robert C. 1998. "New Micro-Institutions for Old Neighborhoods." Paper presented at the American Law and Economics Association, University of California at Berkeley.

———. 1996. "Controlling Chronic Misconduct in City Spaces: Of Panhandlers, Skid Rows, and Public-Space Zoning." *Yale Law Journal* 105: 1165.

———. 1991. *Order without Law: How Neighbors Settle Disputes.* Cambridge, MA: Harvard University Press.

———. 1977. "Suburban Growth Controls: An Economic and Legal Analysis." *Yale Law Journal* 86: 385.

Elster, Jon. 1995. "Strategic Uses of Argument." In *Barriers to Conflict Resolution,* edited by Kenneth Arrow, Robert H. Mnookin, Lee Ross, Amos Tversky, and Robert Wilson, 236–57. New York: W. W. Norton.

Emons, Winand. 1998 or 1999. "Imperfect Tests and Natural Insurance Monopolies." Dept. of Economics Discussion Paper, University of Bern. 97-04.

———. 1996. "Credance Goods Monopolists." Paper presented at the Law and Economics Seminar, University of California at Berkeley.

———. 1994. "The Provision of Environmental Protection Measures under Incomplete Information: An Introduction to the Theory of Mechnism Design." *International Review of Law and Economics* 14: 479–91.

Epstein, David, and Sharyn O'Halloran. 1995. "A Theory of Strategic Oversight: Congress, Lobbyists, and the Bureaucracy." *Journal of Law, Economics, and Organization* 11: 227–55.

Epstein, Edwin M. 1979. "The Emergence of Political Action Committees." In *Political Finance*, edited by Herbert E. Alexander, *Sage Electoral Studies Yearbook*, 159–97. Beverly Hills, CA: Sage Publications.

Epstein, Richard. 1992. *Forbidden Grounds: The Case against Employment Discrimination Laws*. Cambridge, MA: Harvard University Press.

———. 1988. "The Supreme Court: 1987 Term. Foreword: Unconstitutional Conditions, State Power, and the Limits of Consent." *Harvard Law Review* 102: 4–104.

———. 1985a. "Judicial Review: Reckoning on Two Kinds of Error." In *Scalia v. Epstein: Two Views on Judicial Activism*. Washington, DC: Cato Institute.

———. 1985b. *Takings: Private Property and the Power of Eminent Domain*. Cambridge, MA: Harvard University Press.

———. 1973. "A Theory of Strict Liability." *Journal of Legal Studies* 2: 151.

Epstein, Richard A., William N. Eskridge, and Philip P. Frickey. 1988. "Unconstitutional Conditions, State Power, and the Limits of Consent." *Harvard Law Review* 102: 4–104.

Eskridge, William N. 1991. "Overriding Supreme Court Statutory Interpretation Decisions." *Yale Law Journal* 101: 331–455.

Eskridge, William N. and Philip P. Frickey. 1988. *Cases and Materials on Legislation: Statutes and the Creation of Public Policy*. St. Paul: West Pub. Co.

———. 1991. "Reneging on History? Playing the Court/Congress/President Civil Rights Game." *California Law Review* 79: 613–83.

Farber, Daniel A. 1991. "Free Speech without Romance: Public Choice and the First Amendment." *Harvard Law Review* 105: 554.

Farber, Daniel A., and Philip P. Frickey. 1991. *Law and Public Choice: A Critical Introduction*. Chicago: University of Chicago Press.

Feldstein, Martin. 1974. "Distributional Preferences in Public Expenditure Analysis." In *Redistribution through Public Choice*, edited by Harold M. Hochman and George E. Peterson, 136–64. New York: Columbia University Press.

Ferejohn, John, and Charles Shipan. 1990. "Congressional Influence on Bureaucracy." *Journal of Law, Economics, and Organization* 6: 1–20.

Fikentscher, Wolfgang. 1993. "From a Centrally Planned Government System to a Rule-of-Law Democracy: Legal, Economic, and Anthropological Considerations." Paper presented at the Brookings Institution, Washington, DC.

Finkelstein, Claire. 1998. "A Puzzle about Hobbes on Self-Defense." Working paper.

Fiorina, Morris P. 1977. *Congress: Keystone of the Washington Establishment*. New Haven: Yale University Press.

Fischel, William A. 1985. *The Economics of Zoning Laws: A Property Rights Approach to American Land Use Controls*. Baltimore: Johns Hopkins University Press.

Fischel, William A., and Perry Shapiro. 1989. "A Constitutional Choice Model of Compensation for Takings." *International Review of Law and Economics* 9: 115–28.

Fletcher, William A. 1990. "Atomic Bomb Testing and the Warner Amendment: A Violation of the Separation of Powers." *Washington Law Review*. 65: 285.

Frank, Robert H. 1988. *Passions within Reason: The Strategic Role of the Emotions*. New York: Norton.

Frey, Bruno S. 1997a. "A Constitution for Knaves Crowds Out Civic Virtues." *Economic Journal* 107: 1043–53.

———. 1997b. *Not Just For the Money*. Cheltanham: Edward Elgar.

———. 1996. "A Directly Democratic and Federal Europe." *Constitutional Political Economy* 7: 267–79.

Frey, Bruno S., and Iris Bohnet. 1994. "The Swiss Experience with Referenda and Federalism." *IDIOMA: Revue de linguistique et de traductologie* 6: 147–60.

Frey, Bruno S., and Reiner Eichenberger. 1997. "FOCJ: A Single European Market for Government," 195–215. In *Constitutional Law and Economics of the European Union*, edited by D. Schmitchen and R. Cooter. Cheltenham, U.K.: Edward Elgar.

Friedman, Milton. 1953. *An Essay in Positive Economics*. Chicago: University of Chicago Press.

Fudenberg, Drew, and Jean Tirole. 1978. *Game Theory*. Cambridge, MA: MIT Press, 1991.

Fuller, Lon. 1978. "The Forms and Limits of Adjudication." *Harvard Law Review* 93: 1.

Gardner, Martin. 1980. "Mathematical Games: From Counting Votes to Making Votes Count—the Mathematics of Elections." *Scientific American*, October 16–26.

Garrett, Geoffrey, R. Daniel Kelemen, and Heiner Schulz. 1998. "The European Court of Justice, National Governments, and Legal Integration in the European Union." *International Organization* 52: 149–76.

Gerhardt, Michael J., and Thomas D. Rowe. 1993. *Constitutional Theory: Arguments and Perspectives*. Charlottesville, VA: Michie Company.

Gibbard, Allan. 1973. "Manipulation of Voting Schemes: A General Result." *Econometrica* 41: 587–601.

Ginsburg, T. 1999. *Growing Constitutions: Judicial Review in New Decocracies*. Ph.D. dissertation, University of California at Berkeley, Jurisprudence and Social Policy Program.

Gluckman, Max. 1965. *The Ideas in Barotse Jurisprudence*. New Haven: Yale University Press.

Goldman, Alvin. 1999. "Democracy." In *Knowledge in a Social World*. New York: Oxford University Press.

Goldwin, R., and W. Schambia. 1982. *How Capitalistic Is the Constitution?* Washington, DC: American Enterprise Institute for Public Policy Research.

Goodman, John C. 1978. "An Economic Theory of the Evolution of the Common Law." *Journal of Legal Studies* 7: 393–406.

Gordley, Jim. 1981. "Equality in Exchange." *California Law Review*. 69: 1587.

Habermas, Jürgen. 1996. *Between Facts and Norms: Contributions to a Discourse Theory of Law and Democracy*. Studies in Contemporary German Social Thought. Cambridge, MA: MIT Press.

Hadfield, Gillian K. 1992. "Bias in the Evolution of Legal Rules." *Georgetown Law Journal* 80: 583–617.

Hamilton, Alexander et al. 1981. *The Federalist Papers: A Collection of Essays Written in Support of the Constitution of the United States: From the Original Text of Alexander Hamilton, James Madison, John Jay*. Baltimore: Johns Hopkins University Press.

———. 1961. *The Federalist Papers No. 51*. Edited by Clinton Rossiter. New York: New American Library.

Hammond, Thomas H., and Gary J. Miller. 1987. "The Core of the Constitution." *American Political Science Review* 81, no. 4: 1155–74.

Hansmann, Henry. 1998. "Ownership of the Firm." *Journal of Law, Economics, and Organization* 4: 267–304.

———. 1990. "When Does Worker Ownership Work? ESOPs, Law Firms, Codetermination, and Economic Democracy." *Yale Law Journal* 99: 1749–1816.

Hansmann, Henry, and Ugo Mattei. 1994. "The Comparative Law and Economics of Trusts." Paper presented at the CLEF, Geneva, Switzerland.

Harsanyi, J. C. 1955. "Cardinal Welfare, Individualistic Ethics, and Interpersonal Comparisons of Utility." *Journal of Political Economy* 63: 309–21.

———. 1953. "Cardinal Utility in Welfare Economics and in the Theory of Risk Taking." *Journal of Political Economy* 61: 434–35.

Hart, H. L. A., and Tony Honore. *Causation in the Law*. 2nd ed. Oxford: Clarendon Press, 1985.

Hasen, Richard L. 1996. "Voting without Law?" *University of Pennsylvania Law Review*. 144: 2135–79.

Head, J. G. 1966. "On Merit Goods." *Finanzarchi* 25: 1–29.

Heckman, James. 1991. "Did Title VII Work?" Paper presented at the American Law and Economics Association, University of Illinois, Champaign.

Hirshleifer, Jack. 1982. "Evolutionary Models in Law and Economics." In *Research in Law and Economics*, vol. 4, edited by Richard O. Zerbe, 1–60. Greenwich, CT: JAI Press.

Hirschman, Albert O. 1977. *The Passions and the Interests*. Princeton: Princeton University Press.

———. 1970. *Exit, Voice, and Loyalty: Responses to Decline in Firms, Organizations and States*. Cambridge, MA: Harvard University Press.

Hobbes, Thomas. 1965. *Hobbes's Leviathan*, ed. William Pogson-Smith. Oxford: Clarendon Press.

Hoffman, Elizabeth, and Matthew Spitzer. 1985a. "Entitlements, Rights, and Fairness: An Experimental Examination of Subjects' Concepts of Distributive Justice." *Journal of Legal Studies* 14: 259.

———. 1985b. "Experimental Law and Economics: An Introduction." *Columbia Law Review* 85: 991–1035.

Hoffman, Elizabeth, et al. 1994. "Preferences, Property Rights, and Anonymity in Bargaining Games." *Games & Economic Behavior* 7: 346.

Hohfeld, Wesley Newcomb. 1964. *Fundamental Legal Conceptions as Applied in Judicial Reasoning*. 1919. Reprint, New Haven: Yale University Press.

Holden, James M. 1955. *Early History of Negotiable Instruments in English Law*. London: University of London.

Hollifield, James F. 1994. "The Migration Crisis in Western Europe: Causes and Consequences." Paper presented at the Migration and Immigration: Trends and Critical Policy Issues Conference, Brookings Institution, Washington DC.

Holmes, Oliver Wendell. 1897. "The Path of the Law." *Harvard Law Review* 10: 459.

Horwitz, Morton. 1977. *The Transformation of American Law* 1780–1860. Cambridge, MA: Harvard University Press.

Howe, Kenneth. 1998. "Big Money Swamps the Ballot." *San Francisco Chronicle*, 19 May, A1, A8–A9.

Hume, Dand. 1987. *Essays—Moral, Political and Literary*, ed. Eugene F. Miller. Indianapolis: Liberty Fund.

Hylton, Keith N. 1993. "Efficiency and Labor Law." *Northwestern University Law Review* 87, no. 2: 471-522.

Ingber, Stanley. 1984. "The Marketplace of Ideas: A Legitimizing Myth." *Duke Law Journal* 1984: 1.

Inman, Robert P., and Daniel L. Rubinfeld. 1997. "The Political Economy of Federalism." In *Perspectives on Public Choice*, edited by Dennis C. Mueller, 73–106. New York: Cambridge University Press.

———. 1979. "The Judicial Pursuit of Local Fiscal Equity." *Harvard Law Review* 92: 1662–1750.

Jacobs, Jane. 1993. *The Death and Life of Great American Cities*. New York: Modern Library.

Jefferson, Thomas. 1984. *Writings*. New York: Library of America.

Kafka, Franz. 1956. *The Trial*. New York: Modern Library.

Kant, Immanuel. 1970. "On a Supposed Right to Tell Lies from Benevolent Motives." In *Kant's Critique of Practical Reason and Other Works on the Theory of Ethics*. Reprinted in *Moral Rules and Particular Circumstances*, edited by Banech A. Brady. Englewood Cliffs, NJ: Prentice Hall.

Kaplow, Louis. 1986. "An Economic Analysis of Legal Transitions." *Harvard Law Review* 99: 509–617.

Kelman, Mark. 1988. "On Democracy-Bashing: A Skeptical Look at the Theoretical and 'Empricial' Practice of the Public Choice Movement." *Virginia Law Review* 74: 199.

Kirchgassner, G., and B. Frey. 1990. "Volksabstimmung und direkte Demokratie: Ein Beitrag zur Verfassungsdiskusssion." In *Wahlen und Wahler—Analysen aus Anlass der Bundestagwahl*, edited by H. D. Klingmann and M. Kaase, 42–69. Opladen: Westdeutscher Verlag.

Klevorick, Alvin K. 1985. "Legal Theory and the Economic Analysis of Torts and Crimes." *Columbia Law Review*. 85: 905–20.

Koetz, Hein. 1997. "Unfair Terms in Consumer Contracts: Recent Developments in Europe from a Comparative and Economic Perspective," 203–15. In *Festskrist til Ole Lando*, edited by L. L. Anderson, J. Fejo, and Ruth Nielsen. Copenhagen.

———. 1996. "A Common Law for Europe." Paper presented at the Annual Lecture on Comparative Law, Law School, University of California at Berkeley.

Kolko, Gabriel. 1967. *The Triumph of Conservatism: A Re-Interpretation of American History, 1900–1916*. Chicago: Quandrangle.

Kornhauser, Lewis. 1986. "Unpacking the Court." *Yale Law Journal* 96: 82.

Krasnow, Diane-Michele. 1991. "The Imbalance of Power and the Presidential Veto: A Case for the Item Veto." *Harvard Journal of Law and Public Policy* 14: 582–613.

Krueger, Anne. 1963. "Economics of Discrimination." *Journal of Political Economy* 71: 481–86.

Kuran, Timur. 1998. "Ethnic Norms and Their Transformation through Reputational Cascades." *Journal of Legal Studies* 27.

Lakoff, George, and Mark Johnson. 1980. *Metaphors We Live By*. Chicago: University of Chicago Press.

Landes, William. 1993. "The Influence of Economics on Law: A Quantitative Study." *Journal of Law and Economics* 36: 385–424.

Landes, William, and Richard A. Posner. 1979. "Adjudication as a Private Good." *Journal of Legal Studies* 8: 235–84.

———. 1975. "The Independent Judiciary in an Interest-Group Perspective." *Journal of Law and Economics* 18: 875.

La Porta, Rafael, Florencio Lopez-de-Silanes, and Andrei Shleifer. 1997. "Legal Determinants of External Finance." *Journal of Finance* 52: 1131–50.

Latham, R., and W. Matthews, eds. 1970. *The Diary of Samuel Pepys*. London: Bell and Sons.

Laver, Michael, and Norman Schofield. 1990a. "Who Gets In?" In *Multiparty Governments*: The *Politics of Coalition in Europe*, 89–143. New York: Oxford University Press.

———. 1990b. *Multiparty Governments: The Politics of Coalition in Europe*. New York: Oxford University Press.

Lessig, Lawrence, and Paul Resnick. 1998. "The Architectures of Mandated Access Controls." Paper presented at the General Aspects of Legal Analysis (GALA) Seminar, Law School, University of California at Berkeley.

Levin, Jonathan, and Barry Nalebuff. 1995. "An Introduction to Vote-Counting Schemes." *Journal of Economic Perspectives* 9: 3–26.

Levine, Michael, and Charles Plott. 1977. "Agenda Influence and Its Implications." *Virginia Law Review* 63: 561.

Levmore, Saul. 1996. "Precommitment Politics." *Virginia Law Review* 82: 567–627.

———. 1992. "Bicameralism: When Are Two Decisions Better Than One?" *International Review of Law and Economics* 12: 145–62.

Lewin, Jeff L., and William N. Trumbull. 1990. "The Social Value of Crimes." *International Review of Law and Economics* 10: 270.

Lewis, David K. 1969. Convention: *A Philosophical Study*. Cambridge, MA: Harvard University Press.

Lewis, Harold S., and Theodore Y. Blumoff. 1992. "Reshaping Section 1983's Asymmetry." *University of Pennsylvania Law Review* 140: 755–850.

Libecap, Gary D. 1989. *Contracting for Property Rights*. New York: Cambridge University Press.

Lijphart, Arend. 1994. *Electoral Systems and Party Systems: Study of Twenty-Seven Democracies, 1945–90*. Oxford: Oxford University Press.

Locke, John. 1961 (1690). *The Second Treatise of Civil Government*. Edited by Thomas I. Cook. New York: Hafner.

Luce, R. Duncan, and Howard Raiffa. 1967. *Games and Decisions: Introduction and Critical Survey*. New York: John Wiley and Sons.

MacCormick, D. Neil. 1997. "Institutional Normative Order: A Conception of Law." *Cornell Law Review* 82: 1051–70.

Macey, J. 1988. "Transaction Costs and the Normative Elements of the Public Choice Model: An Application to Constitutional Theory." *Virginia Law Review* 74: 471–518.

———. 1986. "Promoting Public-Regarding Legislation through Statutory Interpretation: An Interest Group Model." *Columbia Law Review* 86: 223.

MacKinnon, Catherine. 1987. *Feminism Unmodified: Discourses on Life and Law*. Cambridge, MA: Harvard University Press.

Madison, James. 1981a. "Federalist 10." In *The Federalist Papers*. Baltimore: Johns Hopkins University Press.

———. 1981b. "The Federalist No. 51." In *The Federalist Papers*. Baltimore: Johns Hopkins University Press.

Marshall, Alfred. 1925. *Principles of Economics*. London: Macmillan and Co.

Martin, Philip L. 1994. "The Impacts of Immigration on Receiving Countries." Paper presented at the Migration and Immigration: Trends and Critical Policy Issues Conference, Brookings Institution, Washington DC.

Mashaw, Jerry L. *Greed, Chaos, and Governance: Using Public Choice to Improve Public Law.* New Haven: Yale University Press, 1997.

―――. 1985. "Prodelegaton: Why Administrators Should Make Political Decisions." *Journal of Law, Economics, and Organizations* 1: 81.

Maslow, A. 1954. *Motivation and Personality.* New York: Harper and Row.

Mason, Sir Anthony. 1986–87. "The Role of a Constitutional Court in a Federation: A Comparison of the Australian and the United States Experience." *Federal Law Review* 16: 1–28.

Mattei, Ugo. 1996. *Comparative Law and Economics.* Ann Arbor: University of Michigan Press.

Mayhew, David R. 1974. *Congress: The Electoral Connection.* New Haven: Yale University Press.

McCubbins, Matthew D., Roger G. Noll, and Barry R. Weingast. 1989. "Structure and Process, Politics and Policy: Administrative Arrangements and the Political Control of Agencies." *Virginia Law Review* 75: 431–82.

McKelvey, R. D. 1979. "General Conditions for Global Intransitivities in Formal Voting Models." *Econometrica* 47, no. 5: 1085–1112.

Memon, P. Ali. 1993. *Keeping Zealand Green: Recent Environmental Reforms.* Otago, New Zealand: University of Otago Press.

Merryman, John Henry. 1985. *The Civil Law Tradition: An Introduction to the Legal Systems of Western Europe and Latin America.* 2nd ed. Stanford: Stanford University Press.

Miceli, Thomas J., and Kathleen Segerson. 1994. "Regulatory Takings: When Should Compensation Be Paid?" *Journal of Legal Studies* 23: 749–76.

―――. 1967. "Property, Utility, and Fairness: Comments on Ethical Foundations of 'Just Compensation' Law." *Harvard Law Review* 80: 1214.

Michelman, Frank. 1988. "Takings" *Columbia Law Review* 88: 1600–1629.

Mill, John Stuart. 1951. *Utilitarianism, Liberty and Representative Government.* New York: Dutton.

―――. 1844. "On the Definition of Political Economy; and on the Method of Investigation Proper to It. In *Essays on Some Unsettled Questions of Political Economy.* London: J. W. Parker.

Miller, Gary J., and Thomas H. Hammond. 1990. "Committees and the Core of the Constitution." *Public Choice* 66: 201–27.

Miller, Gary J., Thomas H. Hammond, and Charles Kile. 1996. "Bicameralism and the Core: An Experimental Test." *Legislative Studies Quarterly* 21, no. 1: 83–103.

Miller, Nicholas. 1983. "Pluralism and Social Choice." *American Political Science Review* 77: 734–47.

Mirrlees, J. 1971. "An Exploration in the Theory of Optimum Income Taxation." *Review of Economic Studies* 38: 175–208.

Moe, Terry, and Michael Caldwell. 1994. "The Institutional Foundations of Democratic Government: A Comparison of Presidential and Parliamentary Systems." *Journal of Institutional and Theoretical Economics* 150: 171–85.

Mueller, Dennis. 1997. *Perspectives on Public Choice.* New York: Cambridge University Press.

―――. 1996. *Constitutional Democracy.* New York: Oxford University Press.

―――. 1989. *Public Choice II.* 1979. Reprint, New York: Cambridge University Press.

Musgrave, Peggy, and Richard Musgrave. 1976. *Public Finance in Theory and Practice.* 2nd ed. New York: McGraw-Hill.

Musgrave, Richard A. 1959. *The Theory of Public Finance: A Study in Public Economy.* New York: McGraw-Hill.

Musgrave, Richard A., and Alan T. Peacock. 1967. *Classics in the Theory of Public Finance.* New York: MacMillan.

Nash, J. 1950. "The Bargaining Problem." *Econometrica* 18: 155–62.

Neustadt, Richard E. 1986. *Presidential Power: The Politics of Leadership from FDR to Carter.* New York: Macmillan.

Niskanen, William A. 1992. "The Case for a New Fiscal Constitution." *Journal of Economic Perspectives* 6: 13–24.

———. 1971. *Bureaucracy and Representative Government.* Chicago: Aldine-Atherton.

Nitzan, Samuel, and Jacob Paroush. 1982. "Optimal Decision Rules in Uncertain Dichotomous Situations." *International Economic Review* 23: 289–97.

North, Douglass. 1995. "Some Fundamental Puzzles in Economic History/Development." Paper presented at the Seminar on Development, Economics Department, University of California at Berkeley, October.

———. 1981. *Structure and Change in Economic History.* New York: W. W. Norton.

Nozick, Robert. 1974. *Anarchy, State, and Utopia.* New York: Basic Books.

Oates, Wallace E. 1990. "Federalism and Government Finance." Paper presented at the Modern Public Finance Conference, University of California, Berkeley.

———. 1972. *Fiscal Federalism.* New York: Harcourt, Brace, Jovanovich.

Oberholzer-Gee, Felix, Iris Bohnet, and Bruno S. Frey. 1997. "Fairness and Competence in Democratic Decisions." *Public Choice* 91: 89–105.

Olson, Mancur. 1993. "Dictatorship, Democracy, and Development." *American Political Science Review* 87: 567–76.

———. 1992. "Democracy, the Rule of Law, and Economic Development." Paper presented at the American Law and Economics Association Annual Meeting.

———. 1969. "The Principle of 'Fiscal Equivalence': The Division of Responsibilities among Different Levels of Government." *American Economic Review* 59: 479–87.

———. 1965. *The Logic of Collective Action: Public Goods and the Theory of Groups.* Cambridge, MA: Harvard University Press.

Ortiz, Daniel R. 1989. "The Myth of Intent in Equal Protection." *Stanford Law Review* 41: 1105.

Ott, Claus, and Hans-Bernd Schafer. 1991. "Emergence and Construction of Efficient Rules in the Legal System of German Civil Law." Paper presented at the European Law and Economics Association Annual Meeting, Copenhagen, Denmark.

Palfrey, Thomas. 1989. "A Mathematical Proof of Duverger's Law." In *Models of Strategic Choice in Politics*, edited by Peter C. Ordeshook, 69–91. Ann Arbor: University of Michigan Press.

———. 1984. "Spatial Equilibrium with Entry." *Review of Economic Studies* 51: 139–56.

Palfrey, Thomas R., and Howard Rosenthal. 1985. "Voter Participation and Strategic Uncertainty." *American Political Science Review* 79: 62.

Parkinson, C. Northcote. 1957. *Parkinson's Law, and Other Studies in Administration.* Boston: Houghton Mifflin.

Passmore, John. 1974. *Man's Responsibility for Nature.* London: Gerald Dudscooke.

Persson, Torsten, Gérard Roland, and Guido Tabellini. 1997. "Separation of Powers and Political Accountability." *Quarterly Journal of Economics* 112: 1163–1202.

Persson, Torsten, and Guido Tabellini. 1996. "Federal Fiscal Constitutions: Risk Sharing and Redistribution." *Journal of Political Economy* 104: 979–1009.

Persson, Torsten, and Guido Tabellini. 1994. "Does Centralization Increase the Size of Government?" *European Economic Review* 38: 765–73.

Peterson, Paul E., and Mark C. Rom. 1990. *Welfare Magnets: A New Case for a National Standard*. Washinton, DC: Brookings Institution.

Pigou, A. C. 1950. *The Economics of Welfare*. 4th ed. London: MacMillan and Co.

Pildes, Richard H., and Cass R. Sunstein. 1995. "Reinventing the Regulatory State." *University of Chicago Law Review* 62: 1–130.

Polsby, Daniel D., and Robert D. Popper. 1993. "Ugly: An Inquiry into the Problem of Racial Gerrymandering under the Voting Rights Act. (Symposium: The Future of Voting Rights after *Shaw v. Reno*)." *Michigan Law Review* 92: 652–82.

Pommerehne, W. 1990. "The Empirical Relevance of Comparative Institutional Analysis." *European Economic Review* 34: 458–68.

Posner, Eric A. Forthcoming. *Law, Cooperation, and Rational Choice*. Cambridge, MA: Harvard University Press.

———. 1996. "Law, Economics and Inefficient Norms." *University of Pennsylvania Law Review* 144: 1697.

Posner, Richard. 1992. *Economic Analysis of Law*. 4th ed. Boston: Little Brown.

———. 1985. "An Economic Theory of the Criminal Law." *Columbia Law Review*. 85: 1193.

———. 1981. *Economics of Justice*. Cambridge, MA: Harvard University Press.

Post, Robert C. 1990. "The Constitutional Concept of Public Discourse: Outrageous Opinion, Democratic Deliberation, and *Hustler Magazine v. Falwell*." *Harvard Law Review*. 103: 601–86.

Powell, G. Bingham. 1982. *Contemporary Democracies: Participation, Stability, and Violence*. Cambridge, MA: Harvard University Press.

Priest, George L. 1987. "Measuring Legal Change." *Journal of Law, Economics, and Organization* 3: 193–225.

———. 1977. "The Common Law Practice and the Selection of Efficient Rules." *Journal of Legal Studies* 6: 65–82.

Provost, Rene. 1992. "Emergency Judicial Relief for Human Rights Violations in Canada and Argentina." *University of Miami Inter-American Law Review* 23: 693.

Radin, Max. 1938. "A Restatement of Hohfeld." *Harvard Law Review* 51: 1141.

Rae, Douglas L. W. 1995. "Using District Magnitude to Regulate Political Party Competition." *Journal of Economic Perspectives* 9: 65–76.

———. 1971. *The Political Consequences of Electoral Laws*. Rev. ed. New Haven: Yale University Press.

Raiffa, Howard. 1968. *Decision Analysis: Introductory Lectures on Choices under Uncertainty*. Reading, MA: Addison-Wesley.

Ramsey, F. P. 1928. "A Mathematical Theory of Savings." *Economic Journal* 38: 543–59.

Ramseyer, J. Mark. 1994. "The Puzzling Independence of Courts: A Comparative Approach." *Journal of Legal Studies* 23: 721–47.

Ramseyer, J. Mark, and Eric Rasmusen. 1996. "Judicial Independence in Civil Law Regimes: Econometrics from Japan." Paper presented at the American Law and Economics Association Annual Meeting, Chicago.

Rasmusen, Eric. 1994. *Games and Information: An Introduction to Game Theory*. 2nd ed. Cambridge, MA: Blackwell.

Rawls, John. 1993. *Political Liberalism*. New York: Columbia University Press.

———. 1971. *A Theory of Justice*. Cambridge, MA: Harvard University. Press.

Regan, Donald. 1972. "The Problem of Social Cost Revisited." *Journal of Law and Economics* 15: 427–37.

Reich, Charles A. 1964. "The New Property." *Yale Law Journal* 73: 733.

Revesz, Richard L. 1996. "Federalism and Interstate Environmental Externalities." *University of Pennsylvania Law Review* 144: 2341–2416.

Riker, William H. 1982a. "The Meaning of Social Choice." In *Liberalism against Populism: A Confrontation between the Theory of Democracy and the Theory of Social Choice*. San Francisco: W.H. Freeman.

———. 1982b. "The Two Party System and Duverger's Law." *American Political Science Review* 76: 753–66.

———. 1962. *The Theory of Political Coalitions*. New Haven: Yale University Press.

Roback, Jennifer. 1989. "Racism as Rent-Seeking." *Economic Inquiry* 27: 661–81.

Robbins, Lionel. 1932. *An Essay on the Nature and Significance of Economic Science*. London: MacMillan.

Rogers, Jim. Forthcoming. *The Early History of the Law of Bills and Notes: A Study of the Origins of Anglo-American Commercial Law*. New York: Cambridge University Press.

Romano, Roberta. 1987. "The Political Economy of Takeover Statutes." *Virginia Law Review* 73: 111.

Romer, Paul M. 1996. "Preferences, Promises, and the Politics of Entitlement." *In Individual and Social Responsibility: Child Care, Education, Medical Care, and Long-Term Care in America*, edited by Victor R. Fuchs, 195–220. Chicago: University of Chicago Press.

Romer, Thomas, and Barry R. Weingast. 1991. "Political Foundations of the Thrift Debacle." In *Politics and Economics in the Eighties*, edited by A. Alesina and G. Carliner. Chicago: University of Chicago Press.

Rose-Ackerman, Susan. 1994. "American Administrative Law under Seige: Is Germany a Model?" *Harvard Law Review* 107: 1279–1302.

———. 1992. "Judicial Review and the Power of the Purse." *International Review of Law and Economics* 12: 191–208.

———. 1988. "Against Ad Hocery: A Comment on Michelman." *Columbia Law Review* 88: 1697–1713.

———. 1985. "Inalienability and the Theory of Property Rights." *Columbia Law Review* 85: 931–61.

Rosenberg, Gerald. 1993. *The Hollow Hope: Can Courts Bring about Social Change?* Chicago: University of Chicago Press.

Rubin, Paul H. 1994. "Growing a Legal System in the Post-Communist Economies." *Cornell International Law Journal* 27: 1.

———. 1977. "Why Is the Common Law Efficient?" *Journal of Legal Studies* 6: 51–64.

Rubin, Paul H., and Martin J. Bailey. 1993. "A Positive Theory of Legal Change." Paper presented at the European Law and Economics Association Annual Meeting, Lund, Sweden.

Rubinstein, Ariel. 1982. "Perfect Equilibrium in a Bargaining Game." *Econometrica* 50: 97–109.

Russell, Bertrand. 1945. *History of Western Philosophy*. New York: Simon and Schuster.

Satterthwaite, Mark. 1975. "Strategy-Proofness and Arrow's Conditions: Existence and Correspondence Theroems for Voting Procedures and Social Welfare Functions." *Journal of Economic Theory* 10: 187–217.

Sax, Joseph L. 1993. "Property Rights and the Economy of Nature: Understanding *Lucas v. South Carolina Coastal Commission*." *Standford Law Review* 45: 1433.

Schelling, Thomas C. 1980. *Strategy of Conflict*. Rev. ed. Cambridge, MA: Harvard University Press.

Schelling, Thomas C. 1978a. *Micromotives and Macrobehavior*. New York: W. W. Norton.

———. 1978b. "Sorting and Mixing: Race and Sex." In *Micromotives and Macrobehavior*, 135–67. New York: W. W. Norton.

Schmidtchen, Dieter, and Robert Cooter, eds. 1997. *Constitutional Law and Economics in the European Union*. Cheltenham and Lyme: Edward Elgar Publishing.

Schultze, Charles L. 1977. *The Public Use of Private Interest*. Washington, DC: Brookings Institution.

Schumpeter, Joseph A. 1986. *History of Economic Analysis*. New York: Oxford University Press.

Schwartz, Alan, and Louis L. Wilde. 1979. "Intervening in Markets on the Basis of Imperfect Information: A Legal and Economic Analysis." *University of Pennsylvania Law Review* 127: 630–82.

Scotchmer, Suzanne. 1994. "Public Goods and the Invisible Hand." In *Modern Public Finance*, edited by J. Quigley and E. Smolensky, 93–119. Cambridge, MA: Harvard University Press.

Sen, Amartya. 1994. "Freedoms and Needs: An Argument for the Primacy of Political Rights." *The New Republic*, 10 and 17 January, p. 31.

———. 1970a. *Collective Choice and Social Welfare*. San Francisco: Holden-Day.

———. 1970b. "The Impossibility of a Paretian Liberal." *Journal of Political Economy* 78: 152–57.

Shapley, Lloyd S., and Bernard Grofman. 1984. "Optimizing Group Judgmental Accuracy in the Presence of Interdependencies." *Public Choice* 43: 329–43.

Shavell, Steven. 1985. "Criminal Law and the Optimal Use of Nonmonetary Sanctions as a Deterrent." *Columbia Law Review* 85: 1193.

———. 1979. "Risk Sharing and Incentives in the Principal and Agent Relationship." *Bell Journal of Economics and Management Science* 10: 55–73.

Shepsle, Kenneth A., and Mark S. Bonchek. 1997. *Analyzing Politics: Rationality, Behavior, and Institutions*. New York: W. W. Norton.

Sidgwick, Henry. 1962. *The Methods of Ethics*. Chicago: University of Chicago Press.

Siegan, B. H. 1980. *Economic Liberties and the Constitution*. Chicago: University of Chicago Press.

Simmons, A. John. 1997. "Justification and Legitimacy." Paper presented at the Law Faculty Seminar, University of California at Berkeley.

Smith, Adam. 1937. *An Inquiry into the Nature and Causes of the Wealth of Nations*. Modern Library Edition. New York: Random House.

Spence, Michael. 1974. *Market Signalling: Informational Transfer in Hiring and Related Screening Processes*. Cambridge, MA: Harvard University Press.

———. 1988. "Antitrust Federalism and Rational Choice Political Economy: A Critique of Capture Theory." *Southern California Law Review* 61: 1293.

Spitzer, Matthew. 1990. "Extensions of Ferejohn and Shipan's Model of Administrative Agency Behavior." *Journal of Law, Economics, and Organization* 6: 29–43.

Spriggs, James F. 1997. "Strategic Choices on the U.S. Supreme Court: The Decision to Join the Majority Opinion." Paper presented at the Bag Lunch Series, Law and Society Center, University of California at Berkeley.

Squire, Lyn, and Herman G. Van der Tak. 1975. *Economic Analysis of Projects*. Baltimore: Johns Hopkins University Press.

Sterns, M. 1999. "Should Justices Ever Switch Votes?: *Miller v Albright* in Social Choice Perspective." Supreme Court Economic Review 7: 87–156.

Steen, Lynn Arthur. 1982. "The Arithmetic of Apportionment." *Science News* 121: 317–18.

Stigler, George. 1975. *The Citizen and the State*. Chicago: University of Chicago Press.

———. 1971. "The Theory of Economic Regulation." *Bell Journal of Economics and Management Science* 2: 3.

Stiglitz, Joseph E. 1982. "The Theory of Local Public Goods Twenty-Five Years after Tiebout: A Perspective." NBER working paper no. 954.

Stratmann, Thomas. 1994. "Who Is Represented and Who Is Paid Off? Evidence from Congressional Voting and Political Action Committees' Contribution on the Influence of Reelection Constituencies." Paper presented at the Economic and Legal Organization Workshop, University of Chicago.

Summers, Robert S. 1987. "How Law Is Formal And Why It Matters." *Cornell Law Review* 82: 1165–1229.

Sunstein, Cass R. 1991. "Constitutionalism and Secession." *University of Chicago Law Review* 58: 633–70.

———. 1987. "Lochner's Legacy." *Columbia Law Review* 87: 873.

Superville, Darlene. 1997. "President Acquires Power of the Pen with Line-Item Veto." *San Francisco Chronicle*, 2 January A3.

Sykes, Alan O. 1996. "The (Limited) Role of Regulatory Harmonization in the International System." Paper presented at the Law and Economics Seminar, School of Law, University of California at Berkeley.

———. 1995. *Product Standards for Internationally Integrated Goods Markets*. Washington, DC: Brookings Institution.

Telser, Lester. 1978. *Economic Theory and the Core*. Chicago: University of Chicago Press.

Thompson, Dennis, and Amy Guttman. 1996. *Democracy and Disagreement*. Cambridge, MA: Belknap Press of Harvard University Press.

Thurow, Lester. 1980. *The Zero-Sum Society: Distribution and the Possibilities for Economic Change*. New York: Basic Books.

Tideman, Nicolaus. 1995. "The Single Transferable Vote." *Journal of Economic Perspectives* 9: 27–38.

Tiebout, Charles. 1956. "A Pure Theory of Local Expenditures." *Journal of Political Economy* 64: 416–24.

Tocqueville, Alexis de. 1945. *Democracy in America*. Edited by Phillips Bradley. Vol. 1. New York: A. A. Knopf.

Toma, Eugenia Froedge. 1983. "Institutional Structures, Regulation, and Producer Gains in the Education Industry." *Journal of Law and Economics* 26: 103–16.

Trebilcock, Michael J. 1997. "What Makes Poor Countries Poor? The Role of Institutional Capital in Economic Development," 15–58. In *The Law and Economics of Development*, edited by Edgardo Buscaglia, William Ratliff, and Robert Cooter. Greenwich, CT: JAI Press.

Tyler, Tom R. 1990. *Why People Obey the Law*. New Haven: Yale University Press.

United Nations Commission on International Trade Law. 1985. "Model Law on International Commercial Arbitration,"

Varian, Hal R. 1992. *Microeconomic Analysis*. 3rd ed. New York: Norton.

Veblen, Thorstein. 1967. *The Theory of the Leisure Class*. New York: Viking Press.

Verhovek, Sam How.1998. "Growing Popularity of Ballot Initiatives Leads to Questions." *New York Times* Nov. 2, A22.

Vickrey, W. 1960. "Utility, Strategy, and Social Decision Rules." *Quarterly Journal of Economics* 74.

Vickrey, W. 1945. "Measuring Marginal Utility by Reactions to Risks." *Econometrica* 13.

Voigt, Stefan. 1997a. "Bargaining for Constitutional Change—Towards an Economic Theory of Constitutional Change." *Diskussions beitrag* 02-1997, Max Planck Institute for Research into Economic Systems.

———. 1997b. "Positive Constitutional Economics—A Survey." *Public Choice* 90: 11–53.

Von Neumann, John, and Oskar Morgenstern. 1944. *Theory of Games and Economic Behavior.* Princeton: Princeton University Press.

———. 1995. "The Dignity of Legislation" (1994 Gerber Lecture). *Maryland Law Review* 54: 801–34.

Waldron, Jeremy. 1999. *The Dignity of Legislation.* New York: Cambridge University Press.

Waldon, Jeremy. 1993. "Liberal Rights: Two Sides of the Coin." In his *Liberal Rights: Collected Papers 1981–1991.* New York: Cambridge University Press.

———. ed. 1987. *Nonsense upon Stilts: Bentham, Burke and Marx on the Rights of Man.* New York: Methuen.

Weber, Max. 1974. "Bureaucracy." In *From Max Weber: Essays in Sociology,* Trans. and ed. H. H. Gerth and C. Wright Mills, sec. 6, p. 214. New York: Oxford University Press.

Weber, Robert J. 1995. "Approval Voting." *Journal of Economic Perspectives* 9: 39–50.

Wellman, Carl. 1985. *A Theory of Rights: Persons under Laws, Institutions and Morals.* Totowa, NJ: Rowman and Allanheld.

Wiecek, William M. 1977. *The Sources of Antislavery Constitutionalism in America, 1760–1848.* Ithaca: Cornell University Press.

Wildermuth, John. 1998. "Prop. 13—The People's Revolution." *San Francisco Chronicle,* 20 May. A1, A10–A11.

Williamson, Oliver E. 1975. *Markets and Hierarchies, Analysis and Antitrust Implications: A Study in the Economics of Internal Organization.* New York: Free Press.

Wilson, William Julius. 1987. *The Truly Disadvantaged: The Inner City, the Urderclass, and Public Policy.* Chicago: University of Chicago Press.

Wittgenstein, Ludwig. 1993. *Philosophical Occasions.* Indianapolis: Hackett Press.

Wittman, Donald. 1989. "Why Democracies Produce Efficient Results." *Journal of Political Economy* 97: 1395–1416.

Wright, Georg Henrik von. 1963. *Norm and Action.* London: Routledge.

Young, Peter Lewis. 1997. "Bougainville Conflict Enters Its Ninth Year." *Jane's Intelligence Review* 9, no. 6: 282.

Young, Peyton. 1995. "Optimal Voting Rules." *Journal of Economic Perspectives* 9: 51–64.

Zerbe, R. O. 1981. *Research in Law and Economics.* Greenwich, CT: JAI Press.

INDEX OF NAMES

CPSIA information can be obtained
at www.ICGtesting.com
Printed in the USA
LVOW04s1031181216
517817LV00003B/70/P

9 780691 096209